MW01520774

The data files used in this text can be downloaded from
www.lpdatafiles.com

Lawrenceville Press

A Guide to Web Development Using Macromedia® Dreamweaver® MX 2004

with Fireworks®, Flash™, and ColdFusion®

Elaine Malfas

Jan Marrelli

Beth Brown

Copyright 2005
by

First Edition

ISBN **1-58003-033-5** (softcover)
ISBN **1-58003-034-3** (hardcover)

All rights reserved. No part of this work covered by the copyright may be reproduced or used in any form or by any means—graphic, electronic, or mechanical, including photocopying, recording, taping, or information storage and retrieval systems—without the written permission of the publisher, with the exception of programs, which may be entered, stored, and executed in a computer system, but not reprinted for publication or resold in any other form.

Printed in the United States of America

All orders including educational, Canadian, foreign, FPO, and APO may be placed by contacting:

Lawrenceville Press, Inc.
P.O. Box 704
Pennington, NJ 08534-0704
(609) 737-1148
(609) 737-8564 fax

This text is available in hardcover and softcover editions.

16 15 14 13 12 11 10 9 8 7 6 5 4 3 2

The text is written and published by Lawrenceville Press, Inc. and is in no way connected with Macromedia® Inc. or the Microsoft® Corporation.

Macromedia®, Macromedia® Dreamweaver®, Macromedia® Fireworks®, and Macromedia® Flash™ are either registered trademarks or trademarks of Macromedia Inc. in the United States and/or other countries. Screen Shots reprinted with permission from Macromedia® Inc.

Microsoft®, Microsoft® Internet Explorer, Microsoft® Notepad and Microsoft® Outlook Express are either registered trademarks or trademarks of the Microsoft Corporation in the United States and/or other countries. Screen Shots and Icons reprinted with permission from Microsoft® Corporation.

Exam_View_ is a registered trademark of FSCreations, Inc.

Names of all other products mentioned herein are used for identification purposes only and may be trademarks of their respective owners.

Ｗe believe the best way to introduce students to web development is with a course that meets two primary expectations. First, students need to understand general design concepts and the process of developing a website from sketches to publishing. Second, students need to transfer this knowledge to web development projects, which requires considerable "hands on" computer experience using web development tools such as Macromedia Dreamweaver, Fireworks, Flash, and ColdFusion. Prior to starting web development, students need a foundation of knowledge that includes an understanding of networks, the Internet and intranets, and copyright issues. A basic understanding of HTML and familiarity with World Wide Web terminology is also required. Students can achieve these expectations with this text. The text is designed to strengthen problem-solving skills, and is written to be used either in a one or two term course.

A Guide to Web Development Using Macromedia Dreamweaver MX 2004 presents material for Dreamweaver, Fireworks, Flash, ColdFusion, Internet Explorer, Outlook Express, and Notepad. The text is written to be appropriate for students at a variety of levels. Chapters introduce all aspects of website development, including web page layout, typography, color, editing, and graphics. Other chapters introduce the Internet and the World Wide Web, publishing a website, and cascading style sheets.

Version 8 Throughout the text, differences for Dreamweaver 8, Flash 8, Fireworks 8, and ColdFusion 7 are indicated with parentheses (*ver.8:*).

Design and Features

Hands-on Practices Concepts are presented, discussed, and then followed by a "hands-on" practice that requires the student to test newly learned skills using the computer. The practices also serve as excellent reference guides for review. Answers to all the practices are included in the Teacher Resource Materials.

Sidebars and Tips Additional topics and tips that complement the text are in the margin.

Chapter Summaries Concepts covered in the chapter are reviewed.

Vocabulary Sections At the end of each chapter is a list of new terms and definitions and a list of commands and buttons covered in the chapter.

Review Questions Numerous review questions provide immediate reinforcement of new concepts. Answers to all review questions are included in the Teacher Resource Materials.

Exercises   Numerous exercises of varying difficulty are appropriate for students with a wide range of abilities. Answers to all exercises are included in the Teacher Resource Materials.

Networks, Internet Explorer, and Outlook Express   Before learning to use Dreamweaver, Chapter 1 introduces students to the Internet, networks, Internet Explorer, and Outlook Express. Also covered is the vocabulary needed to understand concepts presented in later chapters.

HTML and CSS   An introduction to HTML is presented before students are introduced to Dreamweaver. CSS style sheets are presented later in the text, after students are familiar with HTML and creating web pages.

Copyright Concerns   The issues related to copyright, copyright protection, copyright infringement, and the use of copyrighted materials are discussed throughout the text.

Web-Related Careers   It is hoped that many students will become interested in IT and web-related careers based upon their experience in this course. Chapter 1 includes information on different careers related to IT and the educational requirements needed to pursue them.

Appendices   Appendix A discusses banner ads and ActionScript. Appendix B discusses digital camera files. Appendix C discusses collaboration for website development using templates. Appendix D lists HTML tags and attributes.

Teacher Resource Materials

Our Teacher Resource Materials correlate directly to the textbook and provide all the additional materials required to offer students an excellent computer applications course. The Teacher Resource Materials feature:

- **cd_contents.htm**   Help files and a guide for using the text and resource materials.

- **Lesson Plans**   Lessons in PDF format keyed to the chapters in the text. Each lesson includes assignments, teaching notes, worksheets, and additional topics.

- **Visual Aids**   Visual aids including PowerPoint presentations display topics keyed to the text.

- **Vocabulary**   Word files of the vocabulary presented in the text.

- **Rubrics**   Rubrics keyed to exercises in the text for assessment.

- **Worksheets**   Problems that supplement the exercises in the text provide additional reinforcement of concepts.

- **Critical Thinking Worksheets**   Thought-provoking written-response questions keyed to concepts practiced in the text.

- **Review Question Answers**   Answers to the review questions that are presented in the text.

- **Data Files**   All files that the student needs to complete the practices and exercises in the text, as well as the files needed to complete the worksheets, quizzes, and tests in the resource materials.

- **Exam***View*® **Software** Question banks keyed to the text and the popular **Exam***View*® software are included to create tests, quizzes, and additional assessment materials.

- **Answer Files** Answers to the practices, exercises, worksheets, and tests.

Acknowledgments

Special thanks to Douglas Jones and Elaine Malfas for the underwater photography used in the SCUBA website. Photographs of Greece and of cacti used in the GREECE and CACTUS websites courtesy of Elaine Malfas.

The success of this and all of our texts is due to the efforts of Heidi Crane, Vice President of Marketing at Lawrenceville Press. Joseph Dupree and Christina Albanesius run our Customer Relations Department and handle the thousands of orders we receive in a friendly and efficient manner. Michael Porter is responsible for the excellent service Lawrenceville Press offers in the shipping of orders.

About the Authors

Elaine Malfas is a graduate of Hartwick College and earned an M.S. degree in Technical Communication from Rensselaer Polytechnic Institute. Ms. Malfas has coauthored numerous computer texts and accompanying Teacher Resource Materials. She has taught computer applications and desktop publishing at the high school level.

Jan Marrelli, a graduate of the University of Western Ontario, has coauthored several computer texts and their accompanying teacher resource materials. She teaches computer programming and applications for the Algoma District School Board. She has also participated in curriculum development and assessment projects for the Ontario Ministry of Education.

Beth A. Brown, a Computer Science graduate of Florida Atlantic University, is director of development at Lawrenceville Press where she has coauthored a number of applications and programming texts and their accompanying Teacher Resource Materials. She has taught computer applications and programming at the high school level.

Chapter Expectations

Chapter 1 – Introducing Networks and the Internet

After completing this chapter, students will be able to:

1. Discuss current computing technologies.
2. Explain what a network is and describe the benefits of using a network.
3. Identify the differences in network topologies.
4. Distinguish between different types of transmission media.
5. Understand network protocols.
6. Apply netiquette rules when using a network.
7. Organize files and folders.
8. Distinguish between an intranet and extranet.
9. Summarize how the Internet works and explain different ways to access the Internet.
10. Identify various Internet services.
11. Describe several categories of websites and the purpose of each.
12. Demonstrate the basic features and functions of Internet Explorer.
13. Use the History list and Favorites list in Internet Explorer.
14. Locate information using search engines and subject trees.
15. Evaluate and cite web pages.
16. Demonstrate the basic features and functions of Outlook Express and apply e-mail etiquette.
17. Analyze Internet privacy issues.
18. Understand the need for an Internet Use Agreement.
19. Discuss social and ethical implications associated with computer use.
20. Describe how copyright applies to material on the Internet.
21. Discuss ethical responsibilities of the web developer.
22. Describe IT careers.

Chapter 2 – HTML

After completing this chapter, students will be able to:

1. Define terminology associated with the World Wide Web.
2. Describe the structure of an HTML document.
3. Create an HTML document using Notepad.
4. View HTML documents in a web browser.
5. Distinguish between the break tag and the paragraph tag.
6. Create headings and horizontal rules.
7. Use attributes to modify HTML elements.
8. Create lists and tables.
9. Create hyperlinks to different HTML documents.
10. Add images to HTML documents.
11. Use comments to clarify HTML for a reader.
12. Apply embedded and linked style sheets to an HTML document.
13. Change the background and text color of an HTML document.
14. Embed scripts and applets into an HTML document.

Chapter 3 – Introducing Dreamweaver

After completing this chapter, students will be able to:

1. Define a website.
2. Create a home page and change the page title.
3. Display a web page in different document views.
4. Understand why tables are used to organize and control the arrangement of content in a web page.
5. Create tables and modify table properties.
6. Edit the content of web page documents and check spelling.
7. Print and close a web page document.
8. Quit Dreamweaver.
9. Edit a website.
10. Create and open web page documents.
11. Create text and external hyperlinks.
12. Display a linked web page in a new window.
13. Display the Dreamweaver site map.

Chapter 4 – Website Development

After completing this chapter, students
will be able to:

1. Outline the steps involved in developing a
   website.
2. Define the purpose and target audience of a
   website.
3. Determine the web pages and navigation
   structure of a website.
4. Determine the content of a website.
5. Distinguish between different types of
   navigation bars.
6. Implement usability standards for web page
   layout.
7. Apply design concepts to a web page.
8. Organize website files and folders.
9. Use the Assets panel.
10. Merge and split table cells.
11. Create and edit library items.
12. Insert a time stamp.
13. Create e-mail hyperlinks.
14. Describe how copyright applies to websites.

Chapter 5 – Images in Dreamweaver and Fireworks

After completing this chapter, students
will be able to:

1. Differentiate between GIF, JPG, and PNG file
   formats.
2. Explain why alternative text should be added
   to an image.
3. Create a graphic hyperlink.
4. Create an image map.
5. Align, resize, and resample images.
6. Demonstrate the basic features and functions
   of Fireworks.
7. Draw objects and add text in Fireworks.
8. Optimize and export a Fireworks document.
9. Create and modify a button symbol in
   Fireworks.
10. Distinguish between the four states of a
    button symbol and change the behavior of a
    state.
11. Export HTML and images from Fireworks.
12. Use an exported HTML document in
    Dreamweaver.
13. Crop images in Fireworks and in
    Dreamweaver.
14. Edit an image in Fireworks from
    Dreamweaver.

Chapter 6 – Typography, Style Sheets, and Color

After completing this chapter, students
will be able to:

1. Define typography and explain how it affects
   the navigation and usability of a website.
2. Explain what a style sheet is using appropriate
   terminology.
3. Link and create a CSS style sheet document.
4. Create and apply a rule, class, and selector
   styles.
5. Check the existing HTML tags of a web page
   document for inconsistencies.
6. Edit, duplicate, delete, and remove styles.
7. Tag indented text and redefine the blockquote
   tag.
8. Create and format numbered and bulleted
   lists.
9. Determine appropriate colors for a web page
   document.
10. Change the background and text color of web
    page document with a style sheet.
11. Create a hyperlink to a named anchor.
12. Create selector styles to change link colors.
13. Use content from external sources in a
    website.
14. Control web page layout using absolute
    positioning.

Chapter 7 – Introducing Flash

After completing this chapter, students
will be able to:

1. Create Flash buttons and Flash text in
   Dreamweaver.
2. Use the Assets panel to access Flash movie
   files.
3. Explain animation.
4. Demonstrate the basic features and functions
   of Flash.
5. Outline the process of creating a Flash movie.
6. Create a frame-by-frame animation.
7. Export Flash documents.
8. Organize and use Flash movie files in
   Dreamweaver.
9. Create an animation using shape tweening.
10. Optimize a Flash movie by creating symbols.
11. Create an animation using motion tweening.
12. Use layers in a Flash document.
13. Animate text.
14. Import sound files and video.

Chapter 8 – Website Content and ColdFusion Technology

After completing this chapter, students will be able to:

1. Discuss advantages of an electronic portfolio over a traditional portfolio.
2. Design an electronic portfolio.
3. Explain the purpose and content of a personal website.
4. Explain the purpose and content of an informational website.
5. Explain the purpose and content of a commercial website.
6. Distinguish between a corporate presence website and an e-commerce website.
7. Create a FAQ page.
8. Import tabular data.
9. Create a site map web page.
10. Create a jump menu.
11. Include a form on a web page.
12. Validate the contents of a form field.
13. Understand how a form allows a user to interacts with a web server.
14. Distinguish between static and dynamic web pages.
15. Use ColdFusion server technology to display dynamic content on a website.

Chapter 9 – Publishing and Promoting a Website

After completing this chapter, students will be able to:

1. Outline the process of publishing a website.
2. Check the spelling and grammar on each web page of a website.
3. Assess the download time of a web page document.
4. Define target browser and determine which target browser should be used to test a site.
5. Preview a website in a target browser.
6. Test the HTML associated with a web page for target browser compatibility.
7. Test a website for broken and missing links.
8. Check a website for HTML problems.
9. Explain what a web host is and distinguish between virtual and non-virtual hosting.
10. Publish a website to a web server and to a local/network server.

11. Update a published site.
12. Use collaboration features in Dreamweaver.
13. Promote a published website.
14. Add meta tags.
15. Describe ways to measure the success of a website.
16. Discuss issues associated with website security.

Table of Contents

Chapter 3 – Introducing Dreamweaver

Chapter 4 – Website Development

Chapter 5 – Images in Dreamweaver and Fireworks

Chapter 6 – Typography, Style Sheets, and Color

Chapter 7 – Introducing Flash

Chapter 8 – Website Content and ColdFusion Technology

Chapter 9 – Publishing and Promoting a Website

Appendix A – Banner Ads and ActionScript

Appendix B – Digital Camera Files

Appendix C – Templates

Appendix D – HTML Tags and Attributes

Index

Chapter 1

Introducing Networks and the Internet

This chapter discusses current computing technologies, networks, the Internet, and the World Wide Web. Issues related to computers, including privacy, viruses, and copyright are also discussed.

Desktop Computing

TIP Desktop computers are often generically referred to as PCs or MACs.

A desktop computer and its components are designed to fit on or under a desk:

Scanner

A scanner is an input device that uses a laser to create a digital image from artwork such as photos and drawings. The digitized image can then be incorporated into an electronic document.

- The physical components of the computer, such as the monitor and system unit, are called *hardware*.

- Data and instructions are entered into the computer using *input devices*, such as a keyboard, mouse, scanner, microphone, digital camera, CD-RW/DVD drive, and disk drive.

- A PC becomes much more versatile when *peripheral devices*, such as printers and scanners, are added. A peripheral device is attached to a *port* on the computer. There are different types of ports, such as serial, parallel, FireWire, USB, and Bluetooth ports.

- Computers process data into useful information. Processed data is conveyed using *output devices*. Monitors and printers display data, CD-RWs, disk drives, and memory keys store data, and speakers communicate audio output.

Printers

A laser printer uses a laser and toner to generate characters and graphics on paper. An ink jet printer uses an ink cartridge to place very small dots of ink onto paper to create characters and graphics.

The *base unit* also contains the *motherboard*, which is the main circuit board. The motherboard contains several components:

- *Expansion boards* are circuit boards that connect to the motherboard to add functionality to the computer. Examples include sound cards and video adapters.

CPU Manufacturers

Intel and AMD are two processor manufacturers. Processors are identified by a model name or number, such as Pentium® 4, Itanium® 2, and Opteron™. The Intel Pentium 4 (P4) CPU has a clock rate of 3.06 GHz. The AMD Opteron CPU has a clock rate of 2.4 GHz. These CPUs contain more than 40 million transistors on a single chip.

Real-time Clock

A battery chip called a real-time clock keeps track of the date and time in a computer even when the computer is off.

integrated circuits
ROM

RAM

Software

Windows, Linux, Unix, and Mac OS X are examples of operating system software. Dreamweaver, Fireworks, Flash, and Microsoft Word are examples of applications software. Applications software is sometimes bundled together in a suite, such as the Studio MX 2004 suite.

- The *CPU* (Central Processing Unit) or processor processes data and controls the flow of data between the computer's other units. Within the CPU is the *ALU* (Arithmetic Logic Unit), which can perform arithmetic and logic operations. It can also make comparisons, which is the basis of the computer's decision-making power. The ALU is so fast that the time needed to carry out a single addition is measured in nanoseconds (billionths of a second). The speed at which a CPU can execute instructions is determined by the computer's *clock rate*. The clock rate is measured in *megahertz* (MHz, million of cycles per second) or *gigahertz* (GHz, billion of cycles per second).

- A *bus* is a set of circuits that connect the CPU to other components. The data bus transfers data between the CPU, memory, and other hardware devices on the motherboard. The *address bus* carries memory addresses that indicate where the data is located and where the data should go. A *control bus* carries control signals. All data flows through the CPU:

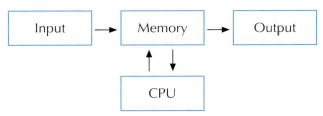

- Memory in the form of *integrated circuits* (ICs) store data electronically. *ROM* (Read Only Memory) contains the most basic operating instructions for the computer. The data in ROM is a permanent part of the computer and cannot be changed. *RAM* (Random Access Memory), also called *primary or main memory*, is memory where data and instructions are stored temporarily. Data stored in RAM can be written to *secondary memory*, which includes any type of storage media, such as a floppy disk, hard disk, memory key, or CD-RW. Secondary memory must be copied into primary memory before it is processed by the CPU. *SRAM* (Static Random Access Memory) is high-speed memory referred to as *cache* (pronounced "cash"). This memory is used to store frequently used data for quick retrieval by an application.

A desktop computer also contains programs, or software. *Operating system software* is run automatically when the computer is turned on and enables the user to communicate with the computer with input devices, such as the mouse and keyboard. *Applications software* is written by programmers to perform a specific task, such as a word processor.

Mobile Computing

Improved technology has allowed the miniaturization of computer components and special long-lasting batteries. Computers now come in many shapes, sizes, and with many levels of features. Among these computers are notebooks, tablets, handhelds, smart phones, and wearables. Because of their portability, these types of computer are classified as mobile computing devices:

Bluetooth

Bluetooth is a wireless technology used to allow mobile computing devices to communicate.

Handheld Computers

Handheld computers are widely used in occupations that require constant travel, such as parcel delivery, meter reading, and sales.

Cross-Platform Connectivity

One issue involved with using so many types of PCs is cross-platform connectivity, which is the ability for one type of PC to link to and share data with a different type of PC. Notebook and desktop PCs typically have good cross-platform connectivity because their file formats can be used on either computer.

MAN and HAN

A MAN (Metropolitan Area Network) and a HAN (Home Area Network) are network technologies classified by the size of a network. A MAN is a high-speed network that typically connects LANs within a city or town. A HAN is used to connect personal devices within the home.

- A *notebook computer* is a portable, lightweight computer with a CPU, memory, and hard disk space comparable to that of a typical desktop computer.

- A *tablet PC* is a computer designed similar to a pad of paper and a pencil. Users simply "write" on a screen with a device called a *stylus* that is shaped like a thin pencil. Handwriting recognition software is used to interpret a user's handwriting. A keyboard can also be attached.

- *Handheld computers*, also called PDAs, are palm-sized and contain applications for storing contact information, schedules, lists, and games. Handhelds come with a stylus for input and have a screen that is several inches vertically. Many types of application software have been written for handhelds, including spreadsheets and word processors. Some handhelds recognize handwriting, have a built-in keyboard, include a cellular phone, and provide Internet access.

- *Smartphones* are cellular phones that are able to send and receive e-mail messages and access the Internet. Some smart phones have digital camera, MP3 player, and color display capabilities.

- *Wearable computers* vary greatly in size and application. MP3 players have been incorporated into clothing, and one type of wearable computer includes voice recognition. Wearable computers are also in the form of goggles, which incorporate a monitor, digital camera, ear bud, and microphone. Wrist-top computers are worn like a traditional wrist watch and work as a pager, provide Internet access, and contain other features usually found in a handheld PC.

Networks

A *network* is a combination of hardware and software that allows computers to exchange data and share software and devices, such as printers. Networks are widely used by businesses, universities, and other organizations because a network:

- allows users to reliably share and exchange data

- can reduce costs by sharing devices such as printers

- offers security options including password protection to restrict access to certain files

- simplifies file management through centralized software updates and file backups

- provides e-mail for network users

Networks are classified by their size, architecture, and topology. A common size classifications is *LAN* (Local-Area Network), which is a network used to connect devices within a small area such as a building or a campus. A *WAN* (Wide-Area Network) is used to connect devices over large geographical distances. A WAN can be one widespread network or it can be a number of LANs linked together.

The computers and other devices in a LAN each contain an expansion card called a *network interface card*:

Network interface card

A cable plugs into the adapter card to connect one device to another to form a LAN. Cables are not required for network cards that have wireless capabilities. Network interface cards are available for desktop and mobile computers and take various other forms including an adapter card, a PC card, or a Flash memory card.

network operating system

Along with the physical, or hardware, aspects of setting up a network, there is also the software aspect. A *network operating system* is software that allow users and devices to communicate over the network. The operating system installed must be capable of supporting networking functions, such as security access features and support for multiple users. Operating systems capable of network functions are available for Linux, Windows, Unix, and Mac. The network architecture, discussed next, must also be considered when choosing a network OS.

network architecture

peer-to-peer

client/server

Network architecture includes the type of computers on the network and determines how network resources are handled. Two common models are peer-to-peer and client/server. In a *peer-to-peer* network, each computer on the network is considered equal in terms of responsibilities and resource sharing. A *client/server network* consists of a group of computers, called *clients*, connected to a server. A *server* is a computer with more RAM, a larger hard disk, and sometimes multiple CPUs that is used to manage network functions.

Physical *topology* refers to the arrangement of the nodes on a network. A *node* is a location on the network with a device capable of processing information, such as a computer or a printer. There are three common physical topologies:

- The bus topology is a physical LAN topology that uses a single central cable, called the *bus* or backbone to attach each node directly:

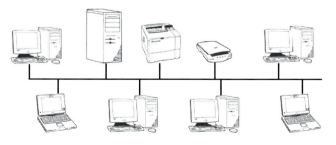

LAN using a bus topology

Transmission Media

Computers must be connected in order to transmit data between the nodes. Cable transmission media includes twisted-pair wiring, coaxial cable, and fiber optic cable.

Wireless transmission media includes infrared signals, broadcast radio, cellular radio, microwaves, and communications satellites.

The amount of data and the speed at which data can travel over a media is called bandwidth, which is measured in bits per second (bps). Each transmission media has a specific length or range restriction, data transmission rate, and cost.

Ethernet

The Ethernet LAN protocol was developed by Bob Metcalfe in 1976. Ethernet uses a bus or star topology with twisted-pair wiring, coaxial cable, or fiber optic cable transmission media. Newer protocols include Fast Ethernet, which operates at 100 Mbps, Gigabit Ethernet which operates at 1 Gbps, and 10G Ethernet, which operates at 10 Gbps.

- In a *star topology*, each node is attached to a *hub*, which is a device that joins communication lines at a central location on the network:

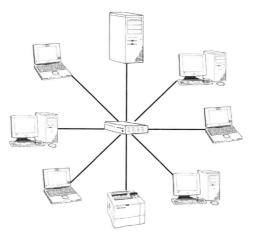

LAN using a star topology

- In a *ring topology*, each node is connected to form a closed loop. A LAN with a ring topology can usually cover a greater distance than a bus or star topology:

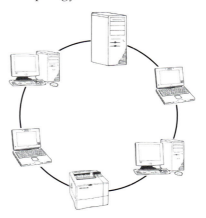

LAN using a ring topology

Wi-Fi

Wi-Fi (Wireless Fidelity) is a term used to describe an 802.11 network, which is a specification or protocol for wireless networks.

- *Wireless networks* use high frequency radio waves or infrared signals instead of cables to transmit data. A router/wireless access point device is used to allow nodes to transfer data wirelessly.

Another type of topology is *logical topology*, which refers to the way data is passed between the nodes on a network. A LAN's logical topology is not always the same as its physical topology.

Network users are given a user name and password to log on to a network through a computer connected to the network. Users are also assigned a level of access to maintain security. Network users should

netiquette   follow a certain etiquette referred to as *netiquette*:

- Do not attempt to access the account of another user without authorization.

- Do not share your password, and change it periodically.

- Use appropriate subject matter and language, and be considerate of other people's beliefs and opinions.

Files and Folders

TIP The original form the file is saved in is referred to as the native format.

A collection of related data stored on a lasting medium, such as a hard disk, is called a *file*. A file can be an application (program) or the product of an application. For example, a word processor application is used to create document files. As another example, a digital camera is used to create photo files. A file is stored on a persistent media so that it is retained even after the computer or computerized device is turned off. A file can be used over and over again whenever the data it stores is needed.

file name

Each file is identified by a unique *file name*. When a new document is created, a temporary generic file name, such as Untitled-1 or Document1 is assigned to the file until it is saved. Applications automatically add an extension to the file name when saved. An extension indicates the file type. For example, Dreamweaver automatically adds the .htm extension to basic HTML documents and .css to cascading style sheets. Extensions are also an indicator of what application the file was created in. For example, Microsoft Word files have a .doc extension.

Changes made to a document after saving are not automatically saved. The file must be saved again, which *overwrites* the original file with the changed file.

File Size Limitations

File size can be decreased or compressed using a compression program, such as WinZip. This technique is often used to accommodate storage device and e-mail account limitations.

Folders are used to organize commonly related files. Like files, folders are also identified by a unique name. Folders are an organizational tool and a folder can contain other folders. For example, the Cats folder shown below is used to store all the folders and files associated with a website about cats:

TIP The Windows operating system allows folder and file directories to be displayed various ways including with details, such as file size and date saved, or as thumbnails, as shown to the right.

The Cats folder contains a notes folder, an images folder, and four HTML files

Intranets, Extranets, and the Internet

An *intranet* is a network that is used by a single organization, such as a corporation or school, and is only accessible by authorized users. The purpose of an intranet is to share information. However, a firewall is also used to lock out unauthorized users. A *firewall* is a network security system that prevents unauthorized network access.

firewall

An *extranet* extends an intranet by providing various levels of accessibility to authorized members of the public. For example, a corporation may extend their intranet to provide access to specific information, such as their ordering system, to registered customers.

The largest and most widely accessed network is the *Internet*, a worldwide network of computers that is not controlled by any one organization. The Internet has had an undeniable impact on modern society because it allows users worldwide to communicate in a matter of seconds.

The Internet is actually numerous networks all linked together through routers. A *router* is a device that can connect different network technologies together. Networks connected to routers use *TCP/IP* (Transmission Control Protocol/Internet Protocol) software to communicate.

Computers on the Internet are either servers or clients. The client is sent information from a server. The client/server structure of the Internet is called *interactive* because the information accessed is a result of selections made by the user. For example, a computer with just minimal software for accessing the Internet is a client. The client user selecting options from the Internet is receiving the information from a server, a computer with additional software and files that is also connected to the Internet. A server that has web server software installed is called a *web server* and is designed to deliver web pages to the client.

> ## History of the Internet
>
> The Internet evolved from ARPANET, a network created in the late 1960s by the Department of Defense's ARPA (Advanced Research Projects Agency), and the theory of open architecture networking.

> ## IP Address
>
> An IP address is an identifier for a computer or device on a TCP/IP network.

> **TIP** Access to the Internet requires telecommunications and the use of an Internet Service Provider (ISP). ISPs are discussed in Chapter 9.

> **TIP** In a wireless network, a router/wireless access point is typically connected by a cable to a cable or DSL modem.

Telecommunications

Telecommunications is the transmitting and receiving of data. Data can be in various forms including voice and video. Telecommunications requires a modem or adapter and a line or cable. The speed of data transmission (sending) and receipt (receiving) is measured in *Kbps* (thousands of bits per second) or *Mbps* (millions of bits per second). Numerous telecommunications options are available, which vary in speed and cost:

- A **conventional modem** uses standard telephone lines to convert analog signals to digital data. A conventional modem is a 56 Kbps modem, which transmits data at 28.8 Kbps and 36.6 Kbps, and receives data at 56 Kbps. Home computers sometimes use a conventional modem.

- A **DSL** (Digital Subscriber Line) modem uses standard telephone lines with data transmission up to 640 Kbps. Data receipt is from 1.5 Mbps to 9 Mbps. A DSL (Asymmetric DSL) is the most common form used.

- A **cable modem** transmits data through a coaxial cable television network. Data transmission is from 2 Mbps to 10 Mbps and data receipt is from 10 Mbps to 36 Mbps.

- **Leased/Dedicated lines** are used by many businesses and schools for Internet access. They allow for a permanent connection to the Internet that is always active. The cost of a leased line is usually a fixed monthly fee. A T-1 carrier is a type of leased line that transmits data at 1.544 Mbps.

- **ISDN** (Integrated Services Digital Network) is a digital telephone network provided by a local phone company. ISDN is capable of transmitting and receiving data at up to 64 Kbps. ISDN requires the use of an ISDN terminal adapter instead of a modem.

Internet Services

World Wide Web

web browser

Internet services include the World Wide Web, e-mail, instant messaging, bulletin board services, and mailing lists. The *World Wide Web* (WWW), also called the *Web* is the most widely used Internet service. The Web can be used to search and access information available on the Internet. A *web browser* application, such as Microsoft Internet Explorer, provides a graphical interface to present information in the form of a website:

A web page that is part of the CNN website

Surfing the Net

"Surfing the net" means to browse web pages looking for information on topics of interest. The phrase was coined in 1992 when a librarian named Jean Armour Polly used a mouse pad with a picture of a surfer on it.

The Web offers access to a multitude of information, and most websites are considered to be in one of the following categories: personal, commercial, informational, media, and portal:

- **Personal websites** are created by individuals for the purpose of displaying information about the individual's hobbies, pets, family members, and so forth.

- **Commercial websites** include *corporate presence websites*, which are created by companies and organizations for the purpose of displaying information about their products or services. It also includes *e-commerce websites*, which are created by businesses for the purpose of selling their products or services online.

Blog

Blog is short for weblog and is a type of website where users can post entries in a journal format.

- **Informational websites** are created for the purpose of displaying factual information about a particular topic and are often created by educational institutions, governments, and organizations.
- **Media websites** are online newspapers and periodicals that are created by companies for the purpose of informing readers about current events and issues.
- **Portal websites** are created by businesses for the purpose of creating a starting point for people to enter the Web. Portals contain hyperlinks to a wide range of topics, such as sport scores and top news stories, and most portals include access to a search engine.

While the Internet and Web were originally developed to help the academic and scientific communities, the Web is being used more and more for advertising and e-commerce. It is common to find advertisements, called *banner ads*, on websites:

A banner ad is designed to entice a user to click it, which in turn displays the advertiser's page. Most websites host banner ads for a fee.

Every web page has a URL (Uniform Resource Locator) associated with it. A *URL* is an address that is interpreted by a web browser to identify the location of a page on the web. For example, consider the URL for the Earth Day Network:

http://www.earthday.net

- **http** is the web protocol used to handle requests and for the transmission of pages between a web server and a web browser.
- **//** separates the protocol from the domain name.
- **www.earthday.net** is the domain name. A *domain name* identifies a particular web page and is made up of a sequence of parts, or subnames, separated by a period. The *subnames* are called labels and may represent a server or organization. The suffix of a domain name is called the *top-level domain* and identifies the type of website. In this case .net indicates the site is a network organization.

e-mail

Another widely used Internet service is *e-mail* or *electronic mail*, which is the sending and receiving of messages and computer files over a communications network, such as a LAN (Local Area Network) or the Internet. E-mail can be received in a matter of seconds, even if the recipient is located half way around the world.

An e-mail address is required in order to send and receive e-mail messages. E-mail addresses are provided when you sign up with an ISP or an online service. A typical e-mail address is similar to:

Web Advertising

The Interactive Advertising Bureau (IAB) sets standards and guidelines for Internet advertising, including guidelines for the size of Banner, Button, Rectangle, Interstitial, Pop-up, Skyscraper, and Webmercial ads.

Top-level Domains

Top-level domains include:
.gov - government agency
.edu - educational institution
.org - non profit organization
.com - commercial business

Each country also as a 2 character top-level domain, such as .uk for the United Kingdom.

TIP Free e-mail accounts, known as browser-based e-mail, are available through numerous sites such as Yahoo! and Hotmail. These accounts require only a web browser.

E-mail Protocols

POP3 is an e-mail protocol that connects to an e-mail server to download messages to a local computer.

IMAP is an e-mail protocol that connects to an e-mail server to read message headers and then the user selects which e-mail messages to download to a local computer.

HTTP is used as an e-mail protocol when a web page is used to access an e-mail account.

E-mail software is also required for sending and receiving e-mail messages. Examples of e-mail software include Outlook, Outlook Express, and Eudora. E-mail software and e-mail etiquette is discussed later in this chapter.

Instant messaging (IM) is a communication tool that allows for *real time*, or immediate text-based communication. Instant messaging allows for private on-line chat sessions and is useful for brief communication that is faster than e-mail.

Sending instant messages requires registering with an instant messaging service, such as Microsoft Windows Messenger or Microsoft MSN Messenger Service, and then adding the instant messaging addresses of the people you want to send instant messages to. These individuals also have to add your instant messaging address to their instant messaging program in order to accept messages from your address. Once this setup is complete, the instant messaging service will automatically indicate which contacts are online to send messages to.

bulletin board service

A *bulletin board service*, sometimes referred to as a BBS, allows a user to participate in a discussion group. There are thousands of bulletin board services with topics ranging from accounting to zoology. Businesses often maintain a bulletin board service for their employees only. Other bulletin board services allow any network user to join.

Network news is a popular BBS available on the Internet. This system uses the term *newsgroup* to refer to an individual bulletin board, and *article* refers to the message posted to the newsgroup. Subscribers of a newsgroup can check for new articles and post (send) articles regarding the topic of discussion. *USENET* refers to the collection of all the servers that offer network news.

mailing list server

A *mailing list server* is a server that manages mailing lists for groups of users. Two mailing list servers are Listserv and Majordomo. Often users subscribe to mailing lists for discussion purposes. When a subscriber posts a message to a mailing list server, every subscriber receives a copy of the message. Subscribers are identified by a single name or e-mail address.

Gopher

Gopher was one of the first widespread Internet browsing services. It is a text-based environment that is used to locate information on the Internet

HTTP

FTP

Internet protocols include *HTTP* (Hypertext Transfer Protocol), which is used for handling the transmission of pages between a web server and a web browser and *FTP* (File Transfer Protocol), which is used to rapidly transfer (upload and download) files from one computer to another over the Internet. FTP is also discussed in Chapter 9.

Telnet

Telnet is a program that is used on networks such as the Internet to allow users to remotely log on to a server on the network. The server can then be controlled from the remote computer. Telnet is commonly used to control web servers.

Using Internet Explorer

A web browser, such as Internet Explorer, is needed to view web pages. Starting Internet Explorer displays a browser window:

Starting Internet Explorer

To start Internet Explorer, select Start → All Programs → Internet Explorer or click the Internet Explorer icon on the Desktop:

- The web page title and the name of browser are displayed in the **title bar**.

- Select commands from menus in the **menu bar**.

- Click a button on the **toolbar** to perform an action.

- Click the **Back button** to display the previously displayed web page.

- Click the **Forward button** to display the next web page from the previously selected pages.

- Click the **Stop button** to stop the transmission of a web page.

- Click the **Refresh button** to update the displayed web page.

- Click the **Home button** to display a preselected web page, which is the web page displayed when Internet Explorer is started.

- Click the **Search button** to display a pane used to locate web pages that contain particular information.

- Click the **Favorites button** to display the *Favorites list*, which is used to maintain a list of web pages.

- Click the **History button** to display the *History list*, which lists the URLs of websites that have been previously visited.

- Click the **Print button** to print the displayed web page(s).

- Type a URL in the **Address bar** and then press Enter or click the **Go button** ( ) to open a web page. Select a previously typed URL from the Address bar list.

- Drag the **scroll bar** to bring unseen parts of the document into view.

- View the progress of a loading web page in the **status bar**.

TIP It is not usually necessary to type the http:// of a URL because the browser will automatically add it.

Header and Footer Codes

To add information to a printout, select File → Page Setup and type a code in the Header or Footer box. Codes include &d for the date, &u for the URL, and &p for the page number.

Web pages do not always print on a single sheet of paper. Therefore, it is important to preview a web page before printing to avoid printing unwanted pages. Select File → Print Preview to display the Print Preview window, which indicates the number of pages that will be printed. Click the Page Setup button (🖼) on the Print Preview window toolbar to add a header and footer to the web page printout. Click Print... to display the Print dialog box. Options in the Print dialog box can then be used to specify which pages should be printed.

Practice: Using Internet Explorer

This practice requires Internet access.

① START INTERNET EXPLORER

  a. Ask your instructor for the appropriate steps to start Internet Explorer. The preselected home page is displayed.

  b. Maximize the window.

  c. What is the URL of the home page?

② GO TO THE MSNBC HOME PAGE

  a. In the Address bar, replace the existing URL with www.msnbc.com, the URL for the MSNBC home page.

  b. Press Enter. The web page is opened.

  c. Use the scroll bar to scroll through the home page.

  d. What is displayed in the title bar?

③ VIEW MSNBC STORIES

  a. Click a hyperlink that interests you.

  b. Continue to surf MSNBC web pages. Realize that a hyperlink may display a web page at a site other than MSNBC. To return to the MSNBC site, click 🔙 Back · on the toolbar.

  c. Which website category would the MSNBC website be in?

④ GO TO THE CNN HOME PAGE

  a. In the Address bar, replace the existing URL with www.cnn.com, the URL for the CNN home page.

  b. Press Enter. The web page is opened. Use the scroll bar to scroll through the CNN home page.

  c. Which website category would the CNN website be in?

⑤ GO TO THE FLORIDA ATLANTIC UNIVERSITY HOME PAGE

  a. In the Address bar, replace the existing URL with www.fau.edu, the URL for the Florida Atlantic University home page.

  b. Press Enter. The web page is opened. Wait until the web page has finished loading, then use the scroll bar if necessary to scroll through the home page.

  c. Which website category would this website be in?

⑥ USE THE HISTORY LIST TO ACCESS WEB PAGES

  a. On the toolbar, click the History button (🕗). The History pane is displayed on the left side of the window.

b. Point to the History pane right border to display a double-headed arrow (↔) and then drag the pane to size the History pane so that it is a little wider.

c. The View button in the History pane can be used to specify how the History list is displayed. In the History pane, click the View button and then select By Order Visited Today:

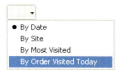

d. Click CNN.com. The CNN home page is displayed.

e. In the History pane, click the View button and then select By Date.

f. Click the Today folder ( Today) if the Today folder is not expanded. In the Today folder, note that a folder is displayed for each of the sites visited today.

g. Click the fau folder:

fau (www.fau.edu)
Welcome to Florida Atlantic ...

The title of the home page is displayed as a hyperlink to the home page. Click the link to display the Florida Atlantic University home page.

h. A pane, such as the History pane, is be displayed in the left side of the window until closed. Click the Close button (×) in the top-right corner of the History pane. The History pane is closed and the web page in the right pane is expanded to fill the space.

⑦ GO TO THE GAP HOME PAGE

a. In the Address bar, replace the existing URL with www.gap.com, the URL for the Gap home page.

b. Press Enter. The web page is opened. Use the scroll bar if necessary to scroll through the Gap's home page.

⑧ ADD A WEB PAGE TO THE FAVORITES LIST

a. On the toolbar, click ⭐ Favorites . The Favorites pane is displayed in the left side of the window. The Favorites pane contains the *Favorites list*, which is used to maintain a list of web pages. Selecting any of the web pages in the list will access that page and display it in the pane in the right side of the window.

b. What pages are displayed in your Favorites list?

c. A Favorites list can be organized using folders. In the Favorites pane, click 📑 Add... . The Add Favorites dialog box is displayed:

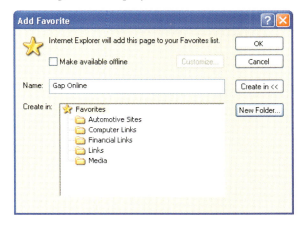

1. Click [New Folder...]. (If the New Folder button is not displayed, click [Create in >>].) The Create New Folder dialog box is displayed:

2. In the Folder name box, type: Shopping Sites

3. Select OK. The dialog box is removed and a folder is added to the Favorites list.

4. Select OK. The dialog box is removed and the current page is added to the Shopping Sites folder in the Favorites list.

⑨ GO TO ANOTHER WEB PAGE

a. In the Address bar, replace the existing URL with www.roots.com, the URL for the Roots home page.

b. Press Enter. The web page is opened.

⑩ RETURN TO A FAVORITE WEB PAGE

a. In the Favorites pane, click the Shopping Sites folder to display the page that was added:

b. Click the link for Gap Online. The selected page is displayed in the right pane.

⑪ DELETE A FOLDER FROM THE FAVORITES LIST

The Organize button in the Favorites pane is used to display a dialog box where folders can be created and renamed, moved, or deleted. The URLs can also be renamed, moved, or deleted.

a. In the Favorites pane, click 🗂 Organize... . The Organize Favorites dialog box is displayed.

b. Click the Shopping Sites folder to select it:

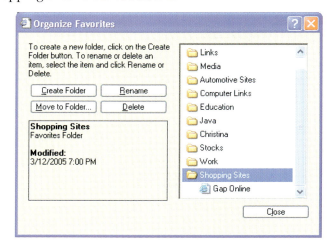

c. Select [Delete]. A warning is displayed. Select Yes to delete the folder and its contents.

d. Select [Close]. The dialog box is removed.

⑫ **CLOSE THE FAVORITES PANE**

⑬ **PRINT A WEB PAGE**

   a. In the Address bar, replace the existing URL with www.earthday.net, the URL for the Earth Day Network home page. Press Enter.

   b. Select File ➔ Print Preview to display the Earth Day Network page as it will appear when printed. The Print Preview window is displayed:

   1. How many pages will be printed?

   2. Click [icon]. The magnification is increased.

   3. Click [icon]. The magnification is decreased.

   4. Select the Page Setup button ([icon]). A dialog box is displayed.

   5. Replace the contents of the Header box with your name. Note the codes in the Footer box.

   6. Click OK. The dialog box is removed.

   7. In the Print Preview window, click [Print...]. A dialog box is displayed.

   8. Select Print. The web page is printed.

   9. Examine the printout. What did the codes in the Footer box represent?

Searching the Web

A *search engine* is a program that searches a database of web pages for keywords and then lists hyperlinks to pages that contain those keywords. Commonly used search engines include:

Yahoo! (www.yahoo.com)
Google (www.google.com)
MSN (www.msn.com)
AOL (www.aol.com)
Excite (www.excite.com)
Ask Jeeves (www.ask.com)
Overture (www.overture.com)
Lycos (www.lycos.com)
WebCrawler (www.webcrawler.com)
FAST Search (www.alltheweb.com)
About.com (www.about.com)
AltaVista (www.altavista.com)
Looksmart (www.looksmart.com)

search criteria

match

A search engine can be queried to display specific web pages. *Search criteria* can include single words or phrases that are then used by the engine to determine a match. A *match* is a web page that contains the search criteria. Surrounding phrases with quotation marks finds web pages that contain the entire phrase. The more specific the search criteria, the better the chance the information will be found.

Most searches yield far too many matches to be useful. Limiting the number of matches to a reasonable number can usually be accomplished by using Boolean logic in the search criteria:

- The + (plus sign) is used in search criteria to limit a search to only web pages that contain all of the specified words. For example, a search for florida +hotel or florida hotel returns only links to pages containing both words. AND can be used in place of + in most search engines.

- **OR** can be used in most search engines to find web pages that contain any one of the words in the criteria. For example, the criteria florida OR hotel returns links to pages containing either of the words.

- The – (minus sign) is used to exclude web pages. For example, a search for shakespeare –play returns links to pages containing the word shakespeare, but eliminates pages that also contain the word play. NOT can be used in place of – in most search engines.

subject tree

Some search engines provide a *subject tree*, or *web directory,* which is a list of sites separated into categories. The term subject tree is used because many of the categories "branch" off into subcategories. These subcategories allow the user to narrow down the subject and display a list of appropriate hyperlinks, which are at the lowest level of the tree.

Search Engines

A search engine usually works by sending out an agent, such as spider. A spider is an application that gathers a list of available web page documents and stores this list in a database that users can search by keywords.

When displaying information, search engines often show "Sponsored Sites Results" first. These are sites that contain the information being searched for but have paid the search engine to list their sites at the top of the list.

Boolean Logic

Boolean logic uses three logical operators:

AND   locates pages that include both words

OR locates pages that include one word or the other or both

NOT   locates pages that include the first word, but not the second word

A boolean expression always evaluates to TRUE or FALSE with pages that match the search condition evaluating to TRUE.

Practice: Searching the Web

Internet Explorer should already be started.

① GO TO THE YAHOO! SEARCH ENGINE

In the Address bar, replace the existing URL with www.yahoo.com, the URL for Yahoo!'s home page, and then press Enter. The Yahoo! home page is displayed.

② TYPE SEARCH CRITERIA

a. In the Search the Web box, type: shakespeare

b. Click Yahoo! Search to start the search. After a few moments a list of website hyperlinks are displayed. How many results matches are there?

c. Scroll down to display the results of the search, then click one of the hyperlinks that interests you. A new page is opened.

③ SELECT OTHER WEB PAGES LOCATED IN THE SEARCH

a. On the toolbar, click   ⓖ Back ▾ . The website hyperlinks are again displayed. Click a different web page hyperlink.

b. Continue this process to access additional pages.

④ DEFINE CRITERIA USING BOOLEAN OPERATORS

a. Refine the search criteria to: shakespeare OR "Globe Theatre" and see how many web page matches there are.

b. Refine the search criteria to: shakespeare +"Globe Theatre" and see how many web page matches there are. Note that there is no space after the + sign.

c. Further refine the criteria to: shakespeare +"Globe Theatre" +reconstruction –usa and see how many web page matches there are.

d. Click a few of the hyperlinks to determine if their web pages include the information that is being searched for.

⑤ GO TO THE YAHOO! HOME PAGE

⑥ USE A SUBJECT TREE TO FIND INFORMATION

a. On the Yahoo! home page, locate the list of Yahoo! Web Directory categories and click the Computers link in the list. Links to Computers subcategories are displayed.

b. Scroll down if necessary and click the Mobile Computing link.

c. In the Mobile Computing subcategories list, click the Wearable Computing link. A list of hyperlinks to appropriate sites is displayed.

d. Click one of the hyperlinks. The corresponding home page is displayed.

Evaluating and Citing Web Pages

Information found at a website, regardless of the category, should be evaluated for accuracy. Anyone can post a website on the Web. There are no rules as to the accuracy or reliability of the information. This means that you must discriminate, read carefully, and check sources.

A few topics to think about and questions to answer when evaluating a source are:

- **Up-to-date**. On what date was the web page last updated? Is the information current?

- **Bias**. Is the information incorrect or incomplete in order to give a particular or slanted view of a topic?

- **Validity**. Is the information truthful and trustworthy? What is the primary source of the information? Information posted by NASA or Yale University is more likely to be valid than information posted by an anonymous person who does not cite sources.

- **Author**. Does the author present his or her credentials? A well established authority in the field you are researching is probably a trustworthy source.

MLA If information from a website is to be referenced or quoted in a report, essay, or other document, a citation must be used to give credit to the original author and allow the reader to locate the cited information. A widely accepted form for citation is published by the Modern Language Association (MLA) in its publication *MLA Handbook for Writers of Research Papers, Fourth Edition*.

In general, a citation for material located at a website should look similar to:

Author's Last Name, First Name MI. Site Title. Access date. Organization name. <URL>.

Citing Online Sources

Online sources of information that are used to support research must be cited. This includes e-mail messages, graphics, sounds, video clips, and newsgroups. The MLA's website (www.mla.org) contains information on how to cite online sources.

A citation of a personal website could look similar to:

Rawlings, Julie. Home page. 23 Dec. 2006. <http://www.lpdatafiles.com/jrawlings/index.htm>.

A citation of an article in an online magazine could look similar to:

Schiffman, Paula. "Making Vinegar at Home." Vinegar Monthly. 4 May 2006. <http://www.lpdatafiles.com/vinegarassoc/journal.asp>.

A citation of a posting to a discussion list could look similar to:

Cruz, Anthony. "Are Orchestras Going Downhill?" online posting. 10 Oct. 2006. Tuscon Annual Ballet Conf. <http://www.lpdatafiles.com/tuscontoes/downhill.txt>.

Practice: Citing a Website

Internet Explorer should already be started.

① SEARCH FOR INFORMATION

Use one of the search engines listed in the "Searching the Web" section to search for web pages about the Egyptian Step Pyramid of Djoser.

② **EVALUATE WEBSITES**

Browse the links to find a web page that contains reliable information. Refer to the "Evaluating and Citing Web" section for a few topics to think about and questions to answer when evaluating a source to be reliable.

③ **CITE THE WEB PAGE**

Use the information on the web page to write a citation on paper.

Using Outlook Express

TIP Most e-mail messaging software has similar features. If you are using a different application you will still be able apply to the concepts discussed in this section to your e-mail software.

Outlook Express is e-mail messaging software that is accessible from Internet Explorer. Click the Mail button arrow (✉·) on the toolbar in Internet Explorer and select Read Mail to start Outlook Express and display the Inbox window:

The Inbox window contains three panes. The pane on the left is the Folders list where e-mail messages are stored. The top pane lists the messages in the selected folder, and the bottom pane displays the selected message.

Click the Create Mail button (📧·) on the toolbar to display a New Message window where an e-mail message can be composed:

Folders List

The Folders list is used to organize e-mail messages. Select File ➙ New Folder to create a new folder. E-mail messages can be dragged from the Inbox to the appropriate folder.

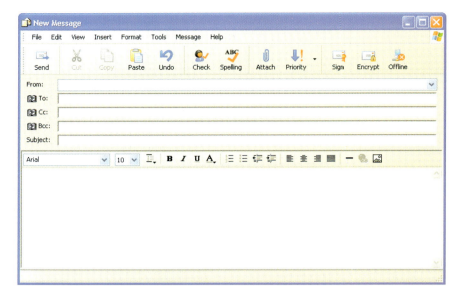

TIP Like the Cc box, the Bcc (blind carbon copy) box is used to type the e-mail address of additional recipients. However, recipients in the To and Cc boxes will not know these recipients received a copy of the e-mail message.

• Type the e-mail address of the recipient in the To box. Click the To button ( ) to display the Select Recipients dialog box where a stored e-mail address can be selected.

• Type the e-mail address of additional recipients in the Cc box. The Cc button ( ) also displays the Select Recipients dialog box.

• Type the message title in the Subject box.

• Type the message in the lower portion of the New Message window.

• Click the Send button ( ) on the New Message toolbar to send the message. It is important to review and spell check the message before sending because once a message is sent it cannot be retrieved.

• Click the Spelling button ( ) on the toolbar to check spelling.

The Attach button is used to send a file with an e-mail message. Click the Attach button ( ) to display the Insert Attachment dialog box:

Signatures

Select Tools ➔ Options and then select the Signatures tab to create a named signature that can be inserted at the bottom of an e-mail message. This saves typing the same information over and over again.

The Look in list and contents box below it are used to navigate to the file to be attached. Click the file name in the contents box and then select Attach to attach a copy of the file to the e-mail message.

When an e-mail message is sent, it resides in an electronic mailbox on a mail server until it is retrieved. Click the Send and Receive All button (📧 ·) on the toolbar to receive messages from the e-mail server and place them in the Inbox folder.

Other commonly used features in Outlook Express include:

Reply button Displays an e-mail message window that includes the original message and the sender's e-mail address in the To box. The Reply button should be used to respond to an e-mail message so that the recipient can refer to the original message.

Forward button Sends a selected e-mail message to another e-mail address that includes the original e-mail message and the original sender's e-mail address. Additional information can be added above the original message.

Print button Prints the displayed e-mail message.

Delete button Places the selected e-mail message in the Deleted Items folder. To permanently deleted the e-mail message, right-click the Deleted Items folder in the Folders list and select Empty 'Deleted Items' Folder and click Yes.

Address Book button Displays the address book for editing purposes.

Find button Searches for specific messages.

quit Outlook Express   Select File → Exit to close the Outlook Express window and remove the application from the computer's memory.

E-mail Etiquette

Rules to follow when composing e-mail messages include:

- Use manners. Include "please" and "thank you" and appropriately address individuals as Mr., Ms., Mrs., Dr., and so on.

- Be concise. Write in short, complete sentences.

- Be professional, which includes using the proper spelling and grammar. E-mail software usually has a built-in spelling checker.

- Re-read a message before it is sent. Always fill in the To box last to avoid sending a message before it is complete.

E-mail messages are not private. An e-mail message goes through several mail servers before it reaches the recipient, making it easily accessible for others to read. Therefore, a certain etiquette needs to be followed:

- Send messages through your account only.

- Use appropriate subject matter and language.

- Be considerate of other people's beliefs and opinions.

When sending e-mail at work or school, it is important to remember that employers and school administrators have the right to read any e-mail messages sent over the corporate or school network, as well as the right to track online activity.

Spam

Along with personal and business messages, most people also receive a lot of "junk e-mail" or spam. Most e-mail software includes features to filter and block messages from specific senders.

Internet Privacy Issues

The growth of the Internet has caused additional concerns about personal privacy. Searching for information on the Internet is not as anonymous as it might seem.

online profiling

The collection of data about consumers visiting a website is a marketing technique known as *online profiling*. When a commercial website is visited, information about the user may be collected using various methods such as cookies or web beacons.

cookie

A *cookie* is a text file created by the server computer when a user enters information into a website. The cookie file is then stored on the user's computer and accessed each time the user visits that website. Cookies are often created when online purchases are made. Although cookies can only store information that the user has selected or entered, their use has raised concerns over privacy issues.

Web beacons, also called *web bugs* or *pixel tags*, are tiny, transparent graphics located on web pages or in e-mail messages that are used in combination with cookies to collect data about web page users or e-mail senders. Usually the monitoring is done by an outside advertising company. The information a web beacon collects includes the IP address of the computer, the URL being visited, the time the web page was viewed, the type of browser being used, and the cookie file.

Before providing a company with personal information through a website, check the site's privacy policy. A *privacy policy* is a legally binding document that explains how any personal information will be used.

Information on a website is sometimes in the form of a downloadable file. *Downloading* is the process of copying a file from a website to the user's computer. For example, virus definitions can be downloaded from a antivirus software company's website and software updates can be down-loaded from the software company's website. When a file is downloaded, the user specifies where the file should be saved on the local computer. Files should only be downloaded from known, authentic websites since downloadable files are often associated with viruses.

The Internet has opened up access to many files that were previously inaccessible. To protect both the privacy of an individual and the accuracy of data stored about individuals, several laws have been passed:

- The **Electronic Communications Privacy Act of 1986 (ECPA)** makes it a crime to access electronic data without authorization. It also prohibits unauthorized release of such data.

- The **Electronic Freedom of Information Act of 1996 (E-FOIA)** requires federal government agencies to make certain agency information available for public inspection and is designed to improve public access to agency records by making more informa-tion available online.

- The **Children's Online Privacy Protection Act of 1998 (COPPA)** requires commercial websites that collect personal information from children under the age of 13 to obtain parental consent.

Spyware

Spyware is software that uses the Internet to gather personal information from an unsuspecting user. Spyware is unknowingly downloaded and installed with another file, such as freeware or shareware programs.

TIP A website's privacy policy is typically found as a link at the bottom of the home page of a website.

Digital Signature

A digital signature is a code that is attached to an electronic message to verify the authenticity of a website or e-mail message. Digital signatures are discussed further in Chapter 9.

Encryption

Encryption is the process of translating data into a code that is not readable without the key to the code. Encryption prevents unauthorized access to the data. Data that is encrypted is referred to as cipher text.

- The **Safety and Freedom through Encryption Act of 1999 (SAFE)** gives Americans the freedom to use any type of encryption to protect their confidential information.

Other laws have been passed that may invade the privacy of some to protect the safety of others. For example, the **Provide Appropriate Tools Required to Intercept and Obstruct Terrorism (PATRIOT) Act of 2001** gives law enforcement the ability to monitor individual's e-mail and web activity.

Internet Acceptable Use Policy

Internet content, unproductive use, and copyright have prompted many schools and businesses to develop an Acceptable Use Policy or Internet Use Agreement. Acceptable Use Policies typically contain rules similar to:

- Use appropriate language.

- Do not reveal personal address or phone numbers.

- Do not access, upload, download, or distribute inappropriate materials.

- Do not access another user's account.

- Use of the network for private business is prohibited.

- Only administrator installed software may be used on the computers. Adding, deleting, or modifying installed software is not permitted.

Internet Filtering Software

Many schools and organizations install Internet filtering software to block offensive material.

The Social and Ethical Implications of Computer Use

The society in which we live has been so profoundly affected by computers that historians refer to the present time as the *information age*. This is due to the our ability to store and manipulate large amounts of information (data) using computers. As an information society, we must consider both the social and ethical implications of our use of computers. By ethical questions we mean asking what are the morally right and wrong ways to use computers.

ergonomics

Ergonomics is the science that studies safe work environments. Many health-related issues, such as carpal tunnel syndrome and computer vision syndrome (CVS) are related to prolonged computer use.

Power and paper waste are environmental concerns associated with computer use. Suggestions for eliminating these concerns include recycling paper and printer toner cartridges and turning off monitors and printers when not in use.

Employee monitoring is an issue associated with computers in the workplace. It is legal for employers to install software programs that monitor employee computer use. As well, e-mail messages can be read without employee notification.

Identity Theft

Identity theft is a growing crime where personal information is stolen electronically in order to make fraudulent purchases or loans.

As discussed in a previous section in the chapter, the invasion of privacy is a serious problem associated with computers. Because computers can store vast amounts of data we must decide what information is proper to store, what is improper, and who should have access to the information. Every time you use a credit card, make a phone call, withdraw money, reserve a flight, or register at school, a computer records the transaction. These records can be used to learn a great deal about you—where you have been, when you were there, and how much money was spent. Should this information be available to everyone?

Computers are also used to store information about your credit rating, which determines your ability to borrow money. If you want to buy a car and finance it at a bank, the bank first checks your credit records on a computer to determine if you have a good credit rating. If you purchase the car and then apply for automobile insurance, another computer will check to determine if you have traffic violations. How do you know if the information being used is accurate? The laws listed below have been passed to help ensure that the right to privacy is not infringed by the improper use of data stored in computer files:

- The **Fair Credit Reporting Act of 1970** gives individuals the right to see information collected about them for use by credit, insurance, and employment agencies. If a person is denied credit they are allowed to see the files used to make the credit determination. If any of the information is incorrect, the person has the right to have it changed. The act also restricts who may access credit files to only those with a court order or the written permission of the individual whose credit is being checked.

- The **Privacy Act of 1974** restricts the way in which personal data can be used by federal agencies. Individuals must be permitted access to information stored about them and may correct any information that is incorrect. Agencies must insure both the security and confidentiality of any sensitive information. Although this law applies only to federal agencies, many states have adopted similar laws.

- The **Financial Privacy Act of 1978** requires that a government authority have a subpoena, summons, or search warrant to access an individual's financial records. When such records are released, the financial institution must notify the individual of who has had access to them.

Protecting Computer Software and Data

copyright

As society becomes more and more reliant on digital information, copyright and exposure to malicious code have become two important issues among computer users. *Copyright* is protection of digital information. Copyright infringement is the illegal use or reproduction of data (text, pictures, music, video, and so on). Laws, such as the NET Act (No Electronic Theft Act) of 1997, protect against copyright infringement. There have been several well-known cases of high penalties for individuals guilty of copyright infringement.

TIP It is usually legal to make one backup copy of a purchased software program.

Copyright infringement includes duplication of computer software when copies are being used by individuals who have not paid for the software. This practice is called *piracy* when illegal copies are distributed. Developing, testing, marketing, and supporting software is an expensive process. If the software developer is then denied rightful compensation, the future development of all software is jeopardized. Therefore, it is important to use only legally acquired copies of software, and to not make illegal copies for others.

Malicious code comes in many forms and is delivered in many ways. A virus, a Trojan horse, and an Internet worm are three forms of malicious code. They can appear on a system through executable programs, scripts, macros, e-mails, and some Internet connections. One devastating effect of malicious code is the destruction of data.

virus

A *virus* is a program or series of instructions that can replicate without the user's knowledge. Often a virus is triggered to run when given a certain signal. For example, a virus might check the computer's clock and then destroy data when a certain time is reached. A virus is easily duplicated when the file is copied, which spreads it to other computers.

Trojan horse

A *Trojan horse* program appears as something else, usually a program that looks trustworthy. Running the program runs the malicious code and damages files on the computer. A *worm* is a program that is able to reproduce itself over a network. *Worms* are a threat because of the way they replicate and use system resources, sometimes causing the system to shut down.

antivirus programs

Malicious code has become so widespread that software called *antivirus programs* must be installed on computers and networks to detect and remove the code before it can replicate or damage data. Precautions can also be taken to prevent damage from malicious code:

- Update antivirus software. An antivirus program can only detect the viruses, Trojan horses, and worms it is aware of. Antivirus programs have a web link for updating the virus definitions on the computer containing the antivirus program.

- Do not open e-mail attachments without scanning for malicious code. One estimate states that 80% of virus infection is through e-mail.

crackers, hackers

Newspapers have carried numerous reports of *crackers*, or *hackers*, gaining access to large computer systems to perform acts of vandalism. This malicious act is illegal and can cause expensive damage. The Electronic Communications Privacy Act of 1986 specifically makes it a federal offense to access electronic data without authorization. Networks usually include a firewall, which is a combination of hardware and software, to help prevent unauthorized access.

The willful destruction of computer data is no different than any other vandalizing of property. Since the damage is done electronically the result is often not as obvious as destroying physical property, but the consequences are much the same. It is estimated that computer crimes cost billions of dollars each year.

phishing

Phishing is the act of sending an e-mail to a user falsely claiming to be a legitimate business in an attempt to trick the user into revealing personal information that could be used for crimes such as identity theft.

The Ethical Responsibilities of the Web Developer

dynamic pages

Websites often contain *dynamic pages* that link to databases to provide the user real-time information. It is extremely difficult, if not impossible, for a web developer to guarantee that data is always valid. A cause for concern is the increased reliance by computer users on the data presented. This places a strong ethical burden on the web developers to ensure, as best they can, the reliability of the data.

As capable as computers have proven to be, we must be cautious when allowing them to replace human beings in areas where judgement is crucial. As intelligent beings, we can often detect that something out of the ordinary has occurred which has not been previously anticipated and then take appropriate actions. Computers will only do what they have been programmed to do, even if it is to perform a dangerous act.

Careers

The growth of the Web has created many new job opportunities in the IT (information technology) field. *IT* encompasses all aspects of computer-related technology.

IT

education requirements

Education requirements for IT careers vary widely. However, a formal education, such as an undergraduate degree in computer science, engineering, or business, is often required. A graduate degree may also be required in highly specialized fields. Some careers require a specialized certification course in an area such as networking. Other skills that are required in this industry are teamwork, problem-solving skills, oral and written communication, up-to-date technical knowledge, and computer experience.

web developer

Web developers design, build, and program websites. They determine the website strategy, which includes the hardware to be used and the design and navigation of the site. They also design tools, such as reports and databases, to measure the success of the website.

Web developers require programming and technical skills. Often the development is divided into back-end development and front-end development. Back-end development involves designing the hardware and database infrastructure, such as where orders are fulfilled. Front-end development involves the navigation and design of the website.

web designer

Web designers create the web page layouts and graphics for websites. The work a web designer does usually determines whether users will stay at a website. Their job involves presenting web pages so they are interesting and accessible.

A web designer requires knowledge of HTML, web implementation software such as Dreamweaver and Flash, and graphic editing software such as Fireworks, Photoshop, or Illustrator. Since technology changes rapidly, web designers must keep up-to-date on new technologies, techniques, and design standards.

webmaster   *Webmaster* responsibilities can include designing and creating web pages and maintaining the site. A webmaster is also responsible for answering e-mail about the website. A webmaster possesses extensive Internet knowledge, programming skills, and design experience.

web author   *Web authors* create textual content for web pages. A web author has good writing skills and carefully considers the text as it will be presented on the Web.

IT Departments and Companies

Most large companies have an IT department. Careers in these departments include the Web careers discussed in the previous section as well as:

intranet analysts
- *Intranet analysts* set up and maintain an intranet for a company or organization. This involves managing company intranet projects, technical support, and creating reports. This job requires technical knowledge of networks, network security features, computers, and software as well as personal communication skills.

network administrator
- A *network administrator* is responsible for a company's network. Duties could include installing the network hardware and software, as well as maintaining the network so it runs properly. LAN manager is another term for network administrator.

There are also many small to large companies that strictly provide IT services. These companies include:

ISP
- *ISPs* (Internet Service Providers) provide access to the Internet. Employees have a wide range of technical knowledge about networks, computers, and software since clients will have a variety of equipment. Personal communication skills are also necessary for sales and technical support.

web host
- *Web hosts* provide space on a server where users can post their web pages. Employees have technical knowledge of networks, computers, and the World Wide Web. Personal communication skills are also necessary for sales and technical support.

Pursuing an IT Career

The growth of the Web has resulted in colleges and universities changing their program offerings to better prepare students for careers in IT. Some degree options that are offered at a variety of schools include:

- Media, Information, and Technoculture
- Computer Arts
- Computer Engineering
- Computer Animation
- Information Technologies Support Services
- International Telecommunications Systems and Service
- Internet Commerce and Technology
- Electronic Media, Arts, and Communication

When selecting a college or university program, factors such as cost, length of program, program location, and course content should be examined. It is always a good idea to visit the school campus before deciding on a program.

A program that sounds interesting at a college or university should be matched to the job market. Employment opportunity ads should be examined to determine the demand for the specific job, job locations, salary range, and educational requirements.

Many colleges and universities are requiring students to submit an electronic portfolio as part of the admissions process. An example electronic portfolio is created in Chapter 8.

It is a good idea to keep an updated list of any acquired computer skills and knowledge in order to update a portfolio, create a resume, or complete a job application. Working through this text will help develop valuable computer skills that could help with a future job including:

- data entry skills
- knowledge of HTML
- website design and development using Dreamweaver

Chapter Summary

A desktop computer and its components are designed to fit on or under a desk. Mobile computers include notebooks, tablets, handhelds, smart phones, and wearables.

A network is a combination of hardware and software that allows computers to exchange data and share software and devices, such as printers. Networks are classified by their size, architecture, topology, and protocol. Network users should use netiquette.

A collection of related data stored on a lasting medium, such as a hard disk, is called a file. A file can be an application (program) or the product of an application. Folders are used to organize commonly related files.

An intranet is a network that is used by a single organization and is only accessible by authorized users. A firewall is a network security system that prevents unauthorized network access. An extranet extends an intranet by providing various levels of accessibility to authorized members of the public. The largest and most widely accessed network is the Internet.

Telecommunications is the transmitting and receiving of data. Telecommunication options include a conventional modem, a DSL modem, a cable modem, leased/dedicated lines, and ISDN.

The most widely used Internet service is the World Wide Web, also called the Web. Another widely used Internet service is e-mail. Other Internet services include instant messaging, BBS, network news, listserv, HTTP, FTP, Telnet, and Gopher.

A web browser, such as Internet Explorer, is needed to view web pages. In Internet Explorer, the History list is a list of the pages that have been visited in the last 20 days and the Favorites list is used to maintain a list of web pages. Web pages do not always print on a single sheet of paper. Therefore, it is important to preview a web page before printing to avoid printing unwanted pages.

A search engine is a program that searches a database of web pages for keywords and then lists hyperlinks to pages that contain those keywords. Search criteria is used by the search engine to determine a match. Limiting the number of matches to a reasonable number can be accomplished using Boolean logic in the search criteria. Some search engines also provide a subject tree, or web directory.

Information found at a website, regardless of the category, should be evaluated for accuracy. There are guidelines for citing electronic material on the Internet. The primary purpose of a citation is to give credit to the original author and allow the reader to locate the cited information.

E-mail software, such as Outlook Express, is used to send and receive e-mail messages. E-mail etiquette should be used when sending e-mail messages.

The growth of the Internet has caused concerns about personal privacy. Online profiling, cookies, and web bugs are all areas of concern. Before providing personal information through a website, check the site's privacy policy. To protect an individual's privacy, several laws have been passed. Concerns about Internet content, unproductive use, and copyright have prompted many schools and businesses to develop an Internet Use Agreement.

Historians refer to our present time as the information age. The potential for the use of computers to invade our right to privacy has prompted legislation to protect individuals. Piracy is the illegal act of duplicating software without permission. A virus is a computer file that erases data and can cause considerable damage.

Web developers should ensure, as best they can, the reliability of the data they provide in dynamic web pages.

The growth of the World Wide Web has created many new job opportunities in the IT field. IT stands for information technology and encompasses all aspects of computer-related technology. Web careers include web developer, web designer, webmaster, and web author. The growth of the Web has resulted in colleges and universities changing their program offerings to better prepare students for careers in web authoring or IT.

Address bus Carries memory addresses that indicate data storage locations.

ALU (Arithmetic Logic Unit) The part of the CPU that handles arithmetic and logic operations.

Antivirus program Software installed on computers and networks to detect and remove viruses.

Applications software Program written to perform a specific task.

Article The message posted to the newsgroup.

Banner ad One type of advertisement on websites.

Base unit Housing that contains the motherboard, CD-RW/DVD drive, disk drive, and hard disk drive.

Bulletin Board Service (BBS) A network service that allows a user to participate in a discussion group.

Bus A central network cable. Also a set of circuits that connect the CPU to other components.

Bus topology A physical LAN topology that uses a single central cable to attach each node directly.

Cable modem A modem that transmits data through a coaxial cable television network.

Cache High-speed memory used to store frequently used data so that it can be quickly retrieved by an application.

Client A computer that is sent information from a server computer.

Client/server network A type of network that consists of a group of computers, called clients connected to a server computer.

Clock rate The speed at which a CPU can execute instructions, measured in megahertz or gigahertz.

Commercial website A business-related website such as corporate presence or e-commerce.

Control bus Carries control signals.

Conventional modem A modem that uses standard telephone lines to convert analog signals to digital data.

Cookie Text file created by the server computer when a user enters information into a website.

Copyright Protects a piece of work from reproduction without permission from the work's author.

Corporate presence website A website created by companies and organizations for the purpose of displaying information about their products or services.

CPU (Central Processing Unit) Processes data and controls the flow of data between the computer's other units. Also contains the ALU. Located on the motherboard.

Cracker Person who accesses a computer system without authorization.

Dedicated line *See* Leased line.

Domain name Part of the URL that identifies a particular web page and is made up of a sequence of parts, or subnames, separated by a period.

Downloading The process of copying a file from a website to the user's computer.

DSL (Digital Subscriber Line) modem A modem that uses standard telephone phone lines. ADSL is the most common form used.

Dynamic pages Web pages that link to databases to provide the user real-time information.

E-commerce website A website created by businesses for the purposes of selling their products or services to consumers online.

E-mail (electronic mail) The sending and receiving of messages and electronic files over a communications network such as a LAN or the Internet.

Ergonomics The science that studies safe work environments.

Expansion boards Circuit boards that connect to the motherboard to add functionality to the computer.

Extranet An extended intranet that provides various levels of access to authorized members of the public.

Favorites list A list of web pages that have been added to the Internet Explorer Favorites list.

File A collection of related data stored on a lasting medium.

File name A unique name used to identify a file.

Firewall   A network security system that prevents unauthorized network access.

Folder   Used to organize commonly related files.

FTP (File Transfer Protocol)   Used to rapidly upload and download files from one computer to another over the Internet.

Gigahertz (GHz)   Billion of cycles per second.

Gopher   One of the first widespread Internet browsing services.

Hacker   *See* Cracker.

Handheld computer   A mobile computing device.

Hardware   The physical components of the computer, such as the monitor and system unit.

History list   A list of URLs and websites that have been visited in the previous days and weeks.

HTTP (Hypertext Transfer Protocol)   Handles the transmission of pages between a web server and a web browser.

Hub   A communication device that joins communication lines at a central location on the network.

Information age   Present time characterized by increasing dependence on the computer's ability to store and manipulate large amounts of information.

Informational website   A website created by educational institutions, governments, and organizations for the purpose of displaying information about a particular topic.

Input device   Device used to enter data and instructions into the computer.

Instant messaging (IM)   A communication tool that allows for real time, or immediate text-based communication.

Integrated circuits (ICs)   Memory that stores data electronically.

Interactive   Information accessed as a result of selections made by the user.

Internet   The largest and most widely accessed network.

Internet Service Providers   A company that provides access to the Internet.

Intranet   A network used by a single organization and only accessible by authorized users.

Intranet analyst   Sets up and maintains intranets for companies or organizations.

ISDN (Integrated Services Digital Network)   A digital telephone network provided by a local telephone company.

IT (Information Technology)   A term that encompasses all aspects of computer-related technology.

Kbps   Thousands of bits per second.

LAN (Local Area Network)   A network used to connect devices within a small area.

Leased line   A telecommunication option used for a permanent connection to the Internet that is always active.

Logical topology   Refers to the way in which data is passed between the nodes on a network.

Mailing list server   A server that manages mailing lists for groups of users.

Main memory   *See* Random Access Memory.

Match   A web page that contains the search criteria.

Mbps   Millions of bits per second.

Media website   Online newspaper and periodicals that are created by companies for the purpose of informing readers about current events and issues.

Megahertz (MHz)   Million of cycles per second.

Minus sign (−)   Used in search criteria to exclude unwanted Web pages.

Modern Language Association (MLA) Organization that publishes standards used for citations.

Motherboard   The main circuit board inside the base unit.

Netiquette   The etiquette that should be followed when using a network.

Network   A combination of software and hardware that allows computers to exchange data and to share software and devices, such as printers.

Network administrator   Responsible for a company's network. Also called LAN Manager.

Network architecture   The structure of a network.

Network interface card   A circuit board that goes into a computer or other device in a LAN.

Network news   A BBS available on the Internet.

Network operating system   Software that allows users and devices to communicate over a network.

Newsgroup   An individual bulletin board.

Node   A location on the network capable of processing information, such as a computer or a printer.

Notebook   A portable, lightweight computer.

Online profiling   A marketing technique that collects online data about consumers.

Operating system   Software that allows the user to communicate with the computer.

Output device   A device used to convey processed data.

Overwrite   Update an original file with changes.

Peer-to-peer network   A type of network that does not have a server.

Peripheral device   A device attached to a PC.

Personal website   A website created by an individual for the purpose of displaying information about themselves.

Phishing   The act of sending an e-mail to a user falsely claiming to be a legitimate business in an attempt to trick the user into revealing personal information that could be used for crimes such as identity theft.

Piracy   Illegally copying or distributing software.

Plus sign (+)   Used in search criteria to limit a search to only those web pages containing two or more specified words.

Port   Used to attach a peripheral device to a computer.

Portal website   A website created by businesses for the purpose of creating a starting point for people to enter the Web.

Primary memory   *See* RAM.

Privacy policy   A legally binding document that explains how any personal information will be used.

Protocol   A standard.

RAM (Random Access Memory)   Memory that temporarily stores data and instructions.

Real time   Occurs immediately.

Ring topology A physical LAN topology where each node is connected to form a closed loop.

ROM (Read Only Memory)   Memory that stores data and is a permanent part of the computer.

Router   A device that connects different network technologies.

Search criteria   A single word or phrase that is used by the search engine to match web pages.

Search engine   A program that searches a database of web pages for keywords and then lists hyperlinks to pages that contain those keywords.

Secondary memory   Any type of storage media, such as a floppy disk, hard disk, memory key, or CD-RW.

Server   A computer used to manage network functions such as communication and data sharing.

Smartphone   Cellular phone that is able to send and receive e-mail messages and access the Internet.

Star topology   A physical LAN topology where each node is attached to a hub.

Stylus   An input device that is shaped like a thin pencil.

Subject tree   A list of sites separated into categories.

Subname   Part of the URL that represents a server or organization. Also called a label.

Tablet PC   A computer designed similar to a pad of paper.

TCP/IP (Transmission Control Protocol/Internet Protocol)   Software used by networks connected to routers to communicate.

Telecommunications   The transmitting and receiving of data.

Telnet   A program that is used on networks such as the Internet to allow users to remotely log on to a server on the network.

Top-level domain   Part of the URL that identifies the type of website.

Topology   The physical or logical arrangement of the nodes on a network.

Transmission media   The media that joins the nodes on a network to enable communication.

Trojan horse Malicious code in the form of a program that appears as something else, usually a program that looks trustworthy.

URL An address that is interpreted by a web browser to identify the location of a page on the Web.

USENET The collection of all the servers that offer network news.

Virus A program that is designed to reproduce itself by copying itself into other programs stored on a computer without the user's knowledge.

WAN (Wide Area Network) A network used to connect computers over large geographical distances.

Wearable computer A mobile computing device that is incorporated into clothing, eyewear, wristwear, and other wearables.

Web *See* World Wide Web.

Web author Writes content for web pages.

Web beacon A tiny, transparent graphic located on a web page used to collect data about the web page user. Also called a web bug or pixel tag.

Web browser Interprets an HTML document to display a Web page.

Web designer Creates the web page layouts and graphics for websites.

Web developer Designs, builds, and programs websites.

Web directory *See* Subject tree.

Web host A company that provides a web server where web authors can post their websites.

Web server A server that has web server software installed and is designed to deliver web pages to clients.

Webmaster Designs and creates web pages, creates graphics for the site, and maintains the site.

Website A series of related web pages.

Wireless network A type of network that does not require the use of cables.

World Wide Web The most widely used Internet service. Used to search and access information available on the Internet.

Internet Explorer Commands and Buttons

Back button Displays the previously selected web page. Found on the toolbar.

Favorites button Displays the Favorites list, which is used to maintain a list of web pages Found on the toolbar.

Forward button Displays the next web page from the previously selected pages. Found on the toolbar.

Go button Opens the web page at the URL that was typed into the Address bar. Found on the Address bar.

History button Displays a pane with the URLs of websites that have been visited in the previous days and weeks. Found on the toolbar.

Home button Displays the History list, which lists the URLs. Found on the toolbar.

Mail button Displays a submenu of Outlook Express commands. Found on the toolbar.

Print button Prints the currently displayed web pages. Found on the toolbar.

Print Preview **command** Displays the web page as it will appear when printed. Found in the File menu.

Refresh button Updates the displayed web page. Found on the toolbar.

Search button Displays a pane used to locate web pages that contain particular information. Found on the toolbar.

Stop button Stops the transmission of a web page. Found on the toolbar.

Outlook Express Commands and Buttons

Address Book button Displays the address book. Found on the toolbar.

Attach button Displays a dialog box that is used to send a file with an e-mail message. Found on the New Message toolbar.

Cc button Displays a dialog box used to select e-mail addresses for additional recipients. Found in the New Message window.

Create Mail button Displays a New Message window used to compose an e-mail message. Found on the toolbar.

Delete button Places the selected e-mail message in the Deleted Items folder. Found on the toolbar.

Exit **command** Closes the Outlook Express window and removes the application from the computer's memory. Found in the File menu.

Find button Searches for specific messages. Found on the toolbar.

Forward button Sends a selected e-mail message to another e-mail address. Found on the toolbar.

Print button Prints the displayed e-mail message. Found on the toolbar.

Reply button Displays an e-mail message window that includes the original message and the sender's e-mail address in the To box. Found on the toolbar.

Send/Receive All button Sends and receives messages from the e-mail server. Found on the toolbar.

Spelling button Checks the spelling in an e-mail message. Found in the New Message window.

To button Displays a dialog box used to select an e-mail address. Found in the New Message window.

1. a) What is hardware?
    b) What are input and output devices used for?
    c) What is a peripheral device?

2. List and describe five components found on the motherboard.

3. List three examples of storage media.

4. Describe the flow of data between the components of a computer, starting with input.

5. Describe one difference between operating system software and applications software.

6. a) List four types of mobile computing devices.
    b) What is a stylus used for?
    c) Describe one type of wearable computer.

7. List four benefits of using a network.

8. a) What are the two common size classifications for networks?
    b) What size classification is used to connect devices over large geographical distances?

9. What is a network operating system?

10. a) What does network architecture refer to?
    b) List two common network architecture models.

11. a) What does physical topology refer to?
    b) What is a node?
    c) Which topology uses a hub?
    d) Which topology connects each node to form a closed loop?
    e) What is the difference between physical and logical topology?

12. List three netiquette rules.

13. a) Why is it important to give files and folders descriptive names?
    b) Why would organizing files into folders be considered a good practice?

14. What is the difference between an intranet and an extranet?

15. a) What is the Internet?
    b) Who controls the Internet?

16. List three telecommunications options.

17. a) If a business needed constant access to the Internet, what type of connection line would be a good choice? Why?
    b) What does a cable modem use instead of analog phone lines?

18. What is the most widely used Internet service?

Answer question 19 using Internet search skills or by discussing the answers with a partner.

19. a) E-commerce websites are often an extension of a traditional or "brick-and-mortar " business. List one traditional business that uses an e-commerce website as a method of extending their business.
    b) Amazon.com is an example of a business that only does transactions on-line. List an example of another business that only conducts business through their website.
    c) Compare shopping at an e-commerce website with traditional shopping. List two advantages and two disadvantages of shopping at an e-commerce website.
    d) List an example of a media website.
    e) Yahoo! is an example of a portal website. List another example of a portal website.

20. a) What is a URL?
    b) Label and describe each part of the URL http://www.lpdatafiles.com.

21. a) What is e-mail?
    b) List one benefit of e-mail over standard mail.
    c) Write your e-mail address and label the parts of the address.
    d) What are the two requirements for sending and receiving e-mail messages?

22. a) What is instant messaging?
    b) What is required to send instant messages?
    c) List two instant messaging services.
    d) List one advantage of sending an instant message instead of an e-mail message.

23. a) What does a bulletin board service allow a user to participate in?
    b) Locate and describe a listserv that is of interest to you.

24. a) What is the History list?
    b) What is the Favorites list used for?

25. a) What is a search engine?
    b) List three commonly used search engines.
    c) Which search engine do you prefer to use, and why?
    d) What is search criteria?
    e) What is a match?

26. Write search criteria to locate web pages that contain the following information:
    a) restaurants in Los Angeles
    b) art museums in Boston
    c) auto repair jobs in Montreal, Canada
    d) mosquitoes and bees, but not ants
    e) the English author Jane Austen
    f) the phrase *to each his own*
    g) George Washington and John Adams, but not Thomas Jefferson
    h) travel to Ireland, but not Dublin

27. What is the purpose of a subject tree?

28. a) List four questions to answer when evaluating a website source.
    b) Why is it necessary to cite sources?
    c) On August 2, 2006 you accessed a posting on the Clewiston Kite Surfing discussion list at http://www.lpdatafiles.com/kitesurf/color.txt. The posting was made by Tara Perez on the topic of kite colors. Write a citation for a research paper that quotes Tara's posting.

29. a) Explain why sending an e-mail message should be thought of the same as sending a postcard.
    b) List three examples of e-mail etiquette.

30. What is online profiling?

31. What is a cookie?

32. a) What is a web beacon?
    b) Who usually monitors the information collected by web beacons?

33. What is a privacy policy?

34. Name and briefly describe one law that helps protect the privacy of an individual.

35. a) List three reasons why many schools have developed an Acceptable Use Policy.
    b) List an example of a rule that typically appears on an Acceptable Use Policy.

36. What can you do if you are turned down for credit at a bank and believe that the data used to deny credit is inaccurate?

37. a) What is necessary for a federal government authority to access an individual's financial records?
    b) What must a financial institution do after releasing an individual's records?

38. a) What is copyright infringement?
    b) What is computer piracy?
    c) What is a computer virus?
    d) What is a computer hacker?
    e) What is a firewall used for?

39. What ethical responsibilities does a web developer have?

40. Describe four IT careers.

41. a) What do ISPs provide?
    b) Which career includes setting up and maintaining an intranet for a company or organization?
    c) What duties are typical of a network administrator?

True/False

42. Determine if each of the following are true or false. If false, explain why.
    a) FireWire and USB are types of ports.
    b) A peer-to-peer network has a server.
    c) A LAN's logical topology is always the same as its physical topology.
    d) The most widely accessed network is the Internet.
    e) A conventional modem transmits data faster than a cable modem.
    f) .com is a top-level domain.
    g) E-mail allows for real-time communication.
    h) E-mail messages are private.
    i) Web pages always print on a single sheet of paper.
    j) Information found at a website is always accurate.
    k) The present time is referred to as the industrial age.
    l) A virus is a harmless computer game.

Exercises

Exercise 1

In this exercise you will research your classroom computer network by answering a series of questions:

- a) Is your computer network a LAN or a WAN?

- b) List one device that is shared on the network.

- c) Locate the cable that plugs into the network interface card on your workstation.

- d) What type of physical topology is used?

- e) What type of transmission media is used?

- f) What network protocol is used?

- g) What operating system is used?

- h) What telecommunication option is used?

- i) Does the school have an intranet?

- j) List four rules on the school's Internet Use Agreement.

Exercise 2

In this exercise you will assess the input and output devices you have access to.

- a) List the input devices accessible on the classroom network. Which of these devices will be helpful in the development of a website?

- b) Describe one additional input device that is not available but would be helpful when developing a website.

- c) List the output devices accessible on the classroom network. List advantages and disadvantages associated with each accessible output device.

Exercise 3

Become familiar with different categories of websites by completing the following steps:

- a) Use the Internet to locate an example of a personal website. List the URL and briefly describe the content at the site.

- b) Use the Internet to locate an example of an e-commerce website. List the URL and briefly describe the products that can be purchased at this site.

- c) Use the Internet to locate an example of an informational website. List the URL and briefly describe the information available at the site.

- d) Use the Internet to locate an example of a media website. Print the home page of the media website and note how up-to-date the content is.

- e) Use the Internet to locate an example of a portal website. Print the home page of the portal website and circle four hyperlinks available on the portal home page.

Exercise 4

Examine and evaluate website content by completing the following steps:

a) Go to the www.cnn.com web page.

b) Read the content on the home page.

c) On what date was the web page last updated?

d) Is the information incorrect or incomplete in order to give a particular or slanted view of a topic? Explain your answer.

e) Is the information truthful and trustworthy? Explain your answer.

f) Describe a banner ads displayed on this site.

g) Go to the www.earthday.net web page.

h) Repeat steps (b) through (g) for the Earth Day Network website.

Exercise 5

You are interested in finding a job in Los Angeles, California and are skilled in website design. A full-time position with a local website design company would be ideal.

a) Conduct a search on the Internet using at least two search engines to find two possible positions. Write a citation for each source.

b) Write a brief description of each of the positions that you found.

c) You also need information on moving to Los Angeles. First, you will want to rent an apartment and cannot afford more than $1,500 a month. Conduct a search on the Internet to come up with brief descriptions of three apartments in Los Angeles that rent for $1,500 or less.

d) Add a paragraph that describes all three apartments, including number of bedrooms and bathrooms and rent per month.

Exercise 6

Your English instructor has assigned a report on the American authors Kurt Vonnegut, Jr. and Ernest Hemingway. Keep in mind that knowledge of information like the titles of their books might help in your search. Because people maintain web pages as homages to their favorite authors, but are not obligated to check their facts for accuracy, it is a good idea to double check the information you find with more than one web page.

a) Conduct a search on the Internet using at least two search engines to find biographical data on each author.

b) Create a folder named American Authors in the Favorites list and add three relevant web pages to this folder.

c) Write a paragraph of biographical information for each author.

d) Write a citation for each source.

Exercise 7

In this exercise you will organize your existing files. You may need to refer to the appropriate operating system chapter on www.lpdatafiles.com to complete this exercise.

a) Examine the files you currently have saved on your computer. Use the appropriate operating system command to rename any files that do not have descriptive names.

b) Use the appropriate operating system commands to organize your existing files into appropriate folders.

Exercise 8

A good friend has been diagnosed with Carpal Tunnel Syndrome and would like you to find out as much as you can about the injury and possible treatments.

a) Conduct a search on the Internet using at least two search engines to find three web pages that have information about Carpal Tunnel Syndrome.

b) Create a folder named: Carpal Tunnel Syndrome in the Favorites list and add relevant web pages to this folder.

c) Write a brief description of the injury.

d) In a second paragraph, write about possible treatments for the injury.

e) Write a citation for each source.

Exercise 9

Expand on the information presented in this chapter by researching one of the following topics:

- Network Protocols
- Operating Systems
- The History of the Internet

a) Use the Internet, magazines, and books to find at least three sources of information.

b) Write a two page report that summarizes your research.

c) Write a citation for each source.

Exercise 10

In this exercise you will research and compare the advantages and cost of obtaining Internet access through three different telecommunication options.

a) Use the Internet and newspapers to find information about ISPs.

b) Compare the costs and the advantages of at least three different telecommunication options.

c) Write a one paragraph conclusion that explains what telecommunication option would be the best choice.

d) Write a citation for each source.

Exercise 11

In this exercise you will further research emerging technologies and find real-life examples of how these technologies have impacted individuals and businesses.

   a) Use the Internet, magazines, and books to learn more about at least three emerging technologies. Look specifically for information on how these emerging technologies impact individuals and businesses. For example, speech recognition technology greatly impacts those individuals who must rely on voice input rather than keyboard input for a PC.

   b) Write a two-page report that summarizes the impact of and lists several functions of the emerging technologies you have researched.

   c) Write a citation for each source.

Exercise 12

Many computer viruses have been associated with e-mail attachments.

   a) Conduct a search on the Internet to find information about a virus associated with an e-mail attachments.

   b) Write a one-paragraph description of the virus. Include details, such as the damage caused by the virus and steps necessary to remove the virus.

   c) Write a citation for each source.

Exercise 13

You have decided to investigate marine biology as a possible career path.

   a) Conduct a search on the Internet using at least two search engines to find three bachelor degree programs in marine biology.

   b) List each program location (college name), the number of credits required to finish the degree, and the tuition cost per credit or per course.

Exercise 14

In this exercise you will investigate bulletin boards and mailing lists.

   a) Join an appropriate bulletin board or mailing list.

   b) Participate on the bulletin board or mailing list as a learner.

   c) Contribute to the bulletin board or mailing list content.

   d) Research the process of starting a bulletin board or mailing list. Present your research in a written report, citing all sources.

Chapter 2

HTML

T his chapter introduces HTML. Using Notepad and viewing an HTML document in a browser are also discussed.

The World Wide Web

The most widely used Internet service is the World Wide Web (WWW), also called the Web. The *Web* is used to search and access information available on the Internet. A *web browser application*, such as Internet Explorer provides a graphic interface to present information from a website. A *website* consists of a series of related web pages. For example, a CNN web page looks similar to:

web browser application

website

Browsers

Commonly used web browser applications include Internet Explorer, Netscape, Opera, Firefox, Amaya, and Safari.

A web page displayed in a web browser

Tim Berners-Lee
1955 –
Tim Berners-Lee is credited with creating the World Wide Web. Berners-Lee now heads a non-profit group, the W3C (World Wide Web Consortium), which sets technical standards for the Web.

Most web pages are created using HTML (HyperText Markup Language) and other code. *HTML* is a markup language that is well suited for the Web because it supports hypertext and multimedia. *Hypertext* is a database system where objects, such as text and images, can be linked. *Multimedia* includes images, video, audio, and Java applets, which can be embedded in an HTML document.

Millions of people all over the world are able to view and author web content because the World Wide Web Consortium (W3C) continuously develops standards for the Web. These standards include HTML standards to ensure that HTML documents display similarly in different browsers and across different platforms. They have also developed Web accessibility standards for those with disabilities.

HTML

HTML uses a set of codes, called *tags*, to "mark up" plain text so that a browser application, such as Internet Explorer, knows how to interpret the text. A tag is comprised of an *element* inside angle brackets (<>). For example, <title> is called the title tag, where title is the element. Tags affect the text they surround, and are usually paired to indicate the start and end of an instruction. A slash (/) before the element indicates the end of an instruction, such as </title>.

A web page with one line of text will be displayed when the HTML document below is opened in a browser.

```
<html>

<head>
<title>An example HTML document</title>
</head>

<body>
<p>Hello world!</p>
</body>

</html>
```

TIP HTML is not case sensitive, so tags may be uppercase or lowercase. This text uses lowercase tags.

Text marked up with <title> and </title> displays An example HTML document in the title bar of the browser window. The text Hello world! is marked to be displayed as a paragraph (<p> and </p>) in the body of the browser window (<body> and </body>). When viewed in Internet Explorer, the document appears similar to:

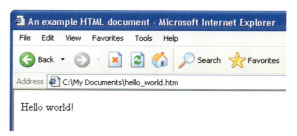

HTML 4

The current version of HTML is HTML 4. HTML 4 is supported by newer browsers.

Validating HTML

HTML documents can be validated to ensure they are meeting W3C standards at http://validator.w3.org.

In order to validate an HTML document, a DTD (document definition tag) must be included as the first line of an HTML document. For example, to check to see if an HTML document meets HTML 4.01 standards, the tag:

<<!DOCTYPE HTML PUBLIC "-//W3C//DTD HTML 4.01// EN" "http://www.w3.org/TR/ hmtl4/stict.dtd"> is included.

HTML documents are plain text files and can be created using any text editor such as Notepad or by using a word processor. In general, the structure of an HTML document should be similar to:

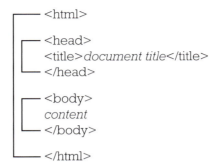

An HTML document contains pairs of tags

The html, head, title, and body tags are called *document tags*:

- The <html> tag tells the browser that the file contains HyperText Markup Language.

- The <head> tag defines the section that contains information about the document, including its title. This section will not be displayed as part of the document content.

- The <title> tag marks the document title. The title section must be within the head section. The document title should be descriptive and meaningful because it is displayed in the title bar of the browser window and is also used when the user adds the document to the Favorites list.

- The <body> tag defines the body section, which contains the document's content. All content must be enclosed in the appropriate tags. For example, on the previous page, the content is marked as a paragraph. Paragraph tags are discussed later in this chapter.

TIP To help make an HTML document easier to understand, place document tags on separate lines, except the title tags, and use blank lines to separate sections of HTML.

HTML documents are *free-form*, which means that spaces and blank lines generally have no effect on how the document is interpreted. Therefore, the document:

```
<html><head><title>An example HTML document</title>
</head>
<body>  <p>Hello world!</p></body></html>
```

TIP A tag should not have any spaces between the opening bracket and the element or slash.

Poorly structured HTML document

displays exactly the same as the HTML document on the previous page. However, editing a poorly structured document can be time-consuming and error-prone.

Starting Notepad

To start Notepad, select Start → All Programs → Accessories → Notepad.

Word Wrap

To make long paragraphs of text easier to read in Notepad, select Format → Word Wrap.

TIP If using a word processor, be sure to save the document as a TXT file.

File Names

File names can be up to 255 characters long and can contain letters, the underscore character (_), and numbers. File names cannot contain colons (:), asterisks (*), question marks (?), and some other special characters. File names for HTML documents should not contain spaces.

Notepad is a text editor that comes with the Windows operating system and is well suited for creating and editing plain text files, such as HTML documents. When Notepad is started, a new, blank document is displayed in the Notepad window. An HTML document can then be typed.

To save an HTML document, select File → Save. The Save As dialog box is displayed the first time a document is saved. Use the Save in list and the contents box below it to navigate to the location where the file is to be saved. Select the Text Documents (*.txt) option in the Save as type list and type a descriptive file name in the File name box:

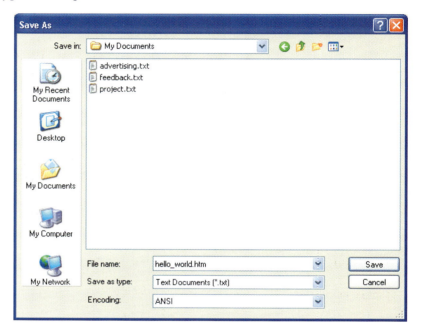

The descriptive file name should be lowercase and should not contain any spaces. The underscore character is used to separate words. The .htm extension needs to be added to the file name so that a browser recognizes the file as an HTML document.

To print a document, select File → Print. Notepad automatically prints a centered header containing the file name and a centered footer containing the page number.

To create a new document, select File → New. To open an existing document, select File → Open, which displays a dialog box. Change the Files of type to All Files to display the HTML document file name in the contents box. Click the appropriate file name and then select Open.

To quit Notepad, select File → Quit. A warning dialog box is displayed if the document has been modified since it was last saved.

Viewing HTML Documents in a Web Browser

TIP An HTML document can be viewed in a browser by locating the document in My Computer and then double-clicking the document.

A web browser is used to access and view HTML documents that have been published to a web server. The web browser first interprets the URL to identify the location of the of the page on the Web and then interprets the HTML document to display a web page in the browser window. In Internet Explorer, select View → Source to view the HTML associated with a displayed web page.

HTML documents saved on a local computer can also be viewed in a browser. In Internet Explorer, select File → Open to display the Open dialog box. Select Browse to display a dialog box, which is used to navigate to the location where the HTML document is saved.

HTML documents that are posted to the Internet are the designer's intellectual property and are protected by copyright. This applies even if a copyright notation (©) is not included on the page.

Multitasking

Multitasking is an operating system feature that allows more than one application to run at a time.

When developing an HTML document, frequent viewing in a browser is usually necessary. This is easily done by having both Notepad and a web browser open at the same time and using the Windows taskbar to switch between the applications. In Internet Explorer, the Refresh button (🔁) is used to check the HTML file for changes and then update the document in the browser window. Any changes made to the HTML document in Notepad must be saved before refreshing the browser.

Practice: first_document.htm

This practice assumes that you have Notepad and Internet Explorer.

① START NOTEPAD

Ask your instructor for the appropriate steps to start Notepad.

② CREATE AN HTML DOCUMENT

Type the following HTML document exactly as shown. Be sure to include a blank line between sections, as indicated, and replace Name with your name:

```
<html>

<head>
<title>First HTML Document</title>
</head>

<body>
<p>My name is Name. Hello world!</p>
</body>

</html>
```

③ SAVE THE HTML DOCUMENT

a. Select File → Save. The Save As dialog box is displayed.

b. Use the Save in list and the contents box below it to select the appropriate location for the file to be saved.

c. In the Save as type list, select Text Documents (*.txt) if it is not already selected.

d. In the File name box, replace the existing text with: first_document.htm

e. Select Save. The document is saved with the name first_document.htm.

④ START INTERNET EXPLORER

Ask your instructor for the appropriate steps to start Internet Explorer.

⑤ OPEN FIRST_DOCUMENT.HTM IN INTERNET EXPLORER

a. Select File → Open. A dialog box is displayed:

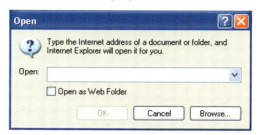

b. Select Browse. A dialog box is displayed.

c. Use the Look in list and the contents box below it to locate the file name first_document.htm.

d. In the contents box, click: first_document.htm

e. Select Open. The dialog box is removed and the location and file name are placed in the Open box.

f. Select OK. The tags are interpreted and the HTML document appears in the browser and the document title appears in the title bar:

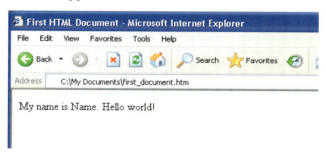

⑥ SWITCH TO NOTEPAD AND MODIFY FIRST_DOCUMENT.HTM

a. On the taskbar, click the Notepad button. The first_document.htm document is displayed.

b. Place the insertion point to the right of the ! in world! and type a space followed by: This is my first HTML document.

c. Save the modified file.

d. Select File → Print and then select Print in the dialog box. A copy of the HTML document is printed.

⑦ SWITCH TO INTERNET EXPLORER AND REFRESH THE VIEW

a. On the taskbar, click the Internet Explorer button. The first_document.htm document is displayed without the additional content.

b. On the toolbar, click the Refresh button (🔄). Internet Explorer updates the displayed document.

Creating Paragraphs and Line Breaks

<p> The body section of an HTML document includes the content and tags that format the content. Text enclosed by <p> and </p> is a paragraph. Lines of paragraph text are automatically wrapped by the browser, and blank space is added after each paragraph.

**
** To move a line of text within a paragraph to the next line, a break tag <br> is used. A break tag does not need to be paired.

Headings

<h1> through <h6> Heading tags are used to emphasize text. There are six levels of headings, which are numbered 1 through 6 and represented with tags <h1> through <h6>. The HTML document below includes all six heading tags:

```
<html>

<head>
<title>Heading Formats</title>
</head>

<body>
<h1>Heading 1</h1>
<h2>Heading 2</h2>
<h3>Heading 3</h3>
<h4>Heading 4</h4>
<h5>Heading 5</h5>
<h6>Heading 6</h6>
</body>

</html>
```

Each heading level has specific formatting associated with it, which includes font size, bold text, and space above and below the heading. Heading 1 has the largest font size and is used to represent the most important information. Heading 6 has the smallest font size. For example, the above HTML document viewed in a browser will look similar to:

Browser Preferences

The formatting associated with heading tags varies between browsers and is dependent on the preferences set by the user.

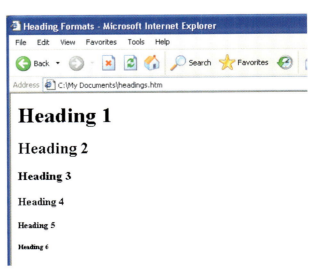

Adding Horizontal Rules

The <hr> tag places a horizontal *rule* (line) across the width of the browser window. This feature is used to divide the text in the browser window into sections for easier reading. The horizontal rule tag does not need to be paired.

attribute

Tags may also contain attributes. An *attribute* is placed in the start tag and set to a value that modifies the element. For example, the horizontal rule width attribute specifies the width of the line in the browser window as a percentage:

```
<hr width="50%">
```

Other attributes of the <hr> tag include:

- size=*"value"* specifies the thickness of the rule in pixels.

- align=*"value"* specifies the rule alignment. The default alignment is center.

Practice: Computer Viruses – part 1 of 5

Internet Explorer and Notepad should already be started.

① SWITCH TO NOTEPAD

② CREATE A NEW HTML DOCUMENT

a. Select File → New.

b. Type the following HTML document exactly as shown, replacing Name with your name:

```
<html>

<head>
<title>Computer Viruses</title>
</head>

<body>
<h1>Computer Viruses</h1>
<hr>
<p>A computer virus is a program that is loaded onto the computer
without the user's knowledge. Computer viruses have varying
effects, such as:<br>
displaying annoying messages<br>
causing programs to run incorrectly<br>
erasing the contents of the hard drive</p>
<p>In order to protect against viruses:<br>
install an antivirus program<br>
update antivirus definitions on a regular basis</p>
<h4>Report by Name</h4>
</body>

</html>
```

③ SAVE THE HTML DOCUMENT

Save the document in the same folder as first_document.htm and name it: computer_viruses.htm.

④ OPEN COMPUTER_VIRUSES.HTM IN INTERNET EXPLORER

a. Switch to Internet Explorer.

b. Select File ➜ Open. A dialog box is displayed.

c. Select Browse. A dialog box is displayed.

d. Use the Look in list and the contents box below it to locate the file name computer_viruses.htm.

e. In the contents box, click: computer_viruses.htm

f. Select Open. The dialog box is removed and the location and file name are placed in the Open box.

g. Select OK. The tags are interpreted and the HTML document appears in the browser:

⑤ PRINT THE HTML DOCUMENT

a. Switch to Notepad.

b. If necessary, make corrections to the HTML document.

c. From Notepad, print a copy of the computer_viruses.htm document.

Creating Lists

bulleted list

Lists are used to organize information. Bulleted and numbered are two types of lists that can be created in an HTML document. A *bulleted list*, also called an *unordered list*, is used when each item is equally important:

Bulleted list tags include:

* <ul> </ul> defines the start and end of a bulleted list
* <li> </li> defines the start and end of an item

numbered list

A *numbered list*, also called an *ordered list*, is used to show priority of importance, for example as steps in a recipe:

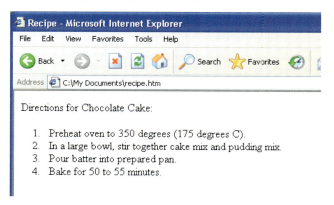

Numbered list tags include:

* <ol> </ol> defines the start and end of a numbered list
* <li> </li> defines the start and end of a list item

Practice: Computer Viruses – part 2 of 5

Internet Explorer and Notepad should already be started with computer_viruses.htm displayed in Notepad.

① MODIFY COMPUTER_VIRUSES.HTM TO INCLUDE LISTS

Modify the BODY section of computer_viruses.htm to include a bulleted and numbered list by removing the existing <br> tags and adding the list tags as shown:

```
<body>
<h1>Computer Viruses</h1>
<hr>
<p>A computer virus is a program that is loaded onto the computer
without the user's knowledge. Computer viruses have varying
effects, such as:</p>
<ul>
<li>displaying annoying messages</li>
<li>causing programs to run incorrectly</li>
<li>erasing the contents of the hard drive</li>
</ul>
<p>In order to protect against viruses:</p>
<ol>
<li>install an antivirus program</li>
<li>update antivirus definitions on a regular basis</li>
</ol>
<h4>Report by Name</h4>

</body>
```

② **SAVE THE MODIFIED COMPUTER_VIRUSES.HTM**

③ **SWITCH TO INTERNET EXPLORER AND REFRESH THE VIEW**

    a. On the taskbar, click the Internet Explorer button. The computer_viruses.htm document is displayed without the modified content.

    b. On the toolbar, click the Refresh button (). The document is updated:

④ **PRINT THE HTML DOCUMENT**

    a. Switch to Notepad.

    b. If necessary, make corrections to the HTML document.

    c. From Notepad, print a copy of the computer_viruses.htm document.

Tables

Tables are used to arrange data in an HTML document:

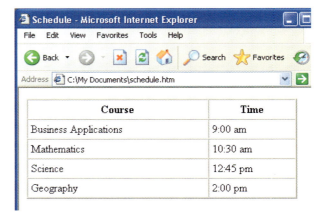

Table tags include:

- \<table> \</table> creates a table
- \<th> \</th> creates a table header, which is a cell with bold, centered text in the first row of the table
- \<tr> \</tr> defines the start and end of a table row
- \<td> \</td> defines the start and end of a table data cell

The table tag may also contain attributes. For example, the border attribute is used to change the thickness of a table border:

```
<table border="2">
```

Table attributes include:

- border="*value*" specifies the thickness of the cell border where value is in pixels
- cellpadding="*value*" sets the amount of space between table cells where value is a number
- width="*value*" specifies the width of a table where value is a number in pixels or as a percentage of the document's width

Hyperlinks

A *hyperlink*, also called a link, is text displayed in a browser window that can be clicked to display a different HTML document in the browser window. Hyperlinks are what make a hypertext system, such as the Web work. Countless documents can all be linked, allowing the user to go from topic to topic, or browse HTML documents. By default, hyperlinks are displayed as blue underlined text in the browser window. Links that have been clicked are referred to as *visited hyperlinks* and display in purple underlined text.

visited hyperlink

TIP Tables can also be used to control the layout of an entire HTML document by placing content in table cells and setting the border attribute to 0.

Pixels

A pixel (picture element) is a single point in a graphic. A graphic is made up of thousands of pixels.

The anchor tag (<a>) is used in an HTML document to mark text that is a link. The href attribute is set in the tag to the name of the linked document:

```
<html>

<head>
<title>Images</title>
</head>

<body>
<p>Images can come from a variety of sources
including <a href="digicam.htm">digital cameras</a>.</p>
</body>

</html>
```

When viewed in a browser, the HTML document above will look similar to:

The text digital cameras is called the hyperlink label. Click digital cameras to display the digicam.htm document.

Practice: Computer Viruses – part 3 of 5

Internet Explorer and Notepad should already be started.

① CREATE A NEW HTML DOCUMENT

a. In Notepad, select File ➞ New.

b. Type the following HTML document exactly as shown, replacing Name with your name:

```
<html>

<head>
<title>Antivirus Program</title>
</head>

<body>
<h2>Checking for Viruses</h2>
<p>A computer can be checked for viruses using an antivirus program. An antivirus program is a utility that scans a hard disk for viruses. If a virus is located, it will be removed by the antivirus program.</p>
<h2>Example Virus Threats</h2>
<table border="2" width="300" cellpadding="5">
<th>Virus</th>
<th>Threat</th>
```

```
<tr><td>Worm MyDoom.p</td>
<td>Low</td></tr>
<tr><td>Worm Blueworm.D</td>
<td>Low</td></tr>
<tr><td>Worm Bagle.AI</td>
<td>Medium</td></tr>
</table>
<h5>Report by: Name</h5>
</body>

</html>
```

② SAVE THE DOCUMENT

a. Save the document in the same folder as computer_viruses.htm and name it: antivirus.htm

b. In Internet Explorer, open antivirus.htm in a browser. The tags are interpreted and the HTML document appears in the browser:

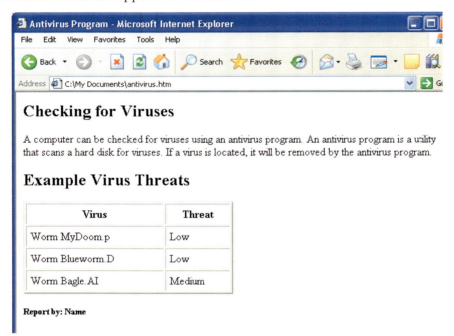

c. If necessary, make corrections to the HTML document.

d. From Notepad, print a copy of the antivirus.htm document.

③ OPEN COMPUTER_VIRUSES.HTM IN NOTEPAD

a. Select File ➡ Open. A dialog box is displayed.

b. In the Files of type list, select All Files.

c. Use the Look in list and the contents box below it to locate computer_viruses.htm.

d. In the contents box, click: computer_viruses.htm.

e. Select Open. The dialog box is removed and the computer_viruses.htm document is displayed in the Notepad window.

④ ADD A HYPERLINK

a. Near the bottom of the body contents, place the insertion point right after the space after the text install an.

b. Type the tag:

```
<a href="antivirus.htm">
```

c. Place the insertion point to the right of the text "antivirus program" and to the left of </li> and then add the tag </a>

Check — The line should look like:

```
install an <a href="antivirus.htm">antivirus program</a></li>
```

d. Save the modified computer_viruses.htm document.

⑤ **TEST THE HYPERLINK**

a. In Internet Explorer, open computer_viruses.htm.

b. Click antivirus program. The antivirus.htm document is displayed in the browser.

⑥ **PRINT THE HTML DOCUMENT**

a. Switch back to Notepad.

b. If necessary, make corrections to the HTML document.

c. From Notepad, print a copy of the computer_viruses.htm document.

GIF, JPG, PNG

GIF (Graphics Interchange Format) format is limited to 256 colors and best used for clip art or logos, JPG (Joint Photographic Experts Group) format supports millions of colors and is best used for photographs. PNG (Portable Network Graphic) format is a newer format only support by recent browser versions. Graphic file formats are discussed in Chapter 5.

Adding Images

Images can be used to enhance the display of an HTML document. The <img src="file name"> tag inserts an image where file name is the file name of the graphic. Image files added to an HTML document should be GIF, JPG, or PNG format. The image tag does not need to be paired.

Attributes of the <img> tag include:

- border=*"value"* specifies the size of the border around the image where value is a number in pixels

- alt=*"value"* specifies alternate text for the graphic where value is the alternative text

- height=*"value"* specifies the height of the image in pixels.

- width=*"value"* specifies the width of the image in pixels.

Accessibility

In response to the ADA (Americans with Disabilities Act), enacted in 1990, the W3C has developed guidelines called the Web Accessibility Initiative (WAI). These guidelines call for alternative text to be provided for any content on a web page that is not text.

Using Comments

Comments are text used to explain and clarify HTML to the reader of an HTML document. They do not appear in a browser window. Comments start with an angle bracket, followed by an exclamation mark and two hyphens. At the end of the comment are two more hyphens and an ending bracket. For example:

```
<!--draws a centered horizontal line across 75% of the screen-->
<hr width="75%">
```

Style Sheets

A *style sheet* is used to define the type, paragraph, and page formats for an HTML document. Style sheets give HTML documents a consistent appearance because they override the browser settings that interpret how tags are displayed.

embedded style sheet

A style sheet can be embedded or linked. An *embedded style sheet* is defined within <style type="text/css"> and </style> tags in the head section of the HTML document. A linked style sheet is a separate file that contains style rules only. *Linked style sheets* are saved with a .css extension and applied using a <link rel="stylesheet" href "style.css" type="text/css"> tag, where style.css is the name of the style sheet.

linked style sheet

rule
selector
declarations

Style sheets can include rules and classes. A *rule* modifies an HTML element and is comprised of a selector and declarations. The *selector* is the HTML element being redefined and the *declarations* are the formats to be applied. Rules are defined using the HTML element name. For example:

p {font-family: Georgia, "Times New Roman", Times, serif;
   font-size: 14px;}

Style Sheet Rule

Font-Family Declarations

Font-family declarations indicate the first font that a browser should display, and then alternate fonts if the first is not installed on the user's computer.

The rule above will automatically display paragraphs in 14 px Georgia. The font-family property can also be specified as generic font, such as serif, sans serif, or monospace and the font-size may be defined in points, pixels, inches, or centimeters (pt, px, in, cm).

A *class* is a set of declarations that can be applied to different tags. Class names begin with a dot (.). For example:

.para_with_space {
    font-family: Georgia, "Times New Roman", Times, serif;
    font-size: 14 px;
    line-height: 28 px;
}

Style Sheet Class

TIP Classes override rules.

The class above can be applied to individual paragraphs to format the paragraph in 14 px Georgia with a line-height of 28 px. For example:

<p class="para_with_space">Spyware is software that collects information without the user's knowledge. The information is usually for advertising purposes.</p>

Adding Color

hexadecimal

Text and background colors are specified using hexadecimal numbers. *Hexadecimal* is a base-16 numbering system that consists of the numbers 0 through 9 and the letters A through F. Color constants and corresponding hexadecimal values include:

Black	(#000000)	Silver	(#C0C0C0)
Gray	(#808080)	White	(#FFFFFF)
Maroon	(#800000)	Red	(#FF0000)

Purple	(#800080)	Fuchsia	(#FF00FF)
Green	(#008000)	Lime	(#00FF00)
Olive	(#808000)	Yellow	(#FFFF00)
Navy	(#000080)	Blue	(#0000FF)
Teal	(#008080)	Aqua	(#00FFFF)

To change the background and text color of an HTML document, the HTML body element is modified in a style sheet rule:

body {background-color : #000000; color : #FFFFFF}

To change the text color of a selected tag, the appropriate HTML element is modified in a style sheet rule. For example:

h1 {color : #0000FF}

Changing Alignment

HTML content is left aligned by default. To change the alignment of an entire HTML document, the HTML body element is modified in a style sheet rule:

body {text-align : center}

To change the alignment of certain parts of a document, modify the appropriate HTML element. For example, the Heading 1 tag is modified in a style sheet rule to be right aligned:

h1 {text-align : right}

Practice: Computer Viruses – part 4 of 5

Internet Explorer and Notepad should already be started with computer_viruses.htm displayed in Notepad.

① MODIFY COMPUTER_VIRUSES.HTM TO INCLUDE AN EMBEDDED STYLE SHEET

Modify the head section of computer_viruses.htm as shown:

```
<html>

<head>
<title>Computer Viruses</title>
<!--apply style sheet rules to the document-->
<style type="text/css">
h1 {color: #FF0000; text-align: center}
p {font-family: Georgia, "Times New Roman", Times, serif;
font-size: 16 px; line-height: 18 px}
ul {font-family: Georgia, "Times New Roman", Times, serif;
font-size: 14 px; line-height: 18 px}
ol {font-family: Georgia, "Times New Roman", Times, serif;
font-size: 14 px; line-height: 18 px}
h4 {text-align:right}
</style>
</head>
```

② ADD AN IMAGE

a. Add the VIRUS.gif image, which is a data file for this text, to the web page by modifying the line of text before the numbered list as shown:

<p><img src="VIRUS.gif" height="150", width="100">In order to protect against viruses:</p>

b. Save the modified computer_viruses.htm.

③ APPLY THE EMBEDDED STYLE SHEET

In Internet Explorer, open computer_viruses.htm. The style sheet rules are applied and the image is added:

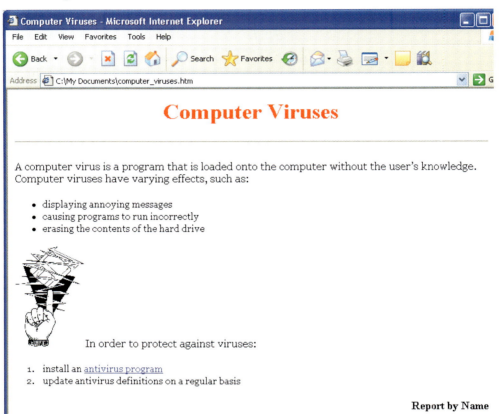

④ CREATE A LINKED STYLE SHEET

a. Switch to Notepad and select File ➡ New.

b. Type the style sheet rules as shown:

h2 {color: #FF0000}
h5 {text-align: right}

c. Select File ➡ Save. A dialog box is displayed:

d. Use the Save in list and the contents box below it to select the same folder location as the antivirus.htm document.

e. In the Save as type list, select Text Documents (*.txt) if it is not already selected.

f. In the File name box, replace the existing text with: antivirus.css

g. Select Save.

⑤ **LINK THE EXTERNAL STYLE SHEET AND ADD AN IMAGE**

a. In Notepad, open antivirus.htm.

b. In the line after the <title> tag in the head section, add the following tag:

```
<link rel="stylesheet" href="antivirus.css" type="text/css">
```

c. Save the modified document.

d. Switch to Internet Explorer and click the antivirus program link. The style sheet rules are applied.

JavaScript

Scripts are used to add dynamic content to an HTML document and consist of a list of commands that execute without user interaction. Scripts are written in a scripting language, such as JavaScript. *JavaScript* is an open scripting language that is interpreted by a browser's built-in JavaScript engine.

The code for a JavaScript is written in an HTML document between <script> and </script> tags or as a separate JavaScript file. Displaying a message in an alert dialog box is one form of dynamic content that can be added to an HTML document using a script:

```
<head>
<title>JavaScript Greeting</title>
<script type="text/javascript">
// Display a greeting
alert("Hello World!");
</script>
</head>
```

- The type attribute in the script tag specifies which **scripting language** is used to define the script.

- // is used to add a single line **comment** that explains the script.

- The **alert function** displays an alert dialog box. The text to be displayed in the dialog box is enclosed in quotation marks.

- A **semicolon** is used to end each JavaScript statement.

The script above is interpreted when the HTML document is loaded:

Java vs. JavaScript

JavaScript is similar to the Java programming language, but it is a separate language.

TIP JavaScript is case sensitive.

JavaScript Files

Scripts can also be written as a separate JavaScript file, which is saved with a .js extension, and then referenced in the script tag.

Another way to add dynamic content is to display a message in the status bar of the browser window:

```
<head>
<title>JavaScript Example</title>
<script type ="text/javascript">
// Display a status bar message
window.defaultStatus="Hello World";
</script>
</head>
```

The script above is interpreted when the document is loaded, and displays a message in the status bar of the browser window:

Note that priority is given to system messages, such as when a page is loading.

Practice: Computer Viruses – part 5 of 5

Internet Explorer and Notepad should already be started.

① ADD JAVASCRIPT

a. In Notepad, open computer_viruses.htm.

b. Modify the head section of computer_viruses.htm to include a script that displays a message in the status bar and an alert dialog box:

```
<html>

<head>
<title>Computer Viruses</title>
<script type="text/javascript">
// Display a greeting
alert("Welcome!");
//Display a message in the status bar
window.defaultStatus="Computer Viruses";
</script>
<!--apply style sheet rules to the document-->
<style type="text/css">
...
</head>
```

c. Save the modified computer_viruses.htm

② TEST THE MODIFIED DOCUMENT

In Internet Explorer, open computer_viruses.htm. The document is interpreted sequentially. Therefore, the alert dialog box is displayed with the greeting first. Click OK. The rest of the HTML document is then interpreted and displayed in the browser window.

Java Applets

A *Java applet* is a small Java application that is embedded in an HTML document and run in a browser window. When a browser interprets a document that contains a Java applet, the program files are downloaded onto the user's machine and then the browser's Java interpreter runs the applet. Java applets are well suited for the Web because they are able to run on different hardware and across different platforms. Applets are secure because they do not have the ability to read or write to files on a user's computer.

Numerous applets can be downloaded from the Web and embedded in an HTML document to add dynamic content. Applets take various forms, such as animated banners, stock ticker tapes, photo cubes, and animated video clips. Original applets can also be created.

A Java applet is embedded in an HTML document within the <applet> and </applet> tags. The tags can surround a text message that will be displayed if the applet cannot run in the browser:

```
<html>

<head>
<title>Embedding an Applet</title>
</head>

<body>
<applet code = "FirstApplet.class" width = "300" height = "60">
<param name="image" value="scenery.gif">
You are unable to view the applet.
</applet>
</body>
```

The <applet> tag has three required attributes:

- code=*"value"* specifies the name of the applets class to run

- width=*"value"* specifies the width for the applet display in pixels

- height=*"value"* specifies the height for the applet display in pixels

Applets may also require parameters. *Parameters* allow users to specify custom values to use in a Java applet. For example, the <param> tag above specifies a specific image file, scenery.gif, to use in the applet.

<object> Tag

The HTML 4 <object> tag allows for multimedia resources, such as video and audio, to be embedded in an HTML document. When interpreting an <object> tag, the browser determines if another application, such as the Windows Media Player, is needed to display the object.

The <object> tag can also be used to embed a media player console in an HTML document using Microsoft ActiveX controls.

Practice: Java Applet

Internet Explorer and Notepad should already be started.

① CREATE A NEW HTML DOCUMENT

a. In Notepad, select File → New.

b. Type the following HTML document as shown:

```
<html>

<head>
<title>Java Applet Example</title>
</head>

<body>
</body>

</html>
```

c. An applet available at the Sun Microsystems website, http://java.sun.com, is an analog clock. Modify the body section of the HTML document as follows, which embeds the JavaClock.class applet data file:

```
<applet code="JavaClock.class" width="150" height="150">
<param name="bgcolor" value="FFFFFF">
<param name="border" value="5">
<param name="ccolor" value="DDDDDD">
<param name="cfont" value="TimesRoman|BOLD|18">
<param name="delay" value="100">
<param name="hhcolor" value="0000FF">
<param name="link" value="http://java.sun.com/">
<param name="mhcolor" value="00FF00">
<param name="ncolor" value="000000">
<param name="nradius" value="80">
<param name="shcolor" value="FF0000">
You are unable to view the applet.
</applet>
```

② SAVE THE HTML DOCUMENT

a. Save the document naming it clock.htm in the classes folder in the CLOCK website included in the data files for this text.

b. Print a copy of the clock.htm document.

c. Quit Notepad.

③ VIEW THE APPLET

a. In Internet Explorer, open clock.htm. The Java applet is displayed:

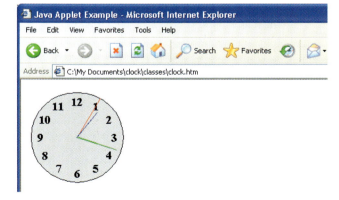

b. Close the browser window.

c. Quit Internet Explorer.

Chapter Summary

Most web pages are created using HTML (HyperText Markup Language) and other code. HTML is a markup language that is well suited for the Web because it supports hypertext and multimedia. HTML (HyperText Markup Language) is a set of special codes, called tags, that are used to "mark up" plain text so that a browser application, such as Internet Explorer, knows how to display the text in a browser window. Text that has been marked up with HTML is called an HTML document.

A tag is comprised of an element inside angle brackets (<>). Tags affect the text they surround, and are usually paired to indicate the start and end of an instruction. A slash (/) before the element indicates the end of an instruction, such as </body>. The html, head, title, and body tags are called document tags. Other tags introduced in this chapter include:

- the paragraph tag, <p>
- the break tag,
- the heading tags, <h1> through <h6>
- the horizontal rule tag, <hr>
- the unordered list tag, <ul>
- the ordered list tag, <ol>
- the table tag, <table>
- the image tag, <img>
- the anchor tag, <a>
- the comment tag, <!--comment-->
- the style sheet tag, <style>

Tags may also contain attributes. An attribute is placed in the start tag and set to a value that modifies the element.

HTML documents are plain text files and can be created using any text editor such as Notepad or a word processor. Both Notepad and Internet Explorer can be running at the same time when developing an HTML document, and the Windows taskbar is used to switch between the applications. The HTML associated with the document in a browser window can be viewed in Internet Explorer. HTML documents that are posted to the Internet are the designer's intellectual property and are protected by copyright. This applies even if a copyright notation (©) is not included on the page.

Scripts are used to add dynamic content to an HTML document. Scripts are written in a scripting language, such as JavaScript. A Java applet is a small Java application that is embedded in an HTML document and run in a browser window.

Vocabulary

Alignment Position of text in a paragraph relative to the sides of the page: left, right, centered, and justified.

Attribute Used to modify an element in an HTML tag.

Bulleted list A list that is used when each item is equally important.

Class A set of declarations that can be applied to different tags.

Comment Text used to explain and clarify HTML for a reader.

Declarations The formats to be applied in a style sheet rule.

Document tags The html, head, title, and body tags.

Element The part of an HTML tag placed inside angle brackets (<>). For example, <title> is called the title tag, where title is the element.

Embedded style sheet A style sheet defined with <style> and </style> tags in the head section of an HTML document.

Free-form Spaces and blank lines generally have no effect on how the document is interpreted. The format of an HTML document.

Hexadecimal A base-16 numbering system that consists of the numbers 0 through 9 and the letters A through F.

HTML (HyperText Markup Language) A set of tags used to "mark up" plain text so that a browser application knows how to display the text.

Hyperlink Text that can be clicked to display another HTML document. Also called a link.

Hypertext A database system where objects, such as text and images, can be linked.

Java applet A small Java application that is embedded in an HTML document and run in a browser window.

JavaScript An open scripting language that is interpreted by a browser's built-in JavaScript engine.

Link *See* Hyperlink.

Linked style sheet A style sheet saved as a separate file with a .css extension and applied using a <link> tag.

Multimedia Images, video, audio, and Java applets embedded in an HTML document.

Numbered list A list that is used to show a priority of importance.

Ordered list *See* Numbered list.

Parameter Specifies custom values to use in a Java applet.

Rule A line in a browser window for dividing content.

Scripts Used to add dynamic content to an HTML document. Scripts are written in a scripting language, such as JavaScript.

Selector The HTML element being redefined in a style sheet rule.

Style sheet Used to define the type, paragraph, and page formats for an HTML document.

Table Arranges data in an HTML document.

Tag Comprised of an element inside angle brackets that is used to "mark up" plain text so that a browser application knows how to display the text.

Unordered list *See* Bulleted list.

Visited hyperlink A link that has been clicked. Visited hyperlinks are displayed in purple underlined text.

Web Tool used to search and access information available on the Internet.

Web browser application Provides a graphic interface to present information in the form of a website.

Website A series of related web pages.

HTML Tags

`<a>` The anchor tag. Links text to another HTML document. Attributes include href.

`<applet>` The applet tag. Embeds an applet in an HTML document. Attributes include code, width, and height.

`<body>` The body tag. Defines the body section, which contains the document's content.

`<br>` The break tag. Moves a line of text within a paragraph to the next line.

`<!--comment-->` A comment tag. Explains and clarifies HTML to the reader.

`<h1>` through `<h6>` The heading tags. Emphasizes text.

`<head>` The head tag. Defines the section that indicates information about the document, including its title.

`<hr>` The horizontal rule tag. Displays a line in the browser window. Attributes include width, align, and size.

`<html>` The HTML tag. Indicates that the file contains HTML.

`<img>` The image tag. Inserts an image. Attributes include border, alt, height, and width.

`<li>` The list item tag. Defines the start and end of an item.

`<link>` The link tag. Links a style sheet.

`<ol>` The ordered list tag. Defines the start and end of a numbered list.

`<p>` The paragraph tag. Formats the content.

`<script>` The script tag. Defines a script.

`<style>` The style sheet tag. Embeds a style sheet.

`<table>` The table tag. Creates a table. Attributes include border, cellpadding, and width.

`<title>` The title tag. Displays the document title in the title bar of the browser window. Must be in the head section of an HTML document.

`<ul>` The unordered list tag. Defines the start and end of a bulleted list.

Notepad Commands

Exit command Quits Notepad. Found in the File menu.

New command Creates a new document. Found in the File menu.

Print command Prints a copy of the document. Found in the File menu.

Save command Displays a dialog box that is used to copy the document to a file. Found in the File menu.

Internet Explorer Commands and Buttons

Open command Displays a dialog box that is used to open an HTML document. Found in the File menu.

Refresh button Checks the HTML file for changes and then updates the page.

Source command Displays the HTML of the current document. Found in the View menu.

1. a) What is the most widely used Internet service?
   b) List two examples of web browsers.

2. a) What is used to create most web pages?
   b) Why is HTML well suited for the Web?
   c) Why is it important for the W3C to develop Web standards?

3. a) What is the element in the tag <html>?
   b) What does a slash (/) before the element indicate?

4. a) List the four document tags.
   b) Why is it important to properly structure an HTML document when HTML is a free-form language?

5. a) What is Notepad?
   b) List three guidelines for the file name of an HTML document.
   c) What does Notepad automatically add to a printed document?

6. List the steps required to open and view an HTML document in a web browser.

7. The HTML document below has five errors. What are they?

```
<html>
<head>
<title>Operating Systems</title>
</body>

<body>
<!--adds a horizontal rule>>
<hr width is "50%">
<p>Every computer must have an operating
system. Types of operating systems include:
</p>
<ul>
<li>Windows<li>
<li>UNIX</li>
<li>Linux</li>
<li>OS/2</li>
</ul>
</head>
</html>
```

8. What happens to any multiple spaces in the text between paragraph tags when a document is viewed in a browser?

9. a) What does a style sheet define?
   b) Why are style sheets used?
   c) What is the difference between an embedded and a linked style sheet?

10. What element is modified to change the background color or alignment of a web page?

11. a) Where are scripts placed in an HTML document?
    b) Write a script to display "Good-bye" in an alert dialog box.
    c) Write a script to display "Today's News" in the status bar of the browser window.

12. a) What is a Java applet?
    b) How is a Java applet interpreted by a web browser?
    c) List two reasons why Java applets are well suited for the Web.

True/False

13. Determine if each of the following are true or false. If false, explain why.
    a) A website consists of a series of web pages.
    b) Hypertext is a database system.
    c) An HTML document must be published to a web server in order to be viewed in a web browser.
    d) The <p> tag moves a line of text within a paragraph to the next line.
    e) The <h1> tag is used to represent the most important information.
    f) A horizontal rule must have a width of 100%.
    g) Comments are displayed on a web page.
    h) Hyperlinks link the pages of a website.
    i) The anchor tag creates a hyperlink.
    j) A rule modifies an HTML element.
    k) Scripts must be placed in the head section of an HTML document.
    l) Java applets are interpreted on web servers.

Exercises

Exercise 1 ——————————————— tourist_attractions.htm

Research tourist attractions in a particular city by using the Internet, magazines, and books and then create an HTML document named tourist_attractions.htm that lists tourist attractions for a particular city. The HTML document should include:

- a comment with your name
- an appropriate title
- the city name in Heading 1 format
- the text Tourist Attractions in Heading 2 format
- a horizontal rule
- at least five tourist attractions, each displayed in a bulleted list
- a style sheet with at least three rules
- a script

Exercise 2 ——————————————— sports_report.htm

Create an HTML document named sports_report.htm that documents recent sports related news. The HTML document should include:

- a comment with your name
- appropriate titles formatted with heading tags
- a horizontal rule
- at least three news stories
- an image
- a style sheet with at least three rules
- a script

Exercise 3 ——————————— html_reference.htm, html_links.htm

Extend your HTML learning and share your knowledge by completing the following steps:

a) Create an "HTML Reference" document named html_reference.htm that lists HTML tags, describes each tag, and provides corresponding examples. Research and include at least three HTML tags not covered in this chapter. The www.w3.org website has information about HTML tags.

b) Create a link to another HTML document named html_links.htm that contains links to HTML reference websites. If necessary, include navigation instructions for the user to locate the appropriate HTML information.

Exercise 4 ——————————————————— passwords.htm

Create an HTML document named passwords.htm that discusses password protocol.

    a) The passwords.htm document should include:

- the title Computer Passwords by Name replacing Name with your name.
- at least one horizontal rule
- the text About Computer Passwords in Heading 2 format
- your name in Heading 4 format
- the following text in the BODY of the document:

  It is important to keep your password a secret so that other individuals cannot gain unauthorized access to your computer. Do not share your password with anyone and if you receive an e-mail requesting your password, even if it looks like it is from a legitimate source, do not provide the requested information. When selecting a password, do not select a password that is easy tc guess. Passwords should be changed frequently.

    b) Find two websites that present guidelines for creating secure passwords. Add the information to the passwords.htm document, and then include citations for the two sources.

Exercise 5 ——————————————— movie.htm, characters.htm, director.htm, favorite_part.htm

Create four HTML documents that detail a movie you have recently seen. Name the HTML documents movie.htm, characters.htm, director.htm, and favorite_part.htm and complete the following steps:

    a) The movie.htm document should include:

- the title Movie Report
- an appropriate background and text color
- the title of the movie in Heading 3 format
- at least one paragraph of at least 30 words summarizing the movie
- a list of hyperlinks below the summary paragraph that link to characters.htm, director.htm, and favorite_part.htm
- your name in Heading 4 format

    b) The characters.htm document should include:

- the title Characters
- an appropriate background and text color
- the title of the movie in Heading 3 format
- the text Characters in Heading 2 format
- one paragraph for each important character in the movie—there should be at least 40 words total on this page
- a hyperlink with the label Home that links to movie.htm
- your name in Heading 4 format

c) The director.htm document should include:

- the title Director
- an appropriate background and text color
- the title of the movie in Heading 3 format
- the text Director in Heading 2 format
- one paragraph of at least 12 words that describe the director, including the date of birth, education, and other biographical information
- a hyperlink with the label Home that links to movie.htm
- your name in Heading 4 format

d) The favorite_part.htm document should include:

- the title Favorite Part
- an appropriate background and text color
- the title of the movie in Heading 3 format
- the text Favorite Part in Heading 2 format
- one paragraph of at least 20 words describing your favorite part of the movie
- a hyperlink with the label Home that links to movie.htm
- your name in Heading 4 format

Exercise 6

Research the history of computers by using the Internet, magazines, and books and then create four linked HTML documents that outline key events in computer history by decade. Describe at least five key events for the 1970s, 1980s, 1990s, and 2000s. Use a style sheet to format the HTML documents.

Exercise 7

Research copyright laws and issues as they pertain to digital information. Present your research in the form of at least two linked HTML documents. Include a third linked HTML document that contains citations, one for each source. Use an established method to cite the sources, such as MLA or APA style.

Exercise 8   technology_report.htm

Research a recently released software application or hardware device. Create an HTML document named technology_report.htm that lists the product specifications and target market for the product. Include your opinion on whether you think the product will be successful or useful.

Exercise 9

Interview a local web developer or designer about the importance of mastering HTML before learning a web development software applications, such as Dreamweaver. Ask which other tools or knowledge they feel are important when designing websites. Document your interview. In small groups, share your interview documentation.

Exercise 10

Collaborate in small groups to create HTML documents that outline the History of the Internet. As a group, present your research to the class by having them view the documents while discussing the research in an oral presentation.

Introducing Dreamweaver

This chapter introduces Dreamweaver and discusses how to create a website and web page documents, add tables and special characters, and create hyperlinks. Printing a web page, checking spelling, using help, and viewing a web page document in a browser are also covered.

Starting Dreamweaver

To start Dreamweaver select Start → All Programs → Macromedia → Macromedia Dreamweaver, or double-click the Dreamweaver icon on the Desktop:

Dreamweaver

Dreamweaver is the web development application that is part of the Macromedia Studio suite. Dreamweaver is used to create websites. The Studio suite also includes Fireworks and Flash, two applications that are introduced later in the text.

The windows, toolbars, and panel groups that are displayed when Dreamweaver is running are collectively called the *workspace*. In the Dreamweaver workspace below, an empty web page document is displayed and the Files panel displays the folder for the active website:

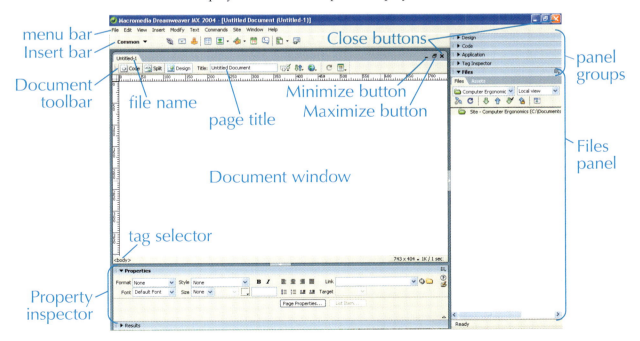

- Select commands from menus in the **menu bar**.

- Add objects to a web page document using buttons in the **Insert bar**.

- Change views and perform some common actions using the **Document toolbar**.

- The **page title** is the text that will be displayed in the title bar of the browser window when a user views the web page.

- The name of the file that stores the web page document is the **file name**.

- Click the **Minimize button** (⊟) to reduce the Document window to a button in the Dreamweaver window.

- Click the **Maximize button** (▣) to expand the Document window in the Dreamweaver window.

- Click a **Close button** (✕) to remove the Document window or the Dreamweaver window.

- Files and folders associated with the active website are displayed in the **Files panel**.

- The **panel groups** contain tools which can be used in developing a website. The **Files panel** is in a panel group.

- The web page document is displayed in the **Document window**.

- Select a tag and its contents using the **Tag selector**.

- Change properties of the selected text or object using the **Property inspector**.

Using Panel Groups

Click the arrow or panel group name to expand the group:

Click 📇 in the right corner of a panel group title bar to display a menu of commands.

Websites

A website consists of one or more web pages with text, graphics, and links used to navigate through the website.

Defining a Website in Dreamweaver

In Dreamweaver, a website needs to be defined before any web page documents are created. This process is called *site definition* or *defining a site*. Select Site → Manage Sites and complete a series of dialog boxes to define a site. The process of defining a site includes specifying a folder name, a server technology, files locations, and remote server options. When the site is defined, a folder is created with the specified name and the folder is displayed in the Files panel. Refer to the Practice below for the dialog boxes displayed during site definition.

Practice: Computer Ergonomics – part 1 of 8

① START DREAMWEAVER

Ask your instructor for the appropriate steps to start Dreamweaver. Note the Insert bar, Property inspector, Files panel, and other parts of the workspace.

② DEFINE A NEW SITE

a. Select Site → Manage Sites. A dialog box is displayed.

b. Select New, and then select Site. A Site Definition dialog box is displayed.

c. Select the Basic tab if those options are not already displayed.

d. In the What would you like to name your site? box type: Computer Ergonomics

e. Select Next. More options are displayed.

f. Select the No, I do not want to use a server technology option:

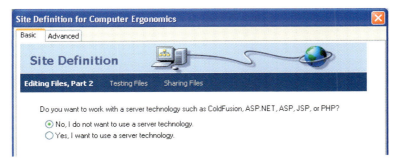

g. Click Next. More options are displayed.

h. Select the Edit local copies on my machine, then upload to server when ready option:

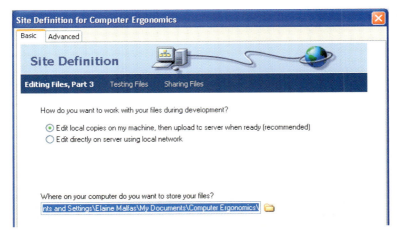

i. Click the folder icon (🗀). A dialog box is displayed for browsing the local disk.

   1. Navigate to the appropriate location where a folder can be created to store the website files.

   2. Click the Create New Folder button:

3. A new folder is created. Type Computer Ergonomics to replace the New Folder name and press Enter.

4. Select Open. The Computer Ergonomics folder appears in the Select list.

5. Select Select to choose the new folder as the website folder.

j. Select Next. More options are displayed.

k. In the How do you connect to your remote server? list, select None:

l. Select Next. A summary is displayed:

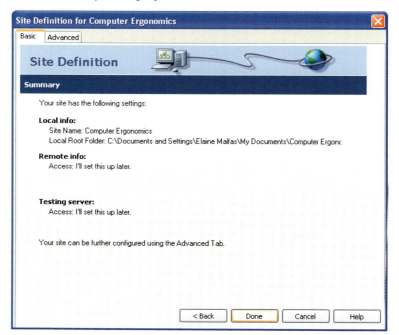

m. Select Done to create the site and return to the Manage Sites dialog box.

n. Select Done. The Site folder is displayed in the Files panel:

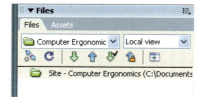

Creating a Web Page Document

create a web page document

A newly defined website does not contain any web page documents. To add a web page document to a website, a document is created and then saved to the website folder that was created during site definition. Select File → New to display a dialog box, then in the General tab options select Basic page, HTML, and then Create to display a new web page document in the Document window.

name a web page document

When a web page document is saved, it must be given a name. File names for web page documents can contain lowercase letters, numbers, and underscores (_). Do not use spaces or uppercase letters, and it is best to not start the file name with a number. These file name guidelines will ensure that the website can be viewed by most users once it is posted to a server and available on the Internet. A file name should also be descriptive of the page contents.

To save a web page document, select File → Save. The Save As dialog box is displayed the first time a web page document is saved:

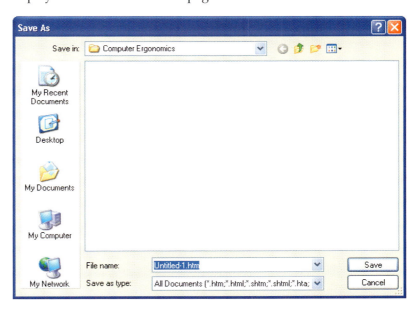

The Save in list and the contents box below it are used to navigate to the location where the file is to be saved. A web page document should be saved in the appropriate website folder. Type a descriptive file name in the File name box and select Save to save the document. The extension .htm is automatically added to the file name.

home page

The *home page* of a website is the main page or starting point of the website. A web page document that is saved with the file name index.htm is automatically designated by Dreamweaver as the home page of the website.

Web page documents can also be created using the Files panel menu:

 Files panel menu

---

Why Save Often?

Saving often when working on a document can help prevent accidental loss. An interruption in power may erase the document in the computer's memory. Saving before printing can also prevent accidental loss.

Home Page File Name

index.htm is usually the best choice for the home page file name because web servers automatically recognize it as the home page of a website.

TIP This method is useful for quickly creating many pages in a new website.

TIP The new file may have a .cfm or other extension, but this can be changed to .htm when typing the new file name.

TIP Spaces can be used in a page title.

Select 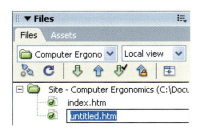 → File → New File in the Files panel to add a new document to the list of documents in the Files panel:

Type a new name with an .htm extension to replace the selected untitled.htm. New web page documents created in this manner are not automatically displayed in a Document window, but can be opened by double-clicking the file name in the Files panel.

The Page Title

The *page title* of a web page is the text displayed in the title bar of the browser window when a user views the web page. The page title also appears in the title bar of the Document window in Dreamweaver. To change the page title of a web page document, select Modify → Page Properties and then select Title/Encoding in the Category list of the dialog box. Type a title in the Title box and select OK.

A fast way to change the page title is to type the new title in the Title box in the Document toolbar and press Enter:

Title box

Viewing a Web Page Document

Design view

Code view

Code and Design view

In Dreamweaver, web page documents are displayed in *Design view* by default, which displays the document similar to how it will appear in a browser window. Changing to *Code view* displays the code generated for the web page, which is useful for studying the HTML and for editing tags and code. A document can be displayed in *Code and Design view*, or Split view, which is a combination of both views. Use the buttons in the Document toolbar to change the view:

Code view \ Design view

Code and Design view

Multiple Browsers

Websites should be previewed in different browsers to detect display differences. Select File → Preview in Browser → Edit Browser List to add an installed browser to the Preview in Browser submenu.

As a web page document is developed, it should be previewed in a browser to see what it will look like to the user. In Dreamweaver, press the F12 key or select File → Preview in Browser and then select a browser from the submenu to preview the active web page document in a browser.

TIP It is a good habit to save a web page document before previewing it in a browser.

A web page document cannot be modified in the browser window. Changes are made by switching back to Dreamweaver and modifying the document in the Document window. Press F12 in Dreamweaver to again view the document in a browser.

Practice: Computer Ergonomics – part 2 of 8

① CREATE A NEW WEB PAGE DOCUMENT

Select File ➔ New. A dialog box is displayed.

    1. Click the General tab to display those options.

    2. In the Category list, select Basic page.

    3. In the Basic page list, select HTML.

    4. Select Create. A web page document is displayed in a Document window.

② SAVE THE DOCUMENT AND DESIGNATE IT AS THE SITE'S HOME PAGE

Select File ➔ Save. A dialog box is displayed.

    1. Use the Save in list to navigate to the Computer Ergonomics folder if it is not already displayed.

    2. In the File name box, replace the existing text with: index.htm

    3. Select Save. The file is saved in the Computer Ergonomics folder with the file name index.htm. The file name is now displayed in the title bar of the Document window and the web page document is listed in the Files panel.

③ CHANGE THE PAGE TITLE AND PREVIEW THE DOCUMENT IN A BROWSER

    a. In the Document toolbar, in the Title box, replace the existing text with: Computer Ergonomics Home Page and then press Enter.

    b. Press F12. A dialog box is displayed with the message "Save changes to index.htm?"

    c. Select Yes. The document is displayed in a browser window and the page title is displayed in the browser's title bar.

    d. Click the Close button (❌) to close the browser window.

④ CHANGE VIEWS

    a. In the Document toolbar, click the Code view button (⟨⟩ Code). The code for the web page document is displayed in the Document window. Note the title tags and the page title:

```
<title>Computer Ergonomics Home Page</title>
```

    b. In the Document toolbar, click the Split button (Split). The Document window is split, with code displayed in the upper half.

    c. In the Document toolbar, click the Design view button (Design). The web page document is again displayed in Design view.

⑤ SAVE THE CHANGES TO THE WEB PAGE DOCUMENT

Select File ➔ Save. The changes are saved.

Using a Table to Arrange Content

The *content* in a web page is the information presented to the user, such as text and graphics. Tables should be used to organize and control the arrangement of content in a web page. A *table* consists of horizontal rows and vertical columns of cells. A *cell* is the intersection of a row and column:

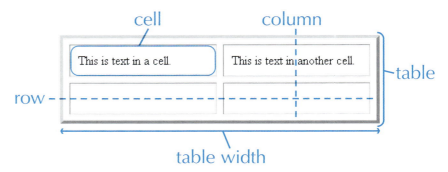

The width of a table can be specified either in pixels or as a percentage of the width of the browser window. A *pixel* is a unit of measurement related to screen resolution. For example, a monitor set to 1024x768 displays 1024 pixels across the screen. Newer monitors can display 1680 or more pixels across the screen.

pixel

A table width specified in pixels is called *fixed width* because the width of the table will not change when a user resizes the browser window. The content will always look the way it was arranged in Dreamweaver during the development of the web page document. However, some content may be hidden if the browser window is sized smaller than the table:

table width

Why Use Tables?

There are millions of potential users that access web pages on the World Wide Web. These users have different monitor sizes, different screen resolutions, and different browsers. Tables are used to control the layout of the content, so that the web page the users view looks similar no matter what monitor size, resolution, or browser they have.

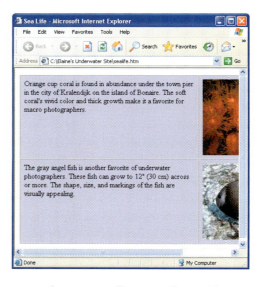

The user now has to scroll vertically and horizontally to view the web page content

To allow a table width to vary, the table width should be specified as a percentage. For example, a table width set to 100% will resize to 100% of the browser window width when the browser window is resized. As the user resizes the browser window, the table expands or contracts:

Liquid Design

Tables with widths specified in percentages are sometimes called liquid or fluid because they change to fill the available space.

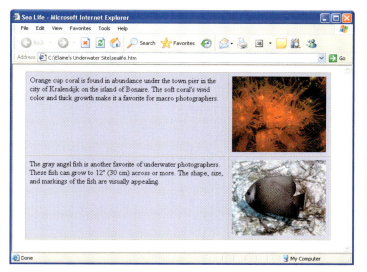
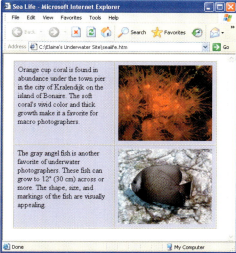

The table adjusts to occupy 100% of the width in the browser window, regardless of window size

However, changing the size of the browser window affects the arrangement of content in a table with widths in percentages. Changing the individual cell widths allows more control of the layout and is discussed later in this chapter.

more table properties

Other table properties include borders, cell padding, and cell spacing:

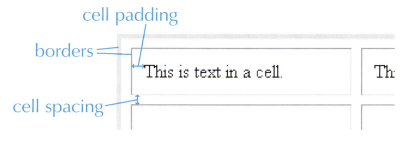

- **Borders** are the lines around the table and the cells. A border size of 0 specifies that no border is displayed. A border size of 1 or more defines the table border thickness in pixels and indicates that the cells will have visible borders.

- **Cell padding** is the number of pixels of blank space between the content in the cell and the cell's boundary. If a cell padding amount is not specified, browsers may assign a value. To avoid this, an amount should be specified. 0 is used if the content should be against the cell boundaries. A larger setting, such as 6 or 8, is used to add space.

- **Cell spacing** is the number of pixels between cells. If a cell spacing amount is not specified, browsers may assign a value. To avoid this, an amount should be specified. 0 specifies no spacing.

Using Borders

Tables used for controlling the layout of text and graphics usually do not have a border. However, borders are used for tables that present numeric data. Tables of numeric data are discussed in Chapter 8.

Creating a Table

Tables are best created in *Standard mode*. Select the Layout category from the pop-up menu in the Insert bar, and then click the Standard mode button to display the document in Standard mode:

Insert bar

Pop-up menu   Table   Standard mode

Select Insert → Table or click the Table button () in the Layout category in the Insert bar to display a dialog box:

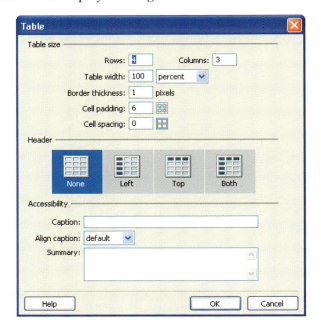

TIP If the Insert Bar is not displayed, select Window → Insert.

Layout Mode

Tables may also be created in Layout mode by drawing cells in the document window.

Accessibility Options

The Accessibility options in the Table dialog box should be used when creating a table of data, not when using tables for layout purposes. Tables of data are discussed in Chapter 8.

- The number of rows and columns for the table is specified in the Rows and Columns boxes.

- To create a table with a variable width, specify 100 and percent for the Table width. For a fixed table width, specify a number of pixels instead of a percentage.

- Values in the Border thickness, Cell padding, and Cell spacing boxes are in pixels.

select a table

A table is automatically selected after being created. When a table is not selected, place the insertion point in any cell in the table and then click the <table> tag in the Tag selector to select the table:

Viewing HTML

When an object in Design view is selected, the corresponding HTML in the document is automatically selected and can be viewed in Code view or Code and Design view.

A table may also be selected by pointing to a border or corner of a table until ⊞ is displayed with the pointer and then clicking to select the table. A selected table has a thick black border around it and square black handles on the bottom and right sides:

100% (533) ▾

TIP In a table with a percentage width, the displayed pixel amount (100% (533) ▾) will vary as the Document window is sized.

A grey area is displayed usually below, or sometimes above, a table and includes the table's width. Any numbers in parentheses indicate actual size. In the table shown above, the width is set to 100%, and this table is currently 533 pixels wide.

When a table is selected, the Property inspector at the bottom of the Dreamweaver workspace displays table properties:

▼ Properties

| Table Id | | Rows | 4 | W | 100 | % ▾ | CellPad | 6 | Align | Default ▾ | Class | None ▾ |
| | ▾ | Cols | 3 | H | | pixels ▾ | CellSpace | 0 | Border | 1 | | |

Bg color ▯ Brdr color ▯

Bg Image ⊕ ▭

table width

- W is the table width. The unit for the value is selected from the adjacent list.

table alignment

- Align is the position of the table within the web page document. A table that has a percentage width is best center aligned so that the table has equal amounts of space on the right and left side. The default is left aligned.

Changing Cell Width and Height

Placing the insertion point in a cell displays the cell properties in the Property inspector at the bottom of the Dreamweaver window:

▼ Properties

| Format | None ▾ | Style | None ▾ | **B** *I* | ≣ ≣ ≣ ≣ | Link | | ▾ ⊕ ▭ |
| Font | Default Font ▾ | Size | None ▾ | | ▾ ▯ | ≣ ≣ ≣ ≣ | Target | ▾ |

| | | Cell | Horz | Default ▾ | W | | No wrap ☐ | Bg | | ⊕ ▭ | Page Properties... |
| | | | Vert | Default ▾ | H | | Header ☐ | Bg ▯ | | Brdr ▯ | |

- W is the width of a cell either in a percentage of the table's width or in a number of pixels. A new value can be typed. The value typed is in pixels unless a percent sign (%) is typed as well.

- H is the height of a cell in a percentage or in pixels. A new value can be typed. If a percent sign (%) is not included when H is set, the amount is in pixels.

Cell widths can be specified as either pixels or percentages, regardless of how a table's width is specified. A single table may contain both cells with widths in pixels and cells with widths in percentages. Note that changing the width of a cell may affect the entire column, because the column's width will be the same as the widest cell in that column. To control the layout of a web page, an amount should always be specified for the width, This will avoid browser window defaults.

The index.htm web page document in the Computer Ergonomics website should be displayed.

① ADD A TABLE

a. In the Insert bar, click the pop-up menu and select Layout. The Layout category is displayed.

b. In the Insert bar, click the Standard mode button if it is not already selected. The web page document is displayed in Standard mode.

c. In the Insert bar, click the Table button (⊞). A dialog box is displayed.

d. In the dialog box, set the options to:

e. Select OK. A table is inserted and the table properties are displayed in the Property inspector.

Check—Your Document window should look similar to:

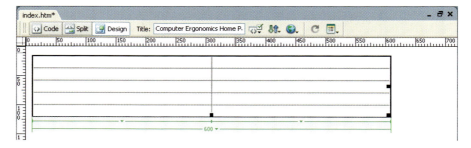

② VIEW THE WEB PAGE DOCUMENT IN A BROWSER

a. Select File ➡ Save. The changes are saved to the document.

b. Press F12. The document is displayed in a browser window. The border is visible because the table was created with a border of 1.

c. Resize the browser window much smaller by dragging the Resize tab in the bottom-right window corner (⬜). (If the window is maximized, click the Restore button (⧉) in the upper-right corner of the browser window before sizing the window.) When the window is sized smaller, notice how the table does not change.

③ CHANGE THE TABLE WIDTH AND ALIGNMENT

a. Close the browser window. Dreamweaver is displayed.

b. In the table, click in any cell. The insertion point is placed.

c. In the Tag selector in the bottom-left corner of the Document window, click the <table> tag. A thick border is displayed around the table indicating that it is selected.

d. In the Property inspector, set Align to Center. The table is centered between the left and right sides of the window.

e. In the Property inspector, set W to 100%. The table width is 100% of the window.

④ VIEW THE WEB PAGE DOCUMENT IN A BROWSER

a. Save the changes and then press F12. The document is displayed in the browser window. The table width fills most of the window.

b. Resize the browser window larger and smaller by dragging the Resize tab in the bottom-right window corner (⬜). The table width changes to fit the window.

⑤ CHANGE THE TABLE BORDER AND CELL PADDING

a. Close the browser window. Dreamweaver is displayed.

b. If the table is no longer selected, point to a corner of the table until ⊞ is displayed with the pointer and then click. The table is selected.

c. In the Property inspector, set Border to 0 and press Enter. The border changes to a dotted line around the cells.

d. Click in any cell. The insertion point is aligned against the left cell border.

e. Select the table.

f. In the Property inspector, set CellPad to 4 and press Enter.

g. Click in any cell. The insertion point is four pixels away from the left cell border. With cell padding, content added to cells will be spaced.

h. Save the changes and then press F12. The document is displayed in the browser window. The border is no longer visible because the Border property was changed to 0.

i. Close the browser window. Dreamweaver is displayed.

Adding and Deleting Rows and Columns in a Table

TIP Right-click in a cell to display a menu of commands for formatting the table, including adding and deleting rows and columns.

After creating a table, a row or column may need to be added or removed. Place the insertion point in a cell and then select Modify ➤ Table ➤ Insert Row or Insert Column to add to the table, or Modify ➤ Table ➤ Delete Row or Delete Column to remove cells. When adding, a row is added above the cell or a column is added to the left of the cell. When deleting, the row or column containing the cell is removed.

TIP Be cautious when deleting rows or columns because a warning is not displayed if the cells have content.

Buttons in the Layout category in the Insert bar can also be used to add or delete rows and columns:

Insert Row Above
Insert Row Below
Insert Column to the Left
Insert Column to the Right

Adding Text Content to a Table

To add text to a table, click in a cell to place the insertion point and then type the text. Press Enter to create a new paragraph in the same cell. HTML paragraphs automatically have extra space below the paragraph.

line break

To have lines of text without extra space between them, insert a line break by pressing Shift+Enter instead of pressing Enter. Another method of inserting a line break is to select Line Break from the Characters button menu in the Text category in the Insert bar:

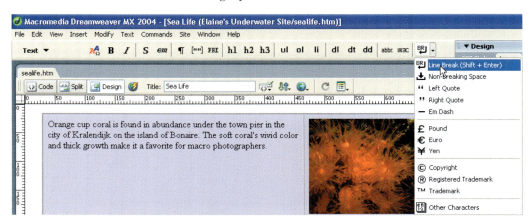

TIP Select Insert → HTML → Special Characters to display a submenu of characters.

The Characters button menu includes other characters such as proper quotation marks, the em dash (—), currency symbols, and the copyright (©) and registered trademark (®) symbols. Click Other Characters in the menu to display a dialog box of additional special characters.

move the insertion point

In a table, press the Tab key to move the insertion point to the next cell or press Shift+Tab to move to the previous cell. The arrow keys also move the insertion point between cells. Pressing the Tab key when the insertion point is in the last cell of a table adds a new row to the table.

cut, copy, and paste

TIP The Clear command does not place the deleted text on the clipboard. The Cut command places text on the clipboard for pasting in another location.

The Edit menu contains commands that are helpful when editing text. The Undo (Ctrl+Z) and Repeat (Ctrl+Y) commands are used to cancel or redo an action. The Cut (Ctrl+X), Copy (Ctrl+C), Paste (Ctrl+V), and Clear commands are used to delete, duplicate, and move content.

Checking Spelling

Dreamweaver includes a spelling checker that can help find misspelled words in a web page document. Select Text ➛ Check Spelling to start checking the spelling from the insertion point. A misspelled word causes a dialog box to be displayed:

TIP To check the spelling of just some of the text in a document, select the text and then start the spell check. Only the selected text will be checked.

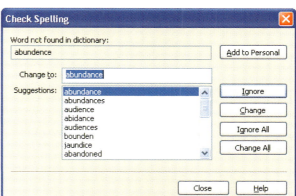

The Importance of Error-Free Content

A web page may be the first impression a user has of a person or a business. Errors such as misspellings make the web page seem unprofessional and less credible.

Select the correct spelling in the Suggestions list and then select Change to change the word and continue checking the spelling. Select Ignore to leave the word unchanged, which is useful for proper names that are not in Dreamweaver's dictionary. Select Ignore All to skip over all occurrences of the word.

Practice: Computer Ergonomics – part 4 of 8

The index.htm web page document in the Computer Ergonomics website should be displayed.

① ADD CONTENT

a. In the table, click in the second cell in the top row (the upper-right cell) to place the insertion point.

b. Type: Computer Workstation Ergonomics

c. In the Insert bar, in the Text category, click the arrow next to the Characters button and select Line Break. The insertion point moves to the next line.

d. Type the following text, but do NOT press the Enter key to end lines of text; allow the text to wrap in the cell:

Ergonomics, also known as human engineering, is the science of designing working environments to be safe and efficient during interaction. Studies show that improper ergonomics can lead to injuries such as MSDs. The ergonomics of a computer workstation include input device ergonomics and posture ergonomics.

e. Press Enter. The insertion point remains in the cell and creates a new paragraph.

f. Type Research by Name replacing Name with your name.

② EDIT CONTENT

a. Select the "Research by Name" text by dragging or triple-clicking in the text.

b. Select Edit ➛ Cut. The text no longer appears in the document.

c. Click in the last cell in the table (the lower-right cell) to place the insertion point.

d. Select Edit ➛ Paste. The text is pasted into the last cell in the table.

e. Click in the blank area below the table to place the insertion point outside of the table. The table adjusts to fit the content:

> Computer Workstation Ergonomics
> Ergonomics, also known as human engineering, is the science of designing working environments to be safe and efficient during interaction. Studies show that improper ergonomics can lead to injuries such as MSDs. The ergonomics of a computer workstation include input device ergonomics and posture ergonomics.
>
>
>
> Research by Sandy
> 100% (658) ▾

③ FORMAT THE CELL WIDTHS

a. Click anywhere in the paragraph about ergonomics to place the insertion point.

b. In the Property inspector, set W to 70% and press Enter. The width of the cell is formatted as 70% of the table's width.

c. Click in the last cell in the table (the lower-right cell). The insertion point is placed.

d. In the Property inspector, set W to 35% and press Enter. The width of the cell does not change because the widest cell in that column is formatted as 70%.

④ DELETE ROWS

a. Place the insertion point in the empty cell below the cell that contains the "Computer Workstation Ergonomics" text.

b. Select Modify ➙ Table ➙ Delete Row. The row is deleted.

c. Select Modify ➙ Table ➙ Delete Row again. Another row is deleted.

d. Select Modify ➙ Table ➙ Delete Row again. The table now only has 2 rows.

Check—Your Document window should look similar to:

> | | Computer Workstation Ergonomics
Ergonomics, also known as human engineering, is the science of designing working environments to be safe and efficient during interaction. Studies show that improper ergonomics can lead to injuries such as MSDs. The ergonomics of a computer workstation include input device ergonomics and posture ergonomics. |
> | --- | --- |
> | | Research by Sandy |
>
> 70% (452) ▾
> 100% (658) ▾

⑤ CHECK THE SPELLING

a. Place the insertion point before the first word in the table.

b. Select Text ➙ Check Spelling. A dialog box is displayed. Dreamweaver finds that the word "MSDs" is not in its dictionary and suggests changing it to "MSD's."

   1. Since the word is correctly spelled as is, select Ignore.

   2. Select Ignore if the spelling of your name is questioned.

   3. Select OK when the message "Spelling check completed." is displayed.

a. Select File ➡ Save. The changes are saved.

b. Press F12. The document, with the modified table, is displayed in a browser.

c. Close the browser window.

Printing a Web Page Document

print from a browser

A web page document is printed from a browser. In Internet Explorer, select File ➡ Print to display a dialog box with printing options, or click the Print button (🖨) in the toolbar to print one copy of a web page without displaying the dialog box.

preview before printing

Long web pages may require several sheets of paper for a printout. In Internet Explorer, select File ➡ Print Preview to display the web page document as it will appear when printed. The number of pages that will print are also indicated. Click Print to display the Print dialog box, which contains options for printing just the current page or a range of pages.

header in Internet Explorer

The header of a printout from Internet Explorer automatically contains the web page title and the page number of the printout. The footer contains the URL. The header and footer are changed by selecting File ➡ Page Setup, which displays the Page Setup dialog box. Information such as your name and the date can be added.

print from Dreamweaver

The code for a web page document can be printed in Dreamweaver by selecting File ➡ Print Code. A footer with the full path and file name and the page number and number of pages is included on the printout.

Closing a Web Page Document and Quitting Dreamweaver

When a web page document is not being worked on, it should be saved and then closed. *Closing a web page document* means that its window is removed from the Dreamweaver workspace and the file is no longer in the computer's memory. Select File ➡ Close or click the Close button in the Document window to close a web page document.

Attempting to close a web page that has been edited but not saved displays a reminder dialog box with the message "Save changes to file name?" Select Yes to save the changes in a file and remove the Document window. Select No to remove the Document window without saving changes. Select Cancel to leave the web page document open without saving changes.

When Dreamweaver is no longer needed, it should be quit properly. *Quitting Dreamweaver* means that its window is removed from the Desktop and the program is no longer in the computer's memory. Select File ➡ Exit to quit Dreamweaver, or click the Close button (❌) in the upper-right corner of the Dreamweaver window to close the application window. Closing an application window quits the application.

TIP If multiple documents are open, select File ➡ Close All to close all of the documents.

Opening a Website for Editing

In the Files panel, Dreamweaver maintains a list of existing websites:

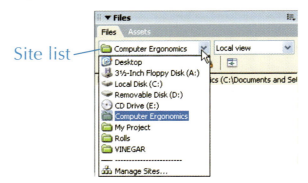

Site list

A website selected from this list will become the active website. If a website is not listed, select Site → Manage Sites and then select New to display the Site Definition dialog box. Select the Advanced tab to display options for defining an existing site:

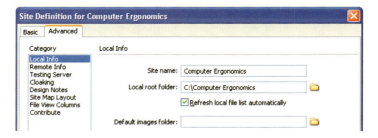

Type a site name in the Site name box, then click the Local root folder folder (📁) and navigate to the location of the website folder. Select OK at the bottom of the Site Definition dialog box to open the site for editing in Dreamweaver and add its name to the Site list in the Files panel.

Practice: Computer Ergonomics – part 5 of 8

The index.htm web page document in the Computer Ergonomics website should be displayed.

① PRINT THE CODE FOR THE INDEX.HTM WEB PAGE

a. Select File → Print Code. A dialog box is displayed.

b. Select OK. The dialog box is removed and the code is printed.

② PRINT THE WEB PAGE DOCUMENT FROM A BROWSER

a. Press F12. The document is displayed in a browser window.

b. Select File → Print. A dialog box is displayed.

c. Select Print. The web page document is printed.

d. Close the browser window.

③ CLOSE THE WEB PAGE DOCUMENT AND QUIT DREAMWEAVER

a. Select File → Close. The Document window is removed.

b. Select File → Exit. The Dreamweaver application window is removed.

④ OPEN A SITE FOR EDITING

Start Dreamweaver. The Files panel may already show Computer Ergonomics as the working website. If not, in the Files panel click the arrow next to the Site list and select Computer Ergonomics.

If Computer Ergonomics is not the active website nor in the Site list, the site needs to be opened for editing. Select Site → Manage Sites. A dialog box is displayed.

1. Click New, and then select Site. A Site Definition dialog box is displayed.

2. Select the Advanced tab.

3. In the Site name box, type: Computer Ergonomics

4. Next to the Local root folder box, click the folder icon (📁). A dialog box is displayed.

   i. Navigate to the Computer Ergonomics website folder.

   ii. Click Select.

5. Select OK. The Manage Sites dialog box is displayed with the Computer Ergonomics site selected.

6. Select Done. The Computer Ergonomics website is the active website.

Opening and Displaying Web Page Documents

Opening a file transfers a copy of the file contents to the computer's memory and displays the file contents in an appropriate window. In Dreamweaver, double-click the file name in the Files panel to open a web page document:

Web page documents may also be opened by selecting File → Open, which displays the Open dialog box. Navigating to the file, clicking the file name, and then selecting Open transfers a copy of the file to a Document window in Dreamweaver.

multiple documents   Several web page documents can be open at the same time, which makes it easy to cut and paste between documents or quickly view different documents. To view an open document that is not displayed, click the document's file name at the top of the Document window:

The file names of open documents are along the top of the Document window when it is maximized

An open document can also be displayed by selecting the file name from the Window menu.

Dreamweaver should be started and the Computer Ergonomics website should be the working site.

① OPEN THE INDEX.HTM WEB PAGE DOCUMENT

In the Files panel, double-click the index.htm file name. The index.htm web page document is opened in a Document window.

② CREATE AND SAVE A NEW WEB PAGE DOCUMENT

a. Select File → New. A dialog box is displayed.

    1. In the Category list, select Basic page.

    2. In the Basic page list, select HTML.

    3. Select Create. A web page document is displayed in a Document window.

b. Select File → Save. A dialog box is displayed.

    1. Use the Save in list to navigate to the Computer Ergonomics folder if it is not already displayed.

    2. In the File name box, replace the existing text with: input_device.htm

    3. Select Save. The file is saved and is now listed in the Files panel.

③ CREATE AND SAVE ANOTHER NEW WEB PAGE DOCUMENT

a. From the Files panel, select ▤ → File → New File. A new document is added to the list in the Files panel.

b. Type posture.htm to replace the untitled.htm file name.

c. In the Files panel, double-click the posture.htm file name. The web page document is displayed in a Document window.

④ CHANGE THE PAGE TITLES AND DISPLAY DIFFERENT DOCUMENTS

a. At the top of the Document window, click input_device.htm. (The Document window must be maximized to show file names.) The web page document is displayed.

b. In the Document toolbar, in the Title box, replace the existing text with Input Device Ergonomics by Name, replacing Name with your name, and then press Enter.

c. At the top of the Document window, click posture.htm. The web page document is displayed.

d. Change the page title to Posture Ergonomics by Name, replacing Name with your name.

⑤ ADD CONTENT

a. Check that the posture.htm web page document is still displayed.

b. In the Insert bar, select the Layout category and then click the Standard mode button if it is not already selected.

c. In the Insert bar, click the Table button. A dialog box is displayed.

d. In the dialog box, set the options to:

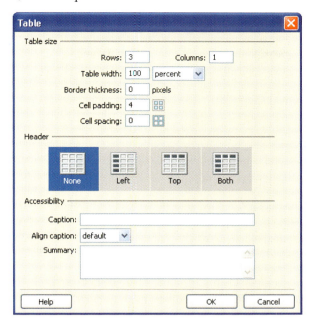

e. Select OK. A table is inserted.

f. Add content as shown below. Allow the text to wrap:

> Your Posture
>
> When working at a computer workstation, your feet should be flat on the floor and your back should be straight. The keyboard should be at a height that allows for neutral hand and wrist positions.
>
> Home

g. Save the modified posture.htm.

h. Display the input_device.htm web page document.

i. Add a table with the same specifications as the posture.htm table.

j. Add content as shown below. Press the Enter key to create new paragraphs where needed:

> Workstation Input Devices
>
> A keyboard and a mouse are the two most frequently used input devices.
>
> Ergonomic aspects related to a keyboard include height, tilt, and keystroke pressure.
>
> Ergonomic aspects related to a mouse include shape, button activation pressure, and ease of movement.
>
> Home

k. Save the modified input_device.htm.

Text Hyperlinks

document-relative hyperlink

Text that can be clicked to display a different web page document in the browser window from the same website is called a *document-relative hyperlink*.

To create a document-relative hyperlink, select the text for the hyperlink and then drag the Point to File icon (⊕) from the Property inspector to a web page document's file name in the Files panel:

In the web page document the linked text is blue and underlined.

A document-relative hyperlink can also be created by selecting text and then clicking the Browse for File icon (📁) in the Property inspector:

TIP Be sure to use the Link list icon in the Property inspector and not the Bg list icon.

The Select File dialog box is displayed with the current website and its web page documents:

Click a file name and then OK to link the selected text to that web page document.

TIP Right-click a hyperlink to display the Change Link and the Remove Tag <a> commands.

The Link list in the Property inspector displays the file name of the linked web page document when the insertion point is in a hyperlink.

Document-relative hyperlinks should be tested in a browser window. If necessary, select the linked text in Dreamweaver and then Modify ➡ Change Link or Modify ➡ Remove Link to change or remove a link.

External Hyperlinks

A hyperlink that displays a web page document in another website is called an *external hyperlink*, also called an *absolute hyperlink*. To create an external hyperlink, select the text for the link and then type the entire URL of the web page to be displayed in the Link box in the Property inspector. Be sure to include the protocol in the URL, such as http://.

External hyperlinks should be tested in a browser window. If necessary, select the linked text in Dreamweaver and then Modify ➡ Change Link or Modify ➡ Remove Link to change or remove a link.

Displaying a Linked Web Page in a New Window

External hyperlinks take the user away from the current website. In cases where the user should be able to easily get back to the original site, a new browser window should open when the link is clicked. Displaying a new window allows the user to browse the other website and then close the window to again display the original website.

To create a link that displays a web page in a new browser window select the hyperlink and then select _blank in the Target list in the Property inspector. Select _self in the Target list in the Property inspector to change a link back to displaying the web page in the current browser window.

Practice: Computer Ergonomics – part 7 of 8

Dreamweaver should be started and the Computer Ergonomics website should be the working site.

① **ADD HYPERLINKS TO THE INDEX PAGE**

    a. Display the index.htm web page document.

    b. Select the text input device ergonomics.

    c. In the Property inspector, next to the Link box, click the Browse for File icon (📁).
A dialog box is displayed.

        1. Click the input_device.htm file name.

        2. Select OK. The dialog box is removed.

    d. Click anywhere to deselect the text. The linked text is blue and underlined.

    e. In the same sentence, select the text posture ergonomics.

    f. In the Property inspector, drag the Point to File icon to the posture.htm file name in the Files panel.

    g. Click in the input device ergonomics hyperlink to place the insertion point. The Link box in the Property inspector displays input_device.htm.

h. Place the insertion point in the posture ergonomics hyperlink. The Link box in the Property inspector displays posture.htm.

i. Save the modified web page document.

② ADD HYPERLINKS TO OTHER PAGES

a. Display the posture.htm web page document.

b. Link the text Home to the index.htm web page document.

c. Save the modified web page document.

d. Display the input_device.htm web page document.

e. Link the text Home to the index.htm web page document.

f. Save the modified web page document.

③ CREATE AN EXTERNAL HYPERLINK

a. Display the index.htm web page document.

b. Select the word Studies.

c. In the Property inspector, in the Link box type http://www.lpdatafiles.com/dmx/studies and press Enter.

d. In the Property inspector, in the Target box select _blank.

e. Click anywhere to deselect the text. The linked text is blue and underlined.

f. Save the modified web page document.

④ TEST THE HYPERLINKS

a. Press F12. The index.htm document is displayed in a browser window.

b. Click the input device ergonomics hyperlink. The Input Device Ergonomics web page is displayed.

c. Click the Home link. The index.htm web page is again displayed.

d. Click posture ergonomics. The Posture Ergonomics web page is displayed.

e. Click Home. The index.htm web page is again displayed.

f. Click the Studies hyperlink. A new browser window is opened and the Studies web page is displayed in the new browser window.

g. Close the browser window. The index.htm web page is again displayed.

⑤ PRINT THE WEB PAGES

a. In the toolbar, click the Print button (🖨). A copy of the web page is printed.

b. Click input devices ergonomics. The Input Device Ergonomics web page is displayed.

c. Print a copy of the Input Device Ergonomics web page.

d. Click Home. The index.htm web page is again displayed.

e. Click posture ergonomics. The Posture Ergonomics web page is displayed.

f. Print a copy of the Posture Ergonomics web page.

g. Close the browser window.

h. Close the posture.htm document and the input_device.htm document.

The Dreamweaver Site Map

Version 8 Dreamweaver 8 differences are indicated with parentheses (*ver.8:*).

In Dreamweaver, a navigational *site map* of the working site can be displayed to help visualize and work with the structure of a website. Click the Expand/Collapse button (🗗) (*ver.8:* 🗗) in the Files panel to expand the Files panel to the size of the workspace, then click the Site Map button (🖧) and select Map and Files to display the site map and files:

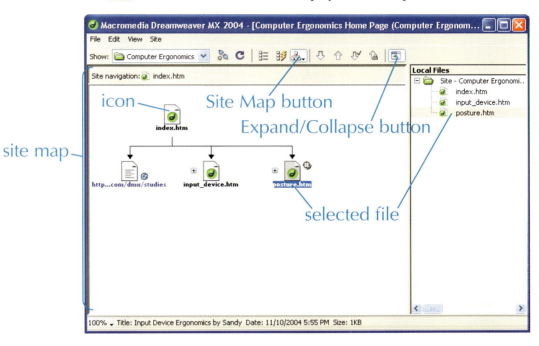

In the expanded Files panel, the site files are listed on the right. The left side contains the site map which consists of icons representing web page documents. Lines and arrows indicate links from one web page document to another. Clicking ⊞ shows the destinations of the links for that web page document. Clicking ⊟ hides them. Colors indicate status:

- red text indicates a broken link
- blue text with a ⊚ indicates an external link

The site map is useful for viewing a website's navigational structure and can also be used to work with the web page documents in the site:

- Select File → Save Site Map to display a dialog box that is used to save the site map as an image file. This image can be used as a reference when developing and maintaining a website.

- Double-click a web page document in the site map to return to the Dreamweaver workspace and open the file.

- In the example above, the index.htm document is the focus of the site map. To change the focus to another web page document, select the document in the site map or file list and then select View → View as Root (*ver.8:* View → Site Map Options → View as Root).

- Select View → Show Page Titles (*ver.8:* View → Site Map Options → Show Page Titles) to display the page titles for each document. Click a title to edit it or type a new title.

Site Map Image File

Select File → Save Site Map to save a BMP image of the site map. BMP and other image file formats are discussed in Chapter 5.

Refresh the Site Map

After making changes, the site map may need to be refreshed by selecting View → Refresh.

The index.htm web page document in the Computer Ergonomics website should be displayed. Dreamweaver 8 differences are indicated with parentheses (*ver.8:*).

① **DISPLAY THE SITE MAP**

    a. In the Files panel, click the Expand/Collapse button (▣) (*ver.8:* ▣). The Files panel expands to the size of the workspace.

    b. Click the Site Map button (▣▾) and from the displayed menu select Map and Files. The site map and files are displayed. Use the scroll bars if necessary to view all of the icons.

    c. Next to the posture.htm icon (▣ posture.htm), click the ⊞. The destinations of the links for that web page document are displayed in a list below it.

    d. Next to the posture.htm icon, click the ⊟. The list is hidden.

② **CHANGE THE FOCUS**

    a. Note that index.htm is currently the icon at the top of the site map.

    b. Click the posture.htm icon to select it.

    c. Select View ➡ View as Root (*ver.8:* View ➡ Site Map Options ➡ View as Root). The posture.htm icon is now the focus, at the top of the site map.

    d. Click the index.htm icon to select it.

    e. Select View ➡ View as Root (*ver.8:* View ➡ Site Map Options ➡ View as Root). The index. htm icon is again at the top of the site map.

③ **DISPLAY PAGE TITLES**

    a. Select View ➡ Show Page Titles (*ver.8:* View ➡ Site Map Options ➡ Show Page Titles). The page title is now displayed below each icon instead of the file name.

    b. Select View ➡ Show Page Titles (*ver.8:* View ➡ Site Map Options ➡ Show Page Titles). The file name is again displayed below each icon.

④ **RETURN TO THE DREAMWEAVER WORKSPACE**

    a. Click the Expand/Collapse button (▣) (*ver.8:* ▣). The Dreamweaver workspace is again displayed.

    b. In the Files panel, click the Expand/Collapse button (▣) (*ver.8:* ▣). The site map is again displayed.

    c. Double-click the posture.htm icon. The Dreamweaver workspace is displayed and the posture.htm web page document is opened.

⑤ **CLOSE THE WEB PAGE DOCUMENTS AND QUIT DREAMWEAVER**

    a. Close the posture.htm Web page document.

    b. Close the index.htm Web page document.

    c. Select File ➡ Exit.

Chapter Summary

The Macromedia Studio suite includes several applications including Dreamweaver, Fireworks, and Flash. The Dreamweaver workspace contains features used in the development of web page documents.

In Dreamweaver, a website needs to be defined before creating any web page documents. Web page documents can be added and saved with descriptive names. A web page document named index.htm is automatically designated by Dreamweaver as the home page of the website. The page title of a web page, displayed in the title bar of a browser window, should also be descriptive.

In Dreamweaver, web page documents are displayed in Design view by default, and can also be displayed in Code view or Code and Design view. The code of a web page document can be printed from Dreamweaver. A browser is used to preview and print web page documents.

Tables are used to control the arrangement of content in a web page. Table width may be a fixed amount or expressed as a percentage of the width of the browser window. A pixel is the unit of measurement used to specify table widths and other measurements in web page documents. Tables are best created in Standard mode.

Cell widths in a table are specified as pixels or percentages, regardless of how a table's width is specified. Rows and columns can be added to or deleted from a table. Text is added in a cell by placing the insertion point and then typing. Special characters are inserted using the Characters button menu in the Text category in the Insert bar. The spelling of text in a document can be checked in Dreamweaver.

A website selected from the Site list in the Files panel becomes the active website. If a website is not listed, the Manage Sites command in the Site menu is used to redefine the site.

Selected text can be designated as a document-relative hyperlink or an external hyperlink using the Property inspector. Commands in the Modify menu are used to edit or remove the hyperlink. The Dreamweaver site map is used to help visualize and work with the structure of a website.

Vocabulary

Absolute hyperlink *See* external hyperlink.

Borders The lines around a table and cells.

Cell The intersection of a row and column in a table.

Cell padding The pixels of blank space between the content in the cell and the cell's boundary.

Cell spacing The pixels of blank space between cells.

Closing a web page document Removing a web page's Document window from the Dreamweaver workspace, which also removes the file from the computer's memory.

Code and Design view A combination of Code and Design view, also called Split view.

Code view Displays the code generated for the web page.

Content The information presented to the user in a web page.

Design view Displays the web page document similar to how it will appear in a browser window.

Document-relative hyperlink Text that can be clicked to display a different web page document in the browser window from the same website.

Document toolbar Area at the top of the Document window that contains buttons and menus for changing views and performing common actions.

Document window Area of the Dreamweaver workspace that contains the web page document.

Dreamweaver An application used to develop websites.

External hyperlink A hyperlink that displays a web page document from another website.

File name The name of the file that stores the web page document.

Files panel Area of the Dreamweaver workspace that displays files and folders associated with the active website.

Fixed width A table width that is specified in pixels. A fixed width table will not change when a user resizes the browser window.

Home page The main page or starting point of the website.

Insert bar Area below the menu bar that contains buttons for adding objects to a web page document.

Menu bar Area at the top of the Dreamweaver workspace that displays the names of menus.

Opening a file The process of transferring a copy of the file contents to the computer's memory, which displays the file in an appropriate window.

Page title The text displayed in the title bar of the browser window when a user views the web page.

Panel groups Tools used in developing a website.

Pixel A unit of measurement related to screen resolution.

Property inspector Area of the Dreamweaver workspace that is used to change properties of the selected text or object.

Quitting Dreamweaver The process of removing the Dreamweaver window from the Desktop, which removes the program from the computer's memory.

Site definition The process of defining a site which includes specifying a folder name, a server technology, files locations, and remote server options.

Site map A map of the structure of the working website.

Standard mode A mode used to create tables.

Table A structure of rows and columns that can be used to organize and control the arrangement of content in a web page.

Tag selector Area at the bottom of the Document window that is used to select a tag and its contents.

Workspace The Dreamweaver application interface, which contains windows, toolbars, and panel groups.

Dreamweaver Commands and Buttons

Change Link command Displays a dialog box used to modify a hyperlink. Found in the Modify menu.

Characters button Displays a menu of special characters to add at the insertion point. Found in the Text category in the Insert bar.

Check Spelling command Finds misspelled words in a web page document. Found in the Text menu.

Clear command Deletes selected content. Found in the Edit menu.

Close command Removes a web page document from the workspace or quits Dreamweaver. Found in the File menu. The button in the upper-right corner of the window can be used instead of the command.

Code and Design view button Splits the Document window to display both code and layout of the document. Found in the Document toolbar.

Code view button Displays the code for a document in the Document window. Found in the Document toolbar.

Copy command Duplicates selected content. Found in the Edit menu.

Cut command Moves selected content to the clipboard. Found in the Edit menu.

Delete Column command Removes a column from a table. Found in Modify → Table.

Delete Row command Deletes a row from a table. Found in Modify → Table.

Design view button Displays the document in the Document window as it will appear in a browser. Found in the Document toolbar.

Exit command Removes the Dreamweaver window from the Desktop.

(ver.8:)Expand/Collapse button Expands or collapses the Files panel. Found in the Files panel.

Insert Column command Inserts a column into a table. Found in Modify → Table. Buttons in the Layout category in the Insert bar can be used instead of the commands.

Insert Row command Inserts a row into a table. Found in Modify → Table. Buttons in the Layout category in the Insert bar can be used instead of the commands.

Maximize button Expands the Document window in the Dreamweaver window.

Minimize button Reduces the Document window to a button in the Dreamweaver window.

New command Displays a dialog box used to create a new web page document. Found in the File menu on the menu bar.

New File command Creates a new web page document and adds it to the list of files in the Files panel. Found in the Files panel group menu.

Manage Sites command Displays a dialog box used to define or edit a website. Found in the Site menu on the menu bar.

Open command Displays a dialog box used to open a web page document. Found in the File menu.

Page Properties command Displays a dialog box used to change the page title for a web page document. Found in the Modify menu.

Paste command Places a copy of the clipboard contents at the insertion point. Found in the Edit menu.

Preview in Browser command Displays a submenu used to view the web page document in a browser window. Found in the File menu. The F12 key can be used instead of the command.

Print Code command Prints the code for a web page document. Found in the File menu.

Remove Link command Removes an existing link. Found in the Modify menu.

Repeat command Used to redo an action. Found in the Edit menu.

Save command Displays a dialog box used to save a web page document. Found in the File menu.

Save Site Map command Displays a dialog box used to save the site map as an image file. Found in the File menu in the expanded Files panel.

Site Map button Displays the site map and files. Found in the expanded Files panel.

Show Page Titles command Displays the page title below each icon in the site map. Found in the View menu in the expanded Files panel (*ver.8:* Found in View → Site Map Options).

Standard **Standard Mode button** Displays a web page document in Standard mode. Found in the Layout category in the Insert bar.

Table command Displays a dialog box used to create a table. Found in the Insert menu. The Table button in the Layout category in the Insert bar can be used instead of the command.

Undo **command** Cancels the last action performed. Found in the Edit menu.

View as Root **command** Changes the focus in the site map to a selected web page document. Found in the View menu in the expanded Files panel (*ver.8:* Found in View → Site Map Options).

1. a) What is Dreamweaver?
   b) What is the Dreamweaver workspace?

2. a) What can be added using the Insert bar?
   b) What does the Files panel display?
   c) What can be changed using the Property inspector?

3. During the site definition process, what is created?

4. List two file name guidelines for web page documents.

5. List the steps required to create a new web page document.

6. a) What is the home page?
   b) What file name is used in Dreamweaver to designate a web page document as the home page of a website?

7. Which panel displays all of the files and folders in a website?

8. a) List two places where the page title of a web page document is displayed.
   b) Can page titles contain spaces?
   c) Describe a fast method of changing the page title.

9. a) What view displays a web page document similar to how it will appear in a browser window?
   b) What view displays the code generated for a web page?

10. a) What key is pressed to view a web page document in a browser window?
    b) Is it possible to modify a web page document in a browser window?

11. What is the information presented in a web page called?

12. a) What is a table used for?
    b) What does a table consist of?
    c) What is a cell?

13. a) What are two ways the width of a table can be specified?
    b) What is a pixel?
    c) What is a fixed width table?

14. a) What does a border size of 0 specify?
    b) What is cell padding?
    c) What is cell spacing?

15. a) What mode should be used to create tables?
    b) List the steps required to create a table.

16. a) List two ways to select a table.
    b) List the steps required to change the width of a cell to 160 pixels.

17. Where is the new row placed when a new row is added to a table?

18. a) How is a line break inserted?
    b) How is a © symbol inserted?
    c) List two ways the insertion point can be moved to the next cell in the table.

19. If a mistake is made, how can the last action be cancelled?

20. Give an example of when you might select Ignore in the Check Spelling dialog box.

21. a) List the steps required to print a web page document from a browser.
    b) List the steps required to determine how many pages will be printed for a web page.
    c) List the steps required to print the code for a web page document.

22. What is the difference between closing a web page and quitting Dreamweaver?

23. List the steps required to open a website for editing that is not listed in the Files panel.

24. List two ways a web page document can be opened in Dreamweaver.

25. a) What is a document-relative hyperlink?
    b) What is the difference between a document-relative hyperlink and an external hyperlink?
    c) When creating a hyperlink, what is selected in the Target list to display a web page in a new browser window?

26. a) Explain two ways the Dreamweaver site map can be useful in the development of a website.
    b) List the steps required to display the page titles for each document in the site map.

True/False

27. Determine if each of the following are true or false. If false, explain why.
    a) A website needs to be defined before any web pages are created.
    b) The extension .htm indicates that a web page document is a home page.
    c) A table with a width of 100 pixels is resized when the browser window is resized.
    d) Cell padding and cell spacing are values that can be expressed in pixels.
    e) When a new column is added to a table, the column is placed to the right of the active cell.
    f) A table can be center aligned.
    g) The header of a printout from Internet Explorer contains the web page title.
    h) More than one web page document can be open in Dreamweaver at the same time.
    i) Once a hyperlink is created it cannot be changed.
    j) A link can display a web page in a new browser window.
    k) Red text next to a document in the site map indicates an external hyperlink.

Exercise 1 ──────────────────────────────Cooking Herbs

Create a new website about cooking with herbs by completing the following steps:

a)   Define a new site named Cooking Herbs in a folder named Cooking Herbs.

b)   Add three web page documents to the Cooking Herbs website naming them index.htm, popular_herbs.htm, and recipes.htm.

c)   Modify the index.htm web page document as follows:

   1.   Change the page title to: Cooking Herbs Home Page

   2.   Add a table with 3 rows and 1 column, a width of 100%, no border, a cell padding of 8, and no cell spacing.

   3.   Add content as shown below. Allow the text to wrap and replace Name with your name:

Cooking Herbs
Herbs have been used in cooking for centuries. Cooking herbs like parsley, thyme, mint, garlic, and chives are among the most popular herbs There are numerous recipes that use cooking herbs: flavored vinegars and oils, salads, stews, soups, entrees, and desserts.
Research by Name

   4.   Link the text popular herbs to popular_herbs.htm.

   5.   Link the text recipes to recipes.htm.

d)   Modify the popular_herbs.htm web page document as follows:

   1.   Change the page title to Popular Herbs - Name replacing Name with your name.

   2.   Add a table with 5 rows and 1 column, a width of 100%, no border, a cell padding of 8, and no cell spacing.

   3.   Add content as shown below. Allow the text to wrap, and insert line breaks after each title:

Popular Herbs There are so many herbs that enhance food. Listed below are just a few.
Garlic A member of the onion family, garlic grows in a bulb that contains many cloves. Garlic cloves are used to flavor all sorts of cooking. Garlic is usually added to olive oil to flavor dishes.
Chives Raw chives are frequently sprinkled on salads, soups, meats, and baked potatoes. Chives are a member of the onion family. Chopped chives are often used in egg and cheese dishes. Cooking chives destroys their flavor, so they are best added at the end of the cooking process.
Dill Often used to make pickles, dill leaves are also used to enhance salads, fish, and sauces. The dill seed oil is used in making gripe water. Dill keeps its flavor even when frozen.
Home

   4.   Link the text Home to index.htm.

e) Modify the recipes.htm web page document as follows:

    1. Change the page title to Recipes by Name replacing Name with your name.

    2. Add a table with 3 rows and 2 columns, a width of 100%, no border, a cell padding of 8, and no cell spacing.

    3. Add content as shown below. Insert line breaks after each of the ingredients and allow the instructions to wrap:

Recipes	
Dill Salad Dressing	Sage Rice
Lemon juice Salad oil Dijon mustard Minced fresh dill Combine the juice and the oil slowly by whisking. Add the mustard and the dill and refrigerate. This dressing can be used on sliced tomatoes or on a salad. Try it with fish or chicken also!	Beef bouillon Rice Butter Chopped fresh sage Cook the rice in the bouillon. Melt butter in a separate pan and add the sage. Stir the melted sage butter into the rice. This dish is excellent served with chicken or veal.
Home	

    4. Link the text Home to index.htm.

f) Check the spelling in each of the web page documents.

g) View each web page document in a browser window and test the hyperlinks.

h) Print a copy of each web page document from the browser.

Exercise 2 ——————————————— Clouds

Create a new website about clouds by completing the following steps:

a) Define a new site named Clouds in a folder named Clouds.

b) Add four web page documents to the Clouds website naming them index.htm, high_clouds.htm, middle_clouds.htm, and low_clouds.htm.

c) Modify the index.htm web page document as follows:

    1. Change the page title to: Clouds Home Page

    2. Add a table with 3 rows and 1 column, a width of 100%, no border, a cell padding of 10, and no cell spacing.

    3. Add content as shown below. Allow the text to wrap and replace Name with your name:

Clouds
Clouds are composed of millions of tiny droplets of water and ice. Clouds can be separated into three categories based on their location in the sky: high, middle, and low.
Research by Name

4. Link the text high to high_clouds.htm.

5. Link the text middle to middle_clouds.htm.

6. Link the text low to low_clouds.htm.

d) Modify the high_clouds.htm web page document as follows:

1. Change the page title to High Clouds - Name replacing Name with your name.

2. Add a table with 3 rows and 1 column, a width of 100%, no border, a cell padding of 10, and no cell spacing.

3. Add content as shown below. Allow the text to wrap.

High Clouds

These are clouds with bases starting at an average of 20,000 feet. Three types of high clouds are Cirrus, Cirrostratus, and Cirrocumulus. Cirrus are thin feather-like crystal clouds. Cirrostratus are thin white clouds that resemble veils. Cirrocumulus are thin clouds that appear as small "cotton patches."

Home

4. Link the text Home to index.htm.

e) Modify the middle_clouds.htm web page document as follows:

1. Change the page title to Middle Clouds - Name replacing Name with your name.

2. Add a table with 3 rows and 1 column, a width of 100%, no border, a cell padding of 10, and no cell spacing.

3. Add content as shown below. Allow the text to wrap.

Middle Clouds

These are clouds with bases starting at about 10,000 feet. Two types of middle clouds are Altostratus and Altocumulus. Altostratus are a grayish or bluish layer of clouds that can obscure the Sun. Altocumulus are a gray or white layer of patches of solid clouds with rounded shapes.

Home

4. Link the text Home to index.htm.

f) Open low_clouds.htm and modify the web page document as follows:

1. Change the page title to Low Clouds - Name replacing Name with your name.

2. Add a table with 3 rows and 1 column, a width of 100%, no border, a cell padding of 10, and no cell spacing.

3. Add content as shown below. Allow the text to wrap.

Low Clouds
These are clouds with bases starting near the Earth's surface to 6,500 feet. Three types of low clouds are Stratus, Stratocumulus, and Cumulus. Stratus are thin, gray sheet-like clouds with low bases and bring drizzle and snow. Stratocumulus are rounded cloud masses that form on top of a layer. Cumulus are fair-weather clouds with flat bases and dome-shaped tops.
Home

4. Link the text Home to index.htm.

g) Check the spelling in each of the web page documents.

h) View each web page document in a browser window and test the hyperlinks.

i) Print a copy of each web page document from the browser.

Exercise 3 ——————————————————————— Sharks

Create a new website about sharks by completing the following steps:

a) Define a new site named Sharks in a folder named Sharks.

b) Add four web page documents to the site naming them index.htm, nurse.htm, zebra.htm, and whale.htm.

c) Modify the index.htm web page document as follows:

1. Change the page title to Sharks.

2. Add a table with 3 rows and 1 column, a width of 600 pixels, a border of 1, a cell padding of 8, and no cell spacing.

3. Set the alignment of the table as centered within the web page document.

4. Add content as shown below. Insert line breaks after each shark name and replace Name with your name:

Sharks
I researched my favorite sharks for this website: Nurse Shark Whale Shark Zebra Shark You can find more information at the Shark Research Institute.
Research by Name

5. Link the text Nurse Shark to nurse.htm.

6. Link the text Whale Shark to whale.htm.

7. Link the text Zebra Shark to zebra.htm.

8. Link the text Shark Research Institute to the URL http://www.sharks.org and set the link to display in a new window.

d) Modify the nurse.htm web page document as follows:

    1. Change the page title to Nurse Shark - Name replacing Name with your name.

    2. Add a table with 3 rows and 1 column, a width of 600 pixels, a border of 1, a cell padding of 8, and no cell spacing.

    3. Set the alignment of the table as centered within the web page document.

    4. Add content as shown below. Allow the text to wrap:

Nurse Shark
Scientific name: Ginglymostoma cirratum This shark is common particularly in the Caribbean. It is sluggish during the day but active at night. It feeds on bottom-dwelling lobsters and other crustaceans, as well as snails, clams, octopus, squid, and any fish slow enough to be caught by its great gulping and inhaling style of feeding. It is a harmless shark unless it is provoked.
Home

    5. Link the text Home to index.htm.

e) Modify the zebra.htm web page document as follows:

    1. Change the page title to Zebra Shark - Name replacing Name with your name.

    2. Add a table with 3 rows and 1 column, a width of 600 pixels, a border of 1, a cell padding of 8, and no cell spacing.

    3. Set the alignment of the table as centered within the web page document.

    4. Add content as shown below. Allow the text to wrap:

Zebra Shark
Scientific name: Stegostoma fasciatum The zebra shark is found over tropical coral reefs. It is distinctive because of its very long, broad tail and its coloring. The juvenile shark has zebra-like stripes of yellow on black. It takes on a yellowish brown color with dark brown spotting as it reaches adulthood. It has pointed teeth, with each tooth having two smaller points. It poses no harm to humans.
Home

    5. Link the text Home to index.htm.

f) Modify the whale.htm web page document as follows:

    1. Change the page title to Whale Shark - Name replacing Name with your name.

    2. Add a table with 3 rows and 1 column, a width of 600 pixels, a border of 1, a cell padding of 8, and no cell spacing.

    3. Set the alignment of the table as centered within the web page document.

4. Add content as shown below. Allow the text to wrap:

Whale Shark
Scientific name: Rhincodon typus The whale shark is the world's largest living fish. It has alternating thin white vertical bars and columns of spots on a dark background. This shark swims slowly near the surface, and it has a huge mouth for consuming small crustacean plankton and small and large fish. The whale shark is found in all tropical and subtropical oceans. Divers and snorkelers can swim with this shark because it is gentle and curious.
Home

5. Link the text Home to index.htm.

g) Check the spelling in each of the web page documents.

h) View each web page document in a browser window and test the hyperlinks.

i) Print a copy of each web page document from the browser.

Exercise 4 ——————————————————— E-commerce

Create a new website about e-commerce by completing the following steps:

a) Define a new site named E-commerce in a folder named E-commerce.

b) Add four web page documents to the site naming them index.htm, b2c.htm, b2b.htm, and c2c.htm.

c) Modify the index.htm web page document as follows:

1. Change the page title to E-commerce Home.

2. Add a table with 3 rows and 1 column, a width of 100%, a border of 1, a cell padding of 10, and no cell spacing.

3. Add content as shown below. Insert line breaks after each type of e-commerce and replace Name with your name:

E-commerce
E-commerce websites are created by companies and organizations for the purpose of selling their products or services online. Three types of e-commerce are: Business to Consumer E-commerce Business to Business E-commerce Consumer to Consumer E-commerce
Research by Name

4. Link the text Business to Consumer E-commerce to b2c.htm.

5. Link the text Business to Business E-commerce to b2b.htm.

6. Link the text Consumer to Consumer E-commerce to c2c.htm.

d) Modify the b2c.htm web page document as follows:

1. Change the page title to B2C - Name replacing Name with your name.

2. Add a table with 3 rows and 1 column, a width of 100%, a border of 1, a cell padding of 10, and no cell spacing.

3. Add content as shown below. Allow the text to wrap:

Business to Consumer E-commerce
Business to Consumer (B2C) is the most common type of e-commerce. In B2C, a business sells goods or services to consumers for their personal use or consumption. Many brick-and-mortar retail establishments have an online presence where consumers can purchase goods. E-commerce has also changed the availability of travel services. Instead of booking through a travel agent, hotel and airline bookings can be made easily online using websites.
Home

4. Link the text Home to index.htm.

e) Modify the b2b.htm web page document as follows:

1. Change the page title to B2B - Name replacing Name with your name.

2. Add a table with 3 rows and 1 column, a width of 100%, a border of 1, a cell padding of 10, and no cell spacing.

3. Add content as shown below. Allow the text to wrap:

Business to Business E-commerce
Business to Business (B2B) is a type of e-commerce where businesses sell products or services to other businesses. For example, many businesses purchase office supplies from an online office supply business.
Home

4. Link the text Home to index.htm.

f) Modify the c2c.htm web page document as follows:

1. Change the page title to C2C - Name replacing Name with your name.

2. Add a table with 3 rows and 1 column, a width of 100%, a border of 1, a cell padding of 10, and no cell spacing.

3. Add content as shown below. Allow the text to wrap:

Consumer to Consumer E-commerce
Consumer to Consumer (C2C) is a type of e-commerce where individuals sell items to others using an intermediary website. Online auctions are one example of C2C e-commerce.
Home

4. Link the text Home to index.htm.

g) Modify the b2c.htm, b2b.htm, and c2c.htm web page document as follows:

    1. Using the Internet, find example sites of each of the three types of e-commerce.

    2. At the bottom of the second row in each table, create an external hyperlink with appropriate text that links to the example website for that type of e-commerce.

    3. Set the link to display in a new window.

h) Check the spelling in each of the web page documents.

i) View each web page document in a browser window and test the hyperlinks.

j) Print a copy of each web page document from the browser.

Exercise 5 ———————————————— Swallowtail Butterflies

Create a new website about swallowtail butterflies by completing the following steps:

a) Define a new site named Swallowtail Butterflies in a folder named Swallowtail Butterflies.

b) Add two web page documents to the Swallowtail Butterflies website naming them index.htm and black_swallowtail.htm.

c) Modify the index.htm web page document as follows:

    1. Change the page title to: Swallowtail Butterflies Home

    2. Add a table with 3 rows and 2 columns, a width of 100%, no border, a cell padding of 6, and no cell spacing.

    3. Set the width of the left cell in the second row to 60%, and set the width of the right cell in the second row to 40%.

    4. Add content as shown below. Allow the text to wrap and replace Name with your name:

Swallowtail Butterflies	
Swallowtail butterflies are found all over the world but live mostly in the tropics. They are brightly colored and have characteristic tail-like projections from their hind wings. The females look different from the males in many of the species. They are often spotted near flowers and are attracted to wet soil, puddles, or ponds.	There are many Swallowtail species. The one I find the most interesting is the Black Swallowtail.
Research by Name	

    5. Link the text Black Swallowtail to black_swallowtail.htm.

d) Modify the black_swallowtail.htm web page document as follows:

    1. Change the page title to Black Swallowtail - Name replacing Name with your name.

    2. Add a table with 2 rows and 2 columns, a width of 100%, no border, a cell padding of 6, and no cell spacing.

    3. Set the width of the left cell in the first row to 25% and set the width of the right cell in the first row to 75%.

4. Add content as shown below. Allow the text to wrap:

Black Swallowtail	This species of butterfly is usually found in open fields and woodland meadows. They always fly near the ground. They have variable markings, but they are mostly black with blue and yellow coloring along the edge of the wings. Some colored spots on the butterfly may be larger and may be orange instead of yellow.
Home	

5. Link the text Home to index.htm.

e) Check the spelling in each of the web page documents.

f) View each web page document in a browser window and test the hyperlinks.

g) Print a copy of each web page document from the browser.

Exercise 6 ———————————————————— Quotations

Create a new website that contains inspirational quotes by completing the following steps:

a) Define a new site named Quotations in a folder named Quotations.

b) Add two web page documents to the Quotations website naming them index.htm and inspirational.htm.

c) Modify the index.htm web page document as follows:

1. Change the page title to: Quotations Home Page

2. Add a table with 3 rows and 1 column, a width of 600 pixels, a border of 2, a cell padding of 8, and no cell spacing.

3. Set the alignment of the table as centered within the web page document.

4. Add content as shown below. Allow the text to wrap and replace Name with your name:

Qutotations
A quotation is a phrase spoken or written by another person. This person is usually famous. It is always nice to have an inspirational quote to live by or to remember when times get tough. There are quotes from people about success, commitment, overcoming obstacles, failure, discipline, and knowledge.
Presented by Name

5. Link the text inspirational quote to inspirational.htm.

d) Modify the inspirational.htm web page document as follows:

1. Change the page title to: Inspirational Quotes

2. Add a table with 5 rows and 2 columns, a width of 600 pixels, a border of 2, a cell padding of 8, and no cell spacing.

3. Set the alignment of the table as centered within the web page document.

4. Set the width of the left cell in the first row to 20% and set the width of the right cell in the first row to 80%.

5. Add content as shown below. Allow the text to wrap and replace Name with your name:

Success	Mistakes are stepping stones to success. --Charles E. Popplestone The only time you'll find success before work is in the dictionary. --Mary B. Smith
Commitment	Commitment is what transforms a promise into reality. --Abraham Lincoln A somebody was once a nobody who wanted to and did. --Anonymous
Overcoming Obstacles	The greater the difficulty, the more glory in surmounting it. --Epicurus Success is to be measured not so much by the position that one has reached in life as by the obstacles which one has overcome while trying to succeed. --Booker T. Washington
Failure	What would you attempt to do if you knew you would not fail? --Robert Schuller Failure is only the opportunity to more intelligently begin. --Kenny Ford
Home	Presented by Name

6. Link the text Home to index.htm.

e) Check the spelling in each of the web page documents.

f) View each web page document in a browser window and test the hyperlinks.

g) Print a copy of each web page document from the browser.

Exercise 7 ——————————————————— Computer Lab

Create a new website about your computer lab and workstation by completing the following steps:

a) Define a new site named Computer Lab in a folder named Computer Lab.

b) Add two web page documents to the website naming them index.htm and lab.htm.

c) Modify the index.htm web page document as follows:

1. Change the page title to: Computer Lab and Workstation Home

2. Add a table with 3 rows and 1 column, a width of 100%, no border, a cell padding of 8, and no cell spacing.

3. Add content as shown below. Allow the text to wrap and replace Name with your name:

Computer Lab and Workstation Information
The workstations in our computer lab use various input devices and output devices. Several titles of software are available on the computers. Files are stored on different types of storage media. I have compiles a listing of what is available in our computer lab.
Prepared by Name

4. Link the text listing to lab.htm.

d) Modify the lab.htm web page document as follows:

    1. Change the page title to Computer Lab Listing - Name replacing Name with your name.

    2. Add a table with 5 rows and 2 columns, a width of 100%, no border, a cell padding of 8, and no cell spacing.

    3. In the first row, in the first column, add the text: Input Devices

    4. Input devices are used to enter data into a computer. Examples of input devices include a keyboard, mouse, scanner, CD/DVD drive, and digital camera. In the first row, in the second column, create a list of the input devices used in your computer lab. Insert line breaks at the end of each input device to create the list.

    5. In the second row, in the first column, add the text: Output Devices

    6. Output devices display or store data. Examples of output devices include a monitor, a printer, and a writable disk drive. In the second row, in the second column, create a list of the output devices used in your computer lab. Insert line breaks at the end of each output device to create the list.

    7. In the third row, in the first column, add the text: Software

    8. In the third row, in the second column, create a list of the software titles available in your computer lab. Insert line breaks at the end of each title to create the list.

    9. In the fourth row, in the first column, add the text: Storage Media

    10. Files are stored on various types of media for later retrieval. Examples of types of storage media include a disk, CD/DVD, or a memory key. In the fourth row, in the second column, create a list of the types of storage media used in your computer lab. Insert line breaks at the end of each type to create the list.

    11. In the last row, in the first column, add the text Home and link it to index.htm.

e) Check the spelling in each of the web page documents.

f) View each web page document in a browser window and test the hyperlinks.

g) Print a copy of each web page document from the browser.

Exercise 8

Select one of the topics listed below. Using the Internet, find at least three websites that provide information on your topic. Create a new website to present your research, and include at least three linked web page documents. Include external hyperlinks to your sources.

- hurricanes
- the Arctic ocean
- earthquakes
- tornadoes
- the ozone layer
- tsunamis

Chapter 4
Website Development

This chapter introduces the overall process of developing a website. The purpose, audience, navigation structure, and content of a website is discussed, as well as implementing design concepts in the web page layout.

Website Development

Website development is the process of planning and creating a website. Planning includes determining the website's purpose, audience, navigation structure, content, and page layout. Dreamweaver is then used to set up the website and create the web pages. Website development can be divided into two stages, planning and implementation:

Planning

1. Define the purpose and target audience.

2. Determine the web pages that will be in the website by sketching the navigation structure. Review and revise the sketches as needed.

3. Determine the content for each web page.

4. Design the web pages by sketching the page layouts. Review and revise the sketches, keeping in mind the four design concepts: appropriateness, placement, consistency, and usability.

Implementation

5. Using Dreamweaver, define the website and organize the files and folders.

6. Create the web pages using Dreamweaver.

7. Review the website in a browser and review a printed copy of each web page.

8. Make changes or corrections.

9. Repeat steps 7 and 8 until complete.

Most of the development process is repetitive: start with something, review it, revise it, review it again, and so on. With experience, you may only need to revise once or twice.

Information Architect

An information architect creates a vision of what a website will look like and defines how it will work. The job invloves all aspects of planning the website and may include assisting with implementation. Careers are discussed in Chapter 1.

Defining the Purpose and Target Audience

purpose

The first step in planning a website is to define the purpose and target audience. The *purpose* is the intent of the website. For example, the purpose of a restaurant's website could be to provide the phone number, location, hours of operation, and menus. Clearly defining the purpose helps to make decisions about the website navigation structure and the content for each web page. Most websites have more than one purpose, so it is best to list as many as possible:

Purposes for a fast-food restaurant's website:

* provide location and contact information
* provide the hours of operation
* provide a fun page for kids
* describe the menus
* provide information about specials and promotions

Purposes for a children's theater website:

* list rehearsal and show times
* describe the theater production company
* provide location and contact information

target audience

Once the purpose is identified, the target audience of the website needs to be defined. The *target audience* is composed of the individuals that are intended to use the website. The content of the website is tailored to the target audience. To define the target audience, describe the intended users. Ask questions such as how old are they, where do they live, what are their interests, and what is their level of education. Answers to these and other questions related to the site can be listed as characteristics which define the target audience, as in the following examples:

Target audience characteristics for a fast-food restaurant website:

* adults, local residents, and travelers
* children who already know and like the restaurant
* people looking for the particular foods offered at the restaurant
* people in a hurry
* people on a budget

Target audience characteristics for a children's theater website:

* parents of children interested in attending or participating in a production
* children interested in attending or participating in a production

Write your answers on paper.

① DETERMINE THE PURPOSE AND TARGET AUDIENCE FOR A PASTA RESTAURANT

You have been asked to develop a website for a pasta restaurant. The owners want to include the address, hours, phone number, lunch and dinner menus, and a few recipes. The restaurant is unique because the pasta and sauces are made fresh daily. The restaurant is family-owned and is popular with tourists as well as local residents.

a. What are the purposes of the website? List as many as possible.

b. Who is the target audience for the website? List characteristics of the audience.

② DETERMINE THE PURPOSE AND TARGET AUDIENCE FOR A BICYCLING CLUB

You have been asked to develop a website for a local bicycling club. The club meets once a month for a breakfast meeting followed by a group ride. They want to have the club president's contact information and a schedule of events on the home page, and other pages with photos and reviews of past rides.

a. What are the purposes of the website? List as many as possible.

b. Who is the target audience for the website? List characteristics of the audience.

Determining the Web Pages and Navigation Structure

navigation structure

The web pages in a website are determined from the purpose and target audience. The home page typically contains links to web pages of specific topics. The organization of the pages in a website is called its *navigation structure*. Using rectangles and lines to represent web pages and their relationships, the navigation structure should be sketched during the planning stage of website development. A sketch usually goes through several revisions before being finalized. This sketch represents the navigation structure of a restaurant's website:

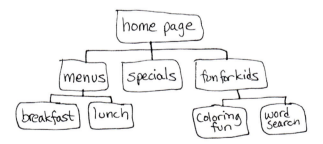

Sticky Notes as a Design Tool

Sticky notes are useful for working on a navigation structure. Using a sticky note for each web page, the notes can be arranged on a table or wall in a hierarchy like a navigation structure sketch. The notes can be rearranged many times to find the best structure.

The arrangement of the pages in a navigation structure should be from general to specific. For example, the menus page is more general than the specific pages for breakfast and lunch. The hierarchy should not be too deep or too shallow and each page should be about one topic.

top-level page

same-level page

The home page is referred to as a *top-level page* because it is at the highest level in the structure. At the second level in the example sketch there are three pages, which are *same-level pages*. This sketch also has web pages at a third level. These third-level pages, such as breakfast and lunch, are also same-level pages with respect to each other.

parent page
child page

In a navigation structure, web pages may also be described in terms of parent and child pages. A *parent page* has at least one page below it, called a *child page*. In the example sketch, the home page is a parent page and pages below it are child pages. The menus page is both a parent page and a child page.

Determining the Content

The *content* of a web page is the text, images, and other objects such as Flash movies that are presented to the user. Content is determined using the navigation structure of a website as a guideline, and then the text and objects for each page are listed on paper. For example, the content of the web pages for a fast-food restaurant's website may be:

- **Home page** Location, hours of operation, contact information, and a brief introduction about what this website offers. Objects include the restaurant's logo and a picture of the restaurant.

- **Menus page** The hours for breakfast and lunch and links to the breakfast and lunch pages. Objects include the restaurant's logo and pictures of food.

- **Specials page** A listing of the current specials. Objects include the restaurant's logo.

- **Fun for kids page** A brief description of the kids web pages and links to the coloring fun page and word search page. Objects include the restaurant's logo and perhaps a cartoon.

- **Breakfast page** The breakfast menu. Objects include the restaurant's logo and pictures of breakfast menu items.

- **Lunch page** The lunch menu. Objects include the restaurant's logo and pictures of lunch menu items.

- **Coloring fun page** An image that kids can color on a printout of the web page. Objects include the restaurant's logo and the coloring image.

- **Word search page** An image of a word search puzzle that kids can complete on a printout of the web page. Objects include the restaurant's logo and the word search image.

Practice: Pasta Restaurant – part 2 of 7

Write your answers on paper.

① **SKETCH THE NAVIGATION STRUCTURE OF THE PASTA RESTAURANT SITE**

    a. Draw a rectangle and label the rectangle "home page." The home page is at the top level.

    b. Below the home page, draw two rectangles in a row and label them "menus" and "recipes" to represent the pages on the second level.

    c. Below the menus page, draw two rectangles in a row and label them "lunch" and "dinner" to represent pages on the third level.

Check—Your sketch should look similar to:

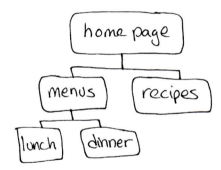

② DETERMINE THE PAGE CONTENT OF THE PASTA RESTAURANT SITE

a. List each of the web pages from the navigation structure created in step 1.

b. Write down the information each web page should present.

c. List possible images for each page. Refer to the previous section "Determining the Content" for examples.

Defining Navigation Bars

A *navigation bar* is a set of hyperlinks that give users a way to display the different pages in a website. A website can contain several types of navigation bars and usually contains more than one type for better usability. For example, this web page includes navigation bars and a breadcrumb trail:

top global navigation bar

The *top global navigation bar* typically contains a link to each page on the first and second levels of the website's navigation structure. The links can be text or images. A top global navigation bar should be placed near the top of each page and should not contain too many links. Eight links is usually the maximum.

bottom global navigation bar

The *bottom global navigation bar* should appear near the bottom of the page and is often centered. This navigation bar should only use text links, in a small size, and should contain links to all of the pages in the website if possible.

the | symbol

Each link in the global navigation bars should be clearly separated. The pipe symbol (|) is often used as a separator when needed. The pipe symbol is created with the | key above the Enter key.

local navigation bar

A *local navigation bar* can be positioned below the top global navigation bar or vertically along the left side of a page. A local navigation bar typically contains links to the child pages of the current page. It may also contain links to pages at the current level of the navigation structure or to locations on the current page. The local navigation bar may not be needed on websites that contain only a few pages.

breadcrumb trail

A *breadcrumb trail*, also called the *path*, is a navigation bar that displays the page names in order of level, from the home page to the current page, based on the navigation structure. Each of the page names, except for the current page name, is a link to the appropriate page. This path gives the user a point of reference and allows the user to navigate by backtracking through the site. Each page name in the path should be separated by a

the > symbol

symbol, most commonly the "greater than" sign (>). A breadcrumb trail does not appear on the home page.

links to the home page

There should always be at least one link on each web page to the home page. Users may be directed to a web page in the website by a link at a search engine, and therefore need a way to find the home page. Home page links are always included in the breadcrumb trail and in the bottom global navigation bar. A logo at the top of a web page is also typically a link to the home page.

The Web Page Layout

A *web page layout* refers to the arrangement of the elements on the page. *Elements* can be in the form of text, images, Flash movies, or other media and include navigation bars, a logo or heading, copyright information, and content. A web page layout should be based on usability standards, which dictate the placement of navigation bars and other elements:

Widths of the Navigation Bar

To control the layout of a table with a percentage width, the cells in the left column are commonly formatted with a fixed width in pixels. This left column often contains the local navigation rail of links to other pages in the website. By specifying a width, the layout of these links remains constant as the user resizes the browser window.

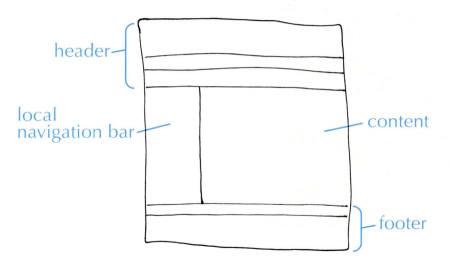

header
The top area of a web page is called the *header* and includes a logo or heading, top global navigation bar, and possibly a breadcrumb trail. The bottom area of the page is called the *footer* and includes a bottom global navigation bar and other information such as a copyright notice, the date of the last update, and a link to contact the author.

footer

sketch the layout
A page layout should be sketched for each page of a website. The sketches should show the general placement of the content elements. The links in the navigation bars can be listed separately or written on the sketch where the links will appear.

Page layout should be similar for each page. By consistently placing elements in the same location, the user quickly becomes familiar with the website and can navigate easily. Because the home page acts as the starting point of a website, it should have a slightly different layout than the other web pages to quickly identify it as the home page.

Practice: Pasta Restaurant — part 3 of 7

Refer to the navigation structure created in the previous practice to complete this practice. Write your answers on paper.

① SKETCH THE HOME PAGE AND DETERMINE THE NAVIGATION BARS

  a. Sketch the home page. The header includes a logo and a top global navigation bar and the footer includes a bottom global navigation bar and copyright notice. Content includes text and a picture.

  b. List the links for the top global navigation bar, which are links to the second level pages.

  c. List the links for the bottom global navigation bar, which are links to the all the pages.

Check—Your sketch should look similar to:

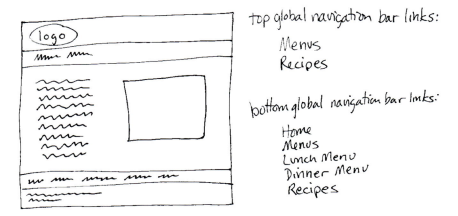

② **SKETCH THE MENUS PAGE AND DETERMINE THE NAVIGATION BARS**

    a. Sketch the menus page. The header includes a logo, top global navigation bar, and a breadcrumb trail. The footer includes a bottom global navigation bar and copyright notice. Content includes text and three pictures.

    b. List the links for the top global navigation bar, which are links to the other pages on the second level of the website and the home page.

    c. List the links for the bottom global navigation bar, which are links to all the pages.

    d. The breadcrumb trail should display <u>Home</u> > Menus, with <u>Home</u> as a link to the home page. Write this information down on your sketch.

③ **SKETCH THE REMAINING PAGES AND DETERMINE THEIR NAVIGATION BARS**

Refer to "The Web Page Layout" section and steps ① and ② in this practice to sketch the recipes, lunch menu, and dinner menu pages. For each web page sketch, list appropriate links for the navigation bars.

Using Metaphors in a Website

Metaphors can help the user understand concepts in a website. For example, e-commerce websites use a shopping cart metaphor by providing links such as "add to cart" and "view cart" so that users feel as if they were shopping in a retail store. However, metaphors only work if they are obvious to the majority of users. If there is a slight possibility that a user may not understand it, then do not use a metaphor.

Concepts of Design

There are four basic concepts to consider when designing a web page: appropriateness, placement, consistency, and usability. Web page design includes the web page's layout and the content elements.

There are no absolute rules for website design, only guidelines that come from design concepts. Although the concepts discussed in this chapter are used frequently to create successful website designs, there are times when they may not yield the best design. With experience, the better choices will become obvious. Keep in mind that a website goes through many changes before it is finished, and good designs result from numerous revisions.

Design Concepts: Appropriateness

The *appropriateness* of a design is how well the elements in the website match the purpose and target audience. Is the text appropriate for the audience? Do the images fit the purpose of the website? Are they appropriate for the audience? What other content would the audience expect to find at this website?

Examine the differences in these two home pages:

Two different designs of the same home page

Websites are Always Under Construction

The nature of the World Wide Web is change. The content of web pages is always changing and being updated. Adding an "under construction" notation or a construction image is not considered good design and could imply that the content on the page is incomplete or false.

The home page on the left conveys immaturity because of inappropriate wording, wild colors, confusing text hyperlinks, and a childish smiling golf ball image. For example, compare the link in the page on the left that reads <u>Might wanna book a tee time online</u> with the same link in the other page <u>Book your tee time</u>. The wording "Might wanna" is too casual and inappropriate for the target audience of a country club. The page on the right has quiet colors and appropriate wording in the text and links. This page invokes a calm, sophisticated feeling, more appropriate for a country club and golfers.

Design Concepts: Placement

The *placement* or arrangement of web page elements should follow generally accepted standards, with a header, a footer, and content in between. These standards are based on user expectations.

user expectations

The expectations continue as the user browses the website. After clicking a link, the user expects to see a web page with similar design but different content. If the design suddenly changes, the links are moved, or the placement is different, they may click away from the website in frustration or confusion.

Within the content are additional elements that require careful placement. The most important elements are those that the user should see first. These elements should be near enough to the top of a web page so

above the fold

that they are visible right away, and do not require the user to scroll. This placement is called *above the fold*, which originally referred to the headlines placed on the top half of a newspaper's front page, above where it is folded in half. News items in this location were sure to be seen first. On a web page, any elements that can be viewed without scrolling are seen first and can influence whether the user clicks on a link to another page in the site or leaves the site.

white space

Another factor in the placement of elements is white space. *White space* is any blank area on a page, regardless of the color. Jamming a page full of elements with little space between them causes visual noise and frustrated users may click away, as illustrated in this web page:

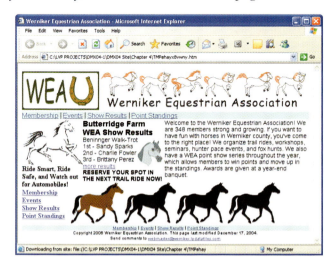

Testing Window Size

The appearance of the web page's layout on different monitors can be checked by using the Window Size button. In Design view, when the Document window is not maximized, click the Window Size button in the status bar to display a menu:

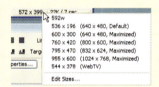

The menu choices correspond to the inside dimensions of a browser window viewed on a monitor of the size given in parentheses. Selecting a size modifies the Document window to reflect how a web page will look when viewed on that monitor.

The shape of white space can emphasize elements and influence the direction that the user's eye travels around the page. Although white space is blank, it is just as important as other elements in the layout of a web page.

Design Concepts: Consistency

Consistency is achieved by repeating the placement and use of elements in web pages. Repetition in the placement of elements creates and maintains expectations for the user. For example, a breadcrumb trail is repeated on every page except the home page. After viewing a couple of pages, the user expects this as a point of reference. The user also subconsciously uses

visual cue

it as a visual cue to know which pages are not the home page. A *visual cue* is a pattern or object that the user sees and identifies quickly after repeated use.

The importance of consistency increases with the number of pages in a website. In a one-page website, consistent visual cues are not needed. In a website with fifteen pages, consistent visual cues help the user navigate and provide a point of reference.

Design Concepts: Usability

Although all of the design concepts are important, if a website isn't usable, it won't get used. The object is to keep users at a website long enough to find information that is useful to them. The *usability* is indicated by how easily the user navigates through the web pages to find the information. Navigation bars makes the site easier to explore. A breadcrumb trail also helps the user understand the current page location in relation to the rest of the website.

Text content on web pages should be limited to only necessary words and paragraphs. The less text there is for users to scan, the faster they will be able to find what they need. Information should be carefully edited to convey a message clearly but without wordiness.

printer-friendly version

Will the user be likely to print out the web page? If so, a link to a *printer-friendly version* of the page may be needed. If a web page looks great in the browser but does not look great printed, the user can click the link to display another web page with the same content set up for printing.

Practice: Pasta Restaurant – part 4 of 7

Refer to the content determined in the previous practice. Write your answers on paper.

① **ANALYZE THE DESIGN OF A WEB PAGE**

Based on the navigation structure shown, analyze the design of the recipes web page in a strawberry farm's website:

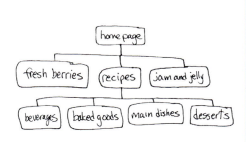

a. Describe the usability and consistency of the top and bottom global navigation bars.

b. Are the links in the local navigation bar appropriate? Explain why or why not.

c. Where is the logo? Where is a more appropriate location for the logo? Why?

d. Describe the appropriateness of the paragraph in the content area.

e. Describe the appropriateness and usability of the links in the content area.

f. How could the footer be improved?

② DESIGN THE PASTA RESTAURANT WEBSITE HOME PAGE

Refine the content layout of the home page for the pasta restaurant. The content of the home page should include:

- a brief statement about the pasta restaurant
- an image related to the restaurant
- the restaurant address, phone number, and hours of business

Check—Your sketch could look similar to:

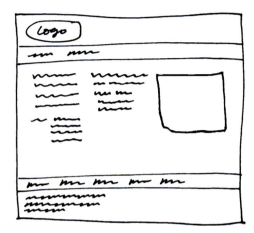

Organizing Files and Folders

root folder

Once the planning stage for a new website is complete, the website can be defined in Dreamweaver as discussed in Chapter 3. The Files panel is then used to organize files and folders for the website. The *root folder* is created during site definition for storing files and folders. To add a new folder to the website, select the root folder in the Files panel and then select ▤ → File → New Folder in the Files panel group. After adding the new folder, it can be renamed:

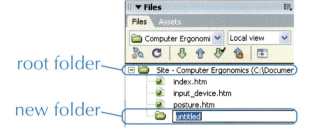

root folder

new folder

> **Folder Structure**
>
> Large websites may use several folders to organize the files. Use as many folders as needed to maintain organization.

Folders are used to organize files. Web page documents have many elements, including images. For better organization, all the image files for a website should be stored together in a folder named images.

existing files

An existing file is added to a site by copying it to a folder in the website's root folder. Select Desktop from the pop-up menu in the Files panel to display a list of files:

TIP In the Files panel, website folders are green (🗀) and other folders are yellow.

Select Desktop from the pop-up menu to display a list of files

Navigate to the existing file and select it, then select 📰 ➙ Edit ➙ Copy. A copy of the file is placed in the computer's memory. Select a website from the Files panel pop-up list to display the site's files and folders in the Files panel, and then select 📰 ➙ Edit ➙ Paste to copy the file to the website.

copy several files   To select several files at once, hold down the Ctrl key while selecting each file. The Copy and Paste commands can then be used to copy or paste all the selected files.

Practice: Pasta Restaurant – part 5 of 7

① START DREAMWEAVER

② DEFINE A NEW SITE

a. Select Site ➙ Manage Sites. A dialog box is displayed.

b. Select New, and then select Site. A Site Definition dialog box is displayed.

c. Select the Basic tab if those options are not already displayed.

d. In the What would you like to name your site? box, type: Pasta Restaurant

e. Select Next. More options are displayed.

f. Select the No, I do not want to use a server technology option and select Next. More options are displayed.

g. Select the Edit local copies on my machine, then upload to server when ready option.

h. Click the folder icon (🗀). A dialog box is displayed for browsing the local disk.

    1. Navigate to the appropriate location where a folder can be created to store the website files.

    2. Click the Create New Folder button (🗁). A new folder is created.

    3. Type Pasta Restaurant to replace the New Folder name and press Enter.

    4. Select Open. The Pasta Restaurant folder appears in the Select list.

    5. Select Select to choose the new folder as the website folder.

i. Select Next. More options are displayed.

j. In the How do you connect to your remote server? list, select None and then select Next. A summary is displayed.

k. Select Done.

l. Select Done to create the site. The Site folder is displayed in the Files panel.

③ CREATE THE HOME PAGE

a. Select File ➙ New. A dialog box is displayed.

    1. Click the General tab to display those options.

2. In the Category list, select Basic page.

3. In the Basic page list, select HTML.

4. Select Create. A web page document is displayed in a Document window.

b. Select File ➔ Save. A dialog box is displayed.

1. Use the Save in list to navigate to the Pasta Restaurant folder if it is not already displayed.

2. In the File name box, replace the existing text with: index.htm

3. Select Save.

c. On the Document toolbar, in the Title box, replace the text Untitled Document with Pasta Restaurant Home Page and press Enter.

④ **CREATE MORE WEB PAGE DOCUMENTS**

a. In the Files panel group, select ▦ ➔ File ➔ New File. A new document is created.

b. Type menus.htm and press Enter to replace the untitled.htm file name.

c. Create three more web page documents naming them: lunch.htm, dinner.htm, and recipes.htm

⑤ **CREATE A FOLDER IN THE WEBSITE**

a. In the Files panel, click the Site root folder to select it.

b. In the Files panel group, select ▦ ➔ File ➔ New Folder. A new folder is added.

c. Type images to replace the untitled folder name and press Enter. This folder will be used to store the images for the website.

Check—Your Files panel should look similar to:

⑥ **ADD IMAGE FILES TO THE IMAGES FOLDER**

a. In the Files panel, select Desktop from the pop-up menu:

A list of files is displayed.

b. In the list of files, navigate to the folder that contains data files for this text.

c. Click the pasta_drawing.gif file to select it.

d. Hold down the Ctrl key and click the pasta_logo.gif file. Two files are selected.

e. In the Files panel group, select ▦ ➔ Edit ➔ Copy.

f. In the Files panel, select Pasta Restaurant from the pop-up menu.

g. In the Files panel, click the images folder in the Pasta Restaurant site to select it.

h. In the Files panel group, select ⊞ ➔ Edit ➔ Paste. Two image files are added to the images folder.

Maintaining Consistency in a Website

Assets panel

Dreamweaver includes the *Assets panel* to help maintain consistency in the content throughout a website. The Assets panel, located in the Files panel group, helps website development by listing images and other objects available in the site:

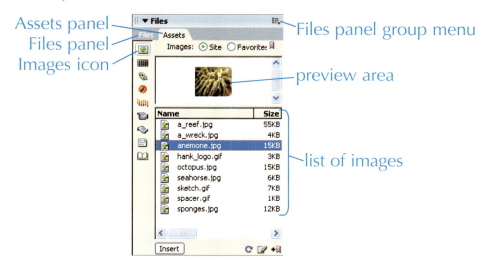

Click the Images icon (⊞) to display the Images category, which lists all the image files in the site. The selected image, anemone.jpg in the example above, is displayed in the preview area. It may be necessary to select ⊞ ➔ Refresh Site List in the Files panel group to update the list of images.

place an image

Drag the image from the Assets panel to an open web page document to place the image, or click [Insert] at the bottom of the Assets panel to place the selected image at the insertion point. (*ver.8:* If the Image Tag Accessibility Attributes dialog box appears when an image is placed, select Cancel to place the image.)

Version 8 Dreamweaver 8 differences are indicated with parentheses (*ver.8:*).

Merging and Splitting Cells

Cells in a table may be merged into one cell or split into separate cells. The Merge cells button (☐) and the Split cell button (ⅢⅠ) in the Property inspector are used to modify selected cells in a table:

Merge cells   Split cell

To merge several cells into one, while leaving the rest of the table as is, select the cells:

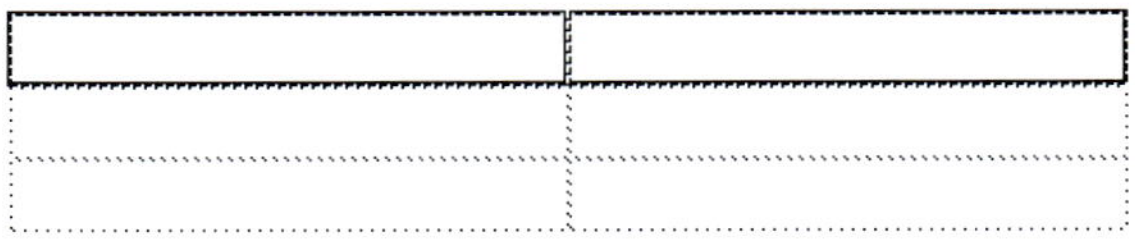

and then click the Merge cells button (⬚):

Cells selected vertically can also be merged:

TIP In the Tag selector, click
<td> to select the cell that
contains the insertion point, or
click <tr> to select that row.

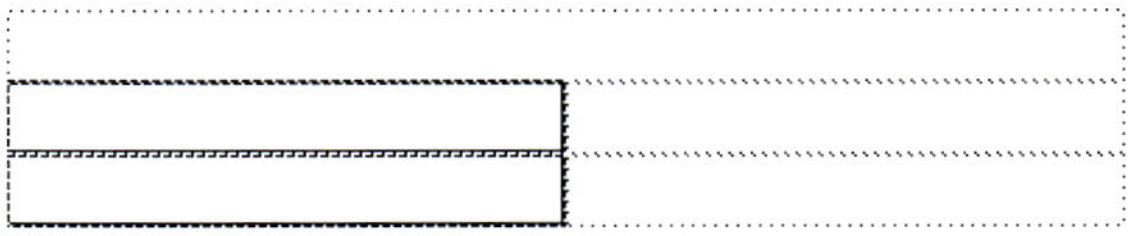

Two cells selected

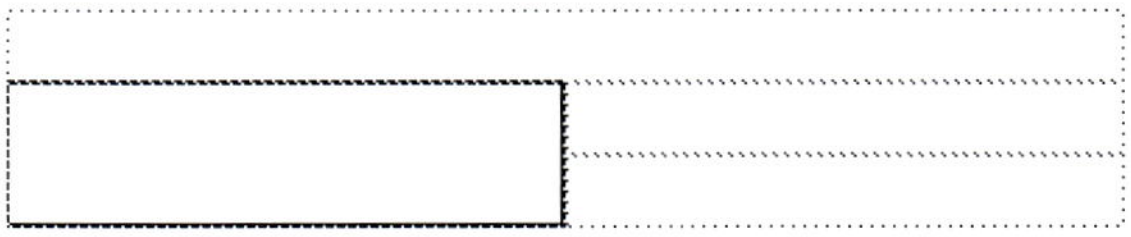

Click the Merge cells button to combine the cells

split a cell A cell can be split into more cells, in a specified number of rows or columns. Place the insertion point in a cell, for example in the lower-right cell of the example above, and click the Split cell button (⌗) in the Property inspector. A dialog box is displayed:

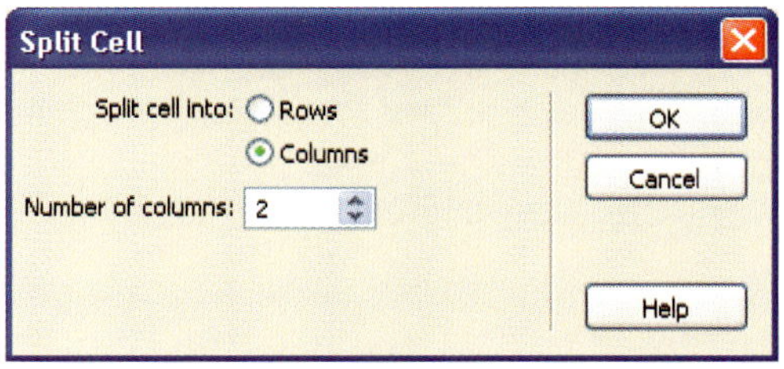

Select Rows or Columns and then specify the number of rows or columns to split the cell into, for example 2 columns in the dialog box shown above. Select OK to divide the cell:

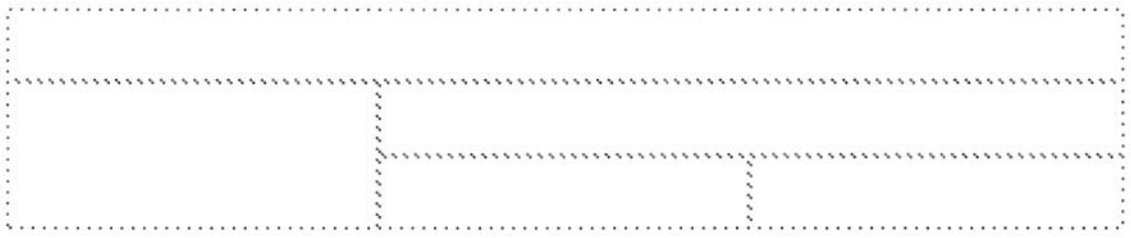

*The bottom-right cell is split into two cells
arranged in a column*

Dreamweaver should be started and the Pasta Restaurant website should be the working site. Dreamweaver 8 differences are indicated with parentheses (*ver.8:*).

① **ADD A TABLE TO THE HOME PAGE**

   a. Display the index.htm web page document.

   b. Insert a table with the following specifications:

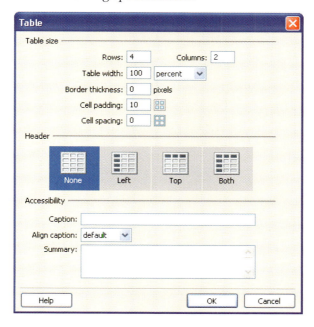

   c. Save the modified index.htm.

② **MERGE CELLS**

   a. Select the two cells in the top row by placing the insertion point in one cell and dragging to the other cell.

   b. In the Property inspector, click the Merge cells button (▭). The two cells are combined:

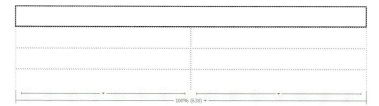

   c. Select the two cells in the second row.

   d. In the Property inspector, click the Merge cells button (▭).

   e. Merge the two cells in the bottom row. The table should now look similar to:

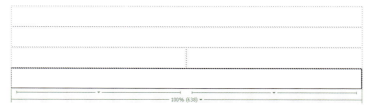

③ **SPLIT CELLS**

    a. Place the insertion point in the second cell in the third row (the far-right cell).

    b. In the Property inspector, click the Split cell button (⬚⬚). A dialog box is displayed.

    c. In the dialog box, set the options to:

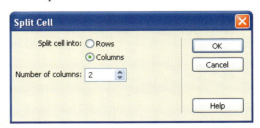

    d. Select OK. The cell is split into two, and the row now contains three cells.

    e. Place the insertion point in the bottom cell of the table.

    f. In the Property inspector, click the Split cell button (⬚⬚). A dialog box is displayed.

    g. In the dialog box, set the options to:

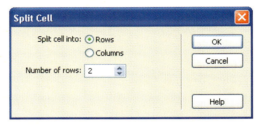

    h. Select OK. The cell is split into two cells:

④ **VIEW THE ASSETS PANEL**

    a. In the Files panel group, click <u>Assets</u>. The Assets panel is displayed.

    b. In the Assets panel, click the Images icon (🖼) if it is not already selected. The images in the site are displayed. If no files are displayed, select 🗒 ➝ Refresh Site List from the Files panel group.

    c. In the Assets panel, click the pasta_logo.gif file to select it. The image is displayed in the preview area.

⑤ **USE THE ASSETS PANEL TO INSERT IMAGES**

    a. Drag the pasta_logo.gif file name from the Assets panel to the top cell in the table. (*ver.8:* If the Image Tag Accessibility Attributes dialog box appears, select Cancel.) The logo now appears in the table.

    b. Drag the pasta_drawing.gif file name from the Assets panel to the far-right cell in the third row in the table. (*ver.8:* If the Image Tag Accessibility Attributes dialog box appears, select Cancel.) The drawing appears in the table:

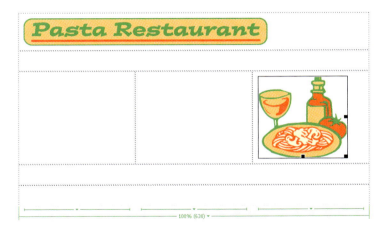

⑥ SAVE, PRINT, AND CLOSE THE INDEX.HTM WEB PAGE DOCUMENT

a. Save the modified index.htm.

b. Press F12. The document is displayed in a browser window.

c. Print a copy of the document.

d. Close the browser window. Dreamweaver is displayed.

e. Close the index.htm document window.

Creating and Editing Library Items

library item

The Library category in the Assets panel lists the library items that are available in the open website. A *library item* is content in a separate file, with a descriptive name, that is used repeatedly in the website. Using library items helps maintain consistency in a website. For example, a library item that consists of a copyright notice could be created and named copyright. Instead of typing the copyright notice on every web page, this library item can be added to each web page. When the copyright notice needs to be changed, only the library item needs to be edited, and then the occurrences of the library item in the web pages can be updated all at once.

Assets panel

Click the Library icon (📖) in the Assets panel to display the Library. Click the New Library Item button (⊞) at the bottom of the Assets panel to create a new, empty library item:

TIP Select 📇 ➜ New Library Item to create a new, empty library item.

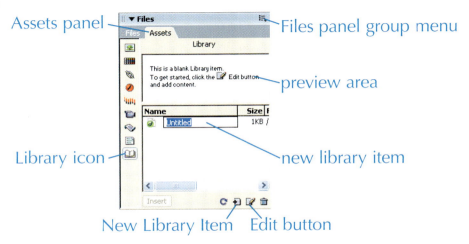

LBI

A library item file is an LBI file. The extension .lbi is automatically added to the file name.

Library folder

create a library item from existing content

place a library item

yellow background

delete a library item

edit a library item

TIP To open the linked library item, right-click a placed library item and select Open Library Item.

break a library item link

Type a new name for the library item to replace the selected Untitled text. To add content, click the Edit button (📝) at the bottom of the Assets panel or double-click the library item. A window is opened and the title bar displays the text <<Library Item>> and the library item name. After adding content in the window, select File ➡ Save to save the changes, then close the window by clicking the Close button. The content of a selected library item appears in the preview area of the Library in the Assets panel. Dreamweaver automatically adds a Library folder to the website root folder when the first library item is created.

A library item may also be created from existing content in a web page document. Select the content and then click the New Library Item button (🔲). After the new library item is named, the selected content in the web page has a yellow background to indicate that it is a library item.

Drag a library item from the Library to an open web page document to place it, or click Insert at the bottom of the Assets panel to place the selected library item at the insertion point. In a web page document, a library item appears with a yellow background. Its does not appear with a yellow background in a browser.

Click the Delete button (🗑) at the bottom of the Assets panel or press the Delete key to delete the selected library item.

To edit an existing library item, select the library item in the Library and then click the Edit button (📝), which opens the item in a window. When changes are saved, a dialog box is displayed that lists all of the web page documents that contain the library item. Click Update to update all of the occurrences of the library item in the website.

A library item in a web page document cannot be edited unless the link between it and the Library is broken. To break the link, select the library item in the web page document and then click Detach from original in the Property inspector. In the web page document, the selected library item will no longer have a yellow background and can now be edited in that web page document. Once the link has been broken, the content that was a library item in the web page document will not be updated if the library item in the Library is changed.

Inserting a Date

time stamp

The footer of a web page should contain a date indicating when the web page was last updated to indicate how current the information is to the users. Instead of typing a new date every time the web page is edited, the date can be in the form of a *time stamp* that changes automatically when a page is modified. Select Insert ➡ Date or click the Date button (📅) in the Common category in the Insert bar to display the Insert Date dialog box:

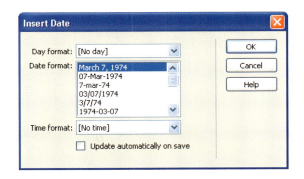

Use the Day format, Date format, and Time format lists to select the format of the date that will appear at the insertion point. The Update automatically on save check box must be selected if the date is to be automatically updated each time the web page document is saved. Select OK to place the time stamp in the web page document at the insertion point.

Outlook Express

Outlook Express is an e-mail software package that is accessible from Internet Explorer. Outlook Express is discussed in Chapter 1.

E-mail Hyperlinks

An *e-mail hyperlink* is a link that allows the user to create and send an e-mail message. When the user clicks an e-mail hyperlink, a new e-mail message window is displayed with the To: address that was specified when the hyperlink was created. After composing the message, the user clicks the Send button to send the message.

An e-mail link to the webmaster is usually included in the footer of a web page. This gives the user a chance to provide feedback about the website, so that improvements and corrections can be made to better meet the needs of the website's users.

To create an e-mail hyperlink, select the text that will be the link in the Document window and then type mailto: followed by the e-mail address in the Link box in the Property inspector:

Webmaster

A webmaster is a person who maintains a website. Webmaster and other careers are discussed in Chapter 1.

An e-mail hyperlink can be tested in a browser window.

Copyright Information

All forms of published work, including a website you may create, are entitled to copyright protection. A web page should include copyright information with a *copyright notice* that contains the text Copyright followed by the year of publication. In addition to a copyright notice, copyright information may also include other statements regarding the use of the website's material and an e-mail hyperlink for sending a request for permission to use the material.

Certificate of Copyright

A publication, such as a website, can be submitted to the United States Copyright Office to receive an official certificate of copyright. Although not required, this certificate can be used in cases of copyright infringement.

TIP The © symbol may be used in place of the word Copyright.

Published work that displays a copyright notice, in this case a website, is protected work and not intended for the public domain. Copyrighted material can be reproduced only with written permission from the owner. However, a website that does not contain a copyright notice is still entitled to copyright protection. Published work should be treated as copyright protected unless explicitly stated as material for the public domain.

Practice: Pasta Restaurant – part 7 of 7

Dreamweaver should be started and the Pasta Restaurant website should be the working site.

① CREATE A LIBRARY ITEM

a. Close any open Document windows.

b. In the Files panel group, click <u>Assets</u> if the Assets panel is not already displayed.

c. In the Assets panel, click the Library icon (📖). The list is empty because no library items exist yet.

d. At the bottom of the Assets panel, click the New Library Item button (🗈). A new item is added to the list.

e. Replace the selected library item name with footer and press Enter.

f. At the bottom of the Assets panel, click the Edit button (✏️). A window is opened.

g. Type the text: Send comments to the webmaster. Last modified

h. Insert a line break after the word "modified" and then type the text:
   Copyright 2006 Pasta Restaurant.

i. Select File ➡ Save. In the Assets panel, the content of the saved selected library item appears in the preview area.

j. Close the library item window.

② EDIT THE FOOTER LIBRARY ITEM

a. In the Assets panel, select the footer library item and click the Edit button (✏️) at the bottom of the Assets panel. The library item is displayed in a window.

b. Select the text: webmaster

c. In the Property inspector, in the Link box type:
   mailto:webmaster@pasta.lpdatafiles.com

d. Press Enter. The text webmaster is now an e-mail hyperlink.

e. Place the insertion point at the end of the word modified and type a space.

f. In the Common category in the Insert bar, click the Date button (📅). A dialog box is displayed.

g. In the dialog box, set the options to:

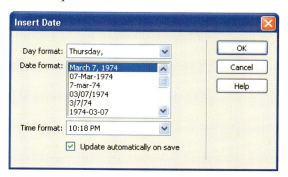

h. Select OK. A time stamp is placed at the insertion point.

i. Select File → Save. The library item is saved.

j. Close the library item window.

③ CREATE ANOTHER LIBRARY ITEM

a. At the bottom of the Assets panel, click the New Library Item button (⊞). A new item is added to the list.

b. Replace the selected library item name with navbar and press Enter.

c. At the bottom of the Assets panel, click the Edit button (✎). A new window is opened.

d. Type the following text, using the | key above the Enter key to create the "pipe" symbol:

Menus | Recipes

e. In the Files panel group, click <u>Files</u>. The list of files in the website is displayed.

f. Link the text Menus to the menus.htm web page document.

g. Link the text Recipes to the recipes.htm web page document.

h. Select File → Save. The library item is saved.

i. In the Files panel group, click <u>Assets</u>. In the Assets panel, the content of the saved library item appears in the preview area.

j. Close the library item window.

④ PLACE LIBRARY ITEMS

a. In the Files panel group, click <u>Files</u>. The list of files in the website is displayed.

b. Double-click the index.htm file name. The web page document is opened.

c. In the Files panel group, click <u>Assets</u>. The Assets panel is displayed.

d. From the Assets panel Library category, drag the navbar library item to the cell in the second row in the table. The <u>Menus</u> and <u>Recipes</u> links in the library item now appear in the cell. Click in a cell to deselect the library item. Note the yellow background behind the links to indicate a library item.

e. From the Assets panel Library category, drag the navbar library item to the cell in the fourth row in the table. The <u>Menus</u> and <u>Recipes</u> links in the library item now appear in the cell.

f. Click in the bottom cell of the table to place the insertion point.

g. In the Assets panel, click the footer library item to select it and then click [Insert] at the bottom of the Assets panel to place the library item at the insertion point. The footer appears, with a yellow background, below the table:

⑤ EDIT A LIBRARY ITEM

a. In the fourth row, click the <u>Menus</u> and <u>Recipes</u> links library item to select it.

b. In the Property inspector, click [Detach from original]. Select **OK** in the warning dialog box. The yellow background no longer appears and the text can be edited.

c. Place the insertion point to the right of <u>Menus</u> and then type:

> | Lunch Menu | Dinner Menu |

Make sure the navigation items are all separated by a pipe symbol (|) with a space on each side.

d. Link the text Lunch Menu to the lunch.htm web page document.

e. Link the text Dinner Menu to the dinner.htm web page document.

⑥ SAVE, PRINT, AND CLOSE THE INDEX.HTM WEB PAGE DOCUMENT

a. Save the modified index.htm.

b. Press F12. The document is displayed in a browser window.

c. Print a copy.

d. Close the browser window. Dreamweaver is displayed.

e. Close the index.htm document window.

f. Quit Dreamweaver.

Chapter Summary

Website development can be divided into two stages, planning and implementation. Planning includes defining the purpose and target audience, determining the web pages in the site, and sketches of the navigation structure and page layouts. Implementation includes creating the website using Dreamweaver, and then reviewing and revising the web pages.

The content of a web page are the elements such as text, images, and navigation bars. Navigation bars help the user navigate through the web pages in a site. Types of navigation bars include the top global navigation bar, bottom global navigation bar, local navigation bar, and breadcrumb trail. A web page layout refers to the placement of the elements on the web page.

There are four basic concepts to consider when designing a web page: appropriateness, placement, consistency, and usability. The appropriateness of a design is how well the elements in the website match the purpose and target audience. The placement of web page elements should follow generally accepted standards, with a header, a footer, and content in between. These standards are based on user expectations. Consistency in placement and use of elements upholds the user's expectations. The usability is indicated by how easily the user navigates through the web pages to find the information.

In Dreamweaver, the Files panel is used to organize files and folders for the website. The root folder is created during site definition and additional folders can be added, such as an images folder. The Assets panel helps website development by listing images and other objects available in the site. The Library category in the Assets panel lists the library items that are available in the open website. A library item is content in a separate file, with a descriptive name, that is used repeatedly in the website.

Cells in a table may be merged into one cell or split into separate cells using buttons in the Property inspector.

A date can be added in the form of a time stamp that changes automatically when a web page is modified.

An e-mail hyperlink is a link that allows the user to create and send an e-mail message. An e-mail link to the webmaster is usually included in the footer of a web page.

All forms of published work, including a website you may create, are entitled to copyright protection. A web page should include copyright information with a copyright notice that contains the text Copyright followed by the year of publication. However, a website that does not contain a copyright notice is still entitled to copyright protection.

Above the fold The placement of the most important elements near the top of a web page so that they are visible without requiring the user to scroll.

Appropriateness A design concept that refers to how well the elements in the website match the purpose and target audience.

Assets panel A panel that helps in website development by gathering a list of objects, such as images, that are available in the site.

Bottom global navigation bar A navigation bar, positioned near the bottom of a web page, that contains links to every page of a website.

Breadcrumb trail A navigation bar that displays the page names in order of level, from the home page to the current page, based on the navigation structure.

Child page A web page that has at least one page above it in the navigation structure of a website.

Consistency A design concept that refers to repetition in the placement and use of elements.

Content The text, images, and other objects presented to the user on a web page.

Copyright notice The text Copyright followed by the year of publication.

Elements Text, images, or other media. Elements on a web page include navigation bars, a logo or heading, copyright information, and content.

E-mail hyperlink A link that allows the user to create and send an e-mail message.

Footer The bottom area of a web page that includes a global navigation bar and other information such as copyright, the date of the last update, and a link to contact the author.

Header The top area of a web page that includes a logo or heading, global navigation bar, and possibly a breadcrumb trail.

Library item Content placed in a separate file, with a descriptive name, that is used repeatedly in a website.

Local navigation bar A navigation bar that typically contains links to the child pages of the current page.

Navigation bar A set of hyperlinks that give users a way to display the different pages in a website.

Navigation structure The organization of the pages in a website.

Parent page A web page that has at least one page below it in the navigation structure of a website.

Path *See* Breadcrumb trail.

Placement A design concept that refers to the arrangement of web page elements.

Printer-friendly version A web page with the same content as another web page, except this page is set up to print.

Purpose The intent of the website.

Root folder The folder created during site definition for storing files and folders.

Same-level page Web pages at the same level in the navigation structure of a website.

Target audience The individuals that are intended to use the website.

Time stamp A date or time that changes automatically when a page is modified.

Top global navigation bar A navigation bar, positioned near the top of a web page, that contains links to the first and second level pages of a website.

Top-level page A web page at the highest level in the navigation structure of a website, usually the home page.

Usability A design concept that refers to how easily the user can navigate through the pages of a website to find information.

Visual cue A pattern or object that the user sees and identifies quickly after repeated use.

Web page design The web page's layout and the content elements.

Web page layout The arrangement of the elements on the page.

Website development The process of planning and creating a website.

White space Any blank area on a page, regardless of the color.

Copy **command** Places a copy of the selected file in the computer's memory. Found in ▤ → Edit → Copy.

▦ Date **command** Inserts a time stamp in a web page document. Found in the Insert menu. The Date button in the Common tab in the Insert bar can be used instead of the command.

🗑 **Delete button** Removes the selected library item from the Library. Found in the Library category in the Assets panel.

[Detach from original] **button** Breaks the link from the selected library item in a web page document to the library item in the Library. Found in the Property inspector.

📝 **Edit button** Opens a window that contains the selected library item. Found in the Library category in the Assets panel.

🖼 **Images icon** Displays the Images category in the Assets panel, with a list of all the images in the site. Found in the Assets panel.

[Insert] **button** Places the selected image or library item at the insertion point. Found in the Assets panel.

📖 **Library icon** Displays the Library category in the Assets panel, with a list of all the library items in the site. Found in the Assets panel.

▭ **Merge cells button** Combines selected cells into one cell. Found in the Property inspector.

New File **command** Creates a new web page document file and adds it to the list of files in the Files panel. Found in the Files panel group menu.

New Folder **command** Creates a new folder and adds it to the list of files and folders in the Files panel. Found in the Files panel group menu.

▤ **New Library Item button** Creates a new library item. Found in the Library category in the Assets panel.

Paste **command** Places a copy of the file in the computer's memory in the selected folder. Found in ▤ → Edit → Paste.

Refresh Site List **command** Updates the list of images in the Assets panel. Found in the Files panel group menu.

⌷ **Split cell button** Displays a dialog box used to divide the selected cell into rows or columns. Found in the Property inspector.

Review Questions

1. a) List four steps involved in the planning stage of website development.
    b) List five steps involved in the implementation stage of website development.

2. Consider a website for a high school soccer team:
    a) List three purposes for the website.
    b) List three characteristics of the target audience for the website.

3. Sketch the navigation structure for an ice cream store's website that contains the following web pages:
    - a home page
    - two second-level pages, one for flavors and one for store hours and other information
    - two child pages of the flavors page, one for ice cream flavors and one for frozen yogurt flavors

4. What is used as a guide when determining web page content?

5. a) List three types of navigation bars used on a web page.
    b) Where should global navigation bars be placed?
    c) How is a breadcrumb trail helpful to the user?

6. List three places on a web page that may have a link to the home page.

7. What does web page layout refer to?

8. a) List three elements that can be found in the header of a web page.
    b) List three elements that can be found in the footer of a web page.

9. List the four basic concepts of design to consider when developing a web page.

10. Would a photograph of a car be appropriate for a web page about gardening? Why or why not?

11. Where do elements need to be placed on a web page in order to be above the fold?

12. a) What is white space?
    b) Why is white space important in the design of a web page?

13. a) How is consistency in a website achieved?
    b) What is a visual cue?

14. a) What is usability?
    b) List two ways to increase the usability of a website.

15. When is the root folder created?

16. a) List the steps required to create a new folder named photos.
    b) List the steps required to add a file named puppies.gif from a folder on your computer's Desktop to the photos folder of a website.

17. a) List the steps required to display a list of the images contained in a website.
    b) What can be done if there are images contained in a website but they are not displayed in the Images category in the Assets panel?

18. List the steps required to place an image in a web page document from the Assets panel.

19. a) List the steps required to merge two cells in a table into one cell.
    b) List the steps required to split a cell into three rows.

20. a) List the steps required to create a new library item named homephone that contains the text 883-555-0303.
    b) What does Dreamweaver automatically add to the root folder after the first library item is created?

21. a) List the steps required to place a library item in a web page document from the Assets panel.
    b) List the steps required to edit a library item in a web page document.

22. Why should a time stamp be used in a web page document instead of typing the date?

23. a) What happens when the user clicks an e-mail hyperlink?
    b) List the steps required to create an e-mail hyperlink with the e-mail address testing@lpdatafiles.com.

24. If a web page does not contain a copyright notice, is the information on the web page entitled to copyright protection?

True/False

25. Determine if each of the following are true or false. If false, explain why.
    a) The navigation structure should be sketched before the purpose and target audience are determined.
    b) Copyright information is typically included in the local navigation bar.
    c) A printer-friendly version of a web page is created in the Assets panel.
    d) If web page elements are above the fold on your computer, they will be above the fold on all computers.
    e) Each web page in a website should contain a link to the home page.
    f) A parent page always has a child page.
    g) Images should be stored in the root folder of a website.
    h) The top area of a web page is called a footer.
    i) Page layout should be different on each page of a website.
    j) The importance of consistency decreases with the number of pages in a website.
    k) Files and folders are organized in the Assets panel.
    l) A library item is edited in the preview area in the Assets panel.
    m) Copyright material can be reproduced only with written permission from the owner.
    n) In a web page document, a library item has a yellow background.

Exercise 1 ———————————————— Hockey League

Create a new website for a local hockey league by completing the following steps:

a) Define a new site named Hockey League in a folder named Hockey League. The purpose of the website is to provide information about the Holyoke Hockey League Association, rules, and a game schedule. The target audience is current and prospective league members and hockey fans of all ages.

b) Add three web page documents to the website, naming them index.htm, rules.htm, and schedule.htm.

c) In the website root folder, create a folder named images. Into the images folder, copy the following image files from the data files for this text:

   - hh_logo.gif
   - hh_map.gif
   - hh_player.gif

d) Modify the index.htm web page document as follows:

   1. Change the page title to: Holyoke Hockey League Association

   2. Insert a table with 6 rows, 1 column, a width of 100%, no border, a cell padding of 6, and no cell spacing.

   3. In the top cell, insert the hh_logo.gif image.

   4. Split the cell in the third row into 2 columns.

   5. Split the cell in the fourth row into 2 columns.

   6. In the left cell of the third row, insert the hh_player.gif image.

   7. In the right cell of the third row, type the following text. Allow the text to wrap and replace Name with your name:

      Name organized the Holyoke Hockey League Association in 1973 to accommodate the growing interest in the sport of ice hockey. Leagues are organized by age, ranging from the Tom Thumb League (5 to 6 years) to the Men's League (35+). For more information, call (561) 555-GOAL.

   8. In the right cell of the fourth row, insert the hh_map.gif image.

   9. In the left cell of the fourth row, type the following text. Allow the text to wrap:

      The hockey arena was built in 1972 through a joint effort of the city and private fund raising. It is a state-of-the-art facility with two Olympic-size sheets of ice. Services include ice time rentals, open skating, open hockey, and a pro shop with skate rental, skate sharpening, and hockey supplies.

e) Create a new library item named navbar that looks similar to:

   Home | Rules | Schedule

   Link the text Home to index.htm, the text Rules to rules.htm, and the text Schedule to schedule.htm.

f) Create a new library item named footer that is similar to the following text. The date should be a time stamp that will automatically update when the web page document is saved:

Copyright 2007 Holyoke Hockey League Association. Send comments to the webmaster. Last modified Monday, March 7, 2007 10:18 AM

Link the text webmaster to the e-mail address webmaster@lpdatafiles.com.

g) Modify the index.htm web page document as follows:

1. In the second row, place the navbar library item. Break the link to the library item and delete the text Home |

2. In the fifth row, place the navbar library item. Break the link to the library item and delete the text Home |

3. In the last row, place the footer library item.

h) Modify the rules.htm web page document as follows:

1. Change the page title to: HHA - Rules

2. Insert a table with 5 rows, 1 column, a width of 100%, no border, a cell padding of 6, and no cell spacing.

3. In the top cell, insert the hh_logo.gif image.

4. In the second row, place the navbar library item. Break the link to the library item and remove the link from the text Rules.

5. In the third row, type the following text. Allow the text to wrap and replace Name with your name:

Rules are in dispute at this time. Please call Name at (561) 555-GOAL for more information.

6. In the fourth row, place the navbar library item. Break the link to the library item and remove the link from the text Rules.

7. In the last row, place the footer library item.

i) Modify the schedule.htm web page document as follows:

1. Change the page title to: HHA - Schedule

2. Insert a table with 5 rows, 1 column, a width of 100%, no border, a cell padding of 6, and no cell spacing.

3. In the top cell, insert the hh_logo.gif image.

4. In the second row, place the navbar library item. Break the link to the library item and remove the link from the text Schedule.

5. In the third row, type the following text. Allow the text to wrap and replace Name with your name:

The new season schedule will be posted any day now. Please call Name at (561) 555-GOAL for more information.

6. In the fourth row, place the navbar library item. Break the link to the library item and remove the link from the text Schedule.

7. In the last row, place the footer library item.

j) Check the spelling in each of the web page documents.

k) View each web page document in a browser window and test the hyperlinks.

l) Print a copy of each web page document from the browser.

Exercise 2 —————————————————— Volcanoes

Create new website about volcanoes by completing the following steps:

a) Define a new site named Volcanoes in a folder named Volcanoes.

b) Add three web page documents to the website, naming them index.htm, lava.htm, and vol_types.htm.

c) In the website root folder, create a folder named images. Into the images folder, copy the following image files from the data files for this text:

- vol_close.jpg
- vol_gas.jpg
- vol_logo.gif
- vol_splash.jpg

d) Modify the index.htm web page document as follows:

1. Change the page title to: About Volcanoes

2. Insert a table with 5 rows, 1 column, a width of 100%, no border, a cell padding of 10, and no cell spacing.

3. In the top cell, insert the vol_logo.gif image.

4. Split the cell in the third row into 2 columns.

5. In the right cell of the third row, insert the vol_close.jpg image.

6. In the left cell of the third row, type the following text. Allow the text to wrap:

A volcano is a location on the surface of the Earth where magma has erupted out of the interior of the planet. Magma is molten rock, which has melted from the extreme heat and pressure inside the Earth. Molten rock on the Earth's surface is called lava. As lava cools, it builds up and forms mountains.

Volcanoes are classified as active or inactive. A volcano is active if it is currently erupting or expected to erupt eventually. Inactive volcanoes are older and have usually erupted many times.

A volcanic eruption occurs when lava, gasses, and other matter come out of a vent. Violent eruptions often include chunks of rock that were blown off the interior walls of the vent. Quiet eruptions consist of lava flowing out of vents.

Eventually, the volcano reaches the cooling stage. While the volcano cools, it reduces in size from erosion.

e) Create a new library item named navbar that looks similar to:

Home | Lava Types | Volcano Types

Link the text Home to index.htm, the text Lava Types to lava.htm, and the text Volcano Types to vol_types.htm.

f) Create a new library item named footer that is similar to the following text, replacing Name with your name. The date should be a time stamp that will automatically update when the web page document is saved:

Send your comments or suggestions to Name. Copyright 2007. Last modified Monday, March 7, 2007 10:20 AM

Link the text Name to the e-mail address webmaster@lpdatafiles.com.

g) Modify the index.htm web page document as follows:

1. In the second row, place the navbar library item. Break the link to the library item and delete the text Home |

2. In the fourth row, place the navbar library item. Break the link to the library item and delete the text Home |

3. In the last row, place the footer library item.

h) Modify the lava.htm web page document as follows:

1. Change the page title to: Types of Lava Rocks

2. Insert a table with 6 rows, 1 column, a width of 100%, no border, a cell padding of 10, and no cell spacing.

3. In the top cell, insert the vol_logo.gif image.

4. In the second row, place the navbar library item. Break the link to the library item and remove the link from the text Lava Types.

5. In the third row, insert the vol_splash.jpg image.

6. In the fourth row, type the following text. Allow the text to wrap:

Types of Lava Rocks: Basalt, Obsidian, Andesite

Basalt (pronounced buh-SALT) is rock composed of mostly feldspar and pyroxene. Dark in color, basalt is considered to be a fine-grained rock. Some varieties of basalt contain iron, silica, or aluminum.

Obsidian (pronounced ub-SID-ee-en) is semi-translucent glass that contains a large amount of silicon. Obsidian is usually black or dark gray in color and occasionally red or brown. Obsidian is formed when lava cools so quickly that it does not have time to crystallize.

Like basalt, andesite (pronounced AN-deh-site) is composed of feldspar and pyroxene and is a fine-grained rock. Andesite is usually light to medium gray in color. Andesite is one of the most common volcanic rocks.

7. In the fifth row, place the navbar library item. Break the link to the library item and remove the link from the text Lava Types.

8. In the last row, place the footer library item.

i) Modify the vol_types.htm web page document as follows:

1. Change the page title to: Types of Volcanoes

2. Insert a table with 6 rows, 1 column, a width of 100%, no border, a cell padding of 10, and no cell spacing.

3. In the top cell, insert the vol_logo.gif image.

4. In the second row, place the navbar library item. Break the link to the library item and remove the link from the text Volcano Types.

5. In the third row, type the following text. Allow the text to wrap:

Types of Volcanoes: Cinder Cones, Shield Volcanoes, Composite Volcanoes

Cinder cone volcanoes are formed from explosive eruptions where materials are ejected high in the air and cool before they hit the ground. Fine-grained rocks are blown away by winds. Coarser rock fragments remain in a cone-shaped pile, which can be hundreds of meters tall.

Shield volcanoes are formed by frequent, quiet eruptions and are much larger in width than in height. As smooth lava flows build up, a dome shape is formed. Shield volcanoes usually change shape when eruptions become explosive late in the life of the volcano.

Composite volcanoes are very large and are formed from alternating explosive eruptions and quiet eruptions. This results in layers of ejected material covered by smooth lava flows. Composite volcanoes are usually symmetrical in shape and can be as high as several kilometers.

6. In the fourth row insert the vol_gas.jpg image.

7. In the fifth row place the navbar library item. Break the link to the library item and remove the link from the text Volcano Types.

8. In the last row place the footer library item.

j) Check the spelling in each of the web page documents.

k) View each web page document in a browser window and test the hyperlinks.

l) Print a copy of each web page document from the browser.

Exercise 3 ———————————————— Lawn Care

Create new website for a lawn care service by completing the following steps:

a) Define a new site named Lawn Care in a folder named Lawn Care.

b) Add three web page documents to the website, naming them index.htm, services.htm, and clients.htm.

c) In the website root folder, create a folder named images. Into the images folder, copy the following image files from the data files for this text:

- lawn_happy.gif
- lawn_logo.gif
- lawn_mower.gif
- lawn_wheel.gif

d) Modify the index.htm web page document as follows:

1. Change the page title to: Smiley's Lawn Care Service

2. Insert a table with 5 rows, 1 column, a width of 100%, no border, a cell padding of 8, and no cell spacing.

3. In the top cell, insert the lawn_logo.gif image.

4. Split the cell in the third row into 2 columns.

5. In the left cell of the third row, type the following text. Allow the text to wrap:

Need lawn care services? Call me! Hi, I'm Smiley, and I have been working in lawn care for over 10 years. I offer many services to both commercial and residential clients. I have a long list of happy customers, and am quite adept at bringing brown lawns back to life.

Call Smiley at 903-555-7979 or e-mail any hour of the day.

6. In the right cell of the third row, insert the lawn_mower.gif image.

7. Link the text services to services.htm, the text happy customers to clients.htm, and the text e-mail to the e-mail address smiley@lpdatafiles.com.

e) Create a new library item named navbar that looks similar to:

Home | Services | Clients

Link the text Home to index.htm, the text Services to services.htm, and the text Clients to clients.htm.

f) Create a new library item named footer that is similar to the following text, replacing Name with your name. The date should be a time stamp that will automatically update when the web page document is saved:

Copyright 2007 Name. Send comments to Smiley. Last modified Monday, March 7, 2007 9:30 AM

Link the text Smiley to the e-mail address smiley@lpdatafiles.com.

g) Modify the index.htm web page document as follows:

1. In the second row place the navbar library item. Break the link to the library item and delete the text Home |

2. In the fourth row place the navbar library item. Break the link to the library item and delete the text Home |

3. In the last row place the footer library item.

h) Modify the clients.htm web page document as follows:

1. Change the page title to: Smiley's Lawn Care Service - Happy Clients

2. Insert a table with 5 rows, 1 column, a width of 100%, no border, a cell padding of 8, and no cell spacing.

3. In the top cell, insert the lawn_logo.gif image.

4. In the second row, place the navbar library item. Break the link to the library item and remove the link from the text Clients.

5. Split the cell in the third row into 2 columns.

6. In the left cell of the third row, type the following text. Insert a line break after each reference:

Happy customers include:

Jerry's Rib Shack
Lake Raton Apartments
Bushnell Condominiums
Featherton Shopping Plaza
Candlewick Mall
Renewal Funeral Home
Terry's Ice Cream
Residents in the Tall Oaks neighborhood
Residents in the Kendall Highlands neighborhood
Residents in the Boynton Ray neighborhood

7. In the right cell of the third row, insert the lawn_happy.gif image.

8. In the fourth row place the navbar library item. Break the link to the library item and remove the link from the text Clients.

9. In the last row place the footer library item.

i) Modify the services.htm web page document as follows:

1. Change the page title to: Smiley's Lawn Care - List of Services

2. Insert a table with 5 rows, 1 column, a width of 100%, no border, a cell padding of 8, and no cell spacing.

3. In the top cell, insert the lawn_logo.gif image.

4. In the second row, place the navbar library item. Break the link to the library item and remove the link from the text Services.

5. Split the cell in the third row into 2 columns.

6. In the left cell of the third row, type the following text. Insert a line break after each service name:

Services Offered

Lawn Mowing
Includes trimming, edging, and removal of clippings.

Tree and Shrub Trimming
Usually done every three to four months.

Weeding
Done by hand, no chemicals used. Includes weeds in plant beds and concrete cracks.

Mulching
Cedar or hardwood mulch applied, fertilizer treatment optional.

Turf Treatments
Aeration, fertilization, and iron and nitrogen treatments are available.

7. In the right cell of the third row, insert the lawn_wheel.gif image.

8. In the fourth row place the navbar library item. Break the link to the library item and remove the link from the text Services.

9. In the last row place the footer library item.

j) Check the spelling in each of the web page documents.

k) View each web page document in a browser window and test the hyperlinks.

l) Print a copy of each web page document from the browser.

Exercise 4 ——————————————————— METEOROLOGY

Modify the METEOROLOGY website by completing the following steps:

a) Open the METEOROLOGY website for editing, a website provided with the data files for this text.

b) In the website root folder, create a folder named images. Into the images folder, copy the following image files from the data files for this text:

- weather_clouds.gif
- weather_logo.gif
- weather_storms.gif
- weather_wind.gif

c) Modify the navigation library item to include the text Wind that is a link to wind.htm. The library item should be similar to:

Home | Clouds | Storms | Wind

Allow Dreamweaver to update all occurrences of the library item.

d) Modify the footer library item as follows:

1. Change the text Name to your name.

2. After the text Last modified insert a time stamp that will automatically update when the web page document is saved. Use a format similar to Monday, March 7, 2007 10:20 AM.

Allow Dreamweaver to update all occurrences of the library item.

e) Modify the index.htm web page document as follows:

1. Change the page title to: Meteorology Home Page

2. In the top cell, insert the weather_logo.gif image.

3. Break the link to the library items in the second row and the last row. Remove the link from the text Home in each of the two rows.

f) Modify the clouds.htm web page document as follows:

1. In the top cell, insert the weather_clouds.gif image.

2. Break the link to the library items in the second row and the last row. Remove the link from the text Clouds in each of the two rows.

g) Modify the storms.htm web page document as follows:

    1. In the top cell, insert the weather_storms.gif image.

    2. Break the link to the library items in the second row and the last row. Remove the link from the text Storms in each of the two rows.

h) Modify the wind.htm web page document as follows:

    1. In the top cell, insert the weather_wind.gif image.

    2. Break the link to the library items in the second row and the last row. Remove the link from the text Wind in each of the two rows.

i) Check the spelling in each of the web page documents.

j) View each web page document in a browser window and test the hyperlinks.

k) Print a copy of each web page document from the browser.

Exercise 5 ———————————————— SEVEN WONDERS

Modify the SEVEN WONDERS website by completing the following steps:

a) Open the SEVEN WONDERS website for editing, a website provided with the data files for this text.

b) In the website root folder, create a folder named images. Into the images folder, copy the following image files from the data files for this text:

- wonder_logo.gif
- wonder_map.gif

c) Modify the navbar library item by linking the last three items to the appropriate web page documents in the website. Save the library item, and allow Dreamweaver to update all occurrences of the library item.

d) Modify the footer library item as follows:

    1. Change the text Name to your name.

    2. After the text Last modified type a space and then insert a time stamp that will automatically update when the web page document is saved. Use a format similar to Monday, March 7, 2007 10:18 AM.

    3. Link the text webmaster to the e-mail address: webmaster@lpdatafiles.com

Allow Dreamweaver to update all occurrences of the library item.

e) Modify the index.htm web page document as follows:

    1. Change the page title to: The SEVEN WONDERS of the Ancient World

    2. Insert a table with 5 rows, 1 column, a width of 100%, no border, a cell padding of 10, and no cell spacing.

    3. In the top cell, insert the wonder_logo.gif image.

    4. In the second row place the navbar library item. Break the link to the library item and delete the text Home |

5. Split the cell in the third row into 2 columns.

6. In the left cell of the third row, insert the wonder_map.gif image.

7. In the right cell of the third row, type the following text. Insert a line break after each wonder:

The Seven Wonders of the Ancient World are architectural and sculptural accomplishments. Only one of the seven (the pyramids) survives today. The Seven Wonders of the Ancient World are:

Temple of Artemis (Diana) at Ephesus
Mausoleum at Halicarnassus
Colossus of Rhodes
Hanging Gardens of Lawnlon
Pyramids of Egypt
Lighthouse of Alexandria
Statue of Zeus (Jupiter) at Olympia

8. In the fourth row place the navbar library item. Break the link to the library item and delete the text Home |

9. In the last row place the footer library item.

f) In each of the other web page documents in the website, break the link to the library items in the second row and the last row, and remove the link from the appropriate text in both rows. Save the modified web page documents.

g) Check the spelling in the index.htm web page document.

h) View each web page document in a browser window and test the hyperlinks.

i) Print a copy of each web page document from the browser.

Exercise 6 ————————————————————Etiquette

Create new website about etiquette by completing the following steps:

a) Define a new site named Etiquette in a folder named Etiquette.

b) Add three web page documents to the website, naming them index.htm, written.htm, and voice.htm.

c) In the website root folder, create a folder named images. Into the images folder, copy the following image files from the data files for this text:

- eti_voice.gif
- eti_write.gif

d) Modify the index.htm web page document as follows:

1. Change the page title to: Etiquette Home Page

2. Insert a table with 5 rows, 1 column, a width of 100%, no border, a cell padding of 10, and no cell spacing.

3. In the top cell, type: Etiquette

4. Split the cell in the third row into 2 columns.

5. In the left cell of the third row, type the following text. Allow the text to wrap:

   Using electronic communication devices requires following a certain etiquette.

6. In the right cell of the third row, type the following text. Press Enter at the end of each line:

   Speaking

   Writing

e) Create a new library item named navbar that looks similar to:

   Home | Voice Etiquette | Written Etiquette

   Link the text Home to index.htm, the text Speaking Etiquette to voice.htm, and the text Writing Etiquette to written.htm.

f) Create a new library item named footer that is similar to the following text, replacing Name with your name. The date should be a time stamp that will automatically update when the web page document is saved:

   Send your comments or suggestions to Name. Copyright 2007. Last modified Monday, March 7, 2007 10:20 AM

   Link the text Name to the e-mail address webmaster@lpdatafiles.com.

g) Modify the index.htm web page document as follows:

   1. In the second row, place the navbar library item. Break the link to the library item and delete the text Home |

   2. In the fourth row, place the navbar library item. Break the link to the library item and delete the text Home |

   3. In the last row, place the footer library item.

h) Modify the written.htm web page document as follows:

   1. Change the page title to: Written Etiquette

   2. Insert a table with 5 rows, 1 column, a width of 100%, no border, a cell padding of 10, and no cell spacing.

   3. In the top cell, type the text: Written Etiquette.

   4. In the second row, place the navbar library item. Break the link to the library item and remove the link from the text Written Etiquette.

   5. Split the cell in the third row into 2 columns.

   6. In the left cell of the third row, insert the eti_write.gif image.

   7. In the right cell of the third row, type the following text. Allow the text to wrap and insert line breaks after each title:

   E-mail Messages
   Use meaningful text in the subject line.

   Text Messages
   Keep the message short.

8. In the fourth row, place the navbar library item. Break the link to the library item and remove the link from the text Written Etiquette.

9. In the last row, place the footer library item.

i) Modify the voice.htm web page document as follows:

1. Change the page title to: Voice Etiquette

2. Insert a table with 5 rows, 1 column, a width of 100%, no border, a cell padding of 10, and no cell spacing.

3. In the top cell, type the text: Voice Etiquette.

4. In the second row, place the navbar library item. Break the link to the library item and remove the link from the text Voice Etiquette.

5. Split the cell in the third row into 2 columns.

6. In the left cell of the third row, insert the eti_voice.gif image.

7. In the right cell of the third row, type the following text. Allow the text to wrap and insert line breaks after each title:

Telephone Calls
Always state your name and the purpose of the call.

Cellular Phones
Refrain from talking on the phone while driving.

Speakerphone
Be sure there is no background noise

Voicemail
Speak slowly and clearly.

8. In the fourth row, place the navbar library item. Break the link to the library item and remove the link from the text Voice Etiquette.

9. In the last row, place the footer library item.

j) Brainstorm in small groups to generate additional etiquette rules.

k) Add the additional rules to the web page documents.

l) Check the spelling in each of the web page documents.

m) View each web page document in a browser window and test the hyperlinks.

n) Print a copy of each web page document from the browser.

Create new website about rubrics by completing the following steps:

a) Define a new site named Rubrics in a folder named Rubrics.

b) Add two web page documents to the website, naming them index.htm and wpd_rubric.htm.

c) Create a new library item named footer that is similar to the following text, replacing Name with your name. The date should be a time stamp that will automatically update when the web page document is saved:

Send your comments or suggestions to Name. Copyright 2007. Last modified Monday, March 7, 2007 10:20 AM

Link the text Name to the e-mail address webmaster@lpdatafiles.com.

d) Modify the index.htm web page document as follows:

1. Change the page title to Name's Rubrics replacing Name with your name.

2. Insert a table with 4 rows, 1 column, a width of 100%, no border, a cell padding of 10, and no cell spacing.

3. In the top cell, type: Rubrics for Web Development

4. In the second row, type the following text. Allow the text to wrap:

Rubrics are used to assess the quality of work. Most rubrics have a scale, criteria to measure, and parallel descriptors that describe what each level of the scale should look like. The criteria defines what will be assessed. It is important to review a rubric before starting a project so that the expectations of the project are clear.

5. In the third row, type the following text:

Web Page Document Rubric

6. Link the text Web Page Document Rubric to wpd_rubric.htm.

7. In the last row, place the footer library item.

e) Modify the wpd_rubric.htm web page document as follows:

1. Change the page title to: Web Page Document Rubric

2. Insert a table with 11 rows, 1 column, a width of 100%, a border of 1, a cell padding of 10, and no cell spacing.

3. In the top cell, type the text: Web Page Document Rubric

4. In the second row, type the following text. Allow the text to wrap:

This rubric can be used to assess the quality of a single web page document.

Instructions: Circle the appropriate number using the following scale:

1-Poor 2–Fair 3-Average 4-Good 5-Excellent

5. In the third row, type the following criteria text:

1. The content of the web page document is appropriate for the target audience.

6. Split the fourth row into five columns and format each cell with a width of 20%.

7. Type a number in each column, from 1 through 5:

1	2	3	4	5

8. In the fifth row, type the following criteria text:

   2. The web page document contains appropriate links to related web page documents.

9. Split the sixth row into five columns, format each cell with a width of 20%, and type a number in each column from 1 through 5

10. In the seventh row, type the following criteria text:

    3. The arrangement of web page elements follows generally accepted standards of a header, footer, and content in between.

11. Split the eighth row into five columns, format each cell with a width of 20%, and type a number in each column from 1 through 5.

12. In the ninth row, type the following text:

    Additional Comments:

    Overall Score: _____

13. In the tenth row, type the text Home and link the text to index.htm.

14. In the last row, place the footer library item.

f) Brainstorm in small groups to generate two additional rubric criteria.

g) Add the criteria to your rubric, adding rows and content as needed.

h) Check the spelling in each of the web page documents.

i) View each web page document in a browser window and test the hyperlinks.

j) Print a copy of each web page document from the browser.

k) In a browser window, view a web page document that a peer has created and print a copy. Use the rubric to evaluate the web page document.

l) Reflect on the design of the rubric. Does it appropriately assess the web page document? Are there criteria that should be added or changed? Make any appropriate revisions and print a copy.

Exercise 8 ———————————————Local Club

Develop a website that is for a local club, such as a bicycling club or a debate club. The website should include news about the club, club events, and appropriate topics for the club. Complete the following steps to finish the website development, writing the answers to parts a, b, c, and d on paper:

a) Determine the purpose and target audience.

b) Determine the web pages and then sketch the navigation structure.

c) Determine the content and navigation links for each page.

d) Sketch the design for each page. Include details about tables.

e) Create the website naming it Local Club.

f) Create web page documents, appropriately named, and add the content.

g) Check the spelling in the web page documents.

h) View each web page document in a browser window and test the hyperlinks.

i) Print a copy of each web page document from the browser.

Exercise 9 ———————————————— Dentist

Develop a website that is for a dentist. The website should include office hours and location, information about the dentist, and educational information about dental hygiene. Complete the following steps to finish the website development, writing the answers to parts a, b, c, and d on paper:

a) Determine the purpose and target audience.

b) Determine the web pages and then sketch the navigation structure.

c) Determine the content and navigation links for each page.

d) Sketch the design for each page. Include details about tables.

e) Create the website naming it Dentist.

f) Create web page documents, appropriately named, and add the content.

g) Check the spelling in the web page documents.

h) View each web page document in a browser window and test the hyperlinks.

i) Print a copy of each web page document from the browser.

Images in Dreamweaver and Fireworks

This chapter introduces graphic file formats and discusses adding graphics to a web page document. Fireworks is introduced, as well as rollover behaviors, exporting HTML, and cropping images.

Graphic File Formats for Web Pages

Images on web pages are usually a GIF or JPG file because these formats are widely supported in browsers. The *GIF* format is best used for graphics that do not contain many colors, such as clip art or logos. GIF graphics are limited to 256 colors. The *JPG* format, also called JPEG, supports millions of colors and is best used for photographs. A third format, PNG, was created in the mid-1990s during a controversy over copyright of the GIF format. The *PNG* format has advantages over GIF and JPG, but it is only supported by the newest browsers and therefore it is currently not a good choice for an image on a web page.

GIF, JPG, and PNG formats are all *bitmap graphics*, which are composed of tiny squares. Each square is a *pixel* and is one solid color. Many pixels of different colors create a bitmap graphic:

1 pixel

The tiny squares are commonly referred to as "dots." The number of *dots per inch (dpi)* is called the *resolution*. The larger the number of dpi, the better the quality of the graphic.

The GIF format has a *transparency* feature which allows one color in the graphic to be a transparent color, a feature not available for JPGs. A transparent color can be used to blend an image with the background color because it allows the background color to show through:

GIF

JPG

PNG

Images and Graphics

The terms "images" and "graphics" are both used to refer to pictures. Pictures may be photographs or drawings.

GIF, JPG, and PNG

GIF (Graphics Interchange Format) format is pronounced either "giff" with a hard g or "jiff." JPG (Joint Photographic Experts Group) format is pronounced "jay-peg." PNG (Portable Network Graphics) format is pronounced "ping."

Background Image

Although there are options for displaying an image as the background of a web page, it is not recommended. Text may become difficult to read, which decreases the usability of the web page.

Two hat GIF graphics on a colored background

In the example above, the GIF on the left has white selected as the transparent color. The GIF on the right does not have any transparent color selected. Transparency is not always used in GIF files, but it is a useful feature to have.

interlaced

GIF files can be *interlaced*, which means that a low-quality version of the graphic appears first and becomes clearer in four horizontal passes as the web page fully loads. This allows the user to see that a graphic is going to be displayed.

compression

Compression is a file format feature that reduces file size, which is helpful because smaller files load faster in a browser window. GIF graphics are compressed but retain all of the original information in a process called *lossless compression*. For JPG graphics the compression is *lossy*, which means that some data in the file is removed in order to reduce the file size. The more compression, the smaller the file, but the lower the image quality:

lossless, lossy

Editing Graphics

Double-clicking a graphic's file name in the Files panel opens the file in an editing program. The program will most likely be Fireworks, but it depends on the preferences set in Dreamweaver.

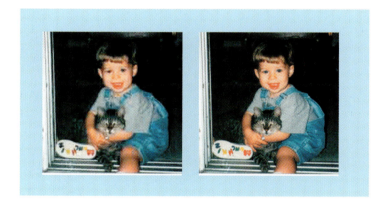

Two JPG graphics with different levels of compression

In the example above, the JPG on the left has more compression and has a lower image quality, with a small file size of 4 KB. The JPG on the right has less compression and a higher image quality, but a larger file size of 20 KB.

progressive

JPG files can be *progressive*, which is similar to an interlaced GIF. When a web page is first loaded into a browser window, a low-quality version of a progressive JPG graphic appears. The graphic becomes clearer as the page fully loads. This allows the user to see that a graphic is going to be displayed.

TIP Digital camera images are discussed in Appendix C.

Alternative Text

One consideration for images in a web page is that some users may not be able to view the images. The user may be visually impaired, or they may have a slow modem connection and therefore have turned images off. *Alternative text* is text added to an image that a voice synthesizer "reads" in place of the image. Alternative text is also displayed as the screen tip that appears when the pointer is paused over an image. In some browsers, alternative text is displayed in place of an image before it loads.

To add alternative text to an image, select the image in the Document window and type the text in the Alt box in the Property inspector:

"Gray Angel fish." is the alternative text for this image

The alternative text can be tested in a browser window by pausing the pointer on the image. A screen tip with the text should appear next to the pointer:

(*ver.8:* The Image Tag Accessibility Attributes dialog box may appear when placing an image. Select Cancel to place the image.)

Accessibility

The Americans with Disabilities Act (ADA), enacted in 1990, calls for accessibility for all persons with disabilities. In response, the W3C developed guidelines called the Web Accessibility Initiative (WAI). Among other issues, these guidelines call for alternative text to be provided for any content that is not text.

TIP Alternative text that ends with a period makes voice synthesizers stop or pause, which helps users understand the content.

Version 8 Dreamweaver 8 differences are indicated with parentheses (*ver.8:*).

Graphic Hyperlinks

A graphic can be formatted as a hyperlink in the same manner as a text hyperlink, using either the Browse for File icon (📁) or the Point to File icon (⊕) in the Property inspector. Unlike text links, a graphic link does not change to blue and underlined. However, when the pointer is moved over a graphic hyperlink in a browser window, the pointer does change to 🖑 and the image's alternative text is displayed.

test and modify a graphic hyperlink

Graphic hyperlinks are tested in a browser window. To modify links, select the linked graphic in Dreamweaver and then select Modify → Change Link or Modify → Remove Link.

Practice: SCUBA – part 1 of 8

Dreamweaver 8 differences are indicated with parentheses (*ver.8:*).

① **OPEN THE SCUBA WEBSITE FOR EDITING**

    a. Start Dreamweaver.

    b. Open the SCUBA website for editing, which is a website provided with the data files for this text.

    c. Familiarize yourself with the files and folders for this website.

d. Open the index.htm web page document and then view the page in a browser.

e. Click the links to explore the other web pages of the website.

f. Close the browser window. Dreamweaver is displayed.

② EDIT THE FOOTER LIBRARY ITEM TO INCLUDE YOUR NAME

a. In the Assets panel, click the Library icon (📖). A list of the website's library items is displayed.

b. In the Assets panel, double-click the footer library item. The library item is displayed in a window.

c. Replace the text Name with your name.

d. Select File ➜ Save. A dialog box is displayed.

    1. Select Update. The occurrence of the library item on each page in the website is updated and a dialog box is displayed with a summary of the changes.

    2. Select Close.

e. Close the library item window.

③ ADD AN IMAGE TO THE INDEX.HTM WEB PAGE DOCUMENT

a. Open the index.htm web page document, if it is not already displayed.

b. In the Assets panel, click the Images icon (🖼). A list of the images in the website's folder is displayed.

c. Drag the sketch.gif file from the Assets panel to the empty cell in the table. (*ver.8:* If the Image Tag Accessibility Attributes dialog box appears, select Cancel.)

Check—Your web page document should look similar to:

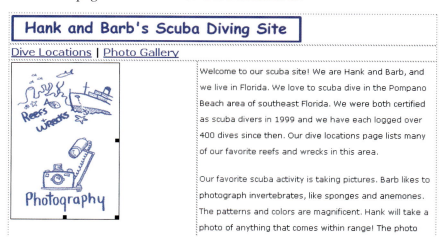

④ ADD ALTERNATIVE TEXT

a. In the web page document, click the image if it is not already selected.

b. In the Property inspector, set Alt to A drawing of a reef, a wreck, and a camera. and press Enter.

c. Save the modified index.htm.

d. Press F12. The document is displayed in a browser window.

e. Move the pointer over the image and stop for a moment. The alternative text appears.

f. Print a copy of the web page.

g. Close the browser window. Dreamweaver is displayed.

h. Close index.htm.

⑤ MAKE A GRAPHIC HYPERLINK

a. Open the photos.htm web page document.

b. In the top cell of the table, click the blue and white logo that reads "Hank and Barb's Scuba Diving Site" to select it.

c. In the Property inspector, next to the Link box, drag the Point to File icon to the index.htm file name in the Files panel. A graphic hyperlink is created.

d. In the Property inspector, set Alt to Link to home page. and press Enter.

e. Save the modified photos.htm.

f. Press F12. The document is displayed in a browser window.

g. Click the logo at the top of the web page to test the hyperlink. The home page is displayed.

h. Close the browser window. Dreamweaver is displayed.

i. Close photos.htm.

⑥ MAKE ANOTHER GRAPHIC HYPERLINK

a. Open the locations.htm web page document.

b. Link the logo in the top cell of the table to the index.htm web page document.

c. Set alternative text for the graphic to: Link to home page.

d. Save the modified locations.htm and then test the graphic hyperlink in a browser.

e. Close the browser window. Dreamweaver is displayed.

f. Close locations.htm.

Creating an Image Map

hotspot

An *image map* is a graphic that contains one or more hotspots. A *hotspot* is an invisible, defined area on a graphic that is a hyperlink. In a browser, when the pointer moves over a hotspot the pointer changes to 🖑 and the hotspot's alternative text is displayed:

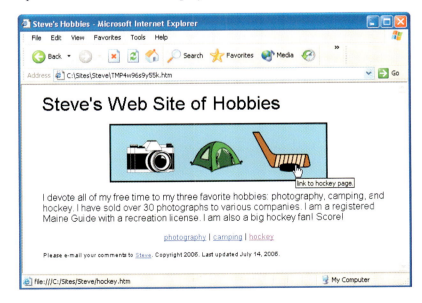

The graphic is an image map with three hotspots

To create an image map, add a graphic to a web page document and then define hotspots on the graphic. Select a graphic in a web page document to display image properties in the Property inspector:

Map box
hotspot tools

- A web page document can have more than one image map, so each image map should be given a unique name in the Map box.

- The **hotspot tools** are used to draw or edit hotspots on the selected graphic. Draw hotspots using the Rectangular Hotspot (☐), Oval Hotspot (◯), and Polygon Hotspot (▽) tools. Select and edit hotspots once they are created using the Pointer Hotspot tool (▶).

To draw a hotspot on a selected graphic, click a hotspot tool. The pointer changes to ✛ when it is moved over the graphic. If the Rectangular Hotspot or Oval Hotspot tool is selected, drag to draw the hotspot. To draw with the Polygon Hotspot tool, click to create the corner points of a shape. With each click, the area between the clicked locations fills in. Double-click to finish the hotspot. Hotspots do not have to perfectly cover an area of the graphic:

A rectangle, oval, and polygon hotspot

Hotspot properties are displayed for a selected hotspot in the Property inspector:

- Link is the web page document linked to the hotspot.

- Alt is the alternative text for the hotspot.

- Click the Pointer Hotspot tool (▶) to select the tool, then click a hotspot to select it. Drag the hotspot or use the arrow keys to move it. Drag a handle to change the shape of a selected hotspot. Press the Delete key to delete a selected hotspot.

Hotspots are tested in a browser window.

Image Maps and Text Hyperlinks

When an image map is used on a web page, the page should also contain text hyperlinks to the same pages that the hotspots are linked to. This avoids usability problems if a browser does not display graphics.

TIP Use the arrow keys to move a selected hotspot.

Dreamweaver should be started and the SCUBA website should be the working site.

① NAME THE IMAGE MAP

a. Open the index.htm web page document.

b. Select the image in the left cell of the third row of the table. Image properties are displayed in the Property inspector.

c. In the Property inspector, set Map to sketch and press Enter.

② CREATE A RECTANGLE HOTSPOT

a. In the Property inspector, click the Rectangular Hotspot tool (▢).

b. Move the pointer over the image. The pointer changes to +.

c. Starting in the upper-left corner of the image, drag down and to the right to draw a rectangle shape on the top half of the sketch, the part with "Reefs and Wrecks." Do not include the camera. If you make a mistake, press the Delete key to delete the shape and try again.

Check—Your image should look similar to:

d. In the Property inspector, next to the Link box, drag the Point to File icon (⊕) to the locations.htm file name in the Files panel.

e. In the Property inspector, set Alt to Link to dive locations information. and press Enter.

③ CREATE A POLYGON HOTSPOT

a. In the Property inspector, click the Polygon Hotspot tool (▽).

b. Move the pointer over the image. The pointer changes to +.

c. Draw a polygon as follows: click near the "P" at the beginning of the word "Photography," then click at the tallest point of the camera drawing, then double-click near the "y" in the word "Photography." A polygon hotspot is created in the shape of a triangle. If you make a mistake, press the delete key to delete the shape and try again.

Check—Your image should look similar to:

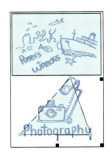

d. Link the hotspot to the photos.htm web page document.

e. In the Property inspector, set Alt to Link to the photo gallery. and press Enter.

④ **EDIT HOTSPOTS**

    a. In the Property inspector, click the Pointer Hotspot tool (🡔).

    b. In the web page document, click the rectangle hotspot. Handles are displayed indicating that it is selected.

    c. In the web page document, click the polygon hotspot. Handles are displayed indicating that it is selected.

    d. Drag the polygon hotspot, adjusting its position over the camera drawing. Drag the handles to edit the shape. Move it to cover as much of the camera and the word "Photography" as possible.

    e. Save the modified index.htm.

⑤ **TEST THE IMAGE MAP IN THE BROWSER WINDOW**

    a. Press F12. The document is displayed in a browser window.

    b. Move the pointer over the image, noting where the pointer changes to 🖑.

    c. Pause the pointer over each hotspot area to check the alternative text.

    d. Click the top hotspot. The Dive Locations web page is displayed. Click the logo at the top of the page to return to the home page.

    e. Click the bottom hotspot. The Photo Gallery web page is displayed. Click the logo at the top of the page to return to the home page.

    f. Print a copy of the web page.

    g. Close the browser window. Dreamweaver is displayed.

    h. Close index.htm.

Using a Spacer GIF

A *spacer GIF* is a GIF image that consists of only 1 pixel and is transparent so that it is not visible in a browser window. A spacer GIF is used to control layout by forcing table cells to a specified width. This is done by inserting a spacer.gif file in a cell, and then changing the width of the spacer gif to the minimum width for the cell if the browser window is resized. For example, the left cell in the table becomes very narrow as the browser window is sized:

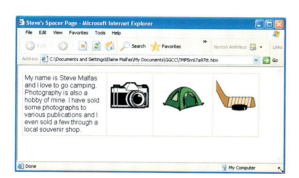

Adding a spacer GIF of width 200 to the left cell ensures that the cell will not be narrower than 200, even when the browser window is resized:

Why use a spacer GIF?

Even though a cell may be set to a specified pixel width, a browser may still resize the cell smaller than the specified number of pixels if the cell contains text that can be wrapped.

Practice: SCUBA – part 3 of 8

Dreamweaver should be started and the SCUBA website should be the working site. Dreamweaver 8 differences are indicated with parentheses (*ver.8:*).

① ADD IMAGES AND ALTERNATIVE TEXT TO A WEB PAGE DOCUMENT

   a. Open photos.htm. There are four empty cells in the table.

   b. In the Assets panel, click the Images icon (🖼).

   c. Drag the anemone.jpg file from the Assets panel to the upper-left empty cell. (*ver.8:* If the Image Tag Accessibility Attributes dialog box appears, select Cancel.)

   d. Select the anemone image, if it is not already selected.

   e. In the Property inspector, set Alt to Anemone photograph. and press Enter.

   f. Drag the sponges.jpg file from the Assets panel to the cell just to the right of the anemone image. (*ver.8:* If the Image Tag Accessibility Attributes dialog box appears, select Cancel.)

   g. Set the sponges alternative text to: Purple sponges photograph.

   h. Add the octopus.jpg file to the lower-left empty cell and set its alternative text to: Octopus eyes photograph.

   i. Add the seahorse.jpg file to the last empty cell and set its alternative text to: Red seahorse photograph.

   j. Save the modified photos.htm.

Check—Your web page document should look similar to:

② **TEST THE TABLE IN THE BROWSER WINDOW**

   a. Press F12. The document is displayed in a browser.

   b. Resize the browser window smaller and observe how the text in the cell next to the photos changes when the window is very narrow.

   c. Close the browser window. Dreamweaver is displayed.

③ **ADD A SPACER GIF**

   a. Click in the blank space below the paragraph that ends "…important!" to place the insertion point.

   b. In the Assets panel, select the spacer.gif file

   c. At the bottom of the Assets panel, click [Insert]. (*ver.8:* If the Image Tag Accessibility Attributes dialog box appears, select Cancel.)

   d. In the Property inspector, set W to 200 and press Enter. The spacer GIF image is resized to 200 pixels wide.

   e. Save the modified photos.htm.

④ **TEST THE TABLE IN THE BROWSER WINDOW**

   a. Press F12. The document is displayed in a browser window.

   b. Resize the browser window much smaller and observe how the text in the cell next to the photos changes when the window is very narrow. It doesn't get any narrower than 200 pixels.

   c. Move the pointer over each image and pause, testing the alternative text.

   d. Print a copy of the web page.

   e. Close the browser window. Dreamweaver is displayed.

Aligning an Image

The horizontal alignment of a selected image can be changed using the alignment buttons in the Property inspector. To change the alignment, select an image and then click either the Align Left button (☰), Align Center button (☰), or the Align Right button (☰). Alignment buttons are also available in the Property inspector when the insertion point is next to an image in a web page document.

Resizing and Resampling an Image

resampling

If the width and height of an image needs to be changed, the image is first resized in the web page document and then resampled. *Resampling* changes the size of the file and correctly adjusts the pixels in the image. An image should not be resized in Dreamweaver and left that way because the image file has not been properly resampled.

To resize an image in a web page document, click the image to select it and display handles:

> **Smaller, not Larger**
>
> In general, images should not be sized larger, only smaller. The image quality decreases if the image is sized larger.

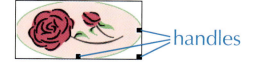

handles

proportionately resize

stretch

Point to a handle until the pointer changes to ↖ and drag to resize the image. Drag the corner handle while pressing the Shift key to *proportionately resize* the image, which keeps the width and height in the same ratio, preventing distortion. Drag any handle without pressing the Shift key to *stretch* the image which causes distortion:

A stretched image is distorted

TIP Select Edit → Undo to reverse resampling.

In the Property inspector, bold numbers are displayed in the W and H boxes for a selected image that has been resized but not yet resampled. Click the Reset icon (↺) to restore the dimensions of the image, or click the Resample button (⟳) to resample the file. Resampling changes the image to the new dimensions, saves the changes to the file, and updates the image in Dreamweaver.

Practice: SCUBA – part 4 of 8

Dreamweaver should be started and the SCUBA website should be the working site.

① **CENTER ALIGN AN IMAGE**

    a. Open the photos.htm web page document, if it is not already displayed.

    b. Click the seahorse image (last image) to select it. Handles are displayed.

    c. In the Property inspector, click the Align Center button (≡). The image is centered.

② **RESIZE AN IMAGE AND RESAMPLE IT**

    a. Click the anemone image to select it. In the Property inspector, note that W is 200 because this image is 200 pixels wide.

    b. Select the octopus image and note the image is 220 pixels wide.

    c. Drag the corner handle to make the octopus smaller. In the Property inspector, the W and H values are now bold because the image's size is different from its actual file's size.

    d. In the Property inspector, click the Reset icon (↺). The image changes back to its original size and proportions and W and H values are no longer bold.

    e. Hold down the Shift key and drag the corner handle of the octopus image until W in the Property inspector is 200. If you have difficulty, click ↺ and try again.

    f. In the Property inspector, click the Resample button (⟳). If a dialog box appears, select OK. The image is resampled to 200 pixels wide, which matches the size of the anemone and sponges images. The seahorse image cannot be changed to match the other images because as images are sized larger they lose quality.

    g. Save the modified photos.htm.

③ **TEST THE TABLE IN THE BROWSER WINDOW**

    a. Press F12. The document is displayed in a browser window.

    b. Print a copy of the web page and then close the browser window.

    c. Close photos.htm.

④ **QUIT DREAMWEAVER**

Introducing Fireworks

Fireworks is the image editing application that is part of the Macromedia Studio suite. Fireworks is used to create and edit images specifically for use on the Web. Fireworks documents are PNG files, which can be exported in other file formats for use in a web page. Images of other file types, such as GIF and JPG, can also be opened and edited directly in Fireworks.

To create a new document in Fireworks, select File → New, which displays the New Document dialog box:

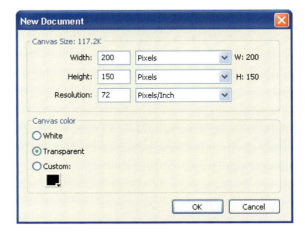

- The Canvas Size is the size of the area where an image is created. The Width and Height of the canvas are usually specified in pixels.

- The Resolution for an image used in a web page should be 72 Pixels/Inch. A larger number would only increase the file size, and not affect how the image looks when viewed on a monitor.

- The Canvas color can be White, Transparent, or a different color. Transparent is often used for an image that will be exported as a GIF, because the GIF file format supports one transparent color. The JPG file format does not support transparency.

Ideally the canvas is set to the exact size of the image, but the canvas can be initially set larger and later modified to fit the image. Select OK to create a new document and display it in a window:

Starting Fireworks

To start Fireworks, select Start → All Programs → Macromedia → Macromedia Fireworks, or double-click the Fireworks icon on the Desktop:

Macromedia
Fireworks MX
2004

Image Placeholder

A placeholder can be used in Dreamweaver in a web page document if an image is not yet created. To add a placeholder, click the Image Placeholder button ( ) in the **Common** category in the Insert bar. Set options in the dialog box and select OK. To create an image in Fireworks, right-click the placeholder and select **Create Image in Fireworks**. A new document is displayed in Fireworks with the same dimensions as the placeholder. After creating the image, select **Done** to save, export, and place the image in Dreamweaver.

Close buttons

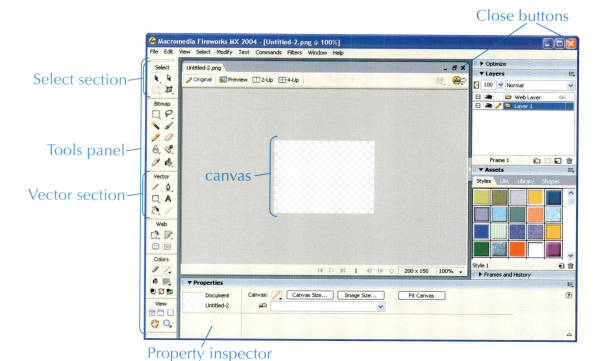

Select section

Tools panel

Vector section

canvas

Property inspector

- Click a **Close button** to remove the document window or the Fireworks window.

- Create and edit images using tools in the **Tools panel**. The tools are divided into sections.

- Select an image using tools in the **Select section**.

- Draw vector graphics using tools in the **Vector section**. A *vector graphic* is composed of lines connected by points, which allows for smooth resizing and a smaller file size than bitmap graphics. Fireworks can be used to create vector graphics as well as bitmap graphics such as GIF or JPG.

- Create and edit images on the **canvas**. A canvas specified as transparent appears as a checkerboard pattern. The pattern does not appear in an image once it has been exported.

- Change properties of the selected text or object using the **Property inspector**.

Select File → Save to save a Fireworks document. Fireworks documents are automatically saved in PNG format. The PNG file should be saved to a location outside of the website and used to export graphics to the website in JPG or GIF format. If a graphic needs to be edited, the PNG file can be edited and exported again. Exporting is discussed later in this chapter.

Native File Format

A native file format is the default format in which an application saves files. Files may be saved or exported in other formats, but are worked on in the native file format. The native file format in Fireworks is PNG. A Fireworks PNG document contains additional information than PNG files used in web pages. To create a PNG for use in a web page, the Fireworks document must be exported as a PNG.

TIP Files that are not directly used in a website are best kept in a folder outside the website root folder.

Drawing Objects in Fireworks

Lines and shapes can be drawn on the canvas using tools in the Vector section in the Tools panel. To draw a line, click the Line tool (/) and then drag on the canvas. To draw a shape, click and hold down the mouse button on the shape tool to display a menu of shape tools:

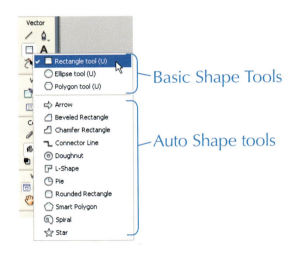

Basic Shape Tools

Auto Shape tools

TIP Hold down the Shift key while dragging the Rectangle or Ellipse tool to draw a square or circle shape.

TIP Hold down the Shift key while dragging the Line tool to constrain the line to 45° angles.

When any shape tool or the Line tool (✎) is selected, the pointer changes to + when it is moved on the canvas. Properties in the Property inspector can be set before or after an object is drawn:

Fill Color box   Stroke Color box   Tip size

- The **Fill Color box** is the color that fills the shape, and the **Stroke Color box** is the color that outlines the shape. A 🖊 indicates transparent, or no color. Click a color box to change the stroke or fill color.

- The **Tip size** affects the thickness of the shape's stroke or line in pixels. Select a different thickness in the list.

When selected, the rectangle and polygon tools have additional options available in the Property inspector:

- For a rectangle, Rectangle roundness rounds the corners.

- For a polygon, the Shape can be either polygon or star. The number of Sides can be specified, as well as the degrees of Angle between the sides of the polygon.

TIP Hold down the Alt key and drag to draw the center of the shape at the location of the pointer.

Most Auto Shape tools also have additional options available in the Property inspector.

Once an object is drawn, use the Pointer tool (▸) in the Select section in the Tools panel to click and select an object, or drag to move an object. Changing the values in the X and Y boxes in the Property inspector also moves a selected object.

Control Points in Auto Shapes

Some Auto Shape objects display control points (◆) when selected. Each control point affects different properties of the object when dragged:

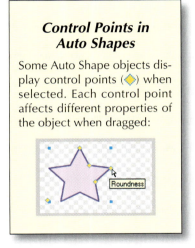

A selected object can be resized using several methods:

- Change the values in the W (width) and H (height) boxes in the Property inspector.

- Use the Pointer tool ( ) in the Select section in the Tools panel to drag a handle. To proportionately resize an object, hold down the Shift key while dragging a corner handle.

- Use the Scale tool ( ) in the Select section in the Tools panel to drag a handle. Dragging a corner handle resizes the object proportionately, and dragging a side handle distorts the shape.

Adding Text in Fireworks

Text can be added to the canvas as a separate object. Select the Text tool (**A**) from the Vector section in the Tools panel and then move the pointer over the canvas. The pointer changes to . Click to create a text block that changes size to accommodate text as it is typed:

a new, empty text block   *the text block after typing*

Properties in the Property inspector can be changed before a text block is created, or after text is typed:

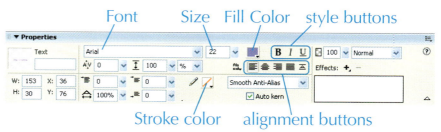

- The Font list is the name that describes the shape and style of the letters in the text. A new font can be selected from the list.

- The Size box is the size of the text. Larger numbers produce larger letters. A new size can be typed or set using the slider.

- The Fill Color box is the text color. Click the Fill Color box and select a different color to change the fill color.

- The style buttons (**B** *I* <u>U</u>) indicate **bold**, *italic*, and <u>underlined</u> text. Click a style button to apply the style. Click the same style button again to remove the style.

- The alignment buttons are used the same way style buttons are used. Alignment buttons indicate the arrangement and position of text in the text block:

Fixed-Width Text Block

Select the Text tool and drag the pointer on the canvas to create a fixed-width text block. The text block will lengthen to accommodate text, but the width will not change.

TIP Fonts, sizes, and text color are discussed in Chapter 6.

TIP To change properties for all of the text in a block, select the block. To change properties for some of the text in a block, select the text.

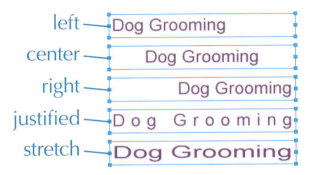

move and resize a text block

Text blocks are objects that are moved and resized in the same manner as shapes. Resizing a text block by dragging a corner handle changes the text block to a fixed width block, and it will no longer change size as more text is typed. However, it can be resized repeatedly by dragging on its handles.

modify text

Select the Text tool and click in the text block to place the insertion point and edit text.

Aligning Objects in Fireworks

Selected objects can be aligned with respect to each other using commands in the Modify → Align submenu. Multiple objects are selected using the Pointer tool ( ) in the Select section in the Tools panel. Drag the pointer to draw a rectangle that touches all of the objects to select them, or hold down the Shift key and click each object:

TIP Select Window → Align to display the Align panel, which can be used to align objects.

Select Modify → Align → Center Vertical to align the centers of the objects on a vertical axis:

Select Modify → Align → Center Horizontal to align the centers of the objects on a horizontal axis:

Additional alignment commands include Left, Right, Top, and Bottom.

Modifying the Canvas

When an image is finished, select Modify → Canvas → Trim Canvas to reduce the canvas to exactly fit the objects. Other commands in the Modify → Canvas submenu can also be used to modify the canvas:

- Fit Canvas is used to increase the size of the canvas enough to fit all of the objects.

- Canvas Size is used to change the dimensions of the canvas size in pixels.

- Canvas Color is used to change the canvas color, such as white or transparent.

Optimizing and Exporting a Fireworks Document

To use a Fireworks document in Dreamweaver, it should be optimized and then exported in a format other than PNG. An *optimized* image has the best possible quality and the smallest possible file size. A small file size allows a web page to load faster in a browser window.

Export Wizard   The Export Wizard is used to choose the best optimization settings and to then export the document. Select File → Export Wizard to display a dialog box. Select the Select an export format option:

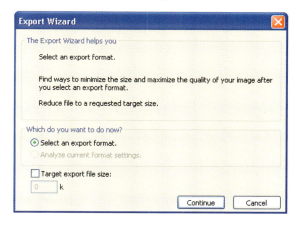

> **Target File Size**
>
> The target file size is the size, in kilobytes, of the exported file. If an approximate file size is known, select **Target export file size** in the first Export Wizard dialog box and type the number of kilobytes in the k box.

Select Continue to display the next dialog box. Select Dreamweaver because the file will be used in Dreamweaver:

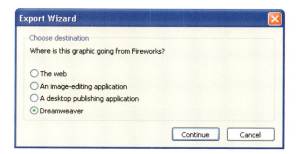

Select Continue to display recommended file formats:

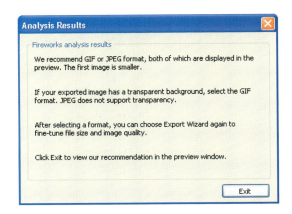

Select Exit to display the Export Preview window:

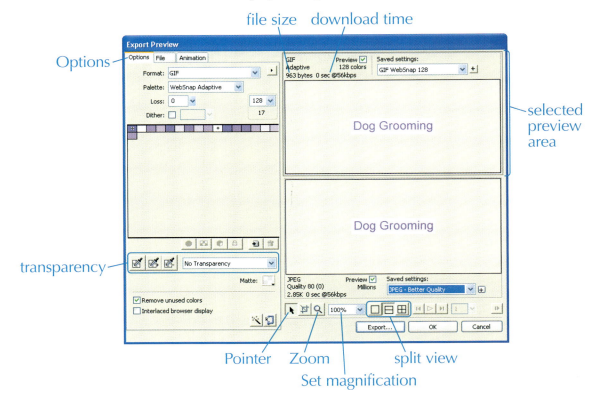

- The **file size** and **download time** are displayed in each preview area and should be considered when choosing between suggested file formats.

- The **preview areas** display the image in the suggested file formats. Settings can be changed in the preview areas, but remember that the window opens with the best choices.

- The **split view buttons** change the number of preview areas that are displayed to one, two, or four. The window opens with the number of preview areas needed to display the suggested file formats.

- The **Set magnification** list changes the magnification of the preview areas with precision. 100% is the best choice when viewing an image for quality.

- Click the **Zoom button** to change the pointer to 🔍 when moved over a preview area. Click to magnify the preview areas. Hold down the Alt key to change the pointer to 🔍. Click to zoom out.

- Click the **Pointer button** and then drag an image to move it in the preview area.

- Click a **transparency button** to change the pointer to 🖉 when it is moved over a color in the color list, and clicking a color selects the transparency color (🖉), adds the color to the transparency (🖉), or removes the transparency color (🖉).

- Select Index transparency in the **Transparency list** if the image should have a transparent background. In the example above, the image should have a transparent background, so GIF would be the best file format choice and the transparency should be changed to Index transparency. Alpha transparency is not supported by all browsers, so it is not yet a good choice.

- Triple-click a preview area to display the optimization settings in the Options tab, where the options can be changed.

With the best preview selected, click Export to display the Export dialog box with a file name already selected:

The extension .gif indicates that the document will be exported as a GIF

The Save in list and the contents box below it are used to navigate to the location where the file is to be saved. A Fireworks image exported for use in a website should be saved in the website's images folder. Type a descriptive name for the image in the File name box, and set the Save as type (*ver.8:* Export) to Images Only. Select Save (*ver.8:* Export) to export the image. In Dreamweaver, the exported image can then be inserted into a web page document.

Version 8 Dreamweaver 8 differences are indicated with parentheses (*ver.8:*).

Dreamweaver 8 differences are indicated with parentheses (*ver.8:*).

① START FIREWORKS

Ask your instructor for the appropriate steps to start Fireworks. Note the canvas, Tools panel, and Property inspector.

② CREATE AND SAVE A NEW FIREWORKS DOCUMENT

Select File → New. A dialog box is displayed.

1. In the dialog box, specify the following:

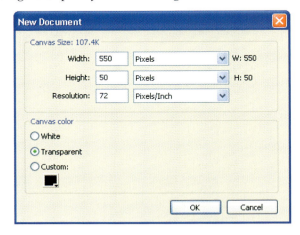

2. Select OK. A new document is created with a transparent canvas that appears as a checkerboard pattern.

③ ADD A TEXT OBJECT AND FORMAT THE TEXT

a. In the Tools panel, in the Vector section, click the Text tool (**A**).

b. Move the pointer over the canvas. The pointer changes to Ⅰ.

c. On the canvas (not the gray document area), click to create a new, empty text block.

d. Type Favorite Reefs and click in the canvas outside of the text block. The text block is selected.

e. If necessary, in the Tools panel, in the Select section, click the Pointer tool ( ) and then drag the text block so that it is entirely on the canvas.

f. In the Property inspector, in the Font list, select Comic Sans MS if it is available or else select Arial. The font of the text is changed.

g. In the Property inspector, in the Size box, set the value to 20 and press Enter. The size of the text is changed.

h. In the Property inspector, click the Fill Color box and select the color that corresponds to #0000CC:

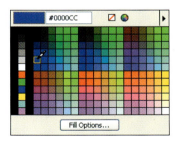

i. In the Property inspector, click the Bold button (**B**). The text is bold.

j. In the Property inspector, set the stroke color to transparent ( ), if it is not already set.

Check—Your canvas should look similar to:

④ **MODIFY THE CANVAS AND SAVE THE DOCUMENT**

a. Select Modify → Canvas → Trim Canvas. The canvas now exactly fits the text.

b. Select File → Save.

  1. Use the Save in list to navigate to a folder that is outside of any website folder.

  2. In the File name box, replace the existing text with: fav_reefs

  3. Select Save. Fireworks automatically adds the .png extension, so the document is saved with the file name fav_reefs.png.

⑤ **EXPORT THE IMAGE**

a. Select File → Export Wizard. A dialog box is displayed.

b. Select the Select an export format option and then select Continue. The next dialog box is displayed.

c. Select Dreamweaver because the file will be used in Dreamweaver, and then select Continue. The next dialog box is displayed.

d. Read the information in the dialog box and then select Exit. The Export Preview window is displayed. The top preview area has GIF settings and the bottom preview area is JPG. The GIF preview is selected, and the GIF settings appear in the Options tab in the left side of the Export Preview window.

  1. In the Transparency list, select Index Transparency.

  2. Click the Zoom button ( ).

  3. Click the top preview area. Both preview areas are zoomed in and the transparent background of the GIF image is more apparent.

  4. Select Export. The Export dialog box is displayed.

    a) Use the Save in list to navigate to the images folder in the SCUBA folder.

    b) In the File name box, type the file name fav_reefs.gif if it is not already there.

    c) Check that in the Save as type (*ver.8:* Export) list the Export Wizard has already selected Images Only, then select Save (*ver.8:* Export). A GIF is exported to the SCUBA website.

⑥ **ADD AN IMAGE TO A WEB PAGE**

a. Start Dreamweaver. The SCUBA website should be the working website.

b. Open the locations.htm web page document.

c. In the left cell of the third row of the table, delete the text: FAVORITE REEFS

d. In the Assets panel, click the Images icon ( ) if it is not already selected. The images in the site are displayed. Select → Refresh Site List . The fav_reefs.gif image is displayed in the list.

e. Drag the fav_reefs.gif file from the Assets panel to the location that contained the deleted text. (*ver.8:* If the Image Tag Accessibility Attributes dialog box appears, select Cancel.)

Check—Your document should look similar to:

⑦ CREATE A SECOND GIF

a. Switch back to Fireworks.

b. Follow steps ② through ⑤ to create a second Fireworks document named fav_wrecks.png that looks similar to:

c. Save the document and then export it to the images folder of the SCUBA website naming it: fav_wrecks.gif

d. Follow step ⑥ to insert the fav_wrecks.gif image into the locations.htm web page document in the right cell of the third row of the table:

e. Save the modified locations.htm.

Creating a Button Symbol in Fireworks

In a web page document, a *button* is an element that indicates to the user that it is a graphic hyperlink by its appearance. A button can be created easily in Fireworks, and then several copies placed together in a Fireworks document to form a navigation bar that can be exported to Dreamweaver.

A button is created by drawing the objects that make up the button, for example a rounded rectangle and a text block:

symbol

The objects are then selected together and made into a single object called a *symbol*. A symbol is similar to a library item in Dreamweaver, except a symbol placed on a canvas does not have to have its link broken to be edited. In Fireworks, symbols appear in the Library panel in the Assets panel group.

Select Modify ➛ Symbol ➛ Convert to Symbol to display a dialog box where a descriptive name should be typed for the symbol:

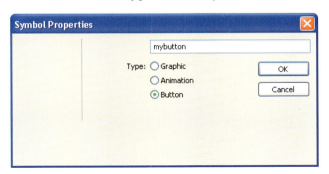

TIP Symbols are useful when graphics need to be used more than once.

Select Button and then OK to convert the selected objects to a button symbol and add the symbol to the Library in the Assets panel:

Items in the Library are stored with the open Fireworks document.

instance

When a symbol is created, the selected objects on the canvas are changed into an *instance* of the symbol, which is a copy of the button symbol:

slice

A symbol is also automatically sliced. *Slicing* is the way Fireworks divides an image so that interactivity can be assigned. The red lines on the canvas are slice boundaries. A button symbol has only one slice—the entire object itself. Therefore interactivity is assigned to the entire button object.

Navigation bars usually have more than one button. More instances can be added to the canvas by dragging the button symbol from the Library to the canvas. Another way to create an instance is to select an instance on the canvas and then select Edit ➛ Clone, which places another button on top of the selected one. The arrow keys can then be used to position the button, or the Pointer tool can be used to drag the button. A document can contain many clones of a symbol:

Each instance of a symbol can be selected individually and its properties changed in the Property inspector:

Text box   Link box   Alt box

- Text is the text displayed on the button. New text can be typed.

- Link is the file name of the document linked to the button. A new file name can be typed or selected from the list.

- Alt is the alternative text for the button. New alternative text can be typed.

preview and test buttons

Click 🖼Preview at the top of the Document window to display the button as it will appear in a website. The preview is interactive, so moving the pointer over or clicking a button displays the interactivity. Click ✏Original to return to the editing view.

Button Symbol Rollover Behavior

A *behavior* is how a symbol interacts with the user. The default behavior for a button symbol is a *rollover*, which allows each state of a button symbol to display a different image. In Fireworks, a button symbol has four states:

- The *Up state* is also called the normal state. A button is in this state when a pointer is not over it or it is not clicked.

- The *Over state* is when the pointer is moved over a button.

- The *Down state* is when a button is clicked.

- The *Over While Down state* is when the pointer is moved over a button that is in the Down state.

To modify the images for each state of a button symbol, double-click a button instance on the canvas or the button symbol's preview in the Library panel to open the Button Editor window:

JavaScript

Rollover behavior is defined with JavaScript code. Fireworks automatically generates the JavaScript for a button.

---

open Fireworks document   button editor for "mybutton" symbol

states

work area

instructions area

- The **work area** is where the button appears and can be edited.
- Click the Up tab, Over tab, Down tab, or Over While Down tab to display the image for a state. Each **state** is edited separately.
- The Active Area tab displays the hotspot area on the button that will trigger the button action.
- The **instructions area** displays descriptions and instructions.

Click a state tab to display the button as it will appear in that state. If the work area is empty, click the Copy Graphic button to copy the button from the previous state into the work area, then make any edits such as color changes. Click Done to make the changes to the button symbol and to all the instances on the canvas. Edits made in the Button Editor window do not affect text, alternative text, and links that were set for each button instance on the canvas.

preview and test buttons   Click ▣ Preview at the top of the Document window to display the button as it will appear in a website. The preview is interactive, so moving the pointer over or clicking a button displays the images for each button state. Click ✎ Original to return to the editing view.

Practice: SCUBA – part 6 of 8

Fireworks should be started.

① **CREATE AND DRAW OBJECTS**

a. In Fireworks, close any open documents.

b. Select File ➜ New. A dialog box is displayed.

1. In the dialog box, set the options to:

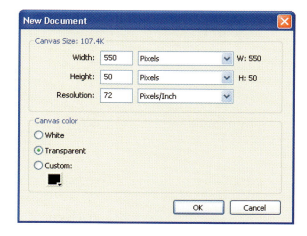

2. Select **OK**. A new document is created with a transparent canvas.

   c. In the Tools panel, in the Vector section, click the Rectangle tool (▢).

   d. On the canvas, draw a rectangle of any size.

   e. In the Property inspector, set **W** to 150 and **H** to 30 and press Enter. The rectangle is resized.

   f. In the Property inspector, click the Fill Color box and select the color that corresponds to #0000CC:

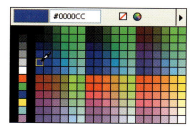

Check—Your canvas should look similar to:

   g. In the Tools panel, in the Vector section, click the Text tool (**A**).

   h. On the rectangle on the canvas, click to create a new, empty text block.

   i. In the Property inspector:

      1. In the **Font** box, select Comic Sans MS if it is available or else select Arial.

      2. In the **Size** box change the value to 20 and press Enter.

      3. Click the Center alignment button (≡) if it is not already selected.

      4. Click the Fill Color box and select the color that corresponds to #FFFFFF:

      5. Click the Bold button (**B**) if it is not already selected.

j. Type button text and then click in the gray area outside of the canvas. Text that is white, centered, Comic Sans MS, bold, and size 20 is displayed.

k. Select File ➡ Save. Save the document in a folder that is outside of any website folder, naming it: divebar.png

② ALIGN THE OBJECTS

a. In the Tools panel, in the Select section, click the Pointer tool ( ).

b. On the canvas, click the rectangle to select it.

c. Hold down the Shift key, and on the canvas, click the text block to select it. Both objects are selected.

d. Select Modify ➡ Align ➡ Center Vertical. The objects are aligned vertically.

e. With both objects still selected, select Modify ➡ Align ➡ Center Horizontal. The objects are aligned horizontally.

f. With both objects selected, drag the objects to the left side of the canvas.

Check—Your canvas should look similar to:

g. Save the modified divebar.png.

③ CONVERT THE OBJECTS TO A BUTTON SYMBOL

a. Select the rectangle and the text block if they are not already selected. Handles are displayed for both objects:

b. Select Modify ➡ Symbol ➡ Convert to Symbol. A dialog box is displayed.

   1. In the Name box, type: blue button

   2. Select Button.

   3. Select OK. The objects are converted to a Button symbol, which is added to the Library. The canvas displays an instance of the button symbol and slice boundaries are displayed.

④ PREVIEW THE BUTTON AND CREATE MORE INSTANCES OF THE BUTTON

a. At the top of the Document window, click ⬛Preview. A preview of the button with correct colors is displayed.

b. At the top of the Document window, click ✏Original. The editing view is displayed.

c. On the canvas, select the instance if it is not already selected.

d. Select Edit ➡ Clone. Another instance is added to the canvas.

e. Hold down the right arrow key until the two instances are next to each other:

f. Select Edit → Clone. Another instance is created.

g. Hold down the right arrow key until the three instances are in a row:

⑤ **CHANGE THE PROPERTIES OF EACH INSTANCE**

a. On the canvas, click the far-left instance to select it.

b. In the Property inspector, set Text to Home and press Enter.

c. In the Property inspector, set Link to index.htm and press Enter.

d. In the Property inspector, set Alt to Link to home page. and press Enter.

e. On the canvas, select the middle button instance and in the Property inspector set the properties to:

- Text: Dive Locations
- Link: locations.htm
- Alt: Link to dive locations information.

f. On the canvas, select the far-right button instance and set the properties to:

- Text: Photo Gallery
- Link: photos.htm
- Alt: Link to the photo gallery.

⑥ **EDIT THE OVER BUTTON STATE IMAGES**

a. On the canvas, double-click any button symbol instance. The Button Editor opens and the blue button button symbol is displayed.

b. In the Button Editor, click the Over tab. No image yet exists for this state.

c. Click Copy Up Graphic. The Up state image is copied to the Over state.

d. In the Button Editor work area, click the text block to select it.

e. In the Property inspector, click the Fill Color box and select the color that corresponds to #33FFFF:

The text is now light blue for the Over state.

⑦ EDIT THE DOWN STATE AND THE OVER WHILE DOWN STATE

a. In the Button Editor, click the Down tab. No image yet exists for this state.

b. Click Copy Over Graphic. The Over state image is copied to the Down state.

c. In the Button Editor work area, click the text block to select it.

d. In the Property inspector, click the Fill Color box and select the color that corresponds to #FFFFFF (white). The text is now white for the down state.

e. In the Button Editor work area, click the rectangle to select it.

f. In the Property inspector, change the Fill Color to #33FFFF:

The rectangle is now light blue for the Down state.

g. In the Button Editor, click the Over While Down tab. No image yet exists for this state.

h. Click Copy Down Graphic. The Down state image is copied to the Over While Down state. This state will remain as is so that nothing changes when the pointer is moved over a button displayed in the Down state.

i. In the Button Editor, click Done. The changes are made to the button symbol and all instances of the symbol on the canvas.

⑧ MODIFY THE CANVAS

Select Modify → Canvas → Trim Canvas. The canvas is reduced in size to exactly fit the instances.

⑨ PREVIEW THE BUTTONS

a. At the top of the Document window, click 🖼Preview. A preview is displayed.

b. Move the pointer over the buttons and click each one.

c. At the top of the Document window, click ✏Original. The editing view is displayed.

d. Save the modified divebar.png.

Exporting HTML and Images from Fireworks

Exporting a Fireworks document with symbol instances generates many files, including a set of image files for rollover behavior states and an HTML file that arranges the objects in the Fireworks document in a table. Also in the HTML file is the code that controls the rollover behavior of the clones. For example, a Fireworks document with a button symbol and three clones generates an HTML document and up to 12 image files, one image file for each state of each button instance.

The Export Wizard can be used to optimize and automatically generate all the files associated with a Fireworks document. Select File → Export Wizard to display the same dialog boxes as shown in the "Optimizing and Exporting" section earlier in this chapter. When the Export Preview dialog box is displayed, select Export to display a dialog box with HTML and Images as the file type:

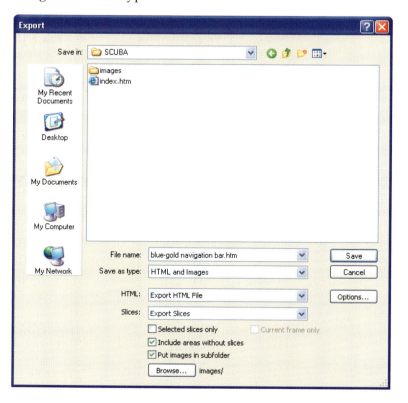

- Use the Save in list and the contents box below it to navigate to the location of the website root folder where the HTML document is to be saved.

- Type a descriptive file name in the File name box.

Version 8 Dreamweaver 8 differences are indicated with parentheses (*ver.8:*).

- The Save as type (*ver.8:* Export) list is set to HTML and Images by the Export Wizard.

- The HTML and the Slices lists should be set as shown in the dialog box above.

- Select the Include Areas without slices check box to ensure that the entire document is exported.

- Select the Put Images in subfolder check box to place image files into the images folder of the website root folder specified in the Save in list.

- Select Save (*ver.8:* Export) to create an HTML document and the image files associated with all the button states.

Chapter 5 Images in Dreamweaver and Fireworks

Using an Exported HTML Document in Dreamweaver

A Fireworks document exported as HTML and Images to a Dreamweaver website is used by following these steps:

1. Open the HTML document that was exported from Fireworks.

2. Select <body> in the Tag selector to select everything in the body of the document.

3. Select Edit ➡ Copy HTML (*ver.8:* Copy) to make a copy of the HTML.

4. Open a web page document and place the insertion point where the exported document should appear.

5. Select Edit ➡ Paste HTML (*ver.8:* Paste) to add the HTML to the document.

edit a Fireworks image from Dreamweaver source file

In Dreamweaver, a selected image from Fireworks can be edited by clicking the Edit button in the Property inspector. Fireworks is started and the PNG *source file*, the PNG file that was created in Fireworks, is displayed. After edits are made and the modified PNG is saved, select Done in the Fireworks document window to close the PNG file. Changes are automatically made to the exported HTML document in Dreamweaver. The HTML that was copied and pasted in Dreamweaver is also updated. Note that changes to links need to be made in Dreamweaver.

Changing Behaviors in Dreamweaver

In Dreamweaver, behaviors for a selected button are listed in the Behaviors panel in the Tag Inspector panel group. Select Window ➡ Behaviors to display the Behaviors panel:

Select 🔳 ➡ Edit Behavior to display a dialog box of all the states for the selected button:

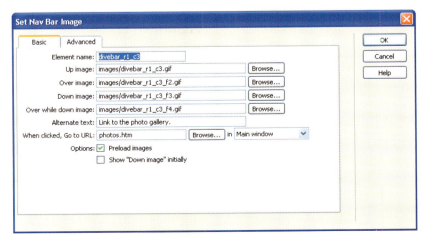

- Change the appearance of a button in a state using the Browse buttons.
- Change the button's link in the When clicked, Go to URL box.
- Select the Show "Down image" initially check box to display the button in the Down state, commonly used for the appearance of a button on the page that it links to.

Select OK to apply the changes to the selected button.

Practice: SCUBA – part 7 of 8

Fireworks should be started and divebar.png should be open. Dreamweaver 8 differences are indicated with parentheses (ver.8:).

① **OPTIMIZE AND EXPORT THE NAVIGATION BAR**

   a. Select File ➝ Export Wizard. A dialog box is displayed.

   b. Select the Select an export format option and then select Continue. The next dialog box is displayed.

   c. Select Dreamweaver because the file will be used in Dreamweaver, and then select Continue. The next dialog box is displayed.

   d. Read the information in the dialog box and then select Exit. The Export Preview window is displayed. The top preview area has GIF settings and the bottom preview area is JPG. The GIF preview is selected, and the GIF settings appear in the Options tab in the left side of the Export Preview window.

   e. In the Transparency list, select Index Transparency.

   f. Select Export. The Export dialog box is displayed. Set the options to:

Select Browse. A dialog box is displayed. Navigate to the images folder in the root folder of the SCUBA website and then select Open.

Chapter 5 Images in Dreamweaver and Fireworks

g. Select Save (*ver.8:* Export). An HTML document named divebar.htm is created in the SCUBA website folder and all the images used in divebar.htm are added to the images folder of the website.

② **SAVE THE MODIFIED DIVEBAR.PNG AND QUIT FIREWORKS**

③ **EDIT THE SCUBA WEBSITE**

  a. Start Dreamweaver. The SCUBA website should be the working website.

  b. In the Files panel, check that the divebar.htm document is in the website's folder.

  c. In the Assets panel, display the Images category. Additional images have been added. If only the few images from earlier practices are displayed, select ▣ ➔ Refresh Site List.

④ **OPEN DIVEBAR.HTM AND COPY THE HTML TO ANOTHER DOCUMENT**

  a. Open the divebar.htm web page document. The document contains the three buttons created in Fireworks in the previous practice.

  b. Select the <body> tag in the Tag selector at the bottom of the Document window. The entire document is selected.

  c. Select Edit ➔ Copy HTML (*ver.8:* Copy). A copy is created of the selected content.

  d. Open the index.htm web page document.

  e. In the cell in the second row of the table, delete the contents.

  f. In the cell in the second row of the table, place the insertion point.

  g. Select Edit ➔ Paste HTML (*ver.8:* Paste). (*ver.8:* The Image Description dialog box appears. Select Cancel.) The copied content is pasted into the cell.

  h. Save and close the modified index.htm.

  i. Close divebar.htm.

⑤ **COPY THE HTML TO OTHER DOCUMENTS**

  a. Open the locations.htm web page document.

  b. In the second row of the table, delete the contents and place the insertion point.

  c. Select Edit ➔ Paste HTML (*ver.8:* Paste). (*ver.8:* The Image Description dialog box appears. Select Cancel.) The copied content is pasted into the cell.

  d. Save and close the modified locations.htm.

  e. Open photos.htm.

  f. In the second row of the table, delete the contents and place the insertion point.

  g. Select Edit ➔ Paste HTML (*ver.8:* Paste). (*ver.8:* The Image Description dialog box appears. Select Cancel.) The copied content is pasted into the cell.

  h. Save the modified photos.htm.

⑥ **TEST THE BUTTONS IN A BROWSER WINDOW**

  a. Press F12. The document is displayed in a browser window.

  b. Move the pointer over the buttons and observe the text changing to light blue for the Over state.

  c. Click the Home button. The index.htm web page document is displayed in the browser window.

  d. Test the buttons on this and the other web page documents.

  e. Close the browser window. Dreamweaver is displayed.

⑦ **CHANGE THE BUTTONS IN EACH WEB PAGE DOCUMENT**

  a. Open photos.htm.

b. Select Window → Behaviors. The Behaviors panel in the Tag Inspector panel group is displayed.

c. In the Document window, click the Photo Gallery button to select it.

d. In the Tag Inspector panel group, select ▦ → Edit Behavior. A dialog box is displayed.

 1. Select the Basic tab if those options are not already displayed.

 2. Select the Show "Down image" initially option.

 3. Select OK. The dialog box is removed and the button is displayed in the Down state.

e. Save and close the modified photos.htm.

f. Open the locations.htm web page document.

g. In the Document window, click the Dive Locations button to select it.

h. In the Tag Inspector panel group, select ▦ → Edit Behavior. A dialog box is displayed.

 1. In the Basic tab, select the Show "Down image" initially option.

 2. Select OK.

i. Save and close the modified locations.htm.

j. Open the index.htm web page document.

k. In the Document window, click the Home button to select it.

l. In the Tag Inspector panel group, select ▦ → Edit Behavior. A dialog box is displayed.

 1. In the Basic tab, select the Show "Down image" initially option.

 2. Select OK.

m. Save the modified index.htm.

⑧ TEST THE BUTTONS IN A BROWSER WINDOW

a. Press F12. The document is displayed in a browser window. The Home button is in the Down state, indicating that the displayed web page is the home page.

b. Move the pointer over the buttons and observe the text changing to light blue for the Over state.

c. Click the Photo Gallery button. The photos.htm web page document is displayed, with the Photo Gallery button in the Down state.

d. Test the buttons on this and the other web page documents.

e. Print a copy of the index.htm and the photos.htm web page documents from the browser.

f. Close the browser window. Dreamweaver is displayed.

g. Close index.htm.

Cropping an Image in Fireworks and in Dreamweaver

There may be occasions when only part of an image is needed. *Cropping* an image trims away areas that are not needed. To crop an image that is open in Fireworks, click the Crop tool (🔲) in the Select section in the Tools panel. Move the pointer over the canvas to change the pointer to ⌐ and then drag to draw a cropping box:

Adjust the cropping box by dragging any handle or by setting the W (width) and H (height) properties in the Property inspector. The arrow keys can also be used to move the cropping box. Double-click in the cropping box or press Enter to crop the image:

The canvas is resized to the cropped image. If a mistake is made, select Edit ➞ Undo Crop Document. Select File ➞ Save to save the changes. Once a cropped image is saved, the trimmed areas cannot be restored.

crop an image in Dreamweaver

Instead of using Fireworks to crop images, an image in a web page document can be cropped directly in Dreamweaver. Select the image in the web page document then click the Crop tool (⬚) in Property inspector. A cropping box appears in the image. (*ver.8:* The cropping box is a solid line.) Adjust the cropping box by dragging handles and using the arrow keys to move the box. Double-click in the box or press Enter to crop the image:

The canvas is resized to include only the cropped image. If a mistake is made, select Edit ➞ Undo Crop. The cropped image can be restored using the Undo command until Dreamweaver is quit.

Editing an Image in Fireworks from Dreamweaver

There may be occasions when an image in a web page document needs to be edited. In Dreamweaver, select an image and then click 🔶 in the Property inspector to start Fireworks and display a dialog box:

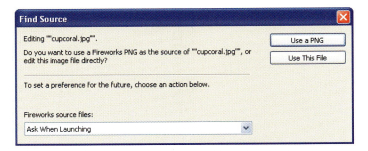

Select Use This File to open the image in Fireworks. After edits such as cropping are made to the image, click Done in the Document window to save the changes to the image, close the file, and update the image in Dreamweaver in the web page document. If the size of the image changed, click 🔁 in the Property inspector in Dreamweaver to adjust the size.

Practice: SCUBA – part 8 of 8

Dreamweaver should be started and the SCUBA website should be the working site. Dreamweaver 8 differences are indicated with parentheses (*ver.8:*).

① **ADD AN IMAGE TO THE LOCATIONS.HTM WEB PAGE DOCUMENT**

  a. Open the locations.htm web page document.

  b. In the Assets panel, display the Images category.

  c. Drag the a_reef.jpg file from the Assets panel to the blank area below the text in the left cell in the table. (*ver.8:* If the Image Tag Accessibility Attributes dialog box appears, select Cancel.) The image is quite large.

② **OPEN THE IMAGE FOR EDITING IN FIREWORKS**

  a. Click the image to select it if it is not already selected.

  b. In the Property inspector, click 🔶. A dialog box is displayed.

  c. Select Use This File. The image is displayed in a Document window in Fireworks.

③ **CROP THE IMAGE IN FIREWORKS**

  a. Click the image to select it if it is not already selected.

  b. In the Tools panel, in the Select section, click the Crop tool (🔲).

  c. Move the pointer over the canvas. The pointer changes to ⼦.

  d. Drag the pointer. A cropping box is drawn.

  e. In the Property inspector, set W to 250 and press Enter. The width of the cropping box is changed.

  f. In the Property inspector, set H box to 200 and press Enter. The height of the cropping box is changed.

  g. Use the arrow keys to move the cropping box to only include the bright fish and the corals beneath it:

h. Press Enter. The image is cropped to the size of the cropping box. Note the width and height of the image in the Property inspector.

④ UPDATE AND FORMAT THE IMAGE IN DREAMWEAVER

    a. In the Document window above the image click Done. The Document window is closed and Dreamweaver is again displayed.

    b. In the Property inspector, click ⟳. The image changes to the new size.

⑤ CROP AN IMAGE IN DREAMWEAVER

    a. From the Images list in the Assets panel, drag the a_wreck.jpg file to the blank area below the text in the right cell in the table. (*ver.8:* If the Image Tag Accessibility Attributes dialog box appears, select Cancel.)

    b. Click the image to select it if it is not already selected.

    c. In the Property inspector, click the Crop tool (▨). A cropping box appears in the image.

    d. Drag the handles of the cropping box so that the diver is <u>not</u> included inside the cropping box (*ver.8:* note the cropping box is a solid line):

    e. Press Enter. The image is cropped.

    f. Save the modified locations.htm.

⑥ VIEW THE DOCUMENT IN A BROWSER

    a. Press F12. The document is displayed in a browser window.

    b. Print a copy.

    c. Close the browser window. Dreamweaver is displayed.

    d. Close locations.htm.

⑦ QUIT DREAMWEAVER

Chapter Summary

Images on web pages are usually a GIF or JPG file because these formats are widely supported in browsers. The GIF format is best used for graphics that do not contain many colors, and the JPG format is best used for photographs. GIF, JPG, and PNG formats are all bitmap graphics made up of pixels.

Alternative text provides text for a voice synthesizer to "read" in place of the image and is displayed as the screen tip that appears when the pointer is paused over an image. Alternative text is typed in the Alt box in the Property inspector.

A graphic can be formatted as a hyperlink in the same manner as a text hyperlink. An image map is a graphic that contains one or more hotspots, which is a defined area on a graphic that is a hyperlink. Hotspots are created using tools in the Property inspector.

A spacer GIF is used to control layout by forcing table cells to a specified width. The horizontal alignment of an image is changed using the alignment buttons in the Property inspector.

If the width and height of an image is changed, the image needs to be resampled which changes the size of the file and correctly adjusts the pixels in the image.

Fireworks is used to create and edit images specifically for use on the web. Fireworks documents are PNG files, which should be saved to a location outside of the website and used to export graphics to the website in JPG or GIF format. In a Fireworks document, lines and shapes can be drawn on the canvas using tools in the Vector section in the Tools panel. Text can be added as a separate object by selecting the Text tool.

To use a Fireworks document in Dreamweaver, it should be optimized and then exported in a format other than PNG using the Export Wizard.

A button can be created easily in Fireworks, and then several copies placed together in a Fireworks document to form a navigation bar that can be exported to Dreamweaver. A button is created by making several objects into a button symbol. Instances of the symbol are then added to the canvas to create a navigation bar. A behavior is how a symbol interacts with the user, and the default behavior for a button symbol is a rollover.

The Export Wizard is used to optimize and automatically generate all the files associated with a Fireworks document. A Fireworks document exported as HTML and images to a Dreamweaver website is used by copying and pasting the HTML.

Cropping an image trims away areas that are not needed. Images can be cropped in Fireworks or in Dreamweaver. A selected image in a web page document in Dreamweaver can be opened and edited in Fireworks by clicking in the Property inspector.

Vocabulary

Alternative text Text added to an image that a voice synthesizer "reads" in place of the image.

Behavior How a symbol interacts with the user.

Bitmap graphic A graphic based on rows and columns of tiny squares.

Button An element that indicates to the user that it is a graphic hyperlink by its appearance.

Canvas In Fireworks, the rectangular area in which an image is created and edited.

Compression A file format feature that reduces file size.

Crop To trim away areas of an image that are no longer needed.

Dots per inch (dpi) The number of pixels in an inch. Measures the resolution of a bitmap graphic.

Down state The button state when a button is clicked.

GIF A file format best used with graphics that do not contain many colors, such as clip art or logos.

Hotspot An invisible, defined area on a graphic that is a hyperlink.

Image map A graphic that contains one or more hotspots.

Instance A copy of a symbol.

Interlaced A GIF file format feature in which a low-quality version of the graphic appears first and becomes clearer in four horizontal passes as the web page fully loads.

JPG A file format that supports millions of colors and is best used for photographs.

Lossless compression Type of compression in which all of the original file information is retained. Used for GIF graphics.

Lossy compression Type of compression in which some data in the file is removed in order to reduce the file size. Used for JPG graphics.

Optimized image The best quality images with the smallest possible file size.

Over state The button state when a pointer is moved over a button.

Over While Down state The button state when a pointer is moved over a button in the Down state.

Pixel A square in a bitmap graphic.

PNG A file format created in the mid-1990s during a controversy over copyright of the GIF format. It is only supported by the newest browsers.

Progressive A JPG file format feature in which a low-quality version of the JPG graphic appears when a web page is first loaded and then becomes clearer as the page fully loads.

Proportionate size The width and height of a graphic are in the same ratio as the original graphic to prevent distortion.

Resample Correctly adjust the pixels in an image.

Resolution The number of dots per inch (dpi) in a graphic.

Rollover The default behavior for a button symbol, which allows each state of a button symbol to display a different image.

Slice The way Fireworks divides an image so that interactivity can be assigned.

Source file The PNG file created in Fireworks that is used to export images to Dreamweaver.

Spacer GIF A transparent GIF image consisting of only 1 pixel that is used to control the layout of a table by forcing table cells to a specified width.

Stretch To distort an image by dragging a handle without holding the Shift key.

Symbol A single object that is similar to a library item in Dreamweaver, except a symbol placed on a canvas does not have to have its link broken to be edited.

Transparency A color that allows the background color to show through.

Up state The button state when a pointer is not over it or it is not clicked. Also called the normal state.

Vector graphic A graphic composed of lines connected by points, which allows for smooth resizing and a smaller file size than bitmap graphics.

Dreamweaver Commands and Buttons

≡ Align Left button Left aligns a selected image. Found in the Property inspector.

≡ Align Center button Center aligns a selected image. Found in the Property inspector.

≡ Align Right button Right aligns a selected image. Found in the Property inspector.

Behaviors **command** Displays the Behaviors panel. Found in the Window menu.

📁 Browse for File icon Displays a dialog box used to locate a destination file for a hyperlink. Found in the Property inspector.

Change Link **command** Modifies an existing link. Found in the Modify menu.

Copy HTML (*ver.8:* Copy) **command** Makes a copy of selected HTML. Found in the Edit menu.

⊠ Crop tool Trims parts of an image that are no longer needed. Found in the Property inspector.

○ Oval Hotspot tool Creates an oval shaped hotspot. Found in the Property inspector.

Paste HTML (*ver.8:* Paste) **command** Pastes copied HTML at the insertion point. Found in the Edit menu.

◉ Point to File icon Points to a destination file for a hyperlink. Found in the Property inspector.

▸ Pointer Hotspot tool Selects a hot spot. Found in the Property inspector.

♡ Polygon Hotspot tool Creates an polygon shaped hotspot. Found in the Property inspector.

▭ Rectangular Hotspot tool Creates a rectangular shaped hotspot. Found in the Property inspector.

Remove Link **command** Removes an existing link. Found in the Modify menu.

Fireworks Commands and Buttons

Center Horizontal **command** Aligns selected objects so that they are horizontally centered with respect to each other. Found in Modify � Align.

Center Vertical **command** Aligns selected objects so that they are vertically centered with respect to each other. Found in Modify ➡ Align.

Clone **command** Creates an instance from a selected instance. Found in the Edit menu.

Convert to Symbol **command** Displays a dialog box used to create a symbol. Found in Modify ➡ Symbol.

⊠ Crop tool Trims parts of an image that are no longer needed. Found in the Select section in the Tools panel.

Export Wizard **command** Displays a series of dialog boxes used to select the best optimization settings and to export a document. Found in the File menu.

╱ Line tool Draws a line on the canvas. Found in the Vector section in the Tools panel.

New **command** Displays a dialog box used to create a new document. Found in the File menu.

▸ Pointer tool Moves and resizes an object. Found in the Select section in the Tools panel.

▭ Rectangle tool Draws a rectangle to the canvas. Found in the Vector section in the Tools panel.

Save **command** Saves the open Fireworks document. Found in the File menu.

▱ Scale tool Resizes a shape. Found in the Select section in the Tools panel.

A Text tool Adds text to the canvas. Found in the Vector section in the Tools panel.

Trim Canvas **command** Reduces the canvas to exactly fit the objects. Found in Modify ➡ Canvas.

1. a) Why are images on web pages usually a GIF or JPG file?
   b) What file format is best used with graphics that do not contain many colors?
   c) How many colors are GIF graphics limited to?
   d) What file format is best used with graphics that are photographs?
   e) Why is the PNG format currently not a good choice for an image on a web page?

2. a) What is a bitmap graphic composed of?
   b) In a bitmap graphic, how is the quality of the graphic measured?

3. What file format allows one color in a graphic to be transparent?

4. Describe how an interlaced GIF graphic is displayed as a web page is loaded.

5. a) What is compression?
   b) What is lossless compression?
   c) What is lossy compression?
   d) What file format has lossless compression?
   e) What file format has lossy compression?

6. Describe how a progressive JPG file is displayed as a web page is loaded.

7. Why should alternative text be added to an image?

8. What happens when the pointer is moved over a graphic hyperlink?

9. a) What is an image map?
   b) What is a hotspot?

10. a) List the three tools that can be used to create hotspots.
    b) List the steps required to delete a hotspot.

11. a) What is a spacer GIF?
    b) Why is a spacer GIF used?

12. List the steps required to change the horizontal alignment of an image to center.

13. If the width and height of an image in a web page document is changed, what should then be done to the image?

14. How can an image be sized proportionately in Dreamweaver?

15. a) What is Fireworks?
    b) What is the file format of a Fireworks document?

16. What should the resolution be set to for an image used in a web page?

17. a) What is a vector graphic composed of?
    b) What is the canvas?

18. Where should a Fireworks document be saved?

19. Describe how shapes and lines are drawn in Fireworks.

20. a) What is the Stroke Color box used to change?
    b) What does the Tip size change?

21. List the steps required to add text to the canvas in Fireworks.

22. List the steps required to align objects so that they are centered vertically with respect to each other.

23. How can the canvas size be reduced to exactly fit the objects?

24. a) What is an optimized image?
    b) What can be used to choose the best optimization settings and to then export the document?

25. a) In a web page document, what does a button represent to a user?
    b) List the steps required to convert two objects to a single symbol.

26. What is an instance of a symbol?

27. What is slicing?

28. a) What is a behavior?
    b) What is the default behavior for a button symbol?

29. List and describe the four states a button symbol has in Fireworks.

30. List the steps required to use an exported HTML document in Dreamweaver.

31. In Dreamweaver, where are the behaviors for a selected button listed?

32. a) Why would you crop an image?
    b) List the steps required to crop an image in Dreamweaver.

33. List the steps required to use Fireworks to edit an image that is in a web page document in Dreamweaver.

True/False

34. Determine if each of the following are true or false. If false, explain why.
    a) Alternative text is displayed as a screen tip that appears when the pointer is paused over an image.
    b) A hotspot is a behavior.
    c) A spacer.gif file contains millions of colors.
    d) Resampling an image changes the size of the file.
    e) The font in a Fireworks document can be changed after the text is typed.
    f) A small file allows a web page to load faster in a browser window.
    g) A graphic hyperlink has a blue underlined border.
    h) The Down State appears when the pointer is moved over a button.
    i) If an image is proportionately resized, the width and height remain in the same ratio.
    j) A document can contain many instances of a symbol.
    k) Cropped parts of an image can be restored after the cropped image is saved.

Exercise 1 ————————————————— GREECE

Use Fireworks and Dreamweaver to modify the GREECE website by completing the following steps:

a) In Dreamweaver, open the GREECE website for editing, which is a website provided with the data files for this text.

b) Edit the footer library item by replacing Name with your name. Allow Dreamweaver to update all occurrences of the library item in the web page documents.

c) Modify the index.htm web page document as follows:

 1. In the right cell of the third row, insert the map_greece.gif image and add alternative text: Map of Greece.

 2. Resize the image proportionately to 280 pixels wide, and then resample the image.

d) Modify the photos.htm web page document as follows:

 1. In the empty cell above the text Cats on the Island of Hydra, insert the image hydra_cats.jpg and add alternative text: Cats on Hydra.

 2. Edit the image in Fireworks to crop it. Use a cropping box of 250 pixels wide and 154 pixels high that includes at least two cats in the image. Save the changes and then update the image in Dreamweaver.

 3. In the other empty cells, insert images and add alternative text as follows:

In the cell above the text	insert the image	and add alternative text
Hydra	hydra_view.jpg	Island of Hydra.
Diros Caves	diros.jpg	Inside the Diros caves.
A Goat	goat.jpg	One of the many goats.
Monemvasia	monemvasia.jpg	The city of Monemvasia.
The Road to Kosmas	road_to_kosmas.jpg	Winding road to Kosmas.

 4. Center align the six images.

e) Switch to Fireworks and create a new document with a width of 660 pixels, a height of 100 pixels, a resolution of 72 pixels/inch, and a transparent canvas. Save the document outside of any website folder naming it: greeknav.png

f) Create a button symbol as follows:

 1. Draw a rectangle with a width of 160 pixels and a height of 36 pixels.

 2. Apply a fill color of #3399FF and a transparent stroke color to the rectangle.

 3. Create a text box with the text button formatted as Verdana font, 24 points in size, center aligned, and #FFFFFF in color.

 4. Align the rectangle and the text block horizontally and vertically.

 5. With both the rectangle and text block selected, convert them to a button symbol named: greek button

g) Create instances of the button symbol and modify them as follows:

    1. Create two more instances of the button symbol on the canvas and then position all three instances next to each other.

    2. Change the properties of each instance, from left to right, as follows:

Text	Link	Alt
Home	index.htm	Link to home page.
Photos	photos.htm	Link to photo page.
Itinerary	itinerary.htm	Link to itinerary page.

Your buttons should look similar to:

h) Double-click any instance to display the button symbol in the Button Editor. Edit the states of the button symbol as follows:

    1. Edit the Over state to be identical to the Up state except change the text color to #FFCCFF.

    2. Edit the Down state to be identical to the Over state except change the rectangle fill color to #3300FF.

    3. Edit the Over While Down state to be identical to the Down state.

i) Finish and export the navigation bar as follows:

    1. Modify the canvas to exactly fit the buttons and then save the modified document.

    2. Use the Export Wizard to export an HTML file named greeknav.htm to the GREECE website. Make sure the images are exported as GIF files, with Index Transparency, to the images folder.

j) In Dreamweaver, modify the GREECE website as follows:

    1. Open greeknav.htm and click the <body> tag to select the entire document.

    2. Copy the HTML.

    3. Paste the HTML in the second row of the index.htm, photos.htm, and itinerary.htm web page documents.

    4. In each web page document, modify the appropriate button to initially appear in the Down state.

k) In the photos.htm and itinerary.htm web page documents, link the logo in the top cell to index.htm.

l) View each web page document in a browser window and test the hyperlinks.

m) Print a copy of each web page document from the browser.

Exercise 2 ——————————————————————————————— CACTUS

Use Fireworks and Dreamweaver to modify the CACTUS website by completing the following steps:

a) In Dreamweaver, open the CACTUS website for editing, which is a website provided with the data files for this text.

b) Edit the footer library item by replacing Name with your name. Allow Dreamweaver to update all occurrences of the library item in the web page documents.

c) Modify the index.htm web page document as follows:

1. In the left cell of the third row, insert the cactus.gif image and add alternative text: Cute cactus.

2. Crop the image in Fireworks using a cropping box of 140 pixels wide that only includes one cactus in the image. Save the changes and then update the image in Dreamweaver.

d) Modify the gallery.htm web page document as follows:

1. In the empty cell above the text Prickly Pear, insert the image prickly_pear.jpg and add alternative text: Prickly pear cactus.

2. Resize the image proportionately to 300 pixels wide, and then resample the image.

3. In the empty cell above the text Agave, insert the image agave.jpg and add alternative text: Agave or century plant.

4. Resize the image proportionately to 300 pixels wide, and then resample the image.

5. In the two remaining cells, insert images and add alternative text as follows:

In the cell above the text	insert the image	and add alternative text
Saguaro	saguaro.jpg	Saguaro cactus.
Cholla	cholla.jpg	Cholla cactus.

6. Center align the four images.

e) Switch to Fireworks and create a new document with a width of 660 pixels, a height of 100 pixels, a resolution of 72 pixels/inch, and a transparent canvas. Save the document outside of any website folder naming it: cactusnav.png

f) Create a button symbol as follows:

1. Draw an ellipse with a width of 180 pixels and a height of 40 pixels.

2. Apply a fill color of #009900 and a transparent stroke color to the ellipse.

3. Create a text box with the text button formatted as Arial font, 18 points in size, center aligned, bold, and #CCFFCC in color.

4. Align the ellipse and the text block horizontally and vertically.

5. With both the ellipse and text block selected, convert them to a button symbol named: cactus button

g) Create instances of the button symbol and modify them as follows:

1. Create two more instances of the button symbol on the canvas and then position all three instances next to each other.

2. Change the properties of each instance, from left to right, as follows:

Text	Link	Alt
Home	index.htm	Link to home page.
Photo Gallery	gallery.htm	Link to photo page.
Cactus Types	types.htm	Link to page about cactus types.

Your buttons should look similar to:

h) Double-click any instance to display the button symbol in the Button Editor. Edit the states of the button symbol as follows:

1. Edit the Over state to be identical to the Up state except change the ellipse fill color to #00CC33.

2. Edit the Down state to be identical to the Over state except change the text color to #FFFFFF.

3. Edit the Over While Down state to be identical to the Down state.

i) Finish and export the navigation bar as follows:

1. Modify the canvas to exactly fit the buttons and then save the modified document.

2. Use the Export Wizard to export an HTML file named cactusnav.htm to the CACTUS website. Make sure the images are exported as GIF files, with Index Transparency, to the images folder.

j) In Dreamweaver, modify the CACTUS website as follows:

1. Open cactusnav.htm and click the <body> tag to select the entire document.

2. Copy the HTML.

3. Paste the HTML in the second row of the index.htm, gallery.htm, and types.htm web page documents.

4. In each web page document, modify the appropriate button to initially appear in the Down state.

k) In the gallery.htm and types.htm web page documents, link the logo in the top cell to index.htm.

l) View each web page document in a browser window and test the hyperlinks.

m) Print a copy of each web page document from the browser.

Use Fireworks and Dreamweaver to modify the FRUIT website by completing the following steps:

a) In Dreamweaver, open the FRUIT website for editing, which is a website provided with the data files for this text.

b) Edit the footer library item by replacing Name with your name. Allow Dreamweaver to update all occurrences of the library item in the web page documents.

c) Modify the index.htm web page document as follows:

   1. In the right cell of the third row, select the fruitbowl.gif image and in the Property inspector set **Map** to fruitbowl and press Enter.

   2. Using the Polygon Hotspot tool, create hotspots on the banana, orange, and apple in the fruitbowl.gif image, linking each hotspot and adding alternative text as follows:

The hotspot	should link to	and have alternative text
banana	banana.htm	Banana information.
orange	orange.htm	Orange information.
apple	apple.htm	Apple information.

d) Start Fireworks and create a new document with a width of 400 pixels, a height of 80 pixels, a resolution of 72 pixels/inch, and a transparent canvas. Save the document outside of any website folder naming it title_banana.png. Create and export a GIF image as follows:

   1. Create a text box with the text About Bananas formatted as Verdana font, 40 points in size, not bold, and #FF3300 in color. Move the text box, if necessary, so that all of the text is visible on the canvas.

   2. Modify the canvas to exactly fit the text.

   3. Using the Export Wizard, export the image as a GIF with Index Transparency, named title_banana.gif, saved in the images folder of the FRUIT website.

e) In Fireworks create two more GIF images, following the instructions in step (d) above, using these file names and text in the images:

     title_orange.png   About Oranges
     title_apple.png   About Apples

Use all of the same color and font properties as listed in step (d). Export the GIFs using the names title_orange.gif and title_apple.gif.

f) In Dreamweaver, modify the FRUIT website as follows:

   1. Open banana.htm and in the third row, insert the title_banana.gif image and add alternative text: About bananas.

   2. Open orange.htm and in the third row, insert the title_orange.gif image and add alternative text: About oranges.

   3. Open apple.htm and in the third row, insert the title_apple.gif image and add alternative text: About apples.

g) Switch to Fireworks and create a new document with a width of 660 pixels, a height of 100 pixels, a resolution of 72 pixels/inch, and a transparent canvas. Save the document outside of any website folder naming it fruitnav.png.

h) Create a button symbol as follows:

1. Select the Rectangle tool and draw a rectangle with a width of 120 pixels and a height of 30 pixels. In the Property inspector, set Rectangle roundness to 70.

2. Apply a fill color of #FF9933 and a transparent stroke color to the rectangle.

3. Create a text box with the text button formatted as Verdana font, 20 points in size, center aligned, bold, and #FFFF00 in color.

4. Align the rectangle and the text block horizontally and vertically.

5. With both the rectangle and text block selected, convert them to a button symbol named: fruit button

i) Create instances of the button symbol and modify them as follows:

1. Create three more instances of the button symbol on the canvas and then position all four instances next to each other, with a little space in between them.

2. Change the properties of each instance, from left to right, as follows:

Text	Link	Alt
Home	index.htm	Link to home page.
Bananas	banana.htm	Link to banana page.
Oranges	orange.htm	Link to orange page.
Apples	apple.htm	Link to apple page.

Your buttons should look similar to:

j) Double-click any instance to display the button symbol in the Button Editor. Edit the states of the button symbol as follows:

1. Edit the Over state to be identical to the Up state except change the rectangle fill color to #FF3300.

2. Edit the Down state so that the text color is #FF9933 and the rectangle has a fill color of #FFFF00.

3. Edit the Over While Down state to be identical to the Down state.

k) Finish and export the navigation bar as follows:

1. Modify the canvas to exactly fit the buttons and then save the modified document.

2. Use the Export Wizard to export an HTML file named fruitnav.htm to the FRUIT website. Make sure the images are exported as GIF files, with Index Transparency, to the images folder.

l) In Dreamweaver, modify the FRUIT website as follows:

1. Open fruitnav.htm and click the <body> tag to select the entire document.

2. Copy the HTML.

3. Paste the HTML in the cell in the second row of the index.htm, banana.htm, orange.htm, and apple.htm web page documents.

4. In each web page document, modify the appropriate button to initially appear in the Down state.

Chapter 5 Images in Dreamweaver and Fireworks

m) In the banana.htm, orange.htm, and apple.htm web page documents, link the logo in the top cell to index.htm.

n) View each web page document in a browser window and test the hyperlinks.

o) Print a copy of each web page document from the browser.

Exercise 4 —————————— COMPUTER MAINTENANCE

Use Fireworks and Dreamweaver to modify the COMPUTER MAINTENANCE website by completing the following steps:

a) In Dreamweaver, open the COMPUTER MAINTENANCE website for editing, which is a website provided with the data files for this text.

b) Edit the footer library item by replacing Name with your name. Allow Dreamweaver to update all occurrences of the library item in the web page documents.

c) Modify the index.htm web page document as follows:

   1. In the top row, insert the com_maint.gif image and add alternative text: Computer maintenance home page.

   2. In Dreamweaver, crop the fish out of the image.

d) Modify the cleaning.htm web page document as follows:

   1. In the top row, insert the com_cleaning.gif image and add alternative text: Cleaning the computer.

   2. In Dreamweaver, crop the fish out of the image.

e) Modify the disks.htm web page document by inserting the com_disks.gif image in the top row and adding alternative text: Disk maintenance.

f) Modify the updates.htm web page document by inserting the com_updates.gif image in the top row and adding alternative text: Software updates.

g) Switch to Fireworks and create a new document with a width of 660 pixels, a height of 100 pixels, a resolution of 72 pixels/inch, and a transparent canvas. Save the document outside of any website folder naming it: maint_nav.png

h) Create a button symbol as follows:

   1. Draw a rectangle with a width of 150 pixels and a height of 55 pixels.

   2. Apply a fill color of #FF9900 and a transparent stroke color to the rectangle.

   3. Create a text box with the text button formatted as Verdana font, 18 points in size, center aligned, bold, and #FFFFFF in color.

   4. Align the rectangle and the text block horizontally and vertically.

   5. With both the rectangle and text block selected, convert them to a button symbol named: maintenance button

i) Create instances of the button symbol and modify them as follows:

1. Create three more instances of the button symbol on the canvas and then position all four instances next to each other, with a little space in between.

2. Change the properties of each instance, from left to right, as follows:

Text	Link	Alt
Home	index.htm	Link to home page.
Cleaning	cleaning.htm	Link to computer cleaning page.
Disks	disks.htm	Link to disk maintenance page.
Updates	updates.htm	Link to software update page.

Your buttons should look similar to:

j) Double-click any instance to display the button symbol in the Button Editor. Edit the states of the button symbol as follows:

1. Edit the Over state to be identical to the Up state except change the text color to #333399.

2. Edit the Down state to be identical to the Over state except change the text color to #FFFFFF and the rectangle fill color to #333399.

3. Edit the Over While Down state to be identical to the Down state.

k) Finish and export the navigation bar as follows:

1. Modify the canvas to exactly fit the buttons and then save the modified document.

2. Use the Export Wizard to export an HTML file named maint_nav.htm to the COMPUTER MAINTENANCE website. Make sure the images are exported as GIF files, with Index Transparency, to the images folder.

l) In Dreamweaver, modify the COMPUTER MAINTENANCE website as follows:

1. Open maint_nav.htm and click the <body> tag to select the entire document.

2. Copy the HTML.

3. Paste the HTML in the second row of the index.htm, cleaning.htm, disks.htm, and updates.htm web page documents.

4. In each web page document, modify the appropriate button to initially appear in the Down state.

m) View each web page document in a browser window and test the hyperlinks.

n) Print a copy of each web page document from the browser.

Exercise 5   SEVEN WONDERS

The SEVEN WONDERS website was last modified in Chapter 4, Exercise 5. Use Dreamweaver to further modify the SEVEN WONDERS website by completing the following steps:

a) In Dreamweaver, open the SEVEN WONDERS website for editing.

b) Modify the index.htm web page document as follows:

    1. In the left cell of the third row, select the wonder_map.gif image and in the Property inspector set **Map** to locations and press Enter.

    2. Create seven rectangular hotspots, one on each word and its corresponding bullet on the wonder_map.gif image, linking each hotspot and adding alternative text as follows:

The hotspot	should link to	and have alternative text
Ephesus	temple.htm	Temple of Artemis at Ephesus.
Halicarnassus	mausoleum.htm	Mausoleum at Halicarnassus.
Rhodes	colossus.htm	Colossus of Rhodes.
Babylon	hanging.htm	Hanging Gardens of Babylon.
Giza	pyramids.htm	Pyramids of Egypt.
Alexandria	lighthouse.htm	Lighthouse of Alexandria.
Olympia	statue.htm	Statue of Zeus at Olympia.

c) View the index.htm web page document in a browser window and test the hyperlinks and alternative text.

d) Print a copy of index.htm from the browser.

Exercise 6   Logos

Develop a website that showcases your talent for creating logos in Fireworks. The website should contain at least:

- at least two web page documents
- at least six logos, created in Fireworks and exported as GIFs
- alternative text
- graphic hyperlinks
- a navigation bar created using button symbols in Fireworks

Preview the website in a browser. When satisfied with the website, print a copy of each web page document from the browser.

The Rubrics website was last modified in Chapter 4, Exercise 7. Use Fireworks and Dreamweaver to further modify the Rubrics website by completing the following steps:

a) Start Fireworks and create a new document with a width of 600 pixels, a height of 70 pixels, a resolution of 72 pixels/inch, and a transparent canvas. Save the document outside of any website folder naming it rubric_logo.png. Create and export a GIF image as follows:

   1. Create a text box with the text Rubrics for Web Development formatted in a font of your choice, 34 points in size, bold, and #9900FF in color.

   2. Modify the canvas to exactly fit the text.

   3. Using the Export Wizard, export the image as a GIF with Index Transparency, named rubric_logo.gif, saved in the images folder of the Rubrics website.

b) In Dreamweaver, open the Rubrics website for editing.

c) Create a new web page document naming it: img_rubric.htm

d) Modify the index.htm web page document as follows:

   1. In the top cell, delete the text Rubrics for Web Development and then insert the rubric_logo.gif image.

   2. In the third row, place the insertion point at the end of the text Web Page Document Rubric, press Enter, and then type the text: Images Rubric

   3. Link the text Images Rubric to img_rubric.htm.

e) Modify the img_rubric.htm web page document as follows:

   1. Change the page title to: Images Rubric

   2. Open the wpd_rubric.htm document, copy the entire table and paste it into the img_rubric.htm web page document.

   3. In the top cell, replace the text with: Images Rubric

   4. In the second row, replace the text single web page document with the text:

      images in a web page document

   5. Replace the first three criteria with these criteria:

      1. The images complement the text and other content of the web page.

      2. The quality of the images enhance the web page content.

      3. Interactive images such as buttons, Flash Text, or graphic hyperlinks enhance the user's experience.

   6. Brainstorm in small groups to generate two additional images rubric criteria. Replace the last two criteria in the rubric with these two.

f) Check the spelling in the img_rubric.htm web page document.

g) View the index.htm and img_rubric.htm web page documents in a browser window.

h) Print a copy of index.htm and img_rubric.htm from the browser.

i) In a browser window, view a web page document that a peer has created and print a copy. Use the rubric to evaluate the images in the web page document.

j) Reflect on the design of the rubric. Does it appropriately assess the images in a web page document? Are there criteria that should be added or changed? Make any appropriate revisions and print a copy.

Exercise 8 —————————————————————— Nav Bar Expert

Develop a website that showcases your talent for creating navigation bars using button symbols in Fireworks. The website should contain at least:

- at least four web page documents, each with a different navigation bar created in Fireworks
- one logo, created in Fireworks and exported as a GIF, placed in the top cell on each page and linked to the home page where appropriate
- alternative text
- graphic hyperlinks

Preview the website in a browser. When satisfied with the website, print a copy of each web page document from the browser.

Exercise 9 —————————————————————— Photographer

Develop a website that showcases a photographer's works. The website should contain at least:

- two web page documents
- at least six JPG images—if you do not have images to use, copy JPG images from the data files provided for this text
- a logo created in Fireworks, placed in the top cell in each web page document, and linked to index.htm
- alternative text
- use of a spacer.gif

Preview the website in a browser. When satisfied with the website, print a copy of each web page document from the browser.

Chapter 5 Images in Dreamweaver and Fireworks

Typography, Style Sheets, and Color

This chapter discusses CSS style sheets and formatting web page documents. Typography, using fonts on the Web, paragraph formats, and formatting background, text, and hyperlink color is discussed.

Typography

Typography refers to the arrangement, shape, size, style, and weight of text. Typography affects the navigation and usability of a website and helps to convey a specific message to the audience.

Making typography choices for a website is more complicated than for a print document. When creating a print document, the text can be presented in any format that is supported by the local monitor and printer. Whereas, web page text has to be formatted so that it appears similarly on various monitor sizes, in different screen resolutions, and in different browsers.

typeface
font

A *typeface* is a set of letters drawn in a specific style. Examples of typefaces include Arial, Times New Roman, and **Verdana**. The word *font* technically refers to a specific size and weight of a typeface, such as 10 point Verdana bold.

Design Considerations: Choosing Fonts

In order for a font to display correctly in a browser, the user must have the font installed on their computer. Dreamweaver only lists commonly available fonts:

Fonts

To ensure that logos and other fancy fonts are displayed as intended on a web page, a graphic is created of the logo and then inserted on the web page.

Dreamweaver also groups fonts so that if a user does not have the first font installed, the next font in the group will be used, and so forth. This is one way to ensure a web page will display similarly on different computers.

The end of each group of fonts lists a font category. If the user doesn't have any of the fonts in the group, a font from the font category is used. Fonts categories include *serif* and *sans serif*. Serifs are small extensions at the ends of the strokes of a character:

serif — The   sans serif — The

Fonts can also be categorized as monospace, cursive, and fantasy.

When designing print documents, serif fonts tend to be easier to read. Because the serifs extend towards the neighboring letters, serif fonts appear closer together, scan easier, and are more readable than sans serif. However, serif fonts are not the best choice for web pages. The clean strokes of sans serif fonts are easier to read on a monitor. Monitor resolution is coarse, which results in serif fonts appearing fuzzy especially if the text is small.

A website should be as readable as possible, allowing the user to scan the text for information. One way to make the text readable is to limit the number of fonts used on the page. Two different fonts should be the maximum for a single web page. More than two fonts decreases usability. Users will also find that text in all capital letters is more difficult to read because our eyes scan for shapes:

EXAMPLE   example

Design Considerations: Font Size

points

The size of printed text is measured vertically in *points*, where one point is 1/72 of an inch. The text in this paragraph is 10 point. In Dreamweaver, text size may be specified as an absolute value in a unit of measure, such as pixels, as a relative size, such as a percentage, or as a named size, such as x-small.

Monitors display in pixels. Therefore, many web designers specify the font size as an absolute value in pixels because pixels are a way to prevent distortion and achieve a consistent look across a variety of web browsers. Fonts set using this method are referred to as "fixed fonts."

Usability is a consideration when choosing sizes for the text on a web page. The font size should be big enough so that the user can easily read the text, but not so big that it appears loud. Sizes from 12 pixels to 16 pixels are a good choice for paragraphs of text, and 14 pixels to 24 pixels for headings. Other size considerations are:

- Text in the top global navigation bar should be in the same size as the text or slightly larger.

- Text in the breadcrumb trail and local navigation bar should be slightly smaller than the top global navigation bar.

TIP *sans* is the French word for "without."

Monospace, Cursive, and Fantasy Fonts

Courier is a common monospace font that most users have installed on their computer. The cursive and fantasy font categories include fonts that are not as common, such as Comic Sans and Impact.

TIP In an e-mail or instant message, text in all capitals is interpreted as screaming.

TIP Text will appear smaller on a Macintosh computer because Mac type displays at 72 pixels per inch and PC type uses 96 pixels per inch.

Text Size in Internet Explorer

To change the display size of relative fonts in Internet Explorer, users can select View → Text Size and then select an appropriate size, such as smaller. This setting will not alter any fixed fonts. However, other browsers do allow fixed fonts to be resized.

- Page footer elements, including the bottom global navigation bar, can be much smaller.

- Serif fonts become difficult to read at small sizes, so use sans serif fonts for any text in a very small size.

Design Considerations: Line Height

Line height is the distance from one line of text to another. Text with greater line height will have more space below it, which gives more separation to lines of text. Line height affects the readability of a document. Lines of text need enough space between them to allow the reader's eye to focus and scan.

The line height is determined by the type size and the line length. The greater the type size, the greater the line height and the longer the lines of text, the greater the line height. Line height is also used to visually connect items on a web page:

Leading

For printed material, *leading* (pronounced "ledding") is the typography term that refers to line height.

Heading   Heading

Subhead   **Subhead**

The line height in the example on the right connects the heading to the subhead better

In Dreamweaver, line height can be specified as a value in a unit of measure, such as pixels or as "normal," which automatically calculates the line height.

Design Considerations: Type Styles

Plain type is referred to as normal, regular, roman, or book style. Type styles, such as *italic* and **bold**, can be applied to normal type to make text stand out and to indicate a heading hierarchy. However, type styles can visually change the meaning of words and should be used with care.

Bold type is said to visually "weigh" more than normal type. Italic style should only be applied to larger text (at least 12 pixels), because it is much more difficult to read on a screen at a smaller size. Underline style should not be applied to text unless it is a hyperlink.

TIP Italic text may not display properly on web pages viewed on a Macintosh computer.

Design Considerations: Alignment

Alignment is a paragraph format that refers to the position of the lines of text relative to the sides of a cell: left, centered, right, and justified:

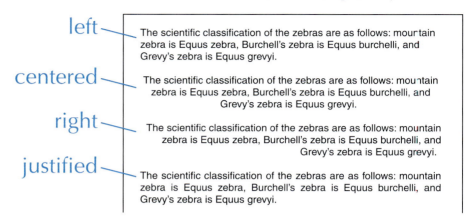

design considerations
Left alignment is the most readable and therefore provides the highest degree of usability. Right alignment is difficult to read in long paragraphs of text. Long paragraphs of centered text are difficult to read, so centered alignment should be used only for headings or short amounts of text. Justified alignment is not recommended because browser support for this format varies.

Links in top and local navigation bars are most readable and usable when left aligned. However, centered alignment is also an acceptable and usable choice for formatting the links in navigation bars. The bottom global navigation bar is often formatted as centered.

Style Sheets

TIP Mastering style sheets requires a basic understanding of HTML, which is covered in Chapter 2.

A *style sheet* defines the type, paragraph, and page formats for a web page document. A single style sheet can be applied to all the pages in a website to achieve a consistent look. Changing the text format of all the web pages in a website is as easy as modifying a single style sheet because updates to the style sheet are automatically applied to linked documents.

The W3C recommends the CSS2 (Cascading Style Sheets, level 2) style sheet language. Multiple style sheets can be applied to a single web page, with the rules in one style sheet layering, or *cascading*, those in another style sheet.

W3C

The World Wide Web Consortium (www.w3c.org) develops design and accessibility standards for the Web.

A CSS style sheet is saved as a separate file in the website folder. Select File → Save All to save the style sheet and any open web page documents. When opened, a style sheet is displayed in a Document window in Code view:

```
index.htm  COFFEE_styles.css*

<> Code    Split    Design    Title:

1  p {
2      font-family: Georgia, "Times New Roman", Times, serif;
3      font-size: 14px;
4  }
5  .para_with_space {
6      font-family: Georgia, "Times New Roman", Times, serif;
7      font-size: 14px;
8      line-height: 28px;
9      text-align: center;
10 }
11
```

Version 8 Dreamweaver 8 differences are indicated with parentheses (*ver.8:*).

In Dreamweaver, the CSS Styles panel is used to link, create, and modify style sheets (*ver.8:* the CSS Styles panel looks different):

TIP Select Window → CSS Styles to display the CSS Styles panel.

To link a style sheet to the open web page document, click the Attach Style Sheet button ( ) (*ver.8:*). The Attach External Style Sheet dialog box is displayed (*ver.8:* the dialog box has an additional option):

Publishing Style Sheets

Style sheets are saved in the website's folder and posted along with a website. The browser displaying the web page must support CSS1 or CSS2. Most newer browser versions support both.

- To create a new CSS style sheet, type a descriptive style sheet name with a .css extension in the File/URL box and then select OK. A warning dialog box is displayed. Select Yes to create a new sheet in the website root folder and display the style sheet name in the CSS Styles panel.

- To link an existing style sheet to the open web page document, click Browse, which displays another dialog box where the style sheet name is selected. The selected style sheet is automatically copied to the website root folder.

- To use a predesigned Dreamweaver style sheet, click sample style sheets, which displays a dialog box with sample style sheets. Select a style sheet and OK.

Creating and Applying a CSS Rule

selector
declaration

A CSS style sheet can include rules. A *rule* modifies an HTML element and is comprised of a selector and declarations. The *selector* is the HTML element being redefined and the *declarations* are the formats to be applied. Rules are defined using the HTML element name. For example, the rule below modifies the paragraph element (<p>) to automatically display paragraphs in 14 px Georgia:

> **TIP** The selector can be any HTML element.

```
1  p {
2      font-family: Georgia, "Times New Roman", Times, serif;
3      font-size: 14px;
4  }
```

To add a new style to a style sheet, click the New CSS Style button (🔲) (*ver.8:* called New CSS Rule button), which displays a dialog box. To create a rule, select Tag (redefines the look of a specific tag) and then select a tag from the Tag list (*ver.8:* the dialog box looks different):

A new rule will be created for the paragraph tag (<p>)

Select OK to display a dialog box where formats for a paragraph and text within a paragraph are set:

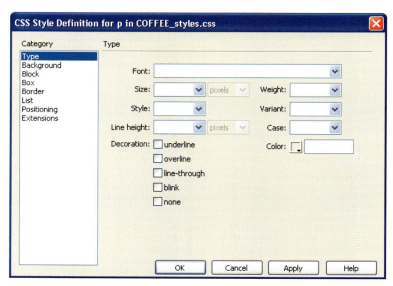

> ### The Style Definition Dialog Box
>
> The **Apply** button can be used to preview the style while keeping the dialog box open for modifications. If necessary, move the dialog box by dragging the title bar.

Each **Category** in the dialog box contains a different set of attributes. Not every attribute affects the tag being redefined. For example, the List category of attributes has no effect on paragraph text. For the p tag, the Type and **Block** categories of attributes can be set. The Type attributes include:

- Font for selecting a font family.
- Size for specifying a type size. Selecting a value enables the units list where pixels should be selected.
- Weight for selecting the thickness of text.
- Style for selecting normal, italic, or oblique.
- Line height for selecting the line height.

The Block category displays attributes that include the Text align list for selecting a paragraph alignment of left, center, right, or justified. Once attributes are selected, select OK to create the style. Rules are automatically applied to any text on the web page document that is within the tags that were redefined.

Oblique vs. Italic Style

Oblique style slants letters. Italic style is an actual different font because it creates structural changes to letters to alter their appearance.

Creating and Applying a CSS Class

A *class* is a set of declarations that can be applied to different tags. Class names must begin with a dot (.). For example:

```
 6  .para_with_space {
 7      font-family: Georgia, "Times New Roman", Times, serif;
 8      font-size: 14px;
 9      line-height: 28px;
10      text-align: center;
11  }
```

The class above can be applied to individual paragraphs to format the paragraph in 14px Georgia with a line-height of 28 px.

A new class is added to a style sheet the same way a rule is created, except that Class (can be applied to any tag) is selected and then a class name typed in the Name box (*ver.8:* the dialog box looks different):

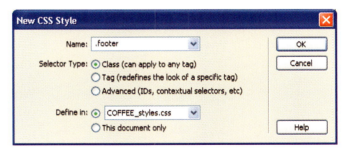

Class Attributes

It is important to keep in mind what the class will be used for. For example, a class that will modify paragraphs should only include attribute settings that apply to paragraphs of text.

Select OK to display a dialog box where attributes are set. The class style can then be applied to selected text. Classes are not automatically applied like rules because classes are created to modify tags, not redefine specific tags. Classes override rules. To apply a class, select the text or table cell and then select the style name in the Style list in the Property inspector:

Dreamweaver will also automatically create a class style if selected text is formatted using options in the Format, Font, Size or Text Color lists in the Property inspector, instead of from the CSS Style Definition dialog box. Automatically created class styles will contain the names .style1, .style2, and so forth. The styles are listed in the Style list in the Property inspector and in the CSS Styles panel (*ver.8:* the CSS Styles panel looks different):

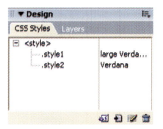

External Style Sheets

External style sheets are saved as a separate document with a .css extension. This allows the style sheet to be applied to multiple pages or sites.

Creating styles in this manner is not considered good design because the automatically generated class styles are placed in an internal style sheet in the HEAD section of the web page document instead of being saved as an external style sheet. Internal style sheets require that changes to styles be made on individual pages and internal style sheets cannot be attached to other web page documents.

Editing HTML Code

Dreamweaver provides a visual environment that allows a page to be designed in Design view while the HTML code is generated in the background. However, when attaching a style sheet, there may be cases, such as formatting inconsistencies, where HTML tags need to be checked in Code view and then modified. For example, Code and Design view can be used to determine if paragraphs of text are enclosed by <p> and </p>:

TIP Enclose text in paragraph tags to have more formatting control.

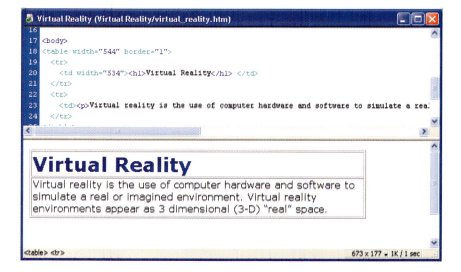

TIP Select Paragraph from the **Format** list in the Property inspector to insert <p> and </p>.

Text that needs to be tagged differently is selected and then a tag button from the **Text** category in the Insert bar is clicked to enclose it. The **Text** category includes many commonly used HTML tags:

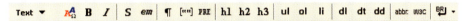

- The Paragraph button (¶) inserts <p> and </p> around selected text.

Tag buttons in the **Text** category in the Insert bar can also used to add formatting to text:

- The Bold (**B**) and Strong (**S**) buttons insert <strong> and </strong> around selected text.
- The Italic (*I*) and Emphasis (*em*) buttons insert <em> and </em> tags around selected text.

Strong text is usually intended to be displayed as bold, and emphasized text as italic. To ensure that text is displayed as intended, these tags should be redefined with CSS styles.

Bold and Italic

The Bold and Italic buttons in the Property inspector can also be used to format text as bold and italic. To remove bold and italic from selected text, deselect the Bold and Italic buttons in the Property inspector.

Practice: COFFEE – part 1 of 7

Dreamweaver 8 differences are indicated with parentheses (*ver.8:*).

① OPEN THE COFFEE WEBSITE FOR EDITING

a. Start Dreamweaver.

b. Open the COFFEE website for editing, which is a website provided with the data files for this text.

c. Familiarize yourself with the files and folders in this website.

d. Open the index.htm web page document and view the page in a browser.

e. Click the links to explore the other web pages of the website.

f. Close the browser window. Dreamweaver is displayed.

g. Open the footer library item.

h. Replace the text Name with your name.

i. Save and close the library item, allowing Dreamweaver to update all the files.

② ATTACH A NEW STYLE SHEET TO INDEX.HTM

a. Display the index.htm web page document, if it is not already displayed.

b. Select Window → CSS Styles if the CSS Styles panel is not already visible.

c. In the bottom of the CSS Styles panel, click the Attach Style Sheet button ( ) (*ver.8:*). A dialog box is displayed.

d. In the File/URL box, type: COFFEE_styles.css

e. Select OK. A dialog box is displayed.

f. Select Yes.

③ CREATE A NEW STYLE

a. In the bottom of the CSS Styles panel, click the New CSS Style button (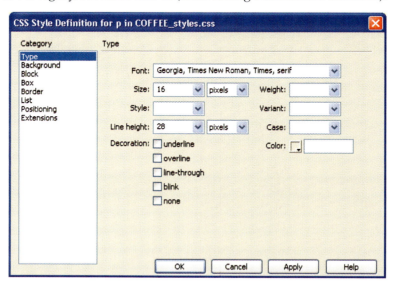) (*ver.8:* called New CSS Rule button). A dialog box is displayed.

     1. Select Tag (redefines the look of a specific tag).

     2. In the Tag list, select p.

     3. In the Define in list, select COFFEE_styles.css.

b. Select OK. A dialog box is displayed (*ver.8:* then select Yes. Another dialog box is displayed).

c. In the Type category, set attributes to (*ver.8:* dialog box name is different):

d. In the Block category, set attributes to:

e. Select OK. A rule is created and applied to the web page document.

④ CHECK THE HTML TAGS AND EMPHASIZE TEXT

a. Scroll the web page document window and note that the sentence that begins "Tips for brewing…" has not changed to reflect the new rule. Place the insertion point in the sentence.

b. Select View → Code and Design to display the HTML for the web page document. Note the text is not enclosed by <p> and </p>.

Chapter 6 Typography, Style Sheets, and Color

c. In the Text category in the Insert bar, click the Paragraph button (¶). <p> and </p> enclose the text, similar to:

```
24    <td><p>Tips for brewing that perfect cup:</p>
25      <ol>
26        <li>Use fresh, high quality coffee.</li>
27        <li>Select the correct grind.</li>
28        <li>Use the proper amount of coffee.</li>
29        <li>Add pure water.</li>
```

In the Design pane, the text displays the formatting of the redefined p tag.

d. In the Design pane, select the entire sentence that begins "Tips for brewing...."

e. In the Text category in the Insert bar, click the Emphasis button (*em*). <em> and </em> enclose the text. In the Design pane, the text is emphasized.

f. Switch to Design view.

⑤ REDEFINE THE EM TAG

a. In the bottom of the CSS Styles panel, click the New CSS Style button (⊞) (*ver.8: called New CSS Rule button*). A dialog box is displayed.

   1. Select Tag (redefines the look of a specific tag).

   2. In the Tag list, select em.

   3. In the Define in list, select COFFEE_styles.css.

b. Select OK. A dialog box is displayed.

c. In the Type category, set Style to italic.

d. Select OK. A rule is created and applied to the web page document.

⑥ CREATE AND APPLY A STYLE

a. In the bottom of the CSS Styles panel, click the New CSS Style button (⊞) (*ver.8: called New CSS Rule button*). A dialog box is displayed.

   1. Select Class (can apply to any tag).

   2. In the Name box, type: .footer

   3. In the Define in list, select COFFEE_styles.css.

b. Select OK. A dialog box is displayed.

c. In the Type category, set attributes to (*ver.8: dialog box name is different*):

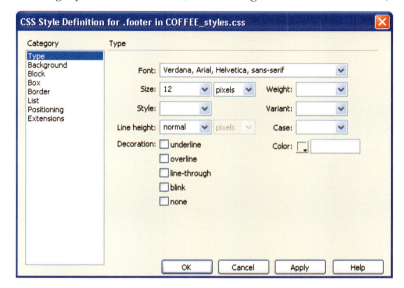

d. In the Block category, set Text align to center.

e. Select OK. A class is created.

f. In the Document window, select the entire bottom navigation bar.

g. In the Property inspector, select footer from the Style list. The style is applied.

h. In the Document window, place the insertion point to the left of the library item in the last row of the table.

i. In the Property inspector, select footer from the Style list. The library item is formatted.

⑦ CREATE AND APPLY A SECOND STYLE

a. In the CSS Styles panel, click the New CSS Style button (▣) (*ver.8:* called New CSS Rule button). A dialog box is displayed.

   1. Select Class (can apply to any tag).

   2. In the Name box, type: .topnavbar

   3. In the Define in list, select COFFEE_styles.css.

b. Select OK. A dialog box is displayed.

c. In the Type category, set the options to (*ver.8:* dialog box name is different):

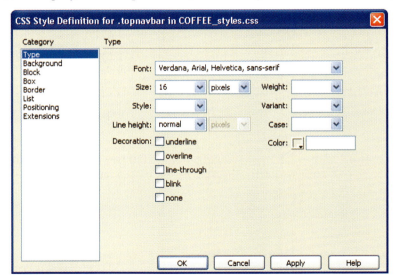

d. In the Block category, set Text align to left.

e. Select OK. A class is created.

f. In the Document window, select the entire top navigation bar.

g. In the Property inspector, select topnavbar from the Style list. The navigation bar is formatted.

⑧ VIEW AND SAVE THE STYLE SHEET

a. In the Files panel, double-click COFFEE_styles.css. The style sheet is displayed in a Document window.

b. Select File ➡ Save All. The style sheet and all open web page documents are saved.

Chapter 6 Typography, Style Sheets, and Color

Working with CSS Styles

The CSS Styles panel is used to edit, duplicate, delete, and remove styles from a document (*ver.8:* the CSS Styles panel looks different):

This style sheet includes three styles

To modify a style, select the style and then click the Edit Style Sheet button ( ) (*ver.8:*), which displays a dialog box where attributes can be modified. To modify any of the styles in the style sheet, double-click a style name in the CSS Styles panel.

A style can be duplicated to create a new, similar style. To duplicate a style, click the style sheet name and then select the Edit Style Sheet button ( ) (*ver.8:*), which displays a dialog box listing all the styles. Select a style name and then the Duplicate button to display a dialog box where the new style is given a name. (*ver.8:* To duplicate a style, right-click the style in the CSS Styles panel and select Duplicate to display a dialog box where the new style is given a name.) The style can then be edited to customize it.

removing a class style

To remove a class style that has been applied to text, select the text and then select None from the Style list in the Property inspector. To remove a rule, the style must be deleted. To delete a style, select the style name in the CSS Styles panel and then click the Delete CSS Style button ( ) (*ver.8:* called Delete CSS Rule button).

Formatting Headings

Headings are used in text to indicate a hierarchy and help with readability. Different levels of headings can be used to further enhance readability. For example, two heading levels are shown below:

Recipes

Vanilla Iced Coffee

A user can more easily scan a long page of text if topics are divided by headings.

Antialiasing

Some web designers create headings in a graphics program because large size fonts can appear jagged on a monitor. The jagged appearance results because web fonts do not have antialiasing, which is a feature that blends pixel edges with the background color to make letters look smoother.

h1 through h6 tags

HTML includes six headings tags, ranging from <h1> through <h6>. Each heading level has specific formatting associated with it, which includes font size, bold text, and space above and below the heading. The largest font size is typically applied to <h1> to represent the highest level or the topic of greatest importance. <h6> typically has the least importance and the smallest font size.

Search Engines

Some search engines rate the relevance of words based on the heading level assigned, with <h1> words having the most relevance.

Only one heading level can be applied to a line of text. To apply a heading tag, place the insertion point in the line of text and select a heading tag button from the Text category in the Insert bar:

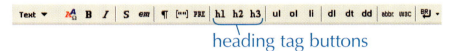

heading tag buttons

TIP Heading tags replace any existing paragraph tags.

The Text category contains buttons for heading level 1, 2, and 3 only. Other heading tags are inserted by selecting a heading level from the Format list in the Property inspector or by selecting Text → Paragraph Format, which displays a menu with all six heading levels.

CSS styles should then be used to redefine the heading tags so that heading formats compliment the paragraph styles. In the CSS Style Definition (*ver.8:* CSS Rule Definition) dialog box, both the Type and Block categories have attributes that can apply to headings.

Practice: COFFEE – part 2 of 7

Dreamweaver should be started and the COFFEE website should be the working site. Dreamweaver 8 differences are indicated with parentheses (*ver.8:*).

① ATTACH THE STYLE SHEET AND APPLY STYLES

a. Display the recipes.htm web page document.

b. Display the CSS Styles panel if it is not already displayed.

c. In the CSS Styles panel, click the Attach Style Sheet button (⬛) (*ver.8:* ⬛). A dialog box is displayed.

d. Select OK. The COFFEE_styles.css style sheet is linked to the recipes.htm web page document.

e. In the Document window, select the entire top navigation bar.

f. In the Property inspector, select topnavbar from the Style list. The navigation bar is formatted.

g. Select the entire bottom navigation bar.

h. In the Property inspector, select footer from the Style list. The bottom navigation bar is formatted.

i. In the last row, place the insertion point to the left of the library item.

j. In the Property inspector, select footer from the Style list. The library item is formatted.

② DUPLICATE A STYLE

a. (*ver.8:* In the CSS Styles panel, click the All button. Next to COFFEE_styles.css click the plus sign if all the styles are not already displayed, then skip to step b.) In the CSS Styles panel, select COFFEE_styles.css and then click the Edit Style Sheet button (⬛) (*ver.8:* ✏). A dialog box is displayed.

b. Select (*ver8:* Right-click) the .topnavbar style and then select Duplicate. A dialog box is displayed.

c. In the Name box, replace the current name with: .btrail

d. Select OK. The new style is listed in the dialog box (ver8: added in the CSS Styles panel).

e. Select Edit (*ver8:* Right-click the new style and select Edit). A dialog box is displayed.

f. In the Type category, set Size to 12 pixels.

g. Select OK and then select Done. (*ver8:* Select OK.)

h. In the recipes.htm Document window, select the entire breadcrumb trail.

i. In the Property inspector, select btrail from the Style list. The breadcrumb trail is formatted.

③ DUPLICATE AND APPLY ANOTHER STYLE

a. (*ver.8:* Skip to step b.) In the CSS Styles panel, select COFFEE_styles.css and then click the Edit Style Sheet button (📝) (*ver.8:* ✏️). A dialog box is displayed.

b. Select (*ver8:* Right-click) the .btrail style and then select Duplicate. A dialog box is displayed.

c. In the Name box, replace the current name with: .localnavbar

d. Select OK. The new style is listed in the dialog box (ver8: added in the CSS Styles panel).

e. Select Edit (*ver8:* Right-click the new style and select Edit). A dialog box is displayed.

f. In the Type category, set Line Height to 35 pixels.

g. In the Block category, set Vertical alignment to top.

h. Select OK and then select Done. (*ver8:* Select OK.)

i. In the recipes.htm Document window, place the insertion point in the local navigation bar.

j. In the Property inspector, select localnavbar from the Style list. The local navigation bar text is formatted and the text is moved to the top of the cell.

k. Select View → Code and Design. The text for the local navigation bar is enclosed by <td> and </td>. The style is affecting the table data, not paragraph text. Paragraph text will not be affected by a vertical alignment setting, like the one used in the localnavbar style.

④ FORMAT HEADINGS

a. In the Design pane, click in the text "Recipes" above "Vanilla Iced Coffee." In the Code pane, the text is enclosed by <p> and </p>.

b. In the Text category in the Insert bar, click the Heading 1 button (**h1**). In the Code pane, the "Recipes" text is now enclosed by <h1> and </h1> instead of <p> and </p>.

c. Below the "Recipes" heading text, place the insertion point in the Vanilla Iced Coffee text.

d. In the Property inspector, select Heading 2 from the Format list. In Code view, the text is now enclosed by <h2> and </h2>.

e. Scroll down and apply the Heading 2 tags to the "Cappuccino" text.

f. Scroll down and apply the Heading 2 tags to the "Cafe au Lait" text.

g. Switch to Design view.

⑤ **CREATE HEADING STYLES**

  a. In the bottom of the CSS Styles panel, click the New CSS Style button (🔲) (*ver.8:* called New CSS Rule button). A dialog box is displayed.

   1. Select Tag (redefines the look of a specific tag).

   2. In the Tag list, select h1.

   3. In the Define in list, select COFFEE_styles.css.

  b. Select OK. A dialog box is displayed.

  c. In the Type category, set attributes to (*ver.8:* dialog box name is different):

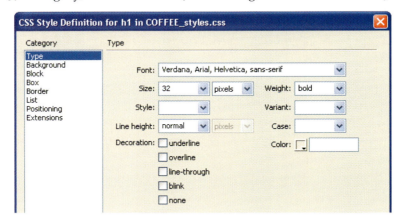

  c. In the Block category, set Text align to left.

  d. Select OK. The dialog box is removed and the heading is formatted.

  e. Create a new style that redefines the h2 tag so that the font family is Verdana, Arial, Helvetica, sans-serif, the size is 18 pixels, the weight is "bold", the height is "normal", and the text alignment is left.

  f. Select File → Save All. The style sheet and all open web page documents are saved.

  g. Display the index.htm web page document. The heading was automatically formatted because the style sheet is already attached.

⑥ **VIEW INDEX.HTM AND RECIPES.HTM IN A BROWSER**

Indenting with Blockquotes

A paragraph that should be set off from other paragraphs, such as a quotation, can be indented. In a web page document, a paragraph is indented by making it a blockquote:

> The Global Bean's mission is to educate coffee lovers about the coffees of the world.
>
> > "A morning without coffee is like sleep."
>
> Coffee tastes are a matter of individual preference. The differences in coffees are found in the country or region of original and the quality of

The second paragraph is a blockquote

Typographer's Quotes

Typographer's quotes (" and ") have a more professional appearance than straight quotes. In Dreamweaver, press Alt+0147 and Alt+0148 to create left and right typographer's quotes.

TIP Unlike heading tags, the blockquote tag does not replace existing tags.

TIP A CSS class style can be created to format blockquote text if the text should have a format different from that applied by the paragraph tag.

A blockquote is a paragraph enclosed by <blockquote> and </blockquote>. To apply a blockquote tag to a selected paragraph, click the Block Quote button ([""]) in the Text category in the Insert bar or click the Text Indent button (±≡) in the Property inspector. Multiple blockquote tags can be inserted to increase the indentation.

Blockquotes are removed from a paragraph by clicking the Text Outdent button (±≡) in the Property inspector. The button may used multiple times to remove levels of blockquotes.

Lists

Lists are used to indicate features, to-do items, or steps in a procedure. *Numbered lists* show a priority of importance for each step:

1. Use fresh, high quality coffee.
2. Select the correct grind.
3. Use the proper amount of coffee.
4. Add pure water.
5. Drink within half an hour of brewing.
6. Store coffee grinds or beans in a cool, dark, airtight container.

To convert selected paragraphs to a numbered list, click the Ordered List button (≔) in the Property inspector. Ordered list (<ol>) and list item (<li>) tags replace any tags originally enclosing the text.

Nested Lists

A sublist, or nested list, can be created within another list. Select the list items to be nested and then select Text → Indent to indent the items and numbers.

bulleted list

A *bulleted list* contains a set of items where each item is equally important. A solid circle (●) called a bullet is typically used to denote each item. To convert selected paragraphs to a bulleted list, click the Unordered List button (≔) in the Property inspector. Unordered list (<ul>) and list item (<li>) tags replace any tags originally enclosing the text.

creating a list style

Lists are formatted by creating and then applying a CSS class style. The Type category in the CSS Style Definition dialog box is used to set attributes to match paragraph text. The List category contains attributes that will apply to list items:

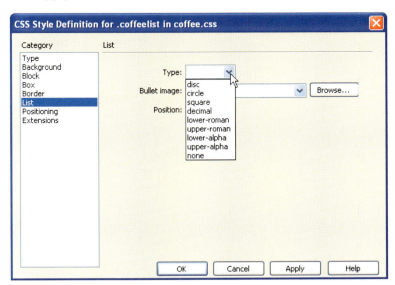

Bullet shapes and number formats can be selected from the Type list.

Dreamweaver should be started and the COFFEE website should be the working site. Dreamweaver 8 differences are indicated with parentheses (*ver.8:*).

① CREATE A BLOCKQUOTE

   a. Display the index.htm web page document.

   b. Click in the paragraph that starts "A morning without coffee…"

   c. In the Property inspector, click the Text Indent button (⊞). The paragraph is indented.

   d. Click the Text Indent button (⊞) again. The paragraph is indented farther.

② CREATE A NUMBERED LIST

   a. Display the recipes.htm web page document.

   b. Scroll to the Vanilla Iced Coffee recipe directions that begin "Combine ingredients…" and select all the text in the directions:

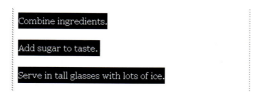

   c. In the Property inspector, click the Ordered List button (⊞). The paragraphs are now a numbered list.

③ CREATE AND APPLY A RULE

   a. In the CSS Styles panel, click the New CSS Style button (⊞) (*ver.8:* called New CSS Rule button). A dialog box is displayed.

      1. Select Tag (redefines the look of a specific tag).

      2. In the Tag list, select ol.

      3. In the Define in list, select COFFEE_styles.css.

   b. Select OK. A dialog box is displayed.

   c. In the Type category, set attributes to (*ver.8:* dialog box name is different):

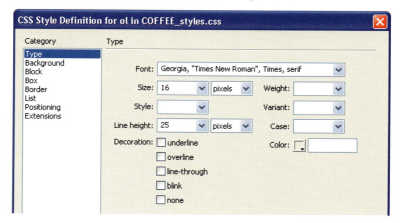

   d. In the List category, set Type to decimal.

   e. Select OK. The dialog box is removed and the recipe steps are formatted.

④ CREATE TWO MORE LISTS

   a. In the recipes.htm web page document, scroll to the Cappuccino recipe directions that begin "Add the expresso…" and select all the text in the directions:

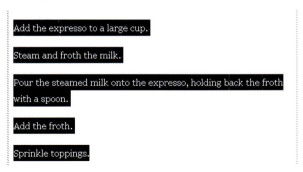

   b. In the Property inspector, click the Ordered List button (⊞). The paragraphs are now a numbered list.

   c. In the recipes.htm web page document, locate the Cafe au Lait recipe directions and format the four recipes steps as an ordered list.

   d. Select File ➜ Save All. The style sheet and all open web page documents are saved.

   e. View the recipes.htm web page document in a browser and then print a copy.

   f. Display the index.htm web page document. The ordered list is formatted because the style sheet is attached.

Using Color in a Website

Color can be added to a web page in many ways: text, page background, and table cells. However, using too many colors can make a web page visually annoying, causing users to click off the site. Color should be used to enhance the design and increase the usability of a website by guiding the user through the navigation aids and making the content more visually scannable.

color wheel   Colors that go together well can be determined with a *color wheel*. On the color wheel, colors from red to violet are arranged chromatically in a circle:

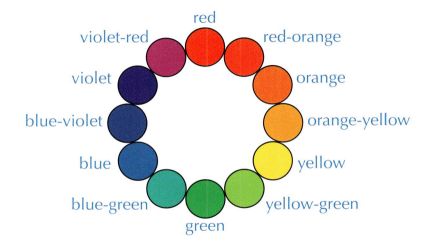

Color Wheel

Occupations that use color wheels include graphic artists, painters, interior designers, and web designers.

The position of a color on the wheel represents its relationship to other colors:

- Colors that are directly opposite each other are **complementary**, such as red and green.

- Three adjacent colors are called **analogous**, such as red, red-orange, and orange.

- Three equally-spaced colors are called **triads**, such as red, blue, and yellow.

Colors are also grouped by temperature:

- Reds, oranges, and yellows are **warm** colors.

- Blues, greens, and violets are **cool** colors.

Choosing two or three colors from the color wheel using one of these methods will ensure that the colors go well together.

consider other elements　　Other elements on a web page should also be considered when choosing colors. For example, a company logo may be red, and cannot be changed, so the other colors chosen should go well with red. Also consider the effect of the color on the user. For example, red is a bright, energetic color, and does not appear soothing or relaxing. Therefore, red is usually not the best color choice for a background or text.

color interaction　　Color interactions should be considered when choosing text and background colors. Black text on a white background is the easiest to read, and white text on a black background is also a readable combination. Colored text can be difficult to read depending on the background color, especially with light-colored text on a light background, or dark on dark:

some color combinations can be difficult to read

Colored text needs to be large enough and contrast with the background enough to be easily read. For example, yellow text can be eye-catching and effective, but it has to be in large letters on a dark background to be readable. However, if all the text is yellow, it would get tiring for the user to read. A bright color, for any element, also is tiring for the user to view. The text and background colors should enhance the usability of a web page, not reduce it.

colors in navigation bars　　One application of cell background color is the top navigation bar and local navigation bar. The top and local navigation bars should be in a different color than the background for maximum usability. The breadcrumb trail and the bottom navigation bar should be in the same color as the page background or in a slightly different color as the navigation bars. When choosing a color for the top and local navigation bars, be careful that the color does not conflict with the hyperlink blue and purple colors.

Changing Background and Text Color

background color

The background of a web page document is changed by redefining the body tag. The Background category in the CSS Style Definition (*ver.8:* CSS Rule Definition) dialog box includes the Background color attribute:

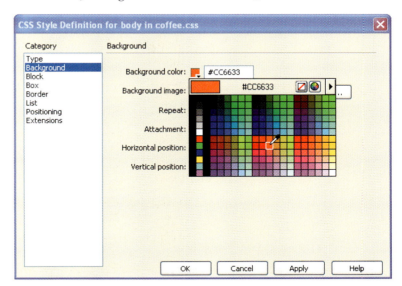

Hexadecimal

When a color is selected, Dreamweaver displays the hexadecimal value associated with the color, such as CC6633. Hexadecimal is a base-16 numbering system that consists of the numbers 0 through 9 and the letters A through F.

The color picker displays a grid of colors to choose from. In addition, the eyedropper can be moved into the document to match a color from the screen. To change the background color for the entire web page, select a color and then select OK.

The body tag should be redefined with a background color even if the color is white. If the color is not formatted and left as Automatic, the web page will display with whatever the user has chosen as the default background color for their browser.

cell background color

The background color of a cell is changed with a CSS class style. The Text category contains the Color attribute that will apply to cells.

text color

Text can be displayed in a different color by changing the Color option in the Type category of a CSS style:

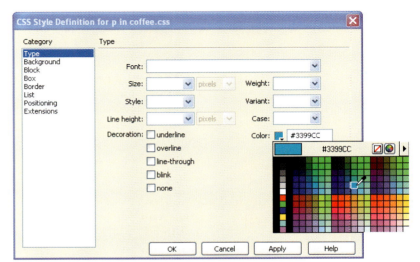

Browser Background and Text Color

In Internet Explorer, a user can select **Tools** → **Internet Options** and then select **Colors** to change the default background and text colors.

Select a color to change the color of text with the applied CSS style.

Dreamweaver should be started and the COFFEE website should be the working site. Dreamweaver 8 differences are indicated with parentheses (*ver.8:*).

① **CHANGE THE WEBSITE BACKGROUND COLOR**

  a. Display the recipes.htm web page document.

  b. In the CSS Styles panel, click the New CSS Style button ( ) (*ver.8:* called New CSS Rule button). A dialog box is displayed.

     1. Select Tag (redefines the look of a specific tag).

     2. In the Tag list, select body.

     3. In the Define in list, select COFFEE_styles.css.

  c. Select OK. A dialog box is displayed.

  d. In the Background category, click the Background color box and select the color that corresponds to #FFFFCC (*ver.8:* dialog box name is different):

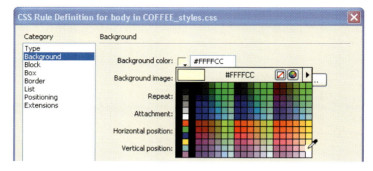

  e. Select OK. A rule is created and applied to the website.

② **CHANGE THE HEADING 2 COLOR**

  a. In the CSS Styles panel, select the h2 class rule and then click the Edit Style sheet button ( ) (*ver.8:*). A dialog box is displayed.

  b. In the Type category, set attributes to (*ver.8:* dialog box name is different):

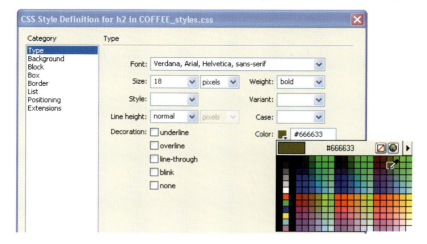

  c. Select OK. The heading level 2 text color is changed.

  d. Select File ➧ Save All. The style sheet and all open web page documents are saved.

③ **VIEW RECIPES.HTM IN A BROWSER**

Hyperlinks to Named Anchors

A long web page is easier to navigate if hyperlinks are provided to different parts of the page. For example, hyperlinks in a local navigation bar can link to sections in a web page. Hyperlinks to different parts of the same page are linked to a *named anchor* that has been created in the page. To create a named anchor, place the insertion point in the location of the anchor and click the Named Anchor button ( ) in the Common category in the Insert bar. A dialog box is displayed:

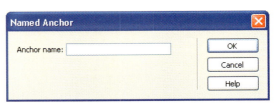

Type a descriptive name for the anchor and then select OK. An anchor icon is added at the insertion point:

Vanilla Iced Coffee

To link selected text to a named anchor, click the Browse for File icon ( ) in the Property inspector and type the anchor name in the Select File dialog box. Selected text can also be linked to a named anchor by dragging the Point to File icon to the anchor icon:

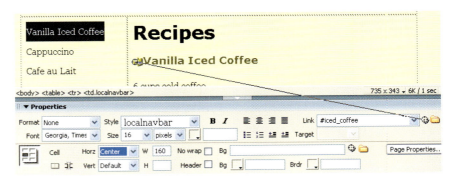

The Link list in the Property inspector displays the anchor name when the insertion point is in a hyperlink.

Links should be tested in a browser window. Links are modified in Dreamweaver by selecting the link text and then selecting Modify → Change Link or Modify → Remove Link.

A link to a named anchor typically causes a page to scroll. To increase usability, there should be another link that takes the user back to the original link location. For example, include a link such as <u>top</u> or <u>Back to top</u> that links to a named anchor near the position of the original hyperlink.

TIP Anchor names must start with a letter, are case-sensitive, and cannot contain spaces.

TIP The anchor icon is not visible when the web page is viewed in a browser.

TIP Be sure to use the Link list icon in the Property inspector and not the Bg list icon.

URL

A named anchor is referenced at the end of a URL, preceded by a # sign. For example, www.lpdatafiles.com/recipes.htm#iced_coffee.

---

modifying and removing links

design considerations

Dreamweaver should be started and the COFFEE website should be the working site. Dreamweaver 8 differences are indicated with parentheses (*ver.8:*).

① CREATE NAMED ANCHORS

   a. Display the recipes.htm web page document.

   b. Place the insertion point to the left of the recipe heading that reads "Vanilla Iced Coffee."

   c. In the **Common** category in the Insert bar, click the Named Anchor button (🔱). A dialog box is displayed.

   d. In the **Anchor name** box, type: iced_coffee

   e. Select **OK**. An anchor icon is displayed in the web page document.

   f. Scroll to the recipe heading that reads "Cappuccino" and insert an anchor named cappuccino to the left of the heading.

   g. Scroll to the recipe heading that reads "Cafe au Lait" and insert an anchor named cafe_au_lait to the left of the heading.

② CREATE HYPERLINKS TO ANCHORS

   a. In the local navigation bar, select the text: Vanilla Iced Coffee

   b. In the Property inspector, drag the Point to File icon to the anchor next to the "Vanilla Iced Coffee" recipe. A hyperlink is created and the anchor name is displayed in the Link box in the Property inspector.

   c. In the local navigation bar, select the text: Cappuccino

   d. Scroll to the recipe heading that reads "Cappuccino" and then drag the Point to File icon to the anchor next to that recipe. A hyperlink is created.

   e. In the local navigation bar, select the text: Cafe au Lait

   f. Scroll to the recipe heading that reads "Cafe au Lait" and then drag the Point to File icon to the anchor next to that recipe. A hyperlink is created.

③ CREATE A BACK TO TOP HYPERLINK

   a. Scroll to the top of the recipes and place the insertion point to the left of the "Recipes" heading.

   b. Insert an anchor named: top

   c. Scroll to the last step of the last recipe.

   d. Place the insertion point just after the period in "…the foam." and then insert a line break.

   e. Type the text: Back to top

   f. Select the Back to top text, scroll to the top of the Document window, and then in the Property inspector, drag the Point to File icon to the anchor next to "Recipes."

   g. Save the modified recipes.htm.

④ VIEW RECIPES.HTM IN A BROWSER AND TEST THE HYPERLINKS

Changing Hyperlink Colors

A lot of design consideration should go into the decision to change hyperlink colors. Users recognize the standard colors: blue for a link and purple for a visited link. However, when appropriately done, nonstandard hyperlink colors can enhance a design.

CSS selector style

Hyperlink colors are changed by creating a *CSS selector style*, which defines a style for a tag and attribute combination. Click the New CSS Style button ( ) (*ver.8:* called New CSS Rule button), which displays a dialog box. Select Advanced (IDs, contextual selectors, etc) (*ver.8:* Advanced (IDs, pseudo-class selectors)) and then make a selection from the Selector list (*ver.8:* dialog box looks different):

> ### Selector Options
>
> link="value" is the HTML attribute that sets the color of links and vlink="value" sets the color of previously visited links.

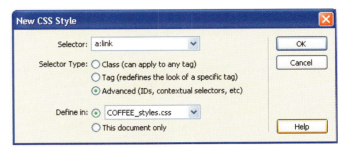

The Selector list contains predefined tag and attribute combinations

Select OK to display a dialog box where color and other formats can be selected from the Type category.

Using Content from Other Sources

Web development often involves collaborating with others to get the content for a website. For example, one person or department may have the responsibility of providing the images for a site, while others are responsible for the copy. *Copy* is a term that refers to text content.

copy

Files that contain copy are typically in text or TXT format to avoid having formatting copied with the text. Notepad is a text editor that can be used to open a text file and then copy and paste text to a Dreamweaver web page document:

TIP Notepad is introduced in Chapter 2.

1. Open the TXT file, which has the .txt extension, in Notepad.
2. Select the text to be placed in a web page document.
3. Select Edit → Copy. The text is placed on the Windows clipboard.

TIP Most word processors have an option that allows files to be saved in TXT format.

4. Display the web page document in Dreamweaver and place the insertion point where the text should be placed.
5. Select Edit → Paste. The copy is pasted at the insertion point.

Dreamweaver should be started and the COFFEE website should be the working site. Dreamweaver 8 differences are indicated with parentheses (*ver.8:*).

① **ADD COPY FROM A TEXT FILE**

  a. Start Notepad.

  b. Open the AFRICA.txt file, a text file provided with the data files for this text.

  c. Select Edit ➝ Select All. All the text is selected.

  d. Select Edit ➝ Copy. The text is copied to the Windows Clipboard.

② **PASTE THE TEXT**

  a. Switch to Dreamweaver.

  b. Display the africa.htm web page document.

  c. Place the insertion point in the empty paragraph below the "Africa" heading.

  d. Select Edit ➝ Paste. The text is pasted.

  e. In the CSS Styles panel, attach the COFFEE_styles.css style sheet.

  f. Apply the topnavbar, localnavbar, btrail, and footer styles appropriately. Remember the footer style will need to be applied to both the bottom navigation bar and the library item.

  g. Save the modified africa.htm and then close the web page document.

③ **ATTACH THE STYLE SHEET TO OTHER PAGES**

  a. Open the coffee_around_world.htm, latin_america.htm, and indonesia.htm web page documents and link the COFFEE_styles.css style sheet.

  b. Apply the topnavbar, localnavbar, btrail, and footer styles appropriately. Remember the footer style will need to be applied to both the bottom navigation bar and the library item.

④ **CHANGE HYPERLINK COLORS**

  a. Display the index.htm web page document.

  b. In the CSS Styles panel, click the New CSS Style button (🔲) (*ver.8:* called New CSS Rule button). A dialog box is displayed.

    1. Select Advanced (IDs, pseudo-class selectors).

    2. In the Selector list, select a:link.

    3. In the Define in list, select COFFEE_styles.css.

  c. Select OK. A dialog box is displayed.

  d. In the Type category, click the Color box and select the color that corresponds to #666633 (*ver.8:* dialog box name is different):

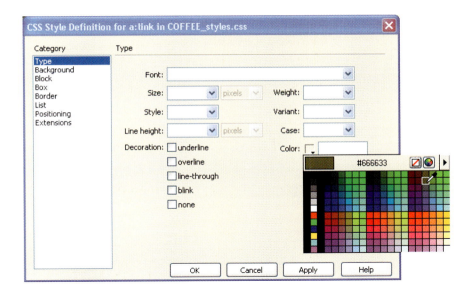

e. Select OK. The hyperlink color is changed.

f. In the CSS Styles panel, click the New CSS Style button (⬛) (*ver.8:* called New CSS Rule button). A dialog box is displayed.

    1. Select Advanced (IDs, pseudo-class selectors).

    2. In the Selector list, select a:visited.

    3. In the Define in list, select COFFEE_styles.css.

g. Select OK. A dialog box is displayed.

h. In the Type category, click the Color box and select the color that corresponds to #993300 (*ver.8:* dialog box name is different):

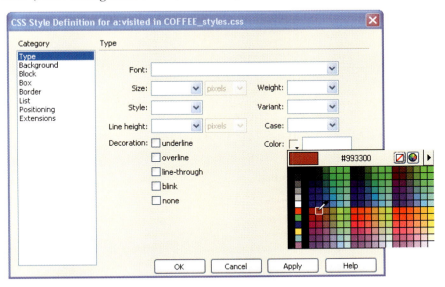

i. Select OK. The visited hyperlink color is changed.

j. Select File ➜ Save All. All open web page documents are saved.

a. View the website in a browser. Note the consistency between the pages.

b. Print a copy of each web page from the browser.

c. Close the browser window.

d. Quit Notepad.

Cascading Style Sheets – Positioning

The start of this chapter explained how typography choices are more complicated for a web page than for a print document. Placement issues are also more complicated. Tables are one way to control the layout of elements on a web page. Another technique used to control layout of elements on a web page is absolute positioning. *Absolute positioning* allows an element, such as an image to be placed at a specific location on a web page. Absolute positioning is specified in a cascading style sheet and is referred to as CSS-P (Cascading Style Sheets-Positioning).

absolute positioning

TIP The # sign creates an ID attribute in the div tag and is used to assign a unique name to the element.

CSS-P requires a CSS style to be defined and then the style is applied to a <div> tag, which represents a specific area on a page. In the CSS Styles panel, click the New CSS Style button (⬛), which displays the New CSS Style dialog box. Select the Advanced option, type a descriptive name in the Name box preceded by a #, and then select OK. The CSS Style Definition dialog box is displayed. Select Positioning to display those options:

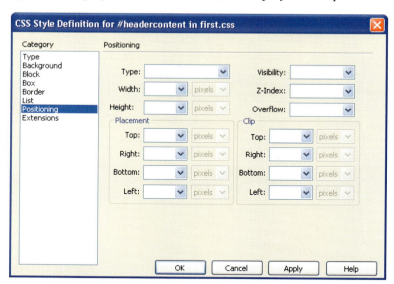

TIP To help with positioning, select View → Rulers to display the ruler.

Select absolute or relative in the Type list. Absolute uses the upper-left corner of the page as the origin for the top and left settings and relative uses the current position as the origin for the specified settings. Placement values can then be entered.

TIP Absolute positioning can be applied to an inline <div> tag instead of a style sheet. Dreamweaver refers to inline <div> tags as layers.

To apply the style to a <div> tag, place the insertion point and then select the Insert Div Tag button (⬛) from the Layout category in the Insert bar, which displays the Insert Div Tag dialog box:

Chapter 6 Typography, Style Sheets, and Color

Select the CSS rule from the ID list and then select the tag placement from the Insert list. The options in the Insert list vary depending on the page elements and whether text is selected.

Practice: COFFEE – part 7 of 7

Dreamweaver should be started and the COFFEE website should be the working site. Dreamweaver 8 differences are indicated with parentheses (*ver.8:*).

① **ADD AN IMAGE USING ABSOLUTE POSITIONING**

    a. Display the coffee_around_world.htm web page document.

    b. In the first cell in the top row, place the insertion point to the right of the Global Bean logo.

    c. In the CSS Styles panel, click the New CSS Style button (🔂) (*ver.8:* called New CSS Rule button). A dialog box is displayed.

        1. Select Advanced (IDs, pseudo-class selectors).

        2. In the Selector list, type: #coffeemap

        3. In the Define in list, select COFFEE_styles.css.

    d. Select OK. A dialog box is displayed.

    e. In the Positioning category, set attributes to (*ver.8:* dialog box name is different):

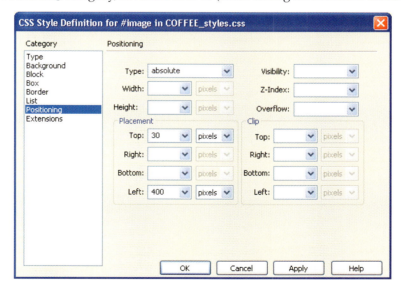

    f. Select OK.

② APPLY THE STYLE TO A <DIV> TAG

a. In the Layout category in the Insert bar, click the Insert Div Tag button (⊞). A dialog box is displayed.

  1. In the ID list, select coffeemap.

b. Select OK. The "coffeemap" area is defined on the page:

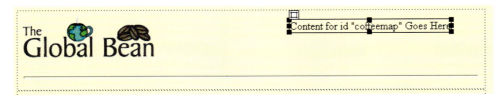

c. In the Files panel, in the images folder, drag the coffeemap.gif image into the "coffeemap" area. (*ver.8:* If the Image Tag Accessibility Attributes dialog box appears, select Cancel.) Note that the image is able to overlap the horizontal rule, creating a layered effect. The image will retain its placement position regardless of the screen resolution or monitor size.

d. Place the insertion point in the "coffeemap" area and delete all of the "Content for id "coffeemap" Goes Here" text.

e. Select File ➜ Save All.

Check — your document should look similar to:

③ VIEW COFFEE_AROUND_WORLD.HTM IN A BROWSER

a. View the coffee_around_world.htm in a browser.

b. Print a copy of coffee_around_world.htm from the browser.

c. Close the browser window.

d. Quit Dreamweaver.

Chapter Summary

Typography refers to the arrangement, shape, size, style, and weight of text. A typeface is a set of letters drawn in a specific style. The word font technically refers to a specific size and weight of a single typeface. In order for a font to display correctly in a browser, the user must have the font installed on their computer.

Font categories include serif and sans serif font. When choosing sizes for the text on a web page, keep usability in mind. Type styles indicate variations of the characters. Line height is the distance from one line of text to another. In a paragraph, left alignment is the most readable and therefore provides the highest degree of usability.

A style sheet defines the type, paragraph, and page formats for a web page document. A single style sheet can be applied to all the pages in a website to achieve a consistent look. The CSS Styles panel is used for linking, creating, and modifying style sheets. A CSS document can have rules, which modify HTML elements and classes, which are a set of declarations that can be applied to different tags.

Headings are used in text to indicate a hierarchy and help with readability. HTML includes six headings tags, ranging from <h1> through <h6>. A paragraph that should be set off from other paragraphs, such as a quotation, can be indented using a blockquote. A numbered list shows a priority of importance for each step. A bulleted list contains a set of items where each item is equally important.

Color can be added to a web page in many ways: text, page background, and table cells. Colors that go together well can be determined with a color wheel. Colored text needs to be large enough and contrast with the background enough to be easily read.

A long web page is easier to navigate if hyperlinks are provided to different parts of the page. Hyperlinks to different parts of the same page are linked to a named anchor. Hyperlink colors can be changed. However, a lot of design consideration should go into the decision to change hyperlink colors because users recognize the standard blue and purple colors.

Web development often involves collaborating with others to get the content for a website. This may require copying and pasting text.

Absolute positioning allows an element, such as an image to be placed at a specific location on a web page. Absolute positioning is specified in a cascading style sheet and is referred to as CSS-P (Cascading Style Sheets-Positioning).

Alignment   A paragraph format that refers to the position of the lines of text relative to the sides of a cell. Paragraph alignments include left, centered, right, and justified.

Analogous   Three adjacent colors on the color wheel.

Bulleted List   A list of items where each item is equally important.

Cascading The effect of applying rules from one style sheet in addition to those in another style sheet.

Class   A set of declarations that can be applied to different tags.

Color wheel   Colors from red to violet that are arranged chromatically in a circle. Used to determine colors that go together well.

Complementary   Colors that are directly opposite each other on the color wheel.

Cool colors   Blue, green, and violet colors.

Copy   Refers to text content.

CSS Selector Style   Defines a style for a tag and attribute combination. Used to change hyperlink colors.

Declarations   The formats to be applied in a rule.

Font   A specific size and weight of a single typeface.

Line Height   The distance from one line of text to another.

Named Anchor   A hyperlink destination that is located on the same web page document as the hyperlink.

Numbered List A list of items where each item has a priority of importance.

Point Unit used to measure the size of printed text. One point is 1/72 of an inch.

Regular   Text that has no style applied to it.

Rule   A selector and its declaration(s) which are used to modify an HTML element.

Sans serif   Characters without the small extensions (serifs) on their ends.

Selector   The HTML element being redefined in a rule.

Serif The small extensions on the ends of the strokes of a character.

Style   Variations of characters including bold and italic.

Style Sheet   Used to define the type, paragraph, and page formats for a web page document.

Triad   Three equally-spaced colors on the color wheel.

Typeface   A set of letters drawn in a specific style.

Typography   The arrangement, shape, size, style, and weight of text.

Warm colors   Red, orange, and yellow colors.

⮥ (*ver.8:* ⬤) **Attach Style Sheet button** Links a style sheet to the open web page document. Found in the CSS Styles panel.

["] **Block Quote button** Indents a paragraph. Found in the Text category in the Insert bar.

B **Bold button** Creates strong text, which is displayed as bold text. Found in the Text category in the Insert bar.

Change Link command Displays a dialog box used to modify a hyperlink. Found in the Modify menu.

Copy command Copies selected text. Found in the Edit menu.

🗑 **Delete CSS Style button** Deletes a style. Found in the CSS Styles panel.

📝 (*ver.8:* ✏) **Edit Style Sheet button** Displays a dialog box used to modify attributes or duplicate styles. Found in the CSS Styles panel.

em **Emphasize button** Creates emphasized text, which is displayed as italic text. Found in the Text category in the Insert bar.

h1 **Heading 1 button** Formats the selected text in heading 1. Found in the Text category in the Insert bar.

I **Italic button** Creates emphasized text, which is displayed as italic text. Found in the Text category in the Insert bar.

⚓ **Named anchor button** Creates a named anchor at the location of the insertion point. Found in the Common category in the Insert bar.

⮥ **New CSS Style button** Adds a new style or a new class to a style sheet. Found in the CSS Styles panel.

:☰ **Ordered list button** Converts selected paragraphs to a numbered list. Found in the Property inspector.

¶ **Paragraph button** Inserts <p> and </p> around selected text. Found in the Text category in the Insert bar.

Paragraph Format command Displays a submenu used to insert heading tags. Found in the Text menu.

Paste command Pastes copied text. Found in the Edit menu.

Remove Link command Removes an existing link. Found in the Modify menu.

Save All command Saves all open documents.

S **Strong button** Creates strong text, which is displayed as bold text. Found in the Text category in the Insert bar.

⬝≡ **Text Indent button** Indents a paragraph. Found in the Property inspector.

⬝≡ **Text Outdent button** Removes blockquotes from a paragraph. Found in the Property inspector.

⦂☰ **Unordered list button** Converts selected paragraphs to a bulleted list. Found in the Property inspector.

Review Questions

1. What does typography refer to?

2. a) What is a typeface?
   b) What is a font?

3. a) Why does Dreamweaver only list commonly available fonts?
   b) List four fonts that are available on most computers.
   c) Why are fonts grouped?
   d) What is the difference between a serif and a sans serif font?

4. a) What is the maximum number of fonts that should be used on a single web page?
   b) List three ways text size can be specified in Dreamweaver.

5. What is line height?

6. a) What can bold type be used to indicate?
   b) What font size should italic style be applied to?

7. a) What does the alignment of text in a paragraph refer to?
   b) List the four paragraph alignments.

8. What does a style sheet define?

9. List the steps required to create a new style sheet named school_styles.css.

10. a) What does a rule modify?
    b) What is a rule comprised of?

11. List the steps required to create a rule for the p tag that sets the size attribute to 14 pixels.

12. What is a class?

13. List the steps required to create and apply a new class named .footer to selected text.

14. List the step required to insert <p> and </p> around selected text.

15. What two buttons can be clicked to display selected text as bold?

16. Why is it often faster to duplicate a style than to create a new one?

17. What are headings used to indicate and help with?

18. List the steps required to indent a paragraph.

19. a) List the steps required to format three paragraphs as items in a numbered list.
    b) What is a bulleted list?

20. a) What are complementary colors?
    b) What are analogous colors?

21. Which color combination would be easier for the user to read: red text on a pink background, or black text on a white background?

22. List the steps required to change the background color of a web page to #CCFF66.

23. a) What is a named anchor?
    b) What type of web page would be most likely to use hyperlinks to named anchors?

24. Why should a lot of design consideration go into the decision to change hyperlink colors?

25. What is copy?

26. List the steps required to copy content from a TXT file into a web page document.

27. What is absolute positioning?

True/False

28. Determine if each of the following are true or false. If false, explain why.
    a) Serifs are the small extensions found on the end of letters.
    b) Text written in all capital letters is easier to read than text written in lowercase letters.
    c) Left alignment is the most readable for paragraph text.
    d) A style sheet can only be applied to the home page of a website.
    e) Class names must begin with a dot.
    f) There are twelve HTML heading tags.
    g) The Unordered List button creates a numbered list.
    h) Red is a warm color.
    i) The background of a web page document is changed by redefining the head tag.

Exercise 1 ——————————— GREECE

The GREECE website was last modified in Chapter 5, Exercise 1. Use Dreamweaver to further modify the GREECE website by completing the following steps:

a) In Dreamweaver, open the GREECE website for editing.

b) Modify the index.htm web page document as follows:

    1. Link a new style sheet named greece_style.css to the web page document.

    2. Select the text in the cell to the left of the map. Tag the text with paragraph tags.

    3. Create a new style that redefines the p tag as follows:

        Type category: set Font to Verdana, Arial, Helvetica, sans-serif, Size to 14 pixels, and Line height to 26 pixels

        Block category: set Text align to left

    4. Create a new class style named .footer that includes the formats:

        Type category: set Font to Verdana, Arial, Helvetica, sans-serif, and Size to 12 pixels

        Block category: set Text align to center

    5. Apply the footer style to the cells containing the bottom navigation bar and the library item.

c) Modify the itinerary.htm web page document as follows:

    1. Link the greece_style.css style sheet to the web page document.

    2. In the first paragraph of the content, tag the text Itinerary with Heading 1 tags.

    3. Tag the text Day 1, Day 2, Day 3, Day 4, Day 5, Day 6, and Day 7 with Heading 2 tags.

    4. Create a new style that redefines the h1 tag as follows:

        Type category: set Font to Verdana, Arial, Helvetica, sans-serif, Size to 30 pixels, and Weight to bold

        Block category: set Text align to left

    5. Create a new style that redefines the h2 tag as follows:

        Type category: set Font to Verdana, Arial, Helvetica, sans-serif, Size to 20 pixels, and Weight to bold

        Block category: set Text align to left

    6. Below Day 1, after the text Stay in Athens., press Enter and then type the text: Back to top

    7. For each of the remaining days, add the text Back to top after the last itinerary item.

    8. Select just the itinerary items (not the text "Back to top") under "Day 1" and tag them as an unordered list.

9. Create unordered lists for the itinerary items in the remaining six days.

10. Create a new style that redefines the ul tag as follows:

> Type category: set Font to Verdana, Arial, Helvetica, sans-serif, Size to 14 pixels, and Line height to 30 pixels
>
> List category: set Type to square

11. To the left of Itinerary, insert an anchor named: top

12. To the left of the "Day 1," insert an anchor named: Day_1

13. To the left of the remaining "Day" headings, insert appropriately named anchors.

14. Below the Itinerary heading, type the following text, inserting a line break at the end of each line:

> Day 1
> Day 2
> Day 3
> Day 4
> Day 5
> Day 6
> Day 7

15. Link Day 1, Day 2, Day 3, Day 4, Day 5, Day 6, and Day 7 to the appropriate named anchor.

16. Link the Back to top text under each "Day" heading to the top anchor.

17. Apply the footer style to the cells containing the bottom navigation bar and the library item.

d) Modify the photos.htm web page document as follows:

1. Link the greece_style.css style sheet to the web page document.

2. Create a new class style named .caption that includes the formats:

> Type category: set Font to Verdana, Arial, Helvetica, sans-serif, Size to 14 pixels, and Weight to bold
>
> Block category: set Text align to center

3. Apply the caption style to the text below each of the photos.

4. Apply the footer style to the cells containing the bottom navigation bar and the library item.

e) View each web page document in a browser window.

f) Print a copy of each web page document from the browser.

Exercise 2 ⟳ ————————————————————— CACTUS

The CACTUS website was last modified in Chapter 5, Exercise 2. Use Dreamweaver to further modify the CACTUS website by completing the following steps:

a) In Dreamweaver, open the CACTUS website for editing.

b) Modify the index.htm web page document as follows:

1. Link a new style sheet named cactus_style.css to the web page document.

2. Create a new style that redefines the p tag as follows:

    Type category: set Font to Georgia, "Times New Roman", Times, serif. Size to 14 pixels, and Line height to 26 pixels

    Block category: set Text align to left

3. Create a new selector style that redefines a:link as follows:

    Type category: set Color to a dark green that corresponds to #009900

4. Create a new selector style that redefines a:visited as follows:

    Type category: set Color to a brown-green that corresponds to #666600

5. Create a new class style named .footer that includes the formats:

    Type category: set Font to Arial, Helvetica, sans-serif, Size to 12 pixels, and Color to a dark green that corresponds to #009900

    Block category: set Text align to center

6. Apply the footer style to the cells containing the bottom navigation bar and the library item.

c) Modify the gallery.htm web page document as follows:

1. Link the cactus_style.css style sheet to the web page document.

2. In the first cell of the content, tag the text A Gallery of Cactus Photographs with Heading 1 tags.

3. Create a new style that redefines the h1 tag as follows:

    Type category: set Font to Arial, Helvetica, sans-serif, Size to 32 pixels, Weight to bold, and Color to a dark green that corresponds to #009900

    Block category: set Text align to center

4. Create a new class style named .caption that includes the formats:

    Type category: set Font to Arial, Helvetica, sans-serif, Size to 16 pixels

    Block category: set Text align to center

5. Apply the caption style to the text below each of the photos.

6. For each caption, select only the cactus name (not the pronunciation text) and then tag the text with <strong> and </strong>.

7. Create a new style that redefines the Strong tag as follows:

    Type category: set Weight to bold

8. Apply the footer style to the cells containing the bottom navigation bar and the library item.

d) Modify the types.htm web page document as follows:

    1. Link the cactus_style.css style sheet to the web page document.

    2. Tag the text Types of Cacti with Heading 1 tags.

    3. Select and tag each of the cacti names in the remaining paragraphs with <strong> and </strong>.

    4. Apply the footer style to the cells containing the bottom navigation bar and the library item.

e) View each web page document in a browser window.

f) Print a copy of each web page document from the browser.

Exercise 3 ────────────────────────── FRUIT

The FRUIT website was last modified in Chapter 5, Exercise 3. Use Dreamweaver to further modify the FRUIT website by completing the following steps:

a) In Dreamweaver, open the FRUIT website for editing.

b) Modify the index.htm web page document as follows:

    1. Link a new style sheet named fruit_style.css to the web page document.

    2. Create a new style that redefines the body tag as follows:

        Background category: set Background color to a light yellow that corresponds to #FFFFCC

    3. Create a new style that redefines the p tag as follows:

        Type category: set Font to Verdana, Arial, Helvetica, sans-serif, Size to 14 pixels, and Line height to 28 pixels

        Block category: set Text align to left

    4. Create a new class style named .footer that includes the formats:

        Type category: set Font to Verdana, Arial, Helvetica, sans-serif, Size to 12 pixels, and Line height to 22 pixels

        Block category: set Text align to left

    5. Apply the footer style to the cells containing the bottom navigation bar and the library item.

c) Modify the apple.htm web page document as follows:

    1. Link the fruit_style.css style sheet to the web page document.

    2. In the first paragraph of the content, tag the text Nutrition with Heading 2 tags.

    3. Tag the text Selection and Storage and Common Types with Heading 2 tags.

    4. Create a new style that redefines the h2 tag as follows:

        Type category: set Font to Verdana, Arial, Helvetica, sans-serif, Size to 22 pixels, and Weight to bold

        Block category: set Text align to left

5. Tag the two paragraphs below the "Nutrition" heading as an unordered list.

6. Tag the two paragraphs below the "Selection and Storage" heading as an unordered list.

7. Tag the four paragraphs below the text "There are thousands of varieties…" as an unordered list.

8. Create a new style that redefines the ul tag as follows:

   Type category: set Font to Verdana, Arial, Helvetica, sans-serif, and Size to 14 pixels

   List category: set Type to disc

9. Apply the footer style to the cells containing the bottom navigation bar and the library item.

d) Modify the banana.htm web page document as follows:

1. Link the fruit_style.css style sheet to the web page document.

2. In the first paragraph of the content, tag the text Nutrition with Heading 2 tags.

3. Tag the text Selection and Storage and Common Types with Heading 2 tags.

4. Tag the two paragraphs below the "Nutrition" heading as an unordered list.

5. Tag the two paragraphs below the "Selection and Storage" heading as an unordered list.

6. Tag the four paragraphs below the "Common Types" heading as an unordered list.

7. Apply the footer style to the cells containing the bottom navigation bar and the library item.

e) Modify the orange.htm web page document as follows:

1. Link the fruit_style.css style sheet to the web page document.

2. In the first paragraph of the content, tag the text Nutrition with Heading 2 tags.

3. Tag the text Selection and Storage and Common Types with Heading 2 tags.

4. Tag the two paragraphs below the "Nutrition" heading as an unordered list.

5. Tag the three paragraphs below the "Selection and Storage" heading as an unordered list.

6. Tag the three paragraphs below the "Common Types" heading as an unordered list.

7. Apply the footer style to the cells containing the bottom navigation bar and the library item.

f) View each web page document in a browser window.

g) Print a copy of each web page document from the browser.

Exercise 4 ✦ ━━━━━━━━━━━━━━━ COMPUTER MAINTENANCE

The COMPUTER MAINTENANCE website was last modified in Chapter 5, Exercise 4. Use Dreamweaver to further modify the COMPUTER MAINTENANCE website by completing the following steps:

a) In Dreamweaver, open the COMPUTER MAINTENANCE website for editing.

b) Modify the index.htm web page document as follows:

   1. Link a new style sheet named com_style.css to the web page document.

   2. Create a new style that redefines the p tag as follows:

      Type category: set Font to Arial, Helvetica, sans-serif, Size to 12 pixels, and Line height to 18 pixels

      Block category: set Text align to left

   3. Create a new class style named .footer that includes the formats:

      Type category: set Font to Arial, Helvetica, sans-serif, Size to 10 pixels, and Line height to 20 pixels

      Block category: set Text align to center

   4. Apply the footer style to the cells containing the bottom navigation bar and the library item.

c) Modify the cleaning.htm, disks.htm, and updates.htm web page documents as follows:

   1. Link the com_styles.css style sheet to the web page documents.

   2. Apply the footer style to the cells containing the bottom navigation bar and the library item.

d) View each web page document in a browser window.

e) Print a copy of each web page document from the browser.

Exercise 5 ———————————————— SEVEN WONDERS

The SEVEN WONDERS website was last modified in Chapter 5, Exercise 5. Use Dreamweaver to further modify the SEVEN WONDERS website by completing the following steps:

a) In Dreamweaver, open the SEVEN WONDERS website for editing.

b) Modify the index.htm web page document as follows:

   1. Link a new style sheet named seven_wonders_style.css to the web page document.

   2. Create a new style that redefines the p tag as follows:

      Type category: set Font to Verdana, Arial, Helvetica, sans-serif, Size to 14 pixels, and Line height to 24 pixels

      Block category: set Text align to left

   3. Create a new class style named .topnavbar that includes the formats:

      Type category: set Font to Verdana, Arial, Helvetica, sans-serif, Size to 12 pixels, and Line height to 24 pixels

      Block category: set Text align to left

   4. Apply the topnavbar style to the cell containing the top navigation bar.

   5. Create a new class style named .footer that includes the formats:

      Type category: set Font to Verdana, Arial, Helvetica, sans-serif, Size to 10 pixels, and Line height to 18 pixels

      Block category: set Text align to left

   6. Apply the footer style to the cells containing the bottom navigation bar and the library item.

c) Modify the colossus.htm web page document as follows:

   1. Link the seven_wonders_style.css style sheet to the web page document.

   2. Tag the text SEVEN WONDERS - Colossus of Rhodes with Heading 1 tags.

   3. Create a new style that redefines the h1 tag as follows:

      Type category: set Font to Verdana, Arial, Helvetica, sans-serif, Size to 28 pixels, and Weight to bold

      Block category: set Text align to left

   4. Apply the footer style to the cells containing the bottom navigation bar and the library item.

d) Modify the hanging.htm, lighthouse.htm, mausoleum.htm, pyramids.htm, statue.htm, and temple.htm web page documents as follows:

   1. Link the seven_wonders_style.css style sheet to the web page document.

   2. Tag the text in the first cell with Heading 1 tags.

   3. Apply the footer style to the cells containing the bottom navigation bar and the library item.

e) View each web page document in a browser window.

f) Print a copy of each web page document from the browser.

Exercise 6

Some of the websites developed in the exercises of Chapters 3 through 5 do not have style sheets attached. Choose one of the following websites and then complete the steps below to attach a style sheet and apply formatting to the website:

Website	Last Modified
Clouds	Chapter 3 Exercise 2
Sharks	Chapter 3 Exercise 3
E-commerce	Chapter 3 Exercise 4
Hockey League	Chapter 4 Exercise 1
Volcanoes	Chapter 4 Exercise 2
Lawn Care	Chapter 4 Exercise 3
METEOROLOGY	Chapter 4 Exercise 4
Etiquette	Chapter 4 Exercise 6

a) Link a new style sheet with an appropriate name to the index.htm web page document.

b) Redefine the body tag if a background color is appropriate for the website.

c) Redefine the p tag to format paragraph text with an appropriate font, font size, line height, and paragraph alignment.

d) Create selector styles that redefine hyperlink colors where appropriate.

e) Create class styles to format navigation bars, breadcrumb trails, and footer text.

f) Link the style sheet to the other web page documents in the website.

g) For each page of the website, do the following:

　　1. Check the document for text that should have been affected when the p tag was redefined in the previous step. Tag text with paragraph tags where needed.

　　2. Create named anchors and links to the named anchors as appropriate.

　　3. Tag text as appropriate using Heading 1 and Heading 2 tags and then redefine the h1 and h2 tags.

　　4. Tag text as appropriate to create lists and then redefine the ol or the ul tag.

　　5. Apply styles as appropriate.

h) Preview the website in a browser. When satisfied with the website, print a copy of each web page document from the browser.

Exercise 7

The Rubrics website was last modified in Chapter 5, Exercise 7. Use Dreamweaver to further modify the Rubrics website by completing the following steps:

a) In Dreamweaver, open the Rubrics website for editing.

b) Create a new web page document naming it: style_rubric.htm

c) Modify the index.htm web page document as follows:

   1. Link a new style sheet named rubric_style.css to the web page document.

   2. Create a new style that redefines the p tag as follows:

      Type category: set Font to Arial, Helvetica, sans-serif, Size to 12 pixels, and Line height to 18 pixels

      Block category: set Text align to left

   3. Check the document for text that should have been affected when the p tag was redefined in the previous step. Tag text with paragraph tags where needed.

   4. Create a new class style named .middle that includes the formats:

      Type category: set Font to Arial, Helvetica, sans-serif, Size to 12 pixels, and Line height to 18 pixels

      Block category: set Text align to center

   5. Apply the middle style to the cell containing the footer library item.

   6. In the third row, place the insertion point at the end of the text Images Rubric, press Enter, and then type the text: Style Sheet Rubric

   7. Link the text Style Sheet Rubric to style_rubric.htm.

   8. Apply the middle style to the cell in the third row.

d) Modify the style_rubric.htm web page document as follows:

   1. Change the page title to: Style Sheet Rubric

   2. Open the wpd_rubric.htm document, copy the entire table and paste it into the style_rubric.htm web page document.

   3. In the top cell, replace the text with: Style Sheet Rubric

   4. In the second row, replace the text single web page document with the text:

      style sheet in a website

   5. Replace the first three criteria with these criteria:

      1. The same style sheet is used in all of the web pages in the website.

      2. The styles enhance the web page content.

      3. The styles enhance the user's experience.

   6. Brainstorm in small groups to generate two additional style sheet rubric criteria. Replace the last two criteria in the rubric with these two.

e) Modify the wpd_rubric, img_rubric.htm, and style_rubric.htm web page documents as follows:

    1. Link the rubric_style.css style sheet to the web page document.

    2. Check the document for text that should have been affected when the p tag was redefined. Tag text with paragraph tags where needed.

    3. Apply the middle style to all the cells that just contain numbers. There should be a row of these cells below each criteria.

    4. Apply the middle style to the cell that contains the link to Home and to the cell that contains the footer library item.

f) Check the spelling in the style_rubric.htm web page document.

g) View the index.htm and style_rubric.htm web page documents in a browser window.

h) Print a copy of index.htm and style_rubric.htm from the browser.

i) In a browser window, view the web pages of a website with a style sheet that a peer has created. Use the style sheet rubric to evaluate the website.

j) Reflect on the design of the rubric. Does it appropriately assess the style sheet of a website? Are there criteria that should be added or changed? Make any appropriate revisions and print a copy.

Chapter 7
Introducing Flash

This chapter introduces Flash and explains how to create Flash movies. Customizing Flash buttons and Flash text in Dreamweaver are also discussed.

Flash

Flash technology is used to create a movie file for a website. A *Flash movie file* can be an animated button, animated text, or an entire web application. For example, the interactive web application shown below was created with Flash:

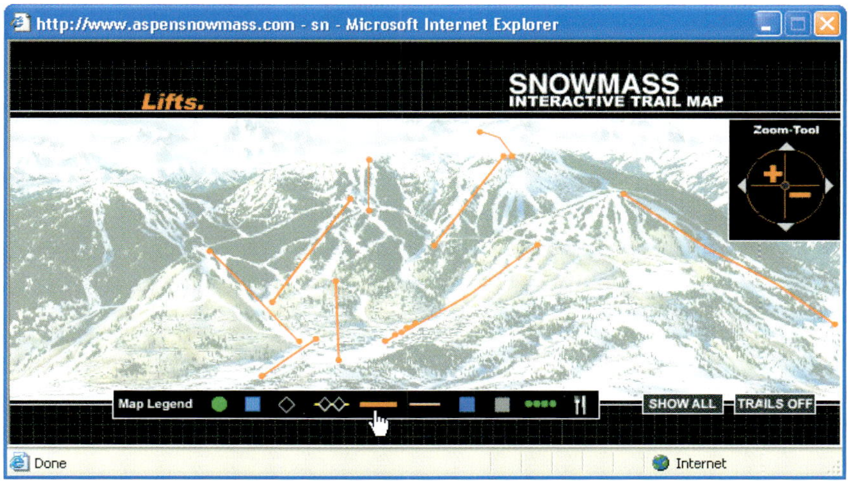

Pointing to a symbol in the Map Legend changes the displayed information in the map

Flash buttons and Flash text can be created directly in Dreamweaver. However, animations beyond these and web applications must be created in Flash, the interactive authoring application that is part of the Macromedia Studio suite.

> ***Flash***
>
> Flash was originally called FutureSplash until the company that developed it was purchased by Macromedia, and the name was changed to Flash.

> ***The Flash Player Plug-in***
>
> The Flash Player is incorporated into the Windows XP operating system and the latest versions of Netscape Navigator, Internet Explorer, and America Online. It can also be downloaded for free at www.macromedia.com.

Creating Flash Buttons in Dreamweaver

Dreamweaver includes predefined Flash buttons that can be added to a web page:

Samples of predefined Flash buttons in Dreamweaver

Flash buttons can have customized text, font, size, and color.

A web page document must be saved before creating a Flash button. To create a Flash button, place the insertion point in the web page document and then click arrow next to the Media button in the **Common** category in the Insert bar and select **Flash Button**:

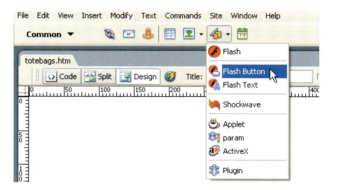

The Insert Flash Button dialog box is displayed:

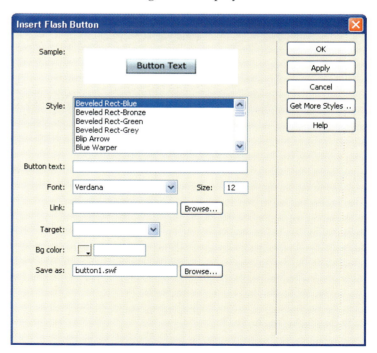

- Point to the button in the Sample area to preview the behavior for the Over state, and click to preview the Down state.

- Different buttons are selected in the Style list.

- Change the text that will be displayed on the button in the Button text box.

- Select a different font for the button text in the Font list.

- Change the point size of the button text in the Size box.

- The file name or URL for the button's hyperlink is added in the Link box. Click Browse to display a dialog box where the web page document file name can be selected.

- Bg color is the background color of the button. This color should match the background of the web page document.

- A Flash button is saved as a Flash movie file with an .swf extension. The Save as box displays the location and name of the Flash movie file. Click Browse to display a dialog box where the appropriate folder can be selected.

Version 8 Dreamweaver 8 differences are indicated with parentheses (*ver.8:*).

TIP Click Apply instead of OK to insert the Flash button in the web page document and leave the dialog box open for editing.

TIP A Flash button can also be edited by clicking ⬚ Edit... in the Property inspector.

Click OK to insert the Flash button into the web page document. (*ver.8: The Flash Accessibility Attributes dialog box may appear when inserting a Flash button. Select Cancel to place the button.*)

To preview a Flash button in Design view, select the button and then click ▶ Play in the Property inspector. Click ■ Stop to end the preview. Flash buttons can also be previewed by viewing the web page document in a browser.

To edit a Flash button, double-click the button to display the Insert Flash Button dialog box.

Arranging Flash Buttons in a Web Page Document

Flash buttons added to a web page document should be arranged in a nested table with each button in a separate cell:

Each cell is sized to the width of the button

To create a nested table, first place the insertion point in the cell of an existing table and then create a new table. A nested table and its cells should be sized in pixels to prevent buttons from wrapping in a browser when the browser window is resized. The table and cell widths can be determined after creating a button by selecting the button and then checking the W property in the Property inspector.

The Align property in the Property inspector can be set to change the alignment within a cell for a selected Flash button.

Dreamweaver 8 differences are indicated with parentheses (*ver.8:*).

① OPEN THE SAMPLER WEBSITE FOR EDITING

a. Start Dreamweaver.

b. Open the SAMPLER website for editing, which is a website provided with the data files for this text.

c. Familiarize yourself with the files and folders for this website.

d. Open the index.htm web page document and view the page in a browser.

e. Click the links to explore the other web pages in the website.

f. Close the browser window. Dreamweaver is displayed.

g. Open the header library item.

h. Replace the text Name with your name.

i. Save and close the library item, allowing Dreamweaver to update all the files.

② INSERT A NESTED TABLE

a. Display the index.htm web page document if it is not already displayed.

b. Place the insertion point in the empty cell in the second row.

c. Add a table with the following specifications:

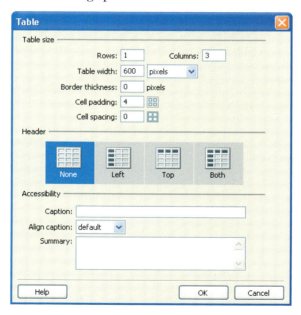

Check—Your index.htm web page document should look similar to:

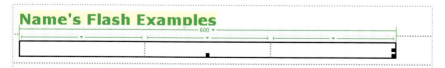

③ INSERT A FLASH BUTTON

a. Place the insertion point in the left cell of the nested table.

b. In the Common category in the Insert bar, click the Media button arrow, then click Flash Button. A dialog box is displayed.

c. In the Style list, select Blue Warper.

d. In the Sample box, point to the sample button to preview the Over state behavior. Click the button to view the Down state behavior.

e. In the Button text box, type: Rollover Text

f. In the Font box, select Verdana.

g. In the Size box, type 12.

h. Next to the Link box, click Browse. A dialog box is displayed.

    1. Select the rollover.htm web page document.

    2. Select OK.

i Next to the Save as box, click Browse. A dialog box is displayed.

    1. In the File name box, type: rollover_text.swf

    2. Select Save.

j. Select OK. (*ver.8:* If the Flash Accessibility Attributes dialog box appears, select Cancel.) The dialog box is removed and the Flash button is inserted in the cell. The nested cell widths may have changed.

④ **RESIZE THE CELLS AND TABLE**

a. Click the Flash button to select it, if it is not already selected. In the Property inspector, the W property displays 103 for the width of the button.

b. Click beside the Flash button to place the insertion point in the same cell. Cell properties are displayed in the Property inspector.

c. In the Property inspector, set W to 103 and press Enter. The cell width changes.

d. Resize the two remaining cells by placing the insertion point in each cell and then setting W to 103 for each.

e. Select the entire nested table and set W to 333 and press Enter.

Check—Your web page document with the nested table should look similar to:

⑤ **VIEW THE DOCUMENT IN A BROWSER**

a. Save the modified index.htm.

b. Press F12. The document is displayed in a browser window.

c. Point to the button. The animated effects play.

d. Click the button. The rollover.htm web page document is displayed.

e. Close the browser window. Dreamweaver is displayed.

Using Flash Movie Files

TIP It may be necessary to select 🔳 → Refresh Site List in the Files panel group to update the list of movies.

Flash movies in a website are listed in the Flash category in the Assets panel. Click the Flash icon (🔶) in the Assets panel to display the list:

The selected image, order.swf in the example above, is displayed in the preview area. Click the ▶ button in the preview area to play the Flash movie and display the ■ button. Click the ■ button to end the movie.

Drag a Flash movie from the Assets panel to an open web page document to place it, or click [Insert] at the bottom of the Assets panel to place the selected movie at the insertion point. (*ver.8:* The Object Tag Accessibility Attributes dialog box may appear when inserting a Flash button. Select Cancel to place the button.)

create a navigation bar   Navigation bars usually have more than one button. Rather than recreating each button from scratch, an existing Flash button in the Assets panel can be placed in a web page document and then modified and saved with a different name. This approach ensures a consistent look among buttons in the same website.

Practice: SAMPLER – part 2 of 10

Dreamweaver should be started and the SAMPLER website should be the working site. Dreamweaver 8 differences are indicated with parentheses (*ver.8:*).

① VIEW THE FLASH CATEGORY IN THE ASSETS PANEL

In the Assets panel, click the Flash icon (🔶). The Flash movie file is displayed. If no file is displayed, select 🔳 → Refresh Site List from the Files panel group.

② CREATE A SECOND BUTTON IN THE NAVIGATION BAR

a. Open the index.htm web page document, if it is not already displayed.

b. In the Assets panel, drag the rollover_text.swf file name to the middle cell of the nested table. (*ver.8:* If the Object Tag Accessibility Attributes dialog box appears, select Cancel.)

c. Double-click the middle Flash button. A dialog box is displayed.

d. In the Button text box, type: Animation

e. Next to the Link box, click Browse. A dialog box is displayed.

   1. Select the animation.htm web page document.

   2. Select OK.

f. Next to the Save as box, click Browse. A dialog box is displayed.

    1. In the File name box, type: animation.swf

    2. Select Save.

g. Select OK. (*ver.8:* If the Flash Accessibility Attributes dialog box appears, select Cancel.) The dialog box is removed and the Flash button is updated.

h. In the Assets panel, select ▦ ➔ Refresh Site List from the Files panel group. The animation.swf Flash movie file is displayed in the list.

③ CREATE A THIRD BUTTON IN THE NAVIGATION BAR

a. In the Assets panel, drag the rollover_text.swf file name to the last cell of the nested table. (*ver.8:* If the Object Tag Accessibility Attributes dialog box appears, select Cancel.)

b. Double-click the button in the last cell. A dialog box is displayed.

c. Change the button text to Video/Sound, link the button to the video_and_sound.htm web page document, and save the button naming it: video_and_sound.swf (*ver.8:* If the Flash Accessibility Attributes dialog box appears, select Cancel.)

d. Save the modified index.htm.

④ VIEW THE DOCUMENT IN A BROWSER AND TEST THE BUTTONS

a. Press F12. The document is displayed in a browser window.

b. Click the Animation button. The animation.htm page is displayed.

c. Click the Home link. The index.htm web page is again displayed.

d. Test the Video/Sound button.

e. Close the browser window.

Creating Flash Text in Dreamweaver

Flash text allows the use of a variety of fonts in a web page document without worrying about whether the user's computer has the font installed. For example, the Flash text below was created with the Blackadder font:

Map and Directions

Flash text can include a rollover color and a link to create a rollover text hyperlink. Text with a rollover behavior can change color when the user points to it in a browser. When the pointer is moved over Flash text that is also a hyperlink, the pointer changes to 🖑.

A web page document must be saved before creating Flash text. To create a Flash button, place the insertion point in the web page document and then click the arrow next to the Media button in the Common category in the Insert bar and select Flash Text. The Insert Flash Text dialog box is displayed:

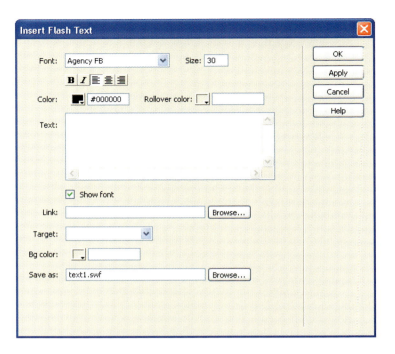

- Select a different font for the text in the Font list.

- Change the point size of the text in the Size box.

- Click a button (**B** *I* ≣ ≣ ≣) to change the style or alignment of the text.

- Select a color for the text using the Color box (◼). The hexadecimal color value, such as #0033CC, can also be typed next to the box.

- Select a color for the rollover behavior using the Rollover color boxes.

- Type the text to be displayed in the Text box. In the Text box, the text will appear in the selected font, but not in the color or size.

- The file name or URL for the text's hyperlink is added in the Link box. Click Browse to display a dialog box where the web page document file name can be selected.

- Bg color is the background color of the text. This color should match the background of the web page document.

- Flash text is saved as a Flash movie file with an .swf extension. The Save as box displays the location and name of the Flash movie file. Click Browse to display a dialog box where the appropriate folder can be selected.

TIP Click Apply instead of OK to insert Flash text in the web page document and leave the dialog box open for editing.

Click OK to insert the Flash text into the web page document.

To preview Flash text in Design view, select the text and then click ▶ Play in the Property inspector. Click ◼ Stop to end the preview. Flash text can also be previewed by viewing the web page document in a browser.

TIP Flash text can also be edited by clicking ✎ Edit... in the Property inspector.

To edit Flash text, double-click the text to display the Insert Flash Text dialog box.

Dreamweaver should be started and the SAMPLER website should be the working site.

① ADD FLASH TEXT TO A TABLE

a. Open the rollover.htm web page document.

b. Place the insertion point in the empty cell in the far right in the fourth row.

c. In the Common category in the Insert bar, click the Media button arrow, then click Flash Text. A dialog box is displayed.

    1. Set Font to a font of your choice.

    2. Set Size to 24.

    3. Set Color to a dark color of your choice.

    4. Set Rollover color to a light color of your choice.

    5. In the Text box, type: Back to the Home Page

    6. Next to the Link box, click Browse. A dialog box is displayed.

        a) Select the index.htm web page document.

        b) Select OK.

    7. Next to the Save as box, click Browse. A dialog box is displayed.

        a) In the File name box, type: home_link.swf

        b) Select Save.

    8. Select OK. (*ver.8:* If the Flash Accessibility Attributes dialog box appears, select Cancel.) The dialog box is removed and the Flash text is inserted in the cell.

d. Save the modified rollover.htm.

② VIEW THE DOCUMENT IN A BROWSER

a. Press F12. The document is displayed in a browser window.

b. Point to the Flash text. Note the rollover color.

c. Click the Flash text. The home page is displayed.

d. Close the browser window.

③ QUIT DREAMWEAVER

What is Animation?

    Animation is the result of many images shown quickly one after the other to create the effect of movement. For example, the following images shown quickly one after the other create the effect of a skateboarder going down a hill:

A Flash movie animation can be broken into components. A *Timeline* correlates images to a particular moment in the movie. At any point in a movie, there is a *frame* with an image. The frame can be several images that are layered. Layers are used because from frame to frame there may be different animation techniques applied. For example, an animation of a skateboarder going down a hill requires only the position of the skateboarder to change. The hill remains unchanged from frame to frame. The hill can be on one layer and the skateboarder on another.

Starting Flash

To start Flash, select Start → All Programs → Macromedia → Macromedia Flash, or double-click the Flash icon on the Desktop:

Macromedia
Flash MX
2004

Introducing Flash

Websites are often designed to include animations beyond rollover text and buttons with special effects. The Flash application, which is part of the Macromedia Studio suite, is used to create custom animations that can include video and sound.

To create a new Flash document, select File → New, which displays a dialog box. Select Flash Document in the General tab and then OK to create the document:

Timeline   Close buttons

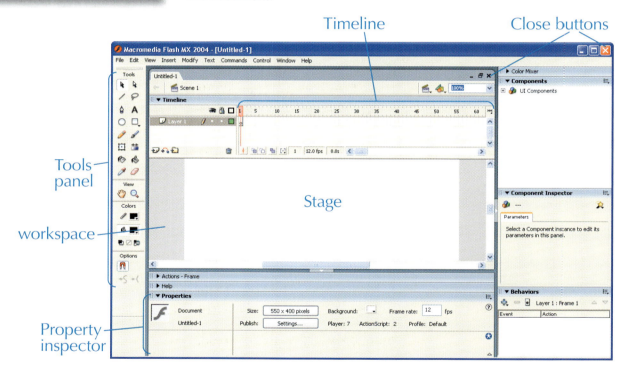

Tools panel

workspace

Property inspector

Flash Native File Format

The native file format in Flash is FLA. A native file format is the default format in which an application saves files. Files may be saved or exported in other formats, but are worked on in the native file format.

- The **Tools panel** contains tools for drawing, painting, and selecting. The tools are divided into sections.

- The **Timeline** correlates images to a frame in the movie.

- Click a **Close button** to remove the document window or the Flash window.

- The **Stage** is the area used to create a Flash movie.

- The **workspace** is the gray area around the Stage, which can be used as a temporary storage area while working.

- Change properties of selected objects in the **Property inspector**.

TIP Files that are not directly used in a website are best kept in a folder outside the website root folder.

Select File ➡ Save to save a Flash document. Flash documents are automatically saved in FLA format. The FLA file should be saved to a location outside of the website's root folder and used to export a movie file to the website in SWF format. The FLA file cannot be used in a web page document. If an SWF movie file needs to be changed, the FLA file can be edited and exported again. Exporting is discussed later in this chapter.

The Flash Tools Panel

vector graphic

Images drawn in Flash are vector graphics. A *vector graphic* is composed of lines connected by points, which allows for smooth resizing and a smaller file size than bitmap graphics.

The tools in the Tools panel are used to create images. Tools include:

- **Selection tool** selects objects.
- **Subselection tool** adjusts *anchor points*, which define sections of a line or shape.
- **Line**, **Oval**, **Rectangle** and **PolyStar tools** draw basic shapes.
- **Pen tool** draws straight or curved lines.
- **Text tool** creates a text block.
- **Pencil tool** draws free-form lines and shapes.
- **Brush tool** paints with brush-like strokes.
- **Paint Bucket tool** fills enclosed areas with a selected color.
- **Eraser tool** deletes parts of a shape.

Tools in the View section include:

- **Hand tool** moves the Stage within the workspace.
- **Zoom tool** changes the magnification level of the Stage.

Tools in the Colors section include:

- **Stroke Color** changes the outline color of the tool.
- **Fill Color** changes the fill color of the tool.

The Options section contains modifier buttons for the tools. Modifiers for the Brush tool include:

- **Brush Mode** changes what is painted.
- **Brush Size** changes the size of the brush stroke.
- **Brush Shape** changes the shape of the brush stroke.

Creating a Flash Movie

The process of creating a Flash movie includes:

• Set Flash document properties.
• Create images.
• Use the Timeline to lay out the sequence of the images.
• Preview the animation.
• Export the document.

A new Flash document is created by selecting File → New. The Property inspector displays the properties for the current Flash document:

• Size is the Stage size, in pixels, which is representative of the size of the movie. Change the Stage size by clicking the button next to Size to display a dialog box. In the dialog box, click Contents to resize the Stage to just accommodate the objects on the Stage.

• Background is the color of the Stage and of the background of the movie. To change the color, click the box and select a color.

• Frame Rate is the number of animation frames to be displayed every second. The default frame rate is 12 frames per second (fps).

Images are created using the Tools panel. To help precisely place objects, rulers and a grid can be displayed. Select View → Rulers to display rulers along the top and left side of the work area. Rulers are scaled in pixels by default. Select View → Grid → Show Grid to display a set of gridlines.

The Timeline is used to lay out the sequence of images:

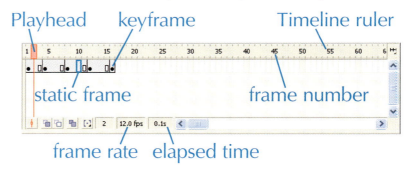

Frame Rates

12 frames per second (fps) is the default frame rate in Flash. Increasing the frame rate results in better-quality animation but requires the computer to process more information in the same period of time. Use 20 fps or less as a guideline to have good-quality animation on most computers.

• Drag the **Playhead** to a frame to display the frame's image on the Stage. When the animation is played, the Playhead moves through the Timeline.

• A **frame** is a point on the Timeline. A **keyframe** is a frame that contains an image that can be edited. A **static frame** contains the same image as the previous frame.

• The **elapsed time** is the time of the animation up to the Playhead.

• The **frame rate** is the rate at which an animation plays in frames per second (fps).

TIP Press Enter to play a movie from the selected frame.

An animation should be previewed to test it. Select Control ➤ Play to preview an animation. Previewing shows if an animation is moving too slowly or too quickly and demonstrates the smoothness of transitions from one image to another. Select Control ➤ Rewind to move the Playhead back to frame 1, or drag the Playhead.

An animation must be exported to be used in a website. Exporting is discussed later in this chapter.

Frame-by-Frame Animation

Frame-by-frame animation is a movie created from a set of specified images. In a new Flash document, the first frame in the Timeline is a blank keyframe. Use tools in the Tools panel to create an image on the Stage for the first keyframe:

Printing in Flash

Select File ➤ Print to print the current frame.

This image was created with the Text and Pencil tools.

add a keyframe

TIP A keyframe can also be added by selecting Insert ➤ Timeline ➤ Keyframe.

Right-click a frame on the Timeline and select Insert Keyframe from the displayed menu to add a keyframe and create static frames between the two keyframes. The image is included in the new keyframe. The image in the new keyframe can then be modified to progress the animation:

A stem and leaf was added to the keyframe at frame 5

The gray static frames are needed to control the rate of animation so that the animation does not play too quickly for the viewer to comprehend. The process of inserting keyframes and modifying the image is repeated until the final frame of the animation:

Final keyframe of the animation

Editing Techniques

remove a frame

To speed up a slow-moving animation, delete a few static frames. The same number of static frames should be removed between each keyframe to keep the animation smooth. Right-click a static frame and select Remove Frames from the menu to delete the frame. To slow down an animation,

add a frame

right-click a frame and select Insert Frame from the menu to add a frame.

onion skinning

To help position and edit images, two or more frames can be displayed at the same time using a technique called *onion skinning*. Click the Onion Skin button ( ) at the bottom of the Timeline to display Onion Skin markers. Drag the right marker in the Timeline ruler to display keyframe images between the markers:

Importing Images

Artwork created in other applications can be imported and used in Flash. Supported file formats include JPG, GIF, PNG, BMP, EMF, EPS, AI, PIC, and WMF. Select File → Import → Import to Stage to display a dialog box where a file is selected.

The current keyframe is darker than the other keyframes

Images that are dimmed cannot be edited, but the Playhead can be dragged to change the current keyframe for editing purposes.

the Transform panel

Common ways to modify an image include scaling, rotating, and skewing objects. To modify a selected object, select Window → Design Panels → Transform, which displays the Transform panel:

The Selection Tool

The Selection tool ( ) is used to select objects. Click once on a shape to select the fill, or double-click a shape to select both the fill and stroke. Multiple shapes can be selected by holding down the Shift key while selecting.

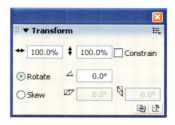

- Type or select a percentage value in the Width ( ) and Height ( ) boxes to adjust the width or height.

- Click Rotate and type an angle to rotate the object.

- Click Skew and type an angle in the Skew Horizontal ( ) or Skew Vertical box ( ) to slant the object.

Practice: SAMPLER – part 4 of 10

Flash 8 differences are indicated with parentheses (*ver.8:*).

① START FLASH

Ask your instructor for the appropriate steps to start Flash. Note the Stage, Tools panel, gray workspace, Timeline, and Property inspector.

② OPEN A FLASH DOCUMENT

a. Select File → Open. A dialog box is displayed.

   1. Use the Look in list to navigate to the folder containing data files for this text.
   2. Select the PURPLE_BALL.fla file.
   3. Select Open. The Flash document is opened and the first frame is displayed on the Stage.

③ PLAY THE FRAME-BY-FRAME ANIMATION

a. Select Control → Play. The animation plays and a purple ball bounces but does not quite land because the animation is not complete.

b. In the Timeline, drag the Playhead back to frame 1. The image for the first keyframe is displayed.

④ USE ONION SKINNING TO VIEW THE FRAMES

a. At the bottom of the Timeline, click the Onion Skin button ( ). Onion Skin markers are displayed on the Timeline ruler.

b. Drag the right Onion Skin marker to the last keyframe (frame 15) to display all of the keyframes. The images are dimmed except the image from frame 1:

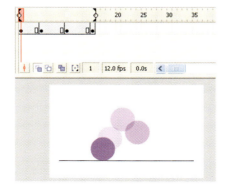

c. Drag the Playhead to the last keyframe. The image in the last frame is in full color and editable.

⑤ **ADD A KEYFRAME**

a. In the Timeline, below the Timeline ruler, right-click frame 20 and select Insert Keyframe. A keyframe is added to the animation. The image from the last keyframe is now displayed on the Stage, and the Onion Skin has advanced to the last frame:

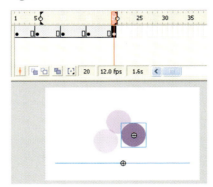

b. Click anywhere in the gray workspace to remove the selection from the ball and surface object.

c. Drag the ball object so that it is just on the surface and slightly to the right:

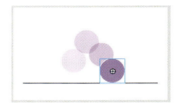

d. Select File ➝ Save. (*ver.8:* If the Flash 8 Compatibility dialog box appears, select Save.) The modified PURPLE_BALL.fla is saved.

⑥ **PLAY THE ANIMATION**

a. Click the Onion Skin button (🔲) to deselect it. The Onion Skin images are no longer displayed.

b. Select Control ➝ Play. The animation plays. The ball bounces from the left to the right.

⑦ **MODIFY THE ANIMATION**

a. In the Timeline, right-click frame 2 and select Remove Frames. A static frame is removed.

b. Remove one static frame after each of the other keyframes, so that your Timeline looks similar to:

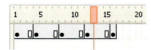

c. Save the modified PURPLE_BALL.fla.

d. Select Control ➝ Rewind. The Playhead moves back to frame 1.

e. Select Control ➝ Play. The animation is faster.

To use a Flash document in Dreamweaver, it must be exported in SWF format so that it can be played with the Flash Player plug-in. To export a Flash document as a movie, select File → Export → Export Movie, which displays the Export Movie dialog box:

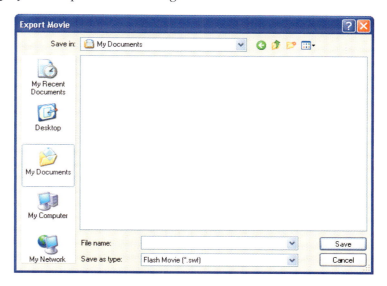

Creating a Media Folder

If a website does not have a media folder when the Flash document is exported, use the Create New Folder button ( ) in the Export Movie dialog box to create a media folder in the website root folder.

Use the Save in list and the contents box below it to navigate to the location where the file is to be saved. A Flash movie exported for use in a website should be saved in a folder named media in the site. Type a descriptive file name for the movie in the File name box, and make sure the Save as type is Flash Movie. Select Save to export the movie and display the Export Flash Player dialog box:

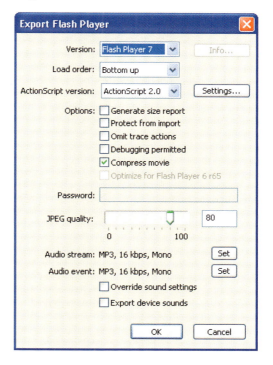

Select OK to complete the export process.

Organizing and Using Flash Movie Files in Dreamweaver

media folder

For better organization, Flash movies created in Flash for a website should be stored together in a media folder that is created in the website root folder.

Flash category in the Assets panel

In Dreamweaver, Flash movie files are displayed in the Flash category in the Assets panel. Select a movie in the Assets panel to display it in the preview area. Click the ▶ button in the preview area to play the Flash movie and display the ■ button. Click the ■ button to end the movie. Select ▤ → Refresh Site List in the Files panel group to update the list of movies in the Assets panel.

insert a Flash movie

Drag a Flash movie from the Assets panel to an open web page document to place it, or click Insert at the bottom of the Assets panel to place the selected movie at the insertion point. When a movie created in Flash is added to a web page document, a placeholder is displayed:

A Flash placeholder varies in size depending on the Stage size

Click the Flash placeholder to display the Flash movie properties in the Property inspector:

- Select the Loop check box to have the movie play continuously. Clear the Loop check box to have the Flash movie play only once when the web page loads in a browser.

preview a Flash movie

- Select the placeholder and then click ▶ Play in the Property inspector to preview the Flash movie in Design view. Click ■ Stop in the Property inspector to end the preview. The Flash movie can also be previewed by viewing the web page document in a browser.

edit a Flash movie

- Click ⊘ Edit... to display a dialog box from which the FLA file corresponding to the movie can be opened for editing in Flash.

Flash should be started and the PURPLE_BALL.fla document displayed. Dreamweaver 8 differences are indicated with parentheses (*ver.8:*).

① CREATE A MOVIE

    a. Select File → Export → Export Movie. A dialog box is displayed.

        1. Use the Save in list to navigate to the SAMPLER website folder. Note that there is no media folder.

        2. At the top of the dialog box, click the Create New Folder button (📁). A folder is added to the website folder.

        3. Replace the existing folder name with: media

        4. Open the media folder.

        5. In the File name box, type: bouncing_ball

        6. Select Save. A dialog box is displayed.

        7. Select OK. The default options are applied and the purple ball animation is exported as an SWF file to the SAMPLER website.

    b. Save and close the PURPLE_BALL.fla document.

② INSERT A FLASH MOVIE IN DREAMWEAVER

    a. Start Dreamweaver. Open SAMPLER for editing if it is not the working website.

    b. Open the animation.htm web page document.

    c. In the Assets panel, click the Flash icon (🔴). If bouncing_ball.swf is not listed, select 📋 → Refresh Site List from the Files panel group.

    d. Drag the bouncing_ball.swf file from the Assets panel to the empty cell next to the text that reads "This example is frame-by-frame animation:" (*ver.8:* If the Object Tag Accessibility Attributes dialog box appears, select Cancel.) A Flash placeholder is displayed:

    e. Save the modified animation.htm.

③ PREVIEW THE FLASH MOVIE

    a. Press F12. The web page document is displayed in a browser. The bouncing ball animation plays continuously.

    b. Close the browser window. Dreamweaver is displayed.

    c. Click the Flash movie placeholder to select it, if it is not already selected.

    d. In the Property inspector, clear the Loop check box.

    e. Save the modified animation.htm and then press F12. The movie plays just once in the browser when the page loads.

    f. Close the browser window. Dreamweaver is displayed.

Shape Tweening

tweened animation

morphing

A *tweened animation* is an animation where Flash generates the keyframes between the first keyframe and the last. One form of tweened animation is *shape tweening*, which is similar to morphing an image. *Morphing* is a technique that turns one shape into another. For example, a square can be turned into a circle:

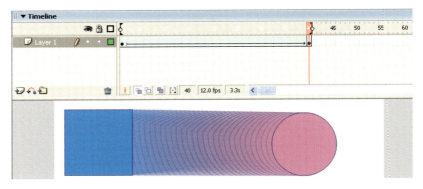

Onion Skin markers show the frames generated by Flash

TIP Shape tweening can only be applied to images that are composed of simple lines and fills.

The steps for creating a shape tweened animation are:

1. Create an image in the first keyframe.
2. Create an end keyframe, delete the image from the first keyframe, and draw a second image.
3. Select any frame between the keyframes.
4. Set Tween to Shape in the Property inspector.
5. Preview the animation.
6. Export the document.

Shape tweening is indicated by green shading and an arrow in the Timeline:

Practice: SAMPLER – part 6 of 10

Dreamweaver 8 differences are indicated with parentheses (*ver.8:*).

① CREATE A NEW FLASH DOCUMENT

a. Start Flash if it is not already running.

b. In Flash, close any open documents, saving if necessary.

c. Select File → New. A dialog box is displayed.

d. Select Flash Document in the General tab and then select OK. A new document with a blank Stage is displayed.

② CREATE THE SHAPE-TWEENING ANIMATION

    a. Scroll the workspace so that the upper-left corner of the Stage is visible.

    b. In the Tools panel, in the Colors section, select a black Fill color ( ).

    c. In the Tools panel, in the Colors section, select a transparent Stroke color ( ).

    d. In the Tools panel, click the Rectangle Tool ( ).

    e. Near the top-left corner of the Stage draw a rectangle.

    f. In the Timeline, right-click frame 20 and select Insert Keyframe. A keyframe is added to the animation with the rectangle image.

    g. Press the Delete key to remove the selected rectangle from the Stage.

    h. In the Tools panel, select a pink Fill color.

    i. In the Tools panel, click the Oval Tool ( ).

    j. Display Onion Skins and move the markers as necessary to see the complete Timeline.

    k. About half way across the stage and level with the rectangle, draw an oval. Use the Onion Skin markers to help with placement.

    l. Deselect the Onion Skin button ( ). The Onion Skins are no longer displayed.

    m. In the Timeline, click frame 10.

    n. In the Property inspector, set Tween to Shape. The static frames are green, an arrow is displayed between the keyframes on the Timeline and the shape in frame 10 is displayed.

③ PLAY THE ANIMATION

    a. Save the document in a folder that is outside of any website folder, naming it: morph_demo.fla

    b. Rewind and then play the animation.

④ CREATE A MOVIE

    a. Select the Selection tool ( ).

    b. Click anywhere in the gray workspace. Document properties are displayed in the Property inspector.

    c. In the Property inspector, click the button next to the Size option. A dialog box is displayed.

        1. Select Contents. The dimensions of the Stage are recalculated based on the amount of space needed by the animation.

        2. Select OK. The Stage is resized.

    d. Save the modified morph_demo.fla.

    e. Select File ➡ Export ➡ Export Movie. A dialog box is displayed.

        1. Navigate to the media folder in the SAMPLER website folder.

        2. In the File name box, type: morphing

        3. Select Save. A dialog box is displayed.

        4. Select OK. The default options are applied and the shape-tweened animation is exported as an SWF file to the SAMPLER website.

    f. Save and close morph_demo.fla.

⑤ INSERT A FLASH MOVIE IN DREAMWEAVER

    a. Switch to Dreamweaver.

    b. Open the SAMPLER website for editing if it is not the working website.

c. Display the animation.htm web page document.

d. Scroll the animation.htm web page document to display the empty cell next to the text that reads "This example is shape-tweened animation:"

e. In the Assets panel, display the Flash category. If morphing.swf is not listed, select ⊞ → Refresh Site List from the Files panel group.

f. Drag the morphing.swf file from the Assets panel to the empty cell to the right of the text that reads "This example is shape tweened animation:" (*ver.8:* If the Object Tag Accessibility Attributes dialog box appears, select Cancel.) A Flash placeholder is displayed.

g. Save the modified animation.htm.

⑥ PREVIEW THE FLASH MOVIE

a. Press F12. The web page document is displayed in a browser and the morphing animation plays continuously, while the frame-by-frame animation plays just once.

b. Close the browser window. Dreamweaver is displayed.

Creating Symbols to Optimize a Flash Movie

optimization techniques

A Flash movie file should be as small a file size as possible to keep web page load times as short as possible. Techniques for optimizing an animation for size include using symbols for images that appear more than once, using tweened animation, and using layers for objects that do not change from frame to frame. Layers are discussed in later in this chapter.

instance

Symbols are stored in a Flash Library and used to create instances on the Stage. An *instance* is a reference to a symbol, rather than a copy of an image. Any image that is used more than once in a movie file should be converted to symbol. This allows the movie file size to be much smaller.

A symbol can be created from a single object or multiple objects selected together. Use the Selection tool and drag to marquee select the object:

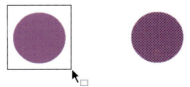

Dragging the Selection tool selects the objects enclosed by the box (the marquee). On the right, the object is selected.

Select Modify → Convert to Symbol to display a dialog box. Type a descriptive name for the symbol and select Graphic to create a graphic symbol:

Select OK to convert the selected objects on the Stage to an instance of the symbol. An instance displays a registration point (⊙) in the center:

the Flash Library   Select Window ➤ Library to display the Flash Library. Click the symbol name in the Library to view the preview area:

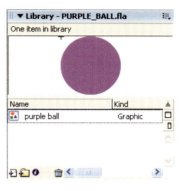

add an instance to the Stage   Drag the symbol name from the Library to the Stage to create an instance of the symbol.

Motion Tweening

In *motion tweening*, a single symbol is tweened to move from a start location to an end location:

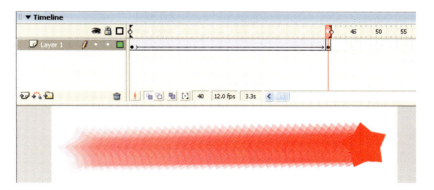

The steps for creating a motion tweened animation are:

1. Create an image and convert it to a graphic symbol.

2. Create a start keyframe with an instance at the starting position.

3. Create an end keyframe with an instance at the ending position.

4. Select a frame between the keyframes.

5. Set Tween to Motion in the Property inspector.

6. Preview the animation.

7. Export the document.

TIP Right-click a frame between keyframes and select Create Motion Tween.

TIP Symbols and editable text blocks can be motion-tweened.

Motion tweening is indicated by lavender shading and an arrow in the Timeline:

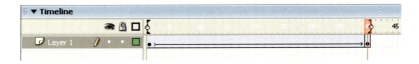

modify the motion

Flash uses the shortest, most direct path from the start position to the end position to fill in the motion tweening. To change the path of the motion, click a frame and then drag the instance in that frame to a new position. For example, in the animation below, frame 20 was clicked and the instance was dragged upwards to change the straight-line path:

Flash makes each frame that changes the path a keyframe and recalculates the motion path.

Practice: SAMPLER – part 7 of 10

Dreamweaver 8 differences are indicated with parentheses (*ver.8:*).

① CREATE A NEW FLASH DOCUMENT

a. In Flash, close any open documents, saving if necessary.

b. Select File → New. A dialog box is displayed.

c. Select Flash Document in the General tab and then select OK. A new document with a blank Stage is displayed.

② CREATE AN IMAGE

a. Scroll so that the upper-left corner of the Stage is visible.

b. Select View → Rulers to display rulers, if they are not already displayed.

c. In the Tools panel, in the Colors section, change the Stroke color and Fill color to a bright yellow:

d. In the Tools panel, click the Oval tool ( ).

e. Hold down the Shift key and drag on the Stage to create a small circle about 50 pixels in diameter.

f. In the Tools panel, change the Stroke and Fill colors to black.

g. In the Tools panel, click the Brush tool ( ).

h. In the Tools panel, in the Options section, set options to:

i. Draw eyes and a smile onto the yellow circle to create a smiley face:

Note: Select Edit ➥ Undo as necessary. Change the brush size if needed.

j. Save the document in a folder that is outside of any website folder, naming it: smiley.fla

③ CREATE A SYMBOL

a. In the Tools panel, click the Selection tool (▶) and then marquee select the smiley face:

b. Select Modify ➥ Convert to Symbol. A dialog box is displayed:

   1. In the Name box, type: smiley_face
   2. Select Graphic.
   3. Select OK. The selected image is converted to a symbol and replaced by an instance of the symbol.

c. Select Window ➥ Library. The Library is displayed. Note the smiley_face symbol name.

d. In the Library, click the smiley_face name to see a preview in the Library.

④ CREATE KEYFRAMES

a. In the Timeline, note that the first frame is already a keyframe. Drag the smiley_face instance on the Stage, leaving some room above the image:

b. In the Timeline, right-click frame 40 and select Insert Keyframe. A keyframe is added to the animation with a smiley_face instance.

c. Drag the smiley_face instance directly across to the right side of the Stage.

⑤ APPLY MOTION TWEENING

a. In the Timeline, click frame 12.

b. In the Property inspector, set Tween to Motion. An arrow is displayed between the starting and ending frames on the Timeline.

c. Save the modified smiley.fla.

d. Select Control ➡ Rewind and then select Control ➡ Play. The smiley face moves across the Stage horizontally.

⑥ MODIFY THE PATH

a. In the Timeline, click the Onion Skin button (🔳). Onion Skin markers are displayed on the Timeline ruler.

b. Drag the Onion Skin markers to display the entire animation. Note the straight path.

c. Deselect the Onion Skin button. The Onion Skins are no longer displayed.

d. Click frame 20. Drag the smiley face up near the top of the Stage. The frame is automatically converted to a keyframe and a symbol is displayed.

e. Display Onion Skins and move the markers as necessary to see the complete motion path. The path is no longer a straight line.

f. Save the modified smiley.fla.

g. Deselect the Onion Skin button. The Onion Skins are no longer displayed.

h. Select Control ➡ Rewind and then select Control ➡ Play. The smiley face moves across the stage along the new motion path.

⑦ CREATE A MOVIE

a. Click anywhere in the gray workspace. Document properties are displayed in the Property inspector.

b. In the Property inspector, click the button next to the Size option. A dialog box is displayed.

   1. Select Contents.

   2. Select OK. The Stage is resized.

c. Save the modified smiley.fla.

d. Select File ➡ Export ➡ Export Movie. A dialog box is displayed.

   1. Navigate to the media folder in the SAMPLER website folder.

   2. In the File name box, type: smiley.swf

   3. Select Save. A dialog box is displayed.

   4. Select OK. The default options are applied and the smiley face animation is exported as an SWF file to the SAMPLER website.

e. Save and close smiley.fla.

⑧ INSERT A FLASH MOVIE IN DREAMWEAVER

a. Switch to Dreamweaver.

b. Open the SAMPLER website for editing if it is not the working website.

c. Display the animation.htm web page document.

d. Scroll the animation.htm web page document to display the empty cell next to the text that reads "This example is motion-tweened animation:"

e. In the Assets panel, display the Flash category and refresh the list.

f. Drag the smiley.swf file from the Assets panel to the empty cell to the right of the text that reads "This example is motion-tweened animation:" (*ver.8:* If the Object Tag Accessibility Attributes dialog box appears, select Cancel.) A Flash placeholder is displayed.

g. Save the modified animation.htm.

⑨ PREVIEW THE FLASH MOVIE

a. Press F12. The web page document is displayed in a browser and the smiley face animation plays in a loop.

b. Close the browser window. Dreamweaver is displayed.

Using Layers

Flash documents of any complexity should be divided into layers. *Layers* can be thought of as transparent sheets of paper with images drawn on them and the sheets placed one on top of the other. The image on one layer can be modified without changing the images on other layers. In animation, an image on one layer can be tweened without affecting the other layers. This allows multiple objects to be motion-tweened and for both motion- and shape-tweening in one document. The document below is divided into layers:

tweening on layers

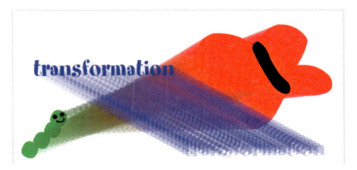

A caterpillar is shape tweened into a butterfly on one layer, and a word is motion tweened from top to bottom on another layer.

create a new layer

Click the Insert layer button (⊞) in the bottom-left corner of the Timeline to add a layer to a document. Layer names appear in the Layers list:

TIP A layer can also be added to a document by selecting Insert → Timeline → Layer.

Layers list

Insert Layer button

name a layer

By default, layers are named Layer 1, Layer 2, and so on. To change a layer name, double-click a name in the Layers list and type a more descriptive name.

The layers in the Layers list are ordered top to bottom, with the top layer Layer 1. Images on Layer 1 appear on top of any images in the layers below. The order of the layers is changed by dragging a layer to a different location in the list:

hide a layer It may be to work on one layer if other layers are temporarily hidden from view. To hide a layer, click to the right of the layer name in the Eye column ( ). An ✗ is displayed in the column.

The text layer is hidden

To display a hidden layer, click the ✗.

lock a layer To lock a layer, which prevents it from being edited, click to the right of the layer name in the Lock column ( ).

delete a layer To delete a layer, click the layer name in the Layers list and then click the Delete Layer button ( ) below the Layers list.

Animating Text

Text can be broken apart into individual characters and then placed onto layers so that a word or phrase can be motion tweened. For example, each letter in a word can move onto the Stage from a different direction or the letters of a word could "dance" on Stage.

create a text block To create a text block in Flash click the Text tool (**A**) in the Tools panel and then click the Stage and type a word or phrase. Use the Property inspector to change font, size, and color properties:

break apart a text block To be animated, the text must be broken up into separate objects, one for each character. Select the text block and then select Modify ➟ Break Apart:

distribute to layers

To allow motion tweening for smooth animation of the text, the characters must be distributed to layers. Select Modify ➞ Timeline ➞ Distribute to Layers to automatically distribute each character to an individual layer with an appropriate name:

TIP Marquee select a single frame to add a keyframe to several layers at once.

At this point, Layer 1 can be deleted because the entire word is no longer needed. Adding a second keyframe creates the end keyframe. In the first keyframe, position each letter to starting position. Finally, motion tweening is applied to each layer. Below is the animated "Howdy" with the Playhead on the first keyframe:

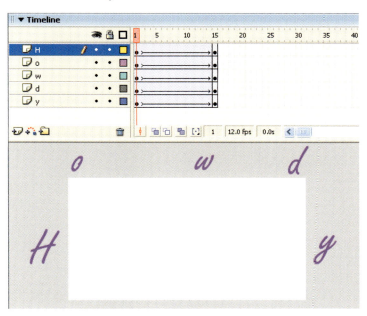

The steps for creating animated text are:

1. Create a text block.

2. Break apart the text block into separate layers.

3. Distribute the separate objects to layers.

4. Delete Layer 1.

5. Insert the last keyframe for each layer.

6. In the first keyframe, position the characters in a start position.

8. Set Tween to Motion in the Property inspector for each layer.

9. Preview the animation.

10. Export the document.

① CREATE A NEW FLASH DOCUMENT AND SIZE THE STAGE

a. In Flash, close any open documents, saving if necessary.

b. Select File → New. A dialog box is displayed.

c. Select Flash Document in the General tab and then select OK. A new document with a blank Stage is displayed.

d. In the Property inspector, click the button next to the Size option. A dialog box is displayed.

    1. Set the Dimensions options to 400 px for the width and 200 px for the height.

    2. Select OK. The Stage is resized.

② CREATE A TEXT ANIMATION

a. In the Tools panel, click the Text tool (**A**).

b. Click the Stage to create a text block.

c. In the Property inspector, select Tahoma for the Font, a Font Size of 72, and a dark green color for the Text (fill).

d. Type: Hola!

e. In the Tools panel, click the Selection tool ( ) and then drag the text block to the center of the Stage.

f. Select Modify → Break Apart. Characters are selected as separate objects.

g. Select Modify → Timeline → Distribute to Layers. A named layer is created for each character in the word Hola!

h. In the Layers list, click Layer 1 to select it.

i. At the bottom of the Layers list, click the Delete Layer button (🗑). Layer 1 is deleted.

j. In layer H, right-click frame 20 and select Insert Keyframe. A keyframe is added.

k. Add a keyframe at frame 20 for each of the remaining layers.

l. In the Timeline, drag the Playhead back to the first frame.

m. Drag each of the characters to a starting position off the Stage, similar to the example of "Howdy" in the previous section.

n. In the H layer, click a frame between the keyframes and then set Tween to Motion in the Property inspector.

o. Set motion tweening for the remaining layers.

③ SAVE THE FLASH DOCUMENT

Save the document in a folder that is outside of any website folder, naming it: hola.fla

④ REWIND AND THEN PLAY THE ANIMATION

Importing Sound Files

Sound can be added to a Flash movie by importing a sound file and then adding the file to a layer. Flash supports sound file formats that include WAV and MP3. Other file formats are available if QuickTime or DirectX is installed on your computer.

QuickTime and DirectX

The latest QuickTime player can be downloaded for free from www.apple.com. The latest DirectX software can be downloaded from www. microsoft.com/directx.

TIP Select Window → Library to display the Library.

Sound files are imported to the document's Library to allow the sound file to be used repeatedly without increasing the Flash movie file size. To import a sound file, select File → Import → Import to Library, which displays the Import to Library dialog box. Select All Sound Formats in the Files of type list and then use the Look in list and the contents box below it to navigate to the file. Select the file and then Open to import the file to the Library.

In an animation, a sound file needs to be on a separate layer with a descriptive name. To add the sound file to the animation, create the start keyframe, drag the sound file from the Library to the Stage, then create the end keyframe. A sound wave is displayed in the Timeline between the keyframes:

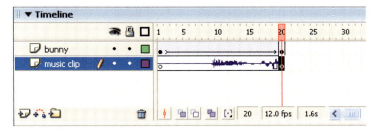

The steps for adding sound to an animation are:

1. Import the sound file to the Library.

2. Create a layer and give it a descriptive name.

3. Create the start keyframe in the sound layer.

4. Display the Library and drag the sound file to the Stage.

5. Create an end keyframe.

6. Preview the animation.

7. Export the document.

sound file properties

When the frames that contain sound are selected, the Property inspector displays their properties:

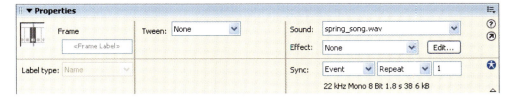

- Select a sound effect such as Fade Out from the Effect list.

- In the Sync options, select Repeat and type the number of times to repeat the sound, or select Loop to play the sound continuously.

This practice assumes you have speakers or headphones and a sound card in your computer. Dreamweaver 8 differences are indicated with parentheses (*ver.8:*).

① ADD SOUND TO THE HOLA ANIMATION

    a. Open the hola.fla document in Flash if it is not already displayed.

    b. Select File → Import → Import to Library. A dialog box is displayed.

        1. Use the Look in list to navigate to the folder containing data files for this text.

        2. In the Files of type list, select All Sound Formats.

        3. Select the HOLA.wav file.

        4. Select Open.

    c. Select Window → Library if the Library window is not already displayed.

    d. Select the H layer and then click the Insert layer button (🗐) below the Layers list.

    e. In the Layers list, double-click the new layer's name and rename it: greeting

    f. In the Timeline, in the greeting layer, click the first keyframe.

    g. From the Library, drag the HOLA.wav file onto the Stage.

    h. In the greeting layer, right-click frame 20 and select Insert Keyframe.

    i. Save the modified hola.fla.

② PLAY THE ANIMATION

③ CREATE A MOVIE

    a. Click anywhere in the gray workspace. Document properties are displayed in the Property inspector.

    b. In the Property inspector, click the button next to the Size option. A dialog box is displayed. Click Contents and then select OK.

    c. Save the modified hola.fla.

    d. Export the movie as an SWF file to the media folder in the SAMPLER website folder, naming it: hola.swf

    e. Save and close hola.fla.

④ INSERT THE FLASH MOVIE IN DREAMWEAVER

    a. Switch to Dreamweaver.

    b. Open the SAMPLER website for editing if it is not the working website.

    c. In the Files panel, open the video_and_sound.htm web page document.

    d. In the Assets panel, display the Flash category and refresh the list.

    e. Drag the hola.swf file from the Assets panel to the empty cell to the right of the text that reads "This example includes sound:" (*ver.8:* If the Object Tag Accessibility Attributes dialog box appears, select Cancel.)

    f. In the Property inspector, deselect Loop. The sound file will play just once when the web page is loaded.

    g. Save the modified video_and_sound.htm.

⑤ PREVIEW THE FLASH MOVIE

    a. Press F12. The web page document is displayed in a browser. The hola animation plays. If you have speakers, you will also hear the sound play.

    b. Close the browser window. Dreamweaver is displayed.

Importing Video

Video can be imported to Flash and then exported as a Flash movie. Supported video file formats include AVI, DV, MPG, MPEG, and MOV, and depend on if QuickTime or DirectX is installed on your computer.

Video Compression

Flash uses the Sorenson Spark codec to import and export video, which is a compression/decompression algorithm.

To import a video into a Flash document, select File → Import → Import to Stage, which displays the Import dialog box. Select All Video Formats in the Files of type list and then use the Look in list and the contents box below it to navigate to the file. Select the file and then Open to display the Video Import Wizard dialog box (*ver.8:* dialog boxes and options selected are different):

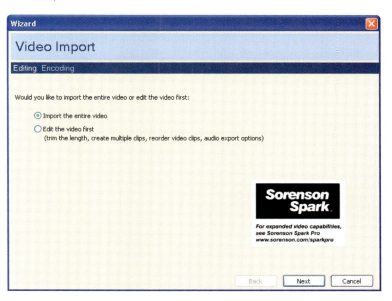

Select Import the entire video then select Next to display more options:

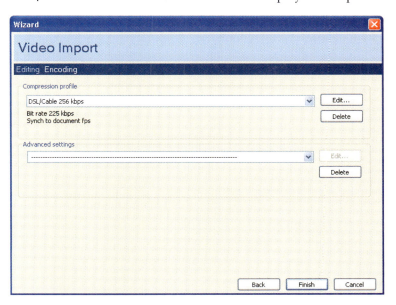

TIP When importing a movie into Flash, select a faster speed for the Compression profile (*ver8:* select a higher quality encoding profile) for a better quality video.

Select DSL/Cable 256 kbps in the Compression profile list and then select Finish. Select Control → Test Movie to play the video and the accompanying audio in Flash.

test a video   To use a video in Dreamweaver, it must be exported in the SWF format, so that it can be played with the Flash Player plug-in. A video exported to the SWF format is considerably smaller than the native file format of the video. Select File ➞ Export Movie to export a movie.

The steps for creating a Flash movie from video are:

1. Import the video file to a new Flash document.

2. Save the Flash document.

3. Preview the movie.

4. Export the document.

Practice: SAMPLER – part 10 of 10

Flash 8 and Dreamweaver 8 differences are indicated with parentheses (*ver.8:*).

① CREATE A NEW FLASH DOCUMENT AND SIZE THE STAGE

a. In Flash, close any open documents, saving if necessary.

b. Select File ➞ New. A dialog box is displayed.

c. Select Flash Document in the General tab and then select OK. A new document with a blank Stage is displayed.

② CREATE A MOVIE FROM VIDEO

a. Select File ➞ Import ➞ Import to Stage. A dialog box is displayed.

    1. Use the Look in list to navigate to the folder containing data files for this text.

    2. In the Files of type list, select All Video Formats.

    3. Select the CHICKENS.avi file.

    4. Select Open. A dialog box is displayed. (*ver.8:* In the dialog box, select Next and in the How would you like to deploy your video? options select Embed video in SWF and play in timeline. Select Next three times and then select Finish. Skip to step 3 to test the movie.)

        a) Select Import the entire video and then select Next.

        b) In the Compression profile list, select DSL/Cable 256 kbps and then select Finish. The video is imported.

    5. A dialog box is displayed with video frame requirements. Select Yes. The first frame of the video is displayed.

③ TEST THE MOVIE

a. Save the document in a folder that is outside of any website folder, naming it: chickens.fla

b. Select Control ➞ Test Movie. The movie is played in a separate window.

c. Close the preview window.

④ CREATE A MOVIE

a. Click anywhere in the gray workspace. Document properties are displayed in the Property inspector.

b. In the Property inspector, click the button next to the Size option. A dialog box is displayed. Click Contents and then select OK. (*ver.8:* The Stage does not change much).

   c. Save the modified chickens.fla.

   d. Export the movie as an SWF file to the media folder in the SAMPLER website folder, naming it: chickens.swf

   e. Save and close chickens.fla.

⑤ **INSERT THE FLASH MOVIE IN DREAMWEAVER**

   a. Switch to Dreamweaver.

   b. Open the SAMPLER website for editing if it is not the working website.

   c. In the Files panel, open the video_and_sound.htm web page document, if it is not already open.

   d. Scroll so that an empty cell is displayed.

   e. In the Assets panel, display the Flash category and refresh the list.

   f. Add the chickens.swf file from the Assets panel to the empty cell to the right of the text that reads "This example is a movie from a video file:" (*ver.8:* If the Object Tag Accessibility Attributes dialog box appears, select Cancel.)

   g. Save the modified video_and_sound.htm.

⑥ **PREVIEW THE FLASH MOVIE**

   a. Press F12. The web page document is displayed in a browser with the movie.

   b. Close the browser window. Dreamweaver is displayed.

⑦ **QUIT DREAMWEAVER AND FLASH**

Chapter Summary

This chapter introduces Flash buttons, Flash text and the Flash application. A Flash movie file can be an animated button, animated text, or an entire web application. Flash buttons and Flash text can be created directly in Dreamweaver, but animations beyond these must be created in Flash.

Dreamweaver includes predefined Flash buttons which are saved as Flash movie files with an .swf extension. In a Dreamweaver document, Flash buttons should be arranged in a nested table with each button in a separate cell.

Flash text allows the use of a variety of fonts in a web page document. Flash text can include a rollover color and a link.

Animation is the result of many images shown quickly one after the other to create the effect of movement. In Flash, a Timeline correlates images to a particular moment in the movie. At any point in a movie, there is a frame with an image. Flash documents are automatically saved in FLA format, which should be saved to a location outside of the website's root folder and used to export a movie file to the website in SWF format.

Images drawn in Flash are vector graphics. The tools in the Tools panel are used to create images. The process of creating a Flash movie includes setting document properties, creating images, and using the Timeline to lay out the sequence of the images. The animation is previewed and then the document is exported.

When creating images in Flash, rulers and a grid can be displayed to help place objects. Onion Skins are also used to help in the placement of objects.

In a new Flash document, the first frame in the Timeline is a blank keyframe. Use tools in the Tools panel to create an image on the Stage for the first keyframe, then add another keyframe which creates static frames between the two keyframes. The image in the new keyframe can then be modified to progress the animation. To speed up or slow down an animation, delete or add static frames.

To use a Flash document in Dreamweaver, it must be exported in SWF format so that it can be played with the Flash Player plug-in. For better organization, Flash movies exported from Flash should be stored in a media folder in the website root folder. In Dreamweaver, Flash movie files are displayed in the Flash category in the Assets panel.

A tweened animation is an animation where Flash generates the keyframes between the first keyframe and the last. In shape tweening, one shape changes into a different shape. In motion tweening, a single symbol moves from a start location to an end location on the Stage. Text can be broken apart into individual characters and then placed onto layers so that a word or phrase can be motion tweened.

A Flash movie file should be as small a file size as possible to keep web page load times as short as possible. Techniques for optimizing an animation for size include using symbols for images that appear more than once, using tweened animation, and using layers for objects that do not change from frame to frame. Symbols are stored in a Flash Library and used to create instances on the Stage. An instance is a reference to a symbol, rather than a copy of an image.

Flash documents of any complexity should be divided into layers so that the image on one layer can be modified without changing the images on other layers. In animation, an image on one layer can be tweened without affecting the other layers. Layer names can be changed and layers can be hidden to help work with the animation.

Sound can be added to a Flash movie by importing a sound file to the document's Library and then adding the file to a layer. Video can also be imported to Flash and then exported as a Flash movie.

Vocabulary

Anchor points   Points that define sections of a line or shape in an object.

Animation   The result of many images shown quickly one after the other to create the effect of movement.

Flash movie file   An animated button, animated text, or an entire web application.

Frame   A Flash movie component that shows an image.

Frame-by-frame animation   A movie created from a set of specified images.

Instance   A reference to a symbol.

Layers   A component of a Flash document that can be compared to images drawn on transparent sheets of paper placed one on top of the other.

Morphing   A technique that turns one shape into another.

Motion tweening   A form of tweened animation where a symbol is tweened to move from a start location to an end location.

Onion skinning   Displaying two or more frames at the same time to help position and edit images.

Property inspector   Area of the Flash window that contains options to modify object properties.

Shape tweening   A form of tweened animation that turns one shape into another.

Stage   The area used to create a Flash movie.

Symbols   Stored in a Flash Library and used to create instances on the Stage.

Timeline   A Flash movie component which correlates images to a particular moment in the movie.

Tools panel   Area of the Flash window that contains tools for drawing, painting, and selecting.

Tweened animation   An animation where Flash generates the keyframes between the first keyframe and the last.

Vector graphic   A graphic that is composed of lines connected by points.

Workspace   The gray area around the Stage, which is used as a temporary storage area while working.

Dreamweaver Commands and Buttons

button   Clicked to play the selected Flash movie. Found in the Assets panel.

button   Clicked to stop the playing of the selected Flash movie. Found in the Assets panel.

Flash icon   Displays a list of all the Flash files in the website. Found in the Assets panel.

Insert button   Inserts the selected movie at the insertion point. Found in the Assets panel.

Play button   Previews a Flash button, Flash text, or a Flash movie. Found in the Property inspector.

Stop button   Stops a Flash button, Flash text, or Flash movie preview. Found in the Property inspector.

Flash Commands and Buttons

Break Apart command Breaks text into separate letter objects. Found in the Modify menu.

Brush Mode Changes what is painted. Found in the Tools panel.

Brush Shape Changes the shape of the brush stroke. Found in the Tools panel.

Brush Size Changes the size of the brush stroke. Found in the Tools panel.

Brush tool Paints with brush-like strokes. Found in the Tools panel.

Convert to Symbol command Displays a dialog box used to convert a selected object to a symbol. Found in the Modify menu.

Delete Layer button Deletes a selected layer. Found below the Layers list.

Distribute to Layers command Automatically distributes separate letter objects to an individual layer and names the layer. Found in Modify → Timeline.

Eraser tool Deletes parts of a shape. Found in the Tools panel.

Export Movie command Displays a dialog box used to export a Flash movie in SWF format. Found in File → Export.

Fill Color Changes the fill color of the tool. Found in the Tools panel.

Hand tool Moves the Stage within the workspace. Found in the Tools panel.

Import to Stage command Displays a dialog box used to import a video into a Flash document. Found in File → Import.

Import to Library command Displays a dialog box used to import a sound file into the Flash Library. Found in File → Import.

Insert Keyframe command Adds a new keyframe and creates static frames between two keyframes. Found in the menu displayed by right-clicking a frame.

Insert Layer button Adds a layer to a document.

Library command Displays the Flash Library. Found in the Window menu.

Line tool Draws a line. Found in the Tools panel.

Onion Skin button Displays Onion Skin markers. Found in the Timeline.

Oval tool Draws an oval shape. Found in the Tools panel.

Paint Bucket tool Fills enclosed areas with a selected color. Found in the Tools panel.

Pen tool Draws straight or curved lines. Found in the Tools panel.

Pencil tool Draws free-form lines and shapes. Found in the Tools panel.

Play command Previews an animation. Found in the Control menu.

PolyStar tool Draws polygons and star shapes. Found in the Tools panel.

Rectangle tool Draws a rectangular shape. Found in the Tools panel.

Rewind command Moves the Playhead to frame 1. Found in the Control menu.

Rulers command Displays rulers along the top and left side of the work area. Found in the View menu.

Selection tool Selects objects. Found in the Tools panel.

Show Grid command Displays a set of gridlines on the Stage. Found in the Grid submenu in the View menu.

Stroke Color Changes the outline color of the tool. Found in the Tools panel.

Subselection tool Adjusts anchor points, which define sections of a line or shape. Found in the Tools panel.

Test Movie command Previews a Flash movie in a separate Flash window. Found in the Control menu.

Text tool Creates a text block. Found in the Tools panel.

Transform command Displays a window used to scale, rotate, and skew an object. Found in Window → Design Panels.

Zoom tool Changes the magnification level of the Stage. Found in the Tools panel.

1. a) What is Flash technology used for?
    b) A Flash movie can be an animated button. List two other examples of what a Flash movie file can be.

2. What application is used to create Flash buttons and Flash text?

3. List the steps required to add a Flash button to a saved web page document.

4. Why should a nested table that has cells sized in pixels be used to arrange Flash buttons in a web page document?

5. In Dreamweaver, where are Flash movies listed?

6. a) Why would Flash text be used?
    b) List the steps required to add Flash text to a saved web page document.
    c) How can Flash text be edited?

7. What is animation?

8. a) What function does a Timeline perform in an animation?
    b) Why is layering used in an animation?

9. a) What is the Stage?
    b) What is the workspace?

10. a) Where should a Flash document be saved?
    b) What format is a Flash document saved in?
    c) What format must a Flash document be exported in so that it can be used in a web page document?

11. a) What is a vector graphic?
    b) How does the file size of a vector-based graphic compare to the file size of a bitmap graphic?

12. What are the tools in the Tools panel used for?

13. List the five steps involved in the process of creating a Flash movie.

14. What is the frame rate?

15. a) What is the Timeline used for?
    b) What does a keyframe contain?
    c) What does a static frame contain?
    d) What is the elapsed time?

16. What does previewing an image show and demonstrate?

17. What is frame-by-frame animation?

18. a) List the steps required to add a keyframe.
    b) Why are static frames needed?

19. What should be done if an animation is moving too slowly?

20. What is onion skinning?

21. List three common ways to modify an image.

22. List the steps required to export a Flash document so that it can be used in Dreamweaver.

23. Where should Flash movies exported in SWF format for a website be stored?

24. What is displayed when a movie created in Flash is added to a web page document?

25. a) What is a tweened animation?
    b) List one type of tweened animation.
    c) What is morphing?

26. List the steps required to create a shape tweened animation.

27. Why should Flash movie files be a small file size?

28. a) Where are symbols stored?
    b) What is an instance?

29. a) List the steps required to convert a selected object to a symbol.
    b) How is an instance of a symbol created?

30. a) What is motion tweening?
    b) What can motion tweening be applied to?

31. List the steps required to create a motion tweened animation.

32. What path does motion tweening use?

33. What can layers be compared to?

34. List the steps required to create a new layer, change the name of the layer to horse, and then hide the layer.

35. List the steps required to animate text so that the individual letters of a word move onto the Stage from different directions.

36. Why are sound files imported to the document's Library?

37. List the steps required to add a sound to an animation.

38. List three video file formats supported by Flash.

39. How do you test a Flash movie that contains a video?

True/False

40. Determine if each of the following are true or false. If false, explain why.
    a) Nested tables ensure the layout of Flash buttons in a Navigation bar.
    b) In Dreamweaver, Flash movie files can be previewed in the Assets panel.
    c) The Timeline is used to control the rollover behavior of Flash text.
    d) Flash documents are automatically saved in SWF format.
    e) The Text tool is used to create a keyframe.
    f) A Flash document is exported in FLA format.
    g) At least two keyframes are required to create a shape tweened animation.
    h) Symbols are stored in the Assets panel.
    i) An instance is a Flash movie file.
    j) A sound file needs to be on a separate layer.
    k) A video exported to SWF format is larger than the video in the native file format.

Exercises

Exercise 1 ——————————————————————— CAT TOYS

Use Flash and Dreamweaver to modify the CAT TOYS website by completing the following steps:

a) In Dreamweaver, open the CAT TOYS website for editing, a website provided with the data files for this text.

b) Modify the copyright info library item by replacing Name with your name. Allow Dreamweaver to update all occurrences of the library item.

c) Modify the index.htm web page document as follows:

   1. In the second row, insert a nested table with 1 row, 2 columns, a width of 400 pixels, no border, a cell padding of 4, and no cell spacing.

   2. In the left cell of the nested table, insert a Flash button in a style of your choice, with the text Rolling Toys and linked to roll.htm. Save the Flash button using the name: bt_roll.swf

   3. In the right cell of the nested table, insert a second Flash button using the bt_roll.swf button with the text Bouncing Toys and linked to bounce.htm. Save the Flash button using the name: bt_bounce.swf

   4. Adjust the widths of the nested table and table cells by previewing the web page document in a browser and setting the W property appropriately in Dreamweaver.

d) Modify the roll.htm web page document as follows:

   1. In the second row, insert a nested table with 1 row, 2 columns, a width of 400 pixels, no border, a cell padding of 4, and no cell spacing.

   2. In the left cell of the nested table, insert a Flash button using the bt_roll.swf button with the text Home and linked to index.htm. Save the Flash button using the name: bt_home.swf

   3. In the right cell of the nested table, insert the bt_bounce.swf Flash button.

   4. Adjust the widths of the nested table and table cells by previewing the web page document in a browser and setting the W property appropriately in Dreamweaver.

e) Modify the bounce.htm web page document as follows:

   1. In the second row, insert a nested table with 1 row, 2 columns, a width of 400 pixels, no border, a cell padding of 4, and no cell spacing.

   2. In the left cell of the nested table, insert the bt_home.swf Flash button.

   3. In the right cell of the nested table, insert the bt_roll.swf Flash button.

   4. Adjust the widths of the nested table and table cells by previewing the web page document in a browser and setting the W property appropriately in Dreamweaver.

f) Modify the index.htm web page document as follows:

   1. In the empty cell below the cat photo, add Flash text in a font of your choice, with a size of 24, a color and rollover color of your choice, using the text See the Rolling Toys! and linked to roll.htm. Save the Flash text using the name: text_roll.swf

2. In the empty cell below the Flash text just added, add Flash text in the same font, size, and colors as the text_roll.swf, using the text See the Bouncing Toys! and linked to bounce.htm. Save the Flash button using the name: text_bounce.swf

g) In the CAT TOYS root folder, create a folder named media.

h) Start Flash and create a new document. Save the document outside of any website folder naming it cattoysinc.fla. Create animated text with sound as follows:

1. Create animated text with letters that start in the left side of the Stage in a pile (on top of each other) and move to the right to recreate the text Cat Toys Inc. in a font and color of your choice and a size of 60.

2. Import the MEOW.wav sound file to the Library. Place the sound file in a new layer named kitty, creating keyframes as necessary.

3. Change the dimensions of the stage to just accommodate the objects.

4. Export the Flash movie to the CAT TOYS media folder naming it: cattoysinc.swf

i) In Flash, create a new document. Save the document outside of any website folder naming it ani_roll.fla. Create a motion-tweened animation as follows:

1. Draw a solid circle in a red color and convert it to a Graphic symbol named toy.

2. Create keyframes and apply motion tweening so that the circle moves in a straight line from the left to the right on the Stage and back again.

3. Change the dimensions of the stage to just accommodate the objects.

4. Export the Flash movie to the CAT TOYS media folder naming it: ani_roll.swf

j) In Flash, create a new document. Save the document outside of any website folder naming it ani_bounce.fla. Create a motion-tweened animation as follows:

1. Draw a solid circle in a red color and convert it to a Graphic symbol named toy.

2. Create keyframes and apply motion tweening so that the circle moves in a straight line from the top to the bottom on the Stage and back again.

3. Change the dimensions of the stage to just accommodate the objects.

4. Export the Flash movie to the CAT TOYS media folder naming it: ani_bounce.swf

k) In Dreamweaver, modify the index.htm web page document by inserting the cattoysinc.swf file in the top cell. With the Flash movie placeholder selected, clear the Loop check box in the Property inspector.

l) In Dreamweaver, modify the roll.htm web page document as follows:

1. Insert the cattoysinc.swf file in the top row and, with the Flash movie placeholder selected, clear the Loop check box in the Property inspector.

2. Insert the ani_roll.swf file in the third row.

m) In Dreamweaver, modify the bounce.htm web page document as follows:

1. Insert the cattoysinc.swf file in the top cell and, with the Flash movie placeholder selected, clear the Loop check box in the Property inspector.

2. Insert the ani_bounce.swf file in the tall empty cell in the left side of the table.

n) View each web page document in a browser window and test the Flash buttons and Flash text.

o) Print a copy of each web page document from the browser.

Use Flash and Dreamweaver to modify the MEASUREMENTS website by completing the following steps:

a) In Dreamweaver, open the MEASUREMENTS website for editing, a website provided with the data files for this text.

b) Modify the footer library item by replacing Name with your name. Allow Dreamweaver to update all occurrences of the library item.

c) Modify the index.htm web page document as follows:

   1. In the top row, add Flash text in a font of your choice, with a size of 38, a color and rollover color of your choice, using the text Scientific Measurement and linked to index.htm. Save the Flash text using the name: logo.swf

   2. In the second row, in the left cell of the nested table, insert a Flash button. The button should be in a style of your choice, with the text SI Derived Units linked to derive.htm and saved using the name bt_derive.swf. If the text does not fit well on the button, change the Size of the text in the Insert Flash Button dialog box until it fits.

   3. In the right cell of the nested table, insert a second Flash button using the bt_derive.swf button with the text SI Prefixes and linked to prefix.htm. Save the Flash button using the name: bt_prefix.swf

   4. Adjust the widths of the nested table and table cells by previewing the web page document in a browser and setting the W property appropriately in Dreamweaver.

d) Modify the prefix.htm web page document as follows:

   1. In the top row, add the Flash text logo.swf.

   2. In the second row, in the left cell of the nested table, insert a Flash button using the bt_prefix.swf button with the text Home and linked to index.htm. Save the Flash button using the name: bt_home.swf

   3. In the right cell of the nested table, insert the bt_derive.swf Flash button.

   4. Adjust the widths of the nested table and table cells by previewing the web page document in a browser and setting the W property appropriately in Dreamweaver.

e) Modify the derive.htm web page document as follows:

   1. In the top row, add the Flash text logo.swf.

   2. In the second row, in the left cell of the nested table, insert the bt_home.swf Flash button.

   3. In the right cell of the nested table, insert the bt_prefix.swf Flash button.

   4. Adjust the widths of the nested table and table cells by previewing the web page document in a browser and setting the W property appropriately in Dreamweaver.

f) View each web page document in a browser window and test the Flash buttons and Flash text.

g) Print a copy of each web page document from the browser.

Exercise 3 ————————————————————Cooking Herbs

The Cooking Herbs website was created in Chapter 3, Exercise 1. Use Flash and Dreamweaver to further modify the Cooking Herbs website by completing the following steps:

a) In Dreamweaver, open the Cooking Herbs website for editing.

b) In the Cooking Herbs website, create a folder named media.

c) Start Flash and create a new document. Save the document outside of any website folder naming it herbstitle.fla. Create animated text as follows:

    1. Create animated text with letters that start in the left side of the Stage in a pile (on top of each other) and move to the right to recreate the text Cooking Herbs in a font and color of your choice and a size of at least 36.

    2. Change the dimensions of the stage to just accommodate the objects.

    3. Export the Flash movie to the Cooking Herbs media folder naming it: herbstitle.swf

d) Modify the index.htm web page document as follows:

    1. Add a new row above the top row in the table.

    2. In the top row, insert the herbstitle.swf file and, with the Flash movie placeholder selected, clear the **Loop** check box in the property inspector.

    3. In the second row, delete the text Cooking Herbs.

    4. In the second row, insert a nested table with 1 row, 2 columns, a width of 400 pixels, no border, a cell padding of 4, and no cell spacing.

    5. In the left cell of the nested table, insert a Flash button in a style of your choice, with the text Herbs and linked to popular_herbs.htm. Save the Flash button using the name: bt_popular.swf

    6. In the right cell of the nested table, insert a second Flash button using the bt_popular.swf button with the text Recipes and linked to recipes.htm. Save the Flash button using the name: bt_recipes.swf

    7. Adjust the widths of the nested table and table cells by previewing the web page document in a browser and setting the W property appropriately in Dreamweaver.

e) Modify the popular_herbs.htm web page document as follows:

    1. Add two new rows above the top row in the table.

    2. In the top row, add the text Popular Herbs and tag the text with Heading 1 tags.

    3. In the second row, insert a nested table with 1 row, 2 columns, a width of 400 pixels, no border, a cell padding of 4, and no cell spacing.

    4. In the left cell of the nested table, insert a Flash button using the bt_popular.swf button with the text Home and linked to index.htm. Save the Flash button using the name: bt_home.swf

    5. In the right cell of the nested table, insert the bt_recipes.swf Flash button.

    6. Adjust the widths of the nested table and table cells by previewing the web page document in a browser and setting the W property appropriately in Dreamweaver.

f) Modify the recipes.htm web page document as follows:

    1. In the top row, merge the two cells into one cell.

    2. Add a new row above the top row in the table.

    3. In the top row, add the text Recipes and tag the text with Heading 1 tags.

    4. In the second row, delete the existing text and then insert a nested table with 1 row, 2 columns, a width of 400 pixels, no border, a cell padding of 4, and no cell spacing.

    5. In the left cell of the nested table, insert the bt_home.swf Flash button.

    6. In the right cell of the nested table, insert the bt_popular.swf Flash button.

    7. Adjust the widths of the nested table and table cells by previewing the web page document in a browser and setting the W property appropriately in Dreamweaver.

e) View each web page document in a browser window and test the Flash buttons and Flash text.

f) Print a copy of each web page document from the browser.

Exercise 4 —————————————————— transformation.fla

Create a Flash file that uses shape tweening to change a red oval into an orange rectangle and then into a blue oval. Save the Flash file naming it transformation.fla.

Exercise 5 —————————————————————— puzzle.fla

Create a Flash file that uses frame-by-frame animation to assemble shapes into a large image. For example, a few squares of varying sizes could fit together to make a large square. Another example would be squares and circles that move into a square or round formation. Save the Flash file naming it puzzle.fla.

Exercise 6 ————————————————————— Flash Logos

Develop a website that showcases your talent for creating logos in Flash. The website should contain:

- at least three web page documents: a home page, a page with logos created in Flash, and a page with logos created using Flash text

- navigation bars that include using Flash buttons

- at least four logos that are created in Flash and exported to the Flash Logos website

- at least four logos created in Dreamweaver with Flash text

Preview the website in a browser. When satisfied with the website, print a copy of each web page document from the browser.

Exercise 7 ——————————————————————— Rubrics

The Rubrics website was last modified in Chapter 6, Exercise 7. Use Dreamweaver to further modify the Rubrics website by completing the following steps:

a) In Dreamweaver, open the Rubrics website for editing.

b) Create a new web page document naming it: flash_rubric.htm

c) Modify the index.htm web page document as follows:

    1. In the third row, place the insertion point at the end of the text Style Sheet Rubric, press Enter, and then type the text: Flash Rubric

    2. Link the text Flash Rubric to flash_rubric.htm.

d) Modify the flash_rubric.htm web page document as follows:

    1. Link the rubric_style.css style sheet to the web page document.

    2. Change the page title to: Flash Rubric

    3. Open the wpd_rubric.htm document, copy the entire table and paste it into the flash_rubric.htm web page document.

    4. In the top cell, replace the text with: Flash Rubric

    5. In the second row, replace the text single web page document with the text:

        Flash in a website

    6. Replace the first three criteria with these criteria:

        1. Flash buttons are consistent throughout the website.

        2. Flash movies enhance the web page content.

        3. Flash text enhances the user's experience.

    7. Brainstorm in small groups to generate two additional Flash rubric criteria. Replace the last two criteria in the rubric with these two.

e) Check the spelling in the flash_rubric.htm web page document.

f) View the index.htm and flash_rubric.htm web page documents in a browser window.

g) Print a copy of index.htm and flash_rubric.htm from the browser.

h) In a browser window, view the web pages of a website that has Flash content and was created by a peer. Use the Flash rubric to evaluate the website.

i) Reflect on the design of the rubric. Does it appropriately assess the Flash content of a website? Are there criteria that should be added or changed? Make any appropriate revisions and print a copy.

Exercise 8 —————————————————— Flash Button Samples

Develop a website named Flash Button Samples that contains many different Flash buttons. The website should contain at least:

- four web page documents, each with a navigation bar created using Flash buttons different from the other web page documents

- one animated text logo, created in Flash and exported to the Flash Button Samples website

Preview the website in a browser. When satisfied with the website, print a copy of each web page document from the browser.

Exercise 9 ——————————————————————— gumball.fla

Create a Flash file that uses motion tweening and layers to recreate a gumball machine that has the gumballs roll out of it through the dispenser opening. Save the Flash file naming it gumball.fla. The gumball machine could look similar to:

Chapter 7 Introducing Flash

Chapter 8

Website Content and ColdFusion Technology

This chapter discusses various website categories including electronic portfolios. Site maps and forms are introduced. ColdFusion technology is also discussed.

Electronic Portfolios

A *portfolio* is a collection of work that clearly illustrates effort, progress, knowledge, achievement, and skills. Traditional portfolios typically take the form of a file folder or a three-ring binder. An *electronic portfolio* stores and presents portfolio content in a digital format such as a website:

Christopher Kemp
Electronic Portfolio
Last updated March 3, 2006

▷ Home   ▷ Academics   ▷ Sports   ▷ Experiences   ▷ Volunteer Work

My academic focus in high school has been Biology and Chemistry. I competed on the school tennis team and wrestling team every school year. I have participated in programs at the local art museum and also for the Restore the Everglades Foundation. I am especially proud of my volunteer work with the Special Olympics. Most of my spare time is devoted to outdoor activities, including hiking, biking, canoeing, and kayaking. I have also been a counselor at a summer camp for pre-teens.

Please request additional information.

Contact Chistopher Kemp with any questions about this electronic portfolio. Copyright 2006.

Electronic portfolios are preferred over traditional portfolios because they:

- are interactive
- can include sound, video, and digital images
- are easy to access, distribute, and share
- take up less space than a binder or stack of work samples
- can be updated easily
- demonstrate technical knowledge

Viewing an Electronic Portfolio

An electronic portfolio website does not necessarily have to be posted on the Internet. It can also be e-mailed or burned to a CD. The user will be able to view the site as long as they have access to a web browser.

Personal Information

An electronic portfolio website contains personal information and therefore should only be posted to a secure server with limited access or distributed on a CD.

College Admission Requirement

Some colleges and universities require an electronic portfolio as part of their admissions process.

The content and design of electronic portfolios will vary depending on the purpose and target audience. For example, an electronic portfolio for admission to college would have a design that reflects individuality and creativity and could include detailed academic and athletic information as well as samples of work. An electronic portfolio for a job search would have a professional appearance and include career objectives, résumé information, work samples, and links to related websites.

In general, the home page of an electronic portfolio website should include an introduction, contact information, and appropriate links. Additional content and design considerations for an electronic portfolio include:

- **Résumé information**, such as education, work experience, volunteer work, awards, and athletic achievements.

- An **e-mail link** to allow portfolio reviewers to send comments, questions, or request additional information.

- The **person's name** on every web page.

- **Work samples,** which may be scanned images or links to files.

Website Categories

Most websites can be classified into general categories by the type of content: personal, informational, and commercial. Within each category there are many specific types of websites. For example, electronic portfolios are a type of personal website.

personal websites

Personal websites typically convey the opinions, hobbies, knowledge, or skills of an individual. The purpose and target audience of a personal website vary depending on the focus of the content. For example, the purpose of the personal website below is to present information about beaches, and the target audience is anyone interested in beach vacations:

Inappropriate Content

A personal website is not an appropriate sounding board for slanderous remarks.

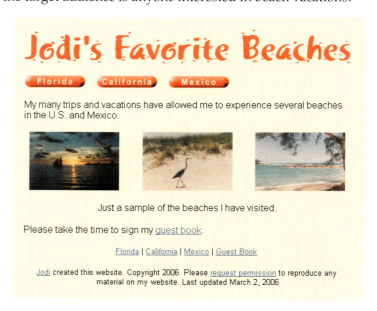

Personal websites may include:

- **information on a topic of interest**, such as sea shells, model airplanes, or competitive swimming.
- a **compilation of likes and dislikes**, such as links to favorite websites or an opinion on a particular topic.
- **personal information**, such as travel photos.

Internet Safety

Never include identifying information, such as a home address, telephone number, or age on a personal website.

informational websites

Informational websites are created for the purpose of displaying factual information about a particular topic and are typically created by educational institutions, governments, and organizations. An informational website can have a variety of content:

- a **site map** for easier navigation
- a **search form** so that users can search the site for information
- a **list of links** to websites that contain related information
- tables of **tabular data**
- **banner ads** or other advertising to help pay for site maintenance

Banner Ads

Banner ads are discussed in Appendix A, Banner Ads and ActionScript.

The purpose of an informational website is to provide factual information, and therefore the site should be updated frequently to keep the content accurate. The target audience varies for informational websites, but all users of this type of website are looking for information that is easy to find.

commercial websites
corporate presence websites

branding

Commercial websites include corporate presence websites and e-commerce websites. *Corporate presence websites* present information about a company's products or services, but do not have online ordering capabilities. The corporate presence website is a form of branding. *Branding* is the technique of raising awareness about a company by making a company logo visible in many places. Successful branding means the user will recognize the logo at a later time, such as when deciding which product to purchase at a store. The Bellur website includes a distinctive logo:

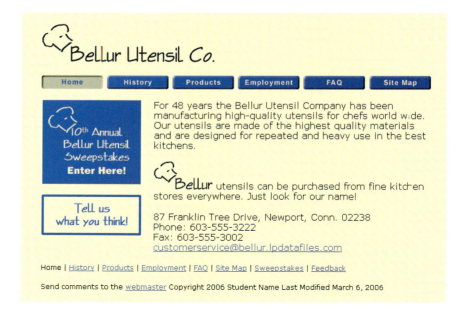

A corporate presence website typically includes:

- a **company history**
- a **list of products** or services
- a **FAQ** page
- a **site map**
- **search** capabilities
- a description of **employment opportunities**
- a **feedback page**
- a **promotion** or contest to keep users returning to the site

The purpose of a corporate presence website is to make users aware of the products and services offered by a company. The target audience varies greatly, but users may be looking for product or service information.

e-commerce websites

E-commerce websites are created by businesses for the purpose of selling their products or services to consumers online:

Amazon.com Inc.

amazon.com is a well known e-commerce website. Founded by Jeff Bezos in 1994, Amazon.com Inc. is an Internet retailer of books, music, toys, electronics, software, and other products.

E-commerce Websites

A company, such as Amazon.com Inc., that does business primarily on the Web is often referred to as dot-com. Other e-commerce websites, such as gap.com, are an extension of an existing brick-and-mortar business, which is a term used to describe a traditional business.

An e-commerce website typically includes:

- product and service **descriptions**
- **visuals** of available products
- **search** capabilities
- a **site map**
- **contact** and **return** information
- a **promotion** or coupon to keep users returning to the site
- **personalized user account** information
- a **shopping cart**

Creating a FAQ Page

A *FAQ* (pronounced *fak*) page is a web page that contains frequently asked questions and their answers. The intent is to answer commonly asked questions quickly without the user having to call or send an e-mail. The FAQ often lists questions about where to find a company's products, use of certain products, what makes a product or service special, and so on:

Depending on the type of company, a FAQ may also list known problems and their solutions or other technical support questions.

① OPEN THE BELLUR WEBSITE FOR EDITING

a. Start Dreamweaver.

b. Open the BELLUR website for editing, which is a website provided with the data files for this text.

c. Familiarize yourself with the files and folders in this website.

d. Open the index.htm web page document and view the page in a browser.

e. Click the links to explore the other web pages of the website.

f. Close the browser window. Dreamweaver is displayed.

g. Close index.htm.

② MODIFY THE FAQ PAGE

a. Open the faq.htm web page document.

b. At the bottom of the list of questions and answers, place the insertion point after the period in craftsmanship. and press Enter.

c. Type the following text, allowing the text to wrap:

Q: What materials are used to make the very comfortable, long-lasting handles of the spoons and spatulas?

d. Insert a line break and then type the following text, allowing the text to wrap:

A: We use a special compound called Typlak, which was developed and is produced by the NowPont Chemical Company.

e. Select all of the questions and answers in the list and apply the faqtext CSS style.

f. Save the modified faq.htm.

③ PREVIEW AND PRINT THE WEB PAGE

a. Press F12. The document is displayed in a browser window.

b. Print the web page.

c. Close the browser window. Dreamweaver is displayed.

d. Close faq.htm.

Importing Tabular Data

Tables are used extensively for web page layout. Tables can also be used to display tabular data. *Tabular data* is data that has been created in another application and saved in a delimited text format, which can be a text (TXT) file. *Tab-delimited* data indicates that each item in each row is separated by a tab character. For example, the tabular data shown below is displayed in a table with nine rows and three columns. A border of 1 adds lines which makes the data easier to read. The event, location, and time data was separated by tabs and saved in a delimited text format before it was imported:

tab-delimited

TIP Select File → Export → Table to export Dreamweaver table data to a text file.

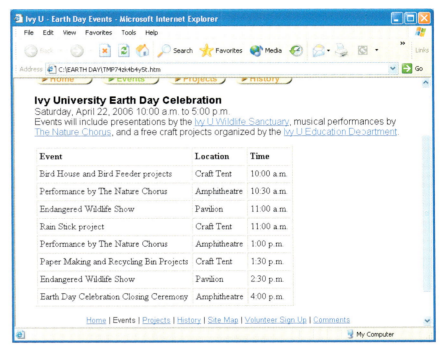

TIP The Insert → Table Objects → Import Tabular Data command can also be used to import tabular data.

To import tabular data and create a table for the data, click the Tabular Data button ( ) in the Layout category in the Insert bar. A dialog box is displayed:

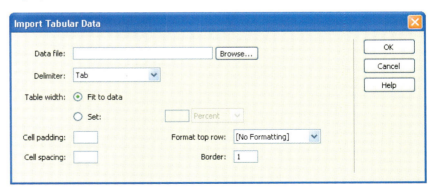

- Use the Browse button to navigate to the file that is to be imported and display the file name in Data File box.
- Select Tab in the Delimiter box for tab-delimited data.
- The Fit to Data option sizes the table to fit all the imported data.

- Set the Cell padding, Cell spacing, and Border options for the new table. It is recommended to include a border of at least 1 for a table of data to make the table more readable.
- Use the Format top row list to format the data in the top row of the table if the top row of the imported data contains column headings.

Select OK to create the table at the insertion point. Cell contents can be further formatted just like any cells in a table.

Practice: BELLUR – part 2 of 5

Dreamweaver should be started and the BELLUR website should be the working site.

① ADD A TABLE OF DATA

a. Open the products.htm web page document.

b. In the empty cell below the text Price List, place the insertion point.

c. In the Layout category in the Insert bar, click the Tabular Data button ( ). A dialog box is displayed.

d. Click Browse. A dialog box is displayed.

  1. Navigate to the root folder of the BELLUR site if it is not already displayed.

  2. Select bellur_price_list.txt and then select Open.

e. In the Import Tabular Data dialog box, set the rest of the options to:

f. Select OK. A new table is created and placed at the insertion point. The table contains data from the bellur_price_list.txt file and the text in the top row is bold.

g. Save the modified products.htm.

② VIEW THE TABLE IN A BROWSER

a. Press F12. The web page document is displayed in a browser window. Scroll to the table and note how the border lines make the data more readable.

b. Print a copy of the web page.

c. Close the browser window. Dreamweaver is displayed.

d. Close products.htm.

Chapter 8 Website Content and ColdFusion Technology

Creating a Site Map

A *site map* is a web page that contains links to information on other pages of the website. The links are usually arranged in alphabetical order or grouped by subject, as in the Earth Day site map:

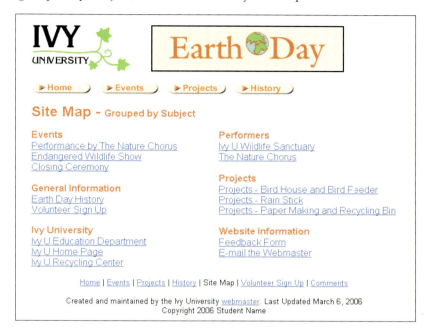

A site map helps users find the web page they are looking for if they cannot find the web page using the navigation bars. The links on a site map web page also provide an overview of the website's contents.

Practice: BELLUR – part 3 of 5

Dreamweaver should be started and the BELLUR website should be the working site.

① **ADD THE LINKS TO THE SITE MAP WEB PAGE DOCUMENT**

   a. Open the site_map.htm web page document.

   b. In the empty cell below the top global navigation bar, place the insertion point.

   c. Type the following text, pressing Enter at the end of each line:

   Bellur Utensil Company Site Map

   Company History

   Employment Opportunities

   FAQ Page

   Feedback Form

   Products and Prices

   Sweepstakes

   d. Select the text Bellur Utensil Company Site Map and apply the sitemaptitle CSS style.

e. Link text to web page documents as follows:

Link the text	to the web page document
Company History	history.htm
Employment Opportunities	employment.htm
FAQ Page	faq.htm
Feedback Form	feedback.htm
Products and Prices	products.htm
Sweepstakes	sweeps.htm

f. Select all the link text and apply the sitemaptext CSS style.

g. Save the modified site_map.htm.

② **VIEW THE SITE MAP IN A BROWSER**

a. Press F12. The web page document is displayed in a browser window. Test the links in the site map.

b. Print a copy of the web page.

c. Close the browser window. Dreamweaver is displayed.

d. Close site_map.htm.

Adding Jump Menus

A *jump menu* is a navigation tool that contains a list of text hyperlinks:

To add a jump menu at the insertion point, click the Jump Menu button (⬛) in the **Forms** category in the Insert bar. A dialog box is displayed:

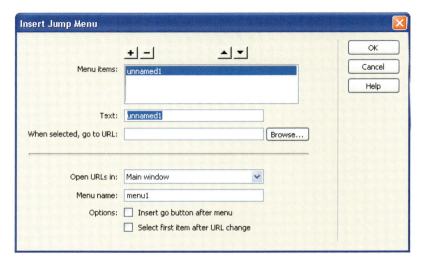

- The text and target URL for the selected menu item are set in the Text box and the When selected, go to URL box.

- Click **+** or **−** to add or delete Menu items.

- Click **▲** and **▼** to move a selected item up or down.

TIP It is a good design to include either a Go button or a first item prompt in a jump menu.

- Select Insert go button after menu to add a Go button (Go) next to the jump menu in the form.

prompt

- Select Select first item after URL change to have the list automatically return to the first item, which should be a prompt. A *prompt* is text in the first menu item that guides the user to select an item from the menu, for example Choose One or Select a Page. A prompt is not a list item that is a link.

test a jump menu

Select OK to create the jump menu. A jump menu can be tested in a browser window.

edit a jump menu

To edit a selected jump menu, double-click the Jump Menu action in the Behaviors panel:

TIP The red outline indicates that the Jump Menu is created within a form. Forms are discussed later in this chapter.

Click List Values... in the Property inspector to edit items in the list.

Practice: BELLUR – part 4 of 5

Dreamweaver should be started and the BELLUR website should be the working site.

① ADD A JUMP MENU

a. Open the index.htm web page document.

b. Place the insertion point to the left of the dark blue "10th Annual Bellur Utensil Sweepstakes" image.

c. In the Forms category in the Insert bar, click the Jump Menu button (🔗). A dialog box is displayed.

  1. In the Text box, type: select a page. A prompt is added.

  2. Click **+**. Another menu item is added.

  3. In the Text box, type: Employment

  4. Click Browse. A dialog box is displayed.

  5. Select employment.htm and then select OK. Employment is added to the Menu items list and the When selected, go to URL box displays employment.htm.

  6. Add the following menu items, selecting the appropriate URLs:

       FAQ

       Feedback

       Home

       History

       Products

       Site Map

       Sweepstakes

7. In the Menu items list, click the History menu item and then click ▲ to move History above Home.

8. Select the Select first item after URL change check box.

9. Select OK. A form is added with a jump menu.

d. Save the modified index.htm.

② **VIEW THE FORM IN A BROWSER**

a. Press F12. The web page document is displayed in a browser window.

b. Print a copy of the web page.

c. Test the jump menu links.

d. Close the browser window. Dreamweaver is displayed.

e. Close index.htm.

Creating a Form

A *form* allows users to communicate and interact with a web server. Forms are used extensively on websites for tasks such as surveys, polls, online ordering, and guest books. The web page below contains a form for a guest book:

> **TIP** The design of a form should be simple to use, easy to understand, and as short as possible.

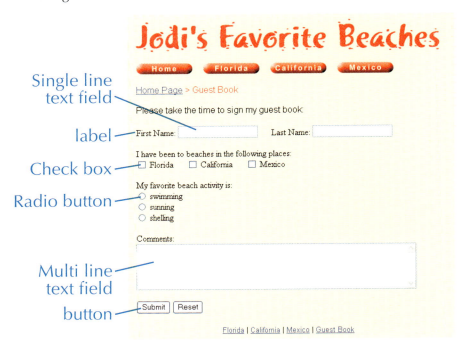

Form objects are used to obtain information from the user in a structured manner:

> **TIP** The size of a form is determined by the form objects that are added. Therefore, a form cannot be sized by dragging.

- **Single line text field** allows the user to type a short amount of text.

- **Labels** describe the purpose of a form object.

- **Check boxes** and **radio buttons** allow the user to select options.

Chapter 8 Website Content and ColdFusion Technology

- **Multi line text field** allow the user to type one or more lines of text.

- **Buttons** are used to send the form results to a file or to an e-mail address, and to clear the form entries.

A form and form objects are created using buttons in the Forms category in the Insert bar:

Form   Text Field   Button   Label

TIP It is possible to have multiple forms on a page, but forms cannot be nested.

A form should be created in a table cell to control the form layout. To create a form, place the insertion point in a table cell and then click the Form button (▢) in the Insert bar. A form indicated by a dashed red outline is created and the insertion point is placed in the form:

TIP Form objects may also be added at the insertion point by selecting commands in the Insert ➜ Form submenu.

To add objects at the insertion point, click a button in the Forms category in the Insert bar. For example, click the Label button (abc), type First Name:, click the Text Field button (▢), press Enter and then click the Button button (▢) to create the form below (*ver.8:* If the Input Tag Accessibility Attributes dialog box appears, select Cancel to insert the object.):

Version 8 Dreamweaver 8 differences are indicated with parentheses (*ver.8:*).

Labels

When the Label button (abc) is clicked, Dreamweaver automatically displays the page in Split view. Typed label text is enclosed in <label> and </label> tags. The <label> tag can then be defined in a style sheet for consistent label formatting.

Form object properties are set in the Property inspector. For example, select a text field to display the following properties:

- Type a name for the form object in the TextField box. Each object in a form should have a descriptive name because the names are included in the file containing the form results. Object names cannot contain spaces.

- Select Multi line to change the field to a multi-line text field.

- Select Password to allow users to enter data, such as a password, secretly. A character, such as •, is displayed on the screen to represent the characters the user is typing.

TIP If the number of characters entered in a text field exceeds the set Char width, the characters will not be viewable but they will be processed by the form.

- Type a value greater than 0 in the Char width box to indicate the number of characters that can be displayed in the text field.

- Type a value greater than 0 in the Max Chars box to indicate the maximum number of characters that the field can accept. The value may be more or less than the number of characters that can be displayed.

- Init val is text that should appear in the text field when the form loads. This property is often left empty. Text can be typed by the user to set the initial value.

A Button form object has the following properties:

- Button name is the form object name.

- Label (*ver.8*: Value) is the text that appears on the button. The Button form object automatically resizes to accommodate the text.

- Action is used to determine what action is taken when the user clicks the button. Submit form sends the form contents to the server. Reset form clears the form fields and allows the user to start over again. None indicates no action.

test form objects Form objects can be tested in a browser window. However, the form will not interact with a server unless a server-side script or application has been defined.

Check Boxes and Radio Buttons

A *Check Box form object* allows the user to select an option by clicking a check box. More than one check box can be selected at the same time. The *Radio Group form object* allows the user to only select one radio button from each group.

Click the Checkbox button (☑) in the Forms category in the Insert bar to add a check box form object. (*ver.8*: If the Input Tag Accessibility Attributes dialog box appears, select Cancel to insert the object.) A check box form object has the following properties:

- CheckBox name is the form object name.

- Checked value indicates the value returned if the user selects the check box, which can be text or a numeric value.

- Initial state sets the check box to checked or unchecked when the form loads.

Radio button form objects should be added in groups. Click the Radio Group button (▤) in the Forms category in the Insert bar, which displays a dialog box:

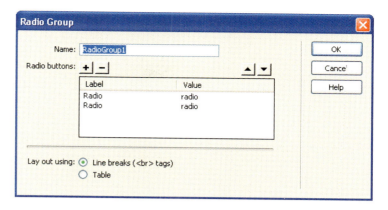

- Type a name for the radio button group in the Name box.

- The radio button group is created with at least two buttons, which are already listed in the Radio buttons list and include labels Radio and the values radio. Select each one and type a new label and value to change the radio buttons. Click **+** to add more radio buttons. Click **−** to delete a selected radio button.

- The Lay out using options indicate the way the radio buttons will be separated in the web page document. Select Line breaks (
 tags) to add a line break after each radio button. The Table value creates a one-column table with each radio button in a separate cell.

Select OK to create the radio buttons in the form at the insertion point.

Scrolling Lists and Drop-Down Menus

Forms often include a scrolling list or a drop-down menu, which allow users to easily select from a list of predetermined choices rather than typing responses. With limited choices, a form is more likely to be completed by the user and the form results are easier to evaluate. A *scrolling list* allows the user to select an option from a list of items by scrolling the list using a scroll bar:

Where do you typically purchase electronics?

scrolling list

Scrolling Lists vs. Drop-down Menus

A scrolling list differs from a drop-down menu in that it has scroll arrows, it can be enabled so that the user can select more than one option, and the height can be set.

A *drop-down menu* allows the user to select an option from a list of items that appear when the user clicks the ⌄ next to the list:

Select product of interest:

drop-down menu

To add a scrolling list, click the List/Menu button (⊞) in the Forms category in the Insert bar. (*ver.8:* If the Input Tag Accessibility Attributes dialog box appears, select Cancel to insert the object.) A scrolling list is created by selecting List in the Property inspector. A name for the list should be typed in the List/Menu box. Click [List Values...] to display a dialog box. The list items are added in this dialog box. Each item should have an Item Label, which is the text that is displayed in the scrolling list, and a value, which is returned to the server:

Click [+] to add an item and click [−] to delete the selected item. The [▲] and [▼] are used to move a selected item up or down in the list. Select OK to add the items to the form object.

In the Property inspector, the scrolling list can be further modified:

- Height is the number of items that should be displayed in the list. The rest of the items will be displayed when the list is scrolled.

- Select Allow multiple to enable the user to select more than one list item.

- Initially selected is the list item that will appear selected in the form object when the web page loads.

To create a drop-down menu, add a List/Menu form object and select Menu in the Property inspector. A name for the menu should be typed in the List/Menu box. Click [List Values...] to display a dialog box. The menu items are added in this dialog box. Each item should have an Item Label, which is the text that is displayed in the menu, and a value, which is returned to the server:

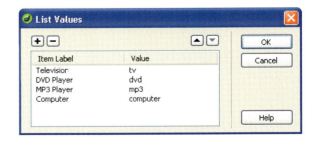

TIP For easy data entry, use the Tab key to move from Item Label to Value.

Click [+] to add an item and click [−] to delete the selected item. The [▲] and [▼] are used to move a selected item up or down in the list. Select OK to add the items to the form object.

In the Property inspector, one menu item can be selected in the Initially selected list, and that item will be selected in the form object when the web page loads.

The Validate Form Action

TIP The Validate Form Action only works with HTML forms.

The Validate Form action can be applied to a form to check the contents of a field for the correct type of data and to see if a value falls within a specified range. For example, a field could be checked to see if the data entered was numeric and in the range of 1 through 10.

To validate a field, name the field in the Property inspector and then select the form's Submit button. Select Window → Behaviors to display the Behaviors panel, click ➕, and select Validate Form to display a dialog box:

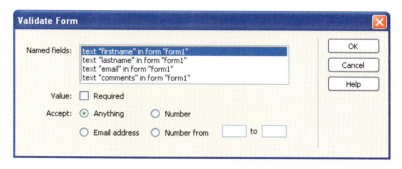

Select the field to validate and then select the Value Required check box to indicate that the field cannot be left blank. The Accept section includes additional options:

- Anything indicates the field can contain any type of data.
- Number indicates the field is to contain only numerals.
- Email address indicates the field will contain the @ symbol.
- Number from is used to specify a numeric range.

Select OK to apply the validation criteria to the field. The Validate Form action will be triggered by an onClick event, which occurs when a user clicks the Submit button.

onBlur and onChange Events

The Validate Form action can also be triggered by an onBlur or onChange event, which both occur when the user moves away from the validated field.

Practice: BELLUR – part 5 of 5

Dreamweaver should be started and the BELLUR website should be the working site. Dreamweaver 8 differences are indicated with parentheses (*ver.8:*).

① **ADD CHECK BOX FORM OBJECTS**

    a. Open the feedback.htm web page document. A form, labels, and text fields have already been added to this web page document.

    b. Place the insertion point to the right of the e-mail address text field and press Enter.

    c. In the Forms category in the Insert bar, click the Label button (abc). The page is displayed in Split view and the insertion point is between <label> and </label> tags. Type: What Bellur utensils do you own? (check all that apply)

d. Switch to Design view and insert a line break.

e. In the Forms category in the Insert bar, click the Checkbox button (☑). (*ver.8:* If the Input Tag Accessibility Attributes dialog box appears, select Cancel.) The logo now appears in A Check Box form object is inserted in the form.

f. In the Property inspector, set CheckBox name to: utility

g. In the Property inspector, set Checked value to: utility spoon

h. Place the insertion point to the right of the check box, type Utility Spoon and insert a line break.

i. In the Forms category in the Insert bar, click the Checkbox button (☑). (*ver.8:* If the Input Tag Accessibility Attributes dialog box appears, select Cancel.)

j. In the Property inspector, set CheckBox name to: perforated

k. In the Property inspector, set Checked value to: perforated spoon

l. Place the insertion point to the right of the check box, type Perforated Spoon and insert a line break.

m. Insert a Check Box form object and in the Property inspector, set CheckBox name to spatula and set Checked value to: spatula

n. Place the insertion point to the right of the check box, type Spatula and insert a line break.

o. Insert a Check Box form object and in the Property inspector, set CheckBox name to none and set Checked value to: none

p. Place the insertion point to the right of the check box, type None and then press Enter.

q. Save the modified feedback.htm.

② ADD A RADIO BUTTON GROUP FORM OBJECT

a. In the Forms category in the Insert bar, click the Label button (abc). The page is displayed in Split view and the insertion point is between <label> and </label> tags. Type: How often do you cook?

b. Switch to Design view and insert a line break.

c. In the Forms category in the Insert bar, click the Radio Group button (▤). A dialog box is displayed.

    1. In the Name box, type: Cook

    2. Click the first Radio label in the list and type: Often

    3. Click the first radio value in the list and type: often

    4. Click the next Radio label in the list and type: Sometimes

    5. Click the next radio value in the list and type: sometimes

    6. Click ➕. Another radio button is added to the list.

    7. Click the new Radio label in the list and type: Rarely

    8. Click the new radio value in the list and type: rarely

    9. Select OK. The radio buttons and labels are added to the form.

d. Save the modified feedback.htm.

Check—Your form should look similar to:

First Name: [   ]   Last Name: [   ]

E-mail address: [   ]

What Bellur utensils do you own? (check all that apply)
☐ Utility Spoon
☐ Perforated Spoon
☐ Spatula
☐ None

How often do you cook?
○ Often
○ Sometimes
○ Rarely

③ ADD A SCROLLING LIST

a. The insertion point should be just below the radio button group. Press the Backspace key to delete the extra line break and then press Enter.

b. In the Forms category in the Insert bar, click the Label button (abc). The page is displayed in Split view and the insertion point is between \<label> and \</label> tags. Type: Where do you purchase other cooking products?

c. Switch to Design view and insert a line break.

d. In the Forms category in the Insert bar, click the List/Menu button (📄). (*ver.8:* If the Input Tag Accessibility Attributes dialog box appears, select Cancel.) A List/Menu form object is added to the form.

e. In the Property inspector, set List/Menu to: where

f. In the Property inspector, select List.

g. In the Property inspector, click [List Values...]. A dialog box is displayed.

    1. In the Item Label list, type: Grocery

    2. Click in the Value list and type: grocery

    3. Click [+]. Another item is added to the list.

    4. For the new item, type Catalog for the Item Label and catalog for the Value.

    5. Add another item and type Specialty Shop for the Item Label and shop for the Value.

    6. Add another item and type Internet for the Item Label and internet for the Value.

    7. Select OK. The dialog box is removed.

h. In the Property inspector, set Height to: 3

i. In the Property inspector, in the Initially selected list select Grocery. The scrolling list now displays three items and Grocery is selected.

j. Save the modified feedback.htm.

④ ADD A POP-UP MENU

a. Place the insertion point to the right of the scrolling list and press Enter.

b. In the Forms category in the Insert bar, click the Label button (abc). The page is displayed in Split view and the insertion point is between \<label> and \</label> tags. Type: What new product would you most likely buy?

c. Switch to Design view and insert a line break.

d. In the Forms category in the Insert bar, click the List/Menu button (📄). (*ver.8:* If the Input Tag Accessibility Attributes dialog box appears, select Cancel.)

e. In the Property inspector, set List/Menu to: newprod

f. In the Property inspector, click [List Values...]. A dialog box is displayed.

    1. Click in the Item Label list and type: Whisk

    2. Click in the Value list and type: whisk

    3. Add another item and type Pasta Fork for the Item Label and pasta for the Value.

    4. Add another item and type Ladle for the Item Label and ladle for the Value.

    5. Select OK. The dialog box is removed.

g. In the Property inspector, in the Initially selected list select Whisk. Whisk is selected in the drop-down menu.

⑤ ADD A MULTI LINE TEXT FIELD

a. Place the insertion point to the right of the drop-down menu and press Enter.

b. In the Forms category in the Insert bar, click the Label button (abc). The page is displayed in Split view and the insertion point is between <label> and </label> tags. Type: Comments:

c. Switch to Design view and insert a line break.

d. In the Forms category in the Insert bar, click the Text Field button (▭). (*ver.8:* If the Input Tag Accessibility Attributes dialog box appears, select Cancel.)

e. In the Property inspector, set TextField to: comments

f. In the Property inspector, select Multi line.

⑥ ADD BUTTON FORM OBJECTS

a. Place the insertion point to the right of the Multi line text field and press Enter.

b. In the Forms category in the Insert bar, click the Button button (▭). A button is inserted.

c. Place the insertion point to the right of the button.

d. In the Forms category in the Insert bar, click the Button button (▭). (*ver.8:* If the Input Tag Accessibility Attributes dialog box appears, select Cancel.)

e. In the Property inspector, set Button name to Clear.

f. In the Property inspector, set Label (*ver.8:* Value) to: Clear Form

g. In the Property inspector, select Reset form.

h. Save the modified feedback.htm.

⑦ VALIDATE FORM OBJECTS

a. Select Window ➡ Behaviors. The Behaviors panel is displayed.

b. In the web page document, click the Submit button to select it.

c. In the Behaviors panel, click +, and select Validate Form from the displayed menu. A dialog box is displayed. Set the firstname field options to:

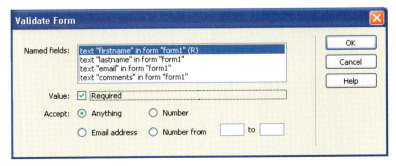

d. In the Named fields list, select the lastname field and set the options to:

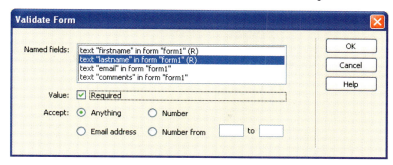

e. In the Named fields list, select the email field and set the options to:

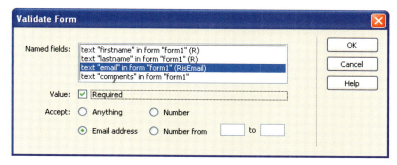

f. Select OK. When the form is posted to a web server, data will be required in the firstname, lastname, and email text field.

g. Saved the modified feedback.htm.

⑧ VIEW THE FORM IN A BROWSER

a. Press F12. The web page document is displayed in a browser window.

b. Print a copy of the web page.

c. Fill out the form and click Clear Form. The form resets.

d. Fill out the form again, leaving the First Name field blank and click Submit. An error dialog box is displayed indicating the firstname field is empty:

e. Test the other validated fields.

f. Close the browser window. Dreamweaver is displayed.

g. Close feedback.htm.

Interactive Forms

A form represents the client side of a client-server relationship because it allows the user to interact with the server. When the user clicks the Submit button, the form information is sent to a server where a *server-side script* or application processes it. Once a form is processed, information is sent back to the user:

server-side script

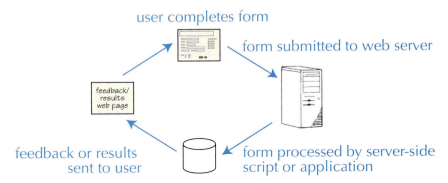

user completes form

form submitted to web server

feedback or results sent to user

form processed by server-side script or application

Forms can be processed by a CGI (Common Gateway Interface) script, ColdFusion page, JSP (JavaServer Page), ASP (Active Server Page) or other application. The server-side script or application used to process the form is defined in the form's **Action** property.

Select a form to display form properties in the Property inspector that allow the server-side script or application to be defined:

TIP Click the <form> tag on the Tag selection bar to select a form.

TIP The information for the Form properties is typically provided by the web host. web hosts are discussed in Chapter 9.

- Type a name for the form in the **Form name** box. A form should be named because it allows the form to be referenced using a script.

- **Action** is the path and file name or script name that will process the contents of the form when the Submit button is clicked.

- **Method** is the method that will transmit the form data to the server. The default method is POST.

- **Enctype** specifies how the information is to be sent, so the web server knows how to interpret the information.

client-side scripts

Simple forms can use JavaScript or VBScript to create a *client-side script* which processes a form on the user's computer instead of sending the information to the web server for processing. For example, a JavaScript could be added to display one message or another when the user clicks the Submit button based on the user's choice of two radio buttons. To create a client-side JavaScript function, select the Submit button in a form and then select **Window → Behaviors** to display the Behaviors panel. In the Behaviors panel, click **+** and select **Call JavaScript**. A dialog box is displayed:

Form Accessibility

To activate accessibility controls for a form, select Edit → Preferences and then select the Form objects checkbox in the Accessibility category.

Type processForm() in the JavaScript dialog box and then add a processForm() JavaScript function to the head section of the web page document to create a client-side script. Adding a processForm() JavaScript function requires knowledge of JavaScript.

Dynamic Web Pages

static web page

A *static web page* contains only text and images. A web page that contains any animation or is interactive is a *dynamic web page*. Dynamic content is content that changes as the source, such as a database, is updated. A website that includes dynamic content on any of the web pages is a *dynamic website*, also called a *web application*. A dynamic website employs a server technology, such as *ColdFusion*, to process input from the user and then send a web page with dynamic content to the user's browser. The information that is returned to the user is from a data source such as a database file.

ColdFusion

The developer edition of ColdFusion is bundled with the Windows version of Studio MX 2004. It can also be downloaded free of charge at www.macromedia.com. The developer edition can be used to develop and test dynamic web applications, but is restricted to one IP address.

To create a website that uses ColdFusion technology, select Site → Manage Sites and complete a series of dialog boxes to define the site. Once the site is defined, select File → New to display a dialog box. In the General tab options select Dynamic page, ColdFusion, and then Create. Change the page title and then save the web page document. The extension .cfm is automatically added to a ColdFusion dynamic page.

The Databases and Bindings panels are used for the rest of the dynamic content setup. Select Window → Databases to display the Databases panel, which displays step-by-step instructions for setting up a page with dynamic content:

TIP The ColdFusion Administrator password is set when ColdFusion is installed.

In the example above, the first three steps have been checked to indicate that they have been completed. To complete step 4, click the <u>RDS log</u> link and type the ColdFusion Administrator password in the displayed dialog box.

Connecting to a Data Source

A *data source* is an external file that is used to display dynamic data on a web page. Databases are the most common way for websites to access dynamic content or data. *Access*, which is the Microsoft Office database **database** application, is an example of a file-based data source. A *database* is a collection of related information organized into tables. A database consists of a series of related records. Within the records, each piece of data is **field** referred to as a *field*. A series of records with the same fields is called a **flat-file database** *flat-file database*. For example, an Access database that consists of one table is considered a flat-file database:

ID	Product	Price	Stock
1	Utility Spoon	$12	124
2	Perforated Spoon	$18	85
3	Spatula	$20	65

Access Table

To connect to a data source, click the Bindings tab in the Application panel and then click the data source link in step 5. The ColdFusion Administrator login screen opens in a new window. Type the password and then click the Login button. The ColdFusion Administrator window is displayed:

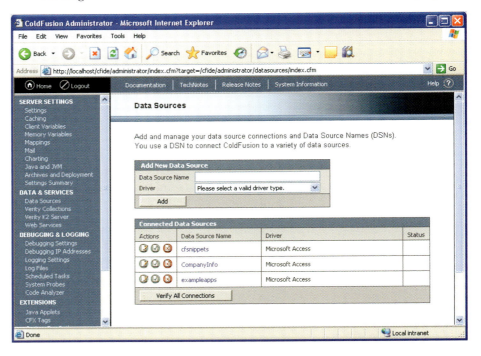

TIP The data source database file should be saved in the db folder in the CFusionMX folder.

Type the data source name in the Data Source Name box and select Microsoft Access from the Driver list and then select Add. Another dialog box is displayed. Select the Database File Browse Server button, locate the data source database file, and select Submit. The database file is displayed in the list of Connected Data Sources.

Creating and Displaying Recordsets

SQL

Databases use a language called SQL (Structured Query Language) to insert, update, and delete data stored within the database.

TIP Recordset names typically start with "rs."

In order to extract data from a data source, the data wanted must be specified. This specified data is called a *recordset*. Dreamweaver provides an interface for creating simple recordsets that do not require a web developer to know SQL. To create a recordset, in the Bindings tab in the Application panel, click and select Recordset (Query) from the menu, which displays a dialog box. Type a name for the recordset in the Name box and select the database file from the Data source list. In the Database items select the database table that contains the data for the recordset and then select Select and OK.

To display the recordset on the web page, select Insert → Application Objects → Dynamic Data → Dynamic Table. A dialog box is displayed where dynamic table options can be selected. Select OK to display the database file fields in the dynamic table. For example:

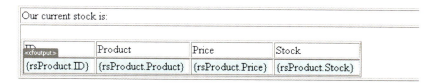

To view the actual data instead of the field placeholders, select View → Live Data:

TIP The Auto refresh check box should be selected when working with Live Data in Dreamweaver.

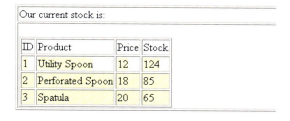

Note that when the database file is updated, the website will also automatically update.

Practice: Bellur Current Stock

Bellur maintains a separate site where fine kitchen stores that sell Bellur products can check in-stock store stock before placing an order. This site requires dynamic content to ensure the stock list is current. This practice creates just one page of the site to illustrate the use of a dynamic content source and ColdFusion technology.

This practice assumes that ColdFusion is installed and the ColdFusion Administrator has been configured. You will need the ColdFusion Administrator password to complete this practice.

① DEFINE A SITE THAT USES COLDFUSION TECHNOLOGY

   a. In Dreamweaver, close any open web page documents.

   b. Select Site → Manage Sites. A dialog box is displayed.

   c. Select New, and then select Site. A Site Definition dialog box is displayed.

   d. Select the Basic tab if those options are not already displayed.

   e. In the What would you like to name your site? box type: BellurCurrentStock

f. Select Next. More options are displayed. Set the options to:

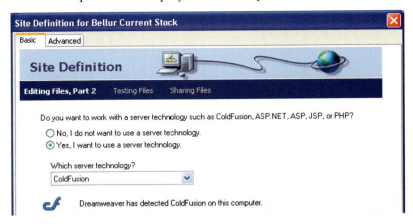

g. Select Next. More options are displayed.

h. Select the Edit and test locally option and do not change the path that is automatically added to the Where on your computer do you want to store your files? box:

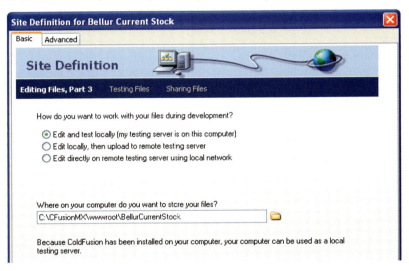

i. Select Next. More options are displayed.

j. Change the What URL would you use to browse to the root of your site? to the path shown below:

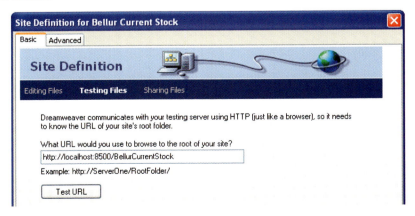

k. Click the Test URL button. A dialog box is displayed indicating the URL test was successful.

l. Select Next. More options are displayed.

m. Select No and then select Next. A summary is displayed:

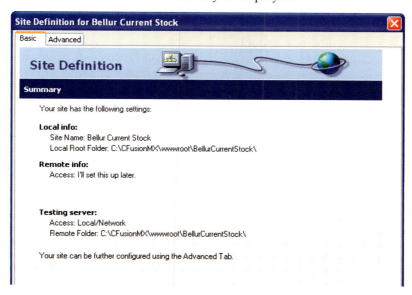

n. Select Done, and then in the next dialog box select Done.

③ CREATE A NEW WEB PAGE DOCUMENT

a. Select File → New. A dialog box is displayed.

    1. Click the General tab to display those options.

    2. In the Category list, select Dynamic page.

    3. In the Dynamic page list, select ColdFusion.

    4. Select Create. A web page document is displayed in a Document window.

b. Change the page title to: Stock

c. Insert a table with the following specifications:

d. In the first table cell, type: Our current stock is:

e. Save the web page document naming it stock.cfm.

④ DISPLAY THE DATABASES PANEL AND SET UP TESTING SERVER

    a. Select Window ➔ Databases. The Databases panel is displayed. Click the Bindings tab:

    b. Click <u>RDS login</u>. A dialog box is displayed:

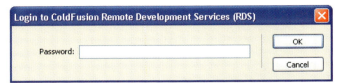

    c. Type the ColdFusion Administrator password that was set when ColdFusion was installed and select OK. A list of existing data sources may now be displayed in the Databases panel.

⑤ CONNECT TO A DATA SOURCE

    a. In the Bindings panel, click <u>data source</u> in step 5. The ColdFusion Administrator login screen opens in a new window.

    b. Type the ColdFusion Administrator password and then click the Login button. The ColdFusion Administrator window is displayed:

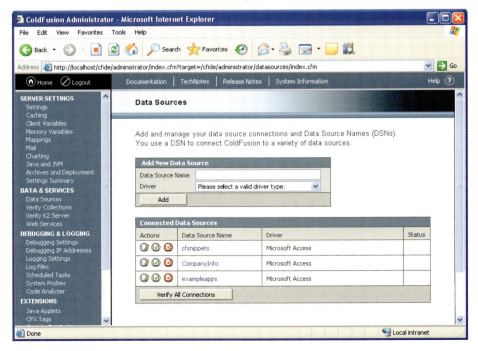

c. In the Data Source Name box, type: Products

d. In the Driver list, select Microsoft Access and then select **Add**. Another dialog box is displayed.

e. Select the Database File **Browse Server** button and locate the bellurstock.mdb data source database file. Select **Apply**.

f. Select **Submit**. The database file is displayed in the list of Connected Data Sources.

g. Close the ColdFusion Administrator window. Dreamweaver is displayed.

⑥ **CREATE A RECORDSET**

a. In the Bindings panel, click ⊞ and select Recordset (Query) from the displayed menu. A dialog box is displayed. Set the options to:

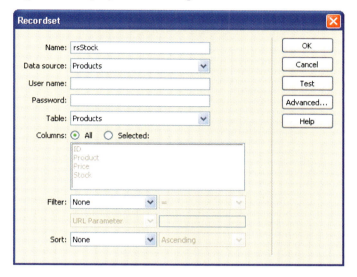

Note: If Products is not listed in the **Table** list, click the Refresh button (↻) in the Databases panel.

b. Select **OK**. The recordset is displayed in the Bindings panel.

⑦ **DISPLAY THE RECORDSET**

a. In the Document window, place the insertion point in the second row in the table.

b. Select Insert ➝ Application Objects ➝ Dynamic Data ➝ Dynamic Table. A dialog box is displayed. Set the options to:

c. Select to **OK**. Database file field placeholders are displayed in the dynamic table.

d. Select View ➝ Live Data. The Database file field placeholders are replaced with values from the database.

e. Save the modified stock.cfm.

f. View the web page in a browser and then print a copy.

g. Close the browser window and quit Dreamweaver.

Chapter Summary

An electronic portfolio stores and presents portfolio content in a digital format, such as a website. Most websites are considered to be in one of the following general categories: personal, commercial, informational, media, or portal. A personal website conveys the opinions, knowledge, or skills of an individual. Informational websites are created for the purpose of displaying factual information about a particular topic. Commercial websites include corporate presence websites and e-commerce websites.

A FAQ page is a page with frequently asked questions and their answers. Tables can be used for displaying tabular data, which is data that has been created in another application and is saved in a delimited text format. A site map is a web page that contains links to information on other pages of the website. A site map is used as a navigational tool. A jump menu contains a set of text hyperlinks and can also be used as a navigation tool.

A form allows users to communicate and interact with a web server. Form objects are used to obtain information from the user in a structured manner. Form objects include labels, text fields, check boxes, radio button groups, buttons, and List/Menu objects. Form objects can be tested in a browser window. A form will not interact with a server unless a server-side script or application has been defined. Form objects can be validated to ensure they contain the correct type of data before the form is processed.

A static web page contains only text and images. A web page that contains any animation or is interactive is a dynamic web page. A website that includes dynamic content on any of the web pages is a dynamic website, also called a web application. A dynamic website employs a server technology, such as ColdFusion. The use of dynamic data requires connecting to a data source and creating a recordset.

Access The Microsoft Office database application.

Branding The technique of raising awareness about a company by making a company logo visible in many places.

Check Box form object A form object that allows the user to select an option by clicking a check box.

Client-side script A script that processes the form on the user's computer.

ColdFusion Macromedia server technology.

Commercial website A type of website classification that includes corporate presence and e-commerce websites.

Corporate presence website A type of website that is created by a company or organization to present information about their products or services, but does not have online ordering capabilities.

Data source An external file used to display dynamic data on a web page.

Database A collection of information organized into tables.

Dot-com A company that does business primarily on the Web.

Drop-down menu A form object that allows the user to select an option from a list of items that appear when the user clicks the ⬇ next to the list.

Dynamic content Content that changes based on source content changes.

Dynamic web page A web page that contains any animation or is interactive.

Dynamic website A website that includes dynamic content on any of the web pages.

E-commerce website A type of website created by businesses for the purpose of selling their products or services to consumers online.

Electronic portfolio Stores and presents portfolio content in a digital format such as a website.

FAQ A web page that contains frequently asked questions and their answers.

Field A piece of data in a record in a database.

Flat-file database A series of records in a database with the same fields.

Form Allows the user to communicate and interact with a web server.

Form object An object in a form that is used to obtain information from the user.

Informational website A type of website created for the purpose of displaying factual information about a particular topic.

Jump menu A navigation tool that contains a list of text hyperlinks.

Personal website A type of website that typically conveys the opinion, hobbies, knowledge, or skills of an individual.

Portfolio A collection of work that clearly illustrates effort, progress, knowledge, achievement, and skills.

Prompt The text in the first menu item of a jump menu that guides the user to select an item from the menu.

Radio Group form object A form object that allows the user to only select one radio button from each group.

Recordset Specified data from a database.

Scrolling list A form object that allows the user to select an option from a list of items by scrolling the list using a scroll bar.

Server-side script A script on a server that processes a form.

Site map A web page that contains links to information on other pages of the website.

Static web page A web page that contains only text and images.

Tab-delimited data Data where each item in each row is separated by a tab character.

Tabular data Data that has been created in another application and is saved in a delimited text format.

Web application *See* Dynamic website.

Behaviors command Displays the Behavior panel. Found in the Window menu.

Button button Inserts a button form object at the insertion point. Found in the Forms category in the Insert bar.

Checkbox button Inserts a checkbox form object at the insertion point. Found in the Forms category in the Insert bar.

Databases command Displays the Databases panel. Found in the Window menu.

Dynamic Table command Displays a recordset in a dynamic table. Found in Insert → Application Objects → Dynamic Data.

Form button Inserts a form at the insertion point. Found in the Forms category in the Insert bar.

Jump Menu button Displays a dialog box used to insert a jump menu at the insertion point. Found in the Forms category in the Insert bar.

Label button Inserts a label form object at the insertion point. Found in the Forms category in the Insert bar.

List/Menu button Inserts a List/Menu form object at the insertion point. Found in the Forms category in the Insert bar.

Radio Group button Displays a dialog box used to insert a radio button group form object at the insertion point. Found in the Forms category in the Insert bar.

Tabular Data button Displays a dialog box used to import tab-delimited data from a file into a table in a web page document. Found in the Layout category in the Insert bar.

Text Field button Inserts a text field form object at the insertion point. Found in the Forms category in the Insert bar.

1. a) What is a portfolio?
   b) What is an electronic portfolio?
   c) List three reasons why electronic portfolios are preferred over traditional portfolios.
   d) List four elements that could be included in an electronic portfolio designed for admission to college.

2. a) List three general website categories.
   b) For each general website category, list a URL that would fit into that category.

3. What does a personal website convey?

4. a) What is the purpose of an informational website?
   b) List three elements or content often included on an informational website.

5. a) What is the purpose of a corporate presence website?
   b) What is branding?
   c) List three elements or content often included on a corporate presence website.

6. a) Describe the difference between a corporate presence website and an e-commerce website.
   b) List two companies that have an e-commerce website and a traditional brick-and-mortar store.

7. a) What does a FAQ page contain?
   b) What is the purpose of a FAQ page?

8. a) What is tabular data?
   b) What does tab-delimited data indicate?

9. a) What is a jump menu?
   b) Describe one advantage of using a jump menu instead of a navigation bar.

10. What are three examples of tasks that forms are used for?

11. a) What is a form object?
    b) List three examples of form objects.

12. List the steps required to create a form.

13. In a text field, what does the Max Chars property set?

14. a) What is a Check Box form object?
    b) What is a Radio Group form object?

15. a) List two objects that allow users to select from a list of predetermined choices on a form.
    b) Why is it better to have limited choices on a form?

16. Why is important to validate form content before it is submitted for processing?

17. What is the difference between a server-side and client-side script?

18. a) What type of content does a static web page contain?
    b) What is a dynamic web page?
    c) What is a dynamic website?
    d) What is ColdFusion?
    e) Why would you install ColdFusion?

19. a) What is a data source?
    b) What is a database?

True/False

20. Determine if each of the following are true or false. If false, explain why.
    a) Electronic portfolios take up less space than a traditional portfolio.
    b) Electronic portfolios must be posted to a website.
    c) Corporate presence websites always offer online ordering.
    d) Branding is a technique used to raise awareness about a company.
    e) Tab-delimited data indicates that each item in each row is separated by a space.
    f) A site map helps users quickly find the web page they are looking for.
    g) A form is more likely to be completed by the user if they have limited choices.
    h) A dynamic web page contains only text and images.
    i) A ColdFusion dynamic web page is saved with a .htm extension.

Exercise 1 ——————————————————— CAKE DELIVERY

Modify the CAKE DELIVERY website by completing the following steps:

a) Open the CAKE DELIVERY website for editing, which is a website provided with the data files for this text.

b) Modify the copyright library item by replacing Name with your name. Allow Dreamweaver to update all occurrences of the library item.

c) Modify the faq.htm web page document as follows:

   1. At the bottom of the list of questions and answers, place the insertion point after the period in the text from us. and press Enter.

   2. Type the following text, inserting a line break at the end of the first line:

      Q: How many calories are in each cake?
      A: One entire cake has 8,867 calories.

d) Modify the win.htm web page document as follows:

   In the empty cell below the text One entry per e-mail address. create a form with labels, text fields, and buttons as follows:

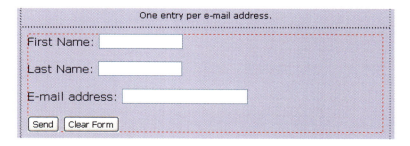

   For each text field, include an appropriate TextField name and set the Char width to approximate the examples above. For each button, include an appropriate Button name and set the appropriate action.

e) Modify the order.htm web page document as follows:

   1. Place the insertion point to the right of the bold text Order a Cake and press Enter.

   2. Add a form at the insertion point.

   3. In the form, insert a nested table with 8 rows, 2 columns, a width of 500 pixels, no border, a cell padding of 10, and no cell spacing.

   4. In the cells of the nested table, add labels, text fields, a scrolling list, radio button groups, a drop-down menu, and buttons as shown on the next page, merging cells as necessary:

Order a Cake

Order placed by:

First Name: [ ]   Last Name: [ ]

Street address: [ ]

City: [ ]   State: [ ]   Zip: [ ]

Phone: [ ]

Place of delivery (if different):

First Name: [ ]   Last Name: [ ]

Street address: [ ]

City: [ ]   State: [ ]   Zip: [ ]

Phone: [ ]

Date of delivery: [ ]

Time:
| before noon |
| between noon and 3 p |

Select a cake flavor:
- ○ chocolate
- ○ white
- ○ yellow
- ○ red velvet
- ○ lemon

Select a frosting type:
- ○ buttercream
- ○ chocolate

Select a frosting color
(only available with
buttercream frosting):
- ○ red
- ○ green
- ○ blue
- ○ pink
- ○ purple
- ○ yellow
- ○ orange
- ○ white

Select a greeting:
[Happy Birthday Name ▾]

If you would like a Name
included in your greeting,
enter it here:
[ ]

[Place Order]   [Clear Form]

For each form object, include an appropriate name. Set the Char width for each text field to approximate the examples above. Use the following list items for the scrolling list and drop-down menu, adding appropriate values for each item:

Scrolling List Items	Drop-down Menu Items
before noon	Happy Birthday Name
between noon and 3 pm	Happy Anniversary Name
between 3 pm and 6 pm	Congratulations Name

f) Modify the feedback.htm web page document as follows:

1. In empty cell below the text We'd love to hear from you! Send us your comments: create a form with labels and form objects as follows:

We'd love to hear from you! Send us your comments:

First Name: [_____]   Last Name: [_____]

E-mail address: [_____]

Please rate your last Carter Cake delivery:
○ Excellent
○ Good
○ Not Quite Satisfactory
○ Terrible
○ I have never ordered.

How would you like us to improve our cakes? Please check all that apply.
☐ More shapes
☐ More sizes
☐ More flavors

Comments and suggestions:
[_____]

[Send Feedback] [Clear Form]

For each form object, include an appropriate name. Set the Char width for each text field to approximate the examples above.

g) Modify the sitemap.htm web page document as follows:

1. In the empty cell in the third row, place the insertion point and type the following text, pressing Enter at the end of each line:

> SITE MAP
> Cakes
> FAQ
> Feedback Form
> Home
> Order a Cake
> Site Map
> Win a Cake

2. Link text to web page documents as follows:

Link the text	to the web page document
Cakes	cakes.htm
FAQ	faq.htm
Feedback Form	feedback.htm
Home	index.htm
Order a Cake	order.htm
Site Map	sitemap.htm
Win a Cake	win.htm

h) Modify the cakes.htm web page document as follows:

   1. Place the insertion point after the bold text Price List and press Enter.

   2. Insert tabular data, using the carterprices.txt tab-delimited file, a table width that fits the data, a cell padding of 8, no cell spacing, a border of 1, and format the top row of data as bold.

i) View each web page document in a browser window.

j) Print a copy of each web page document from the browser.

Exercise 2 ———————————————————————— MEASUREMENTS

The MEASUREMENTS website was last modified in Chapter 7, Exercise 2. Modify the MEASUREMENTS website by completing the following steps:

a) In Dreamweaver, open the MEASUREMENTS website for editing.

b) Modify the index.htm web page document as follows:

   1. In the empty cell in the right side of the third row, place the insertion point.

   2. Insert tabular data, using the si_base_units.txt tab-delimited file, a table width that fits the data, a cell padding of 6, no cell spacing, a border of 1, and format the top row of data as bold.

   3. Near the bottom of the web page document, place the insertion point after the period in the text table at right. and press Enter.

   4. Type the following text, allowing the text to wrap:

      For more information on the International System of Units, visit the website of the Bureau International des Poids et Mesures (BIPM), which is based in France.

   5. Link the text Bureau International des Poids et Mesures (BIPM) using an external hyperlink to the following URL: http://www.bipm.fr/en/home/

c) Modify the prefix.htm web page document as follows:

   1. Near the bottom of the web page document, place the insertion point below the text SI Prefix Chart.

   2. Insert tabular data, using the si_prefixes.txt tab-delimited file, a table width that fits the data, a cell padding of 6, no cell spacing, a border of 1, and format the top row of data as bold.

d) Modify the derive.htm web page document as follows:

   1. Near the bottom of the web page document, place the insertion point below the text SI Derived Units Chart.

   2. Insert tabular data, using the si_derive.txt tab-delimited file, a table width that fits the data, a cell padding of 6, no cell spacing, a border of 1, and format the top row of data as bold.

e) View each web page document in a browser window.

f) Print a copy of each web page document from the browser.

Exercise 3 ———————————————————Cooking Herbs

The Cooking Herbs website was last modified in Chapter 7, Exercise 3. Modify the Cooking Herbs website by completing the following steps:

a) In Dreamweaver, open the Cooking Herbs website for editing.

b) Modify the recipes.htm web page document as follows:

    1. In the bottom row, merge the two cells.

    2. Insert a row above the bottom row and place the insertion point in the new row.

    3. Create a form with labels, text fields, and buttons as follows:

For each text field, include an appropriate TextField name. For the Multi line text field, set the Char width to 50 and Num Lines to 6. For the other text fields, set the Char width to approximate the examples above. For each button, include an appropriate Button name and set the appropriate action.

c) Modify the index.htm web page document as follows:

    1. In the cell below the top global navigation bar, place the insertion point before the text Herbs have been used and press Enter.

    2. Move the insertion point to the blank paragraph just created above the text Herbs have been used.

    3. Add a form at the insertion point.

    4. In the form, add a jump menu that contains the following menu items:

Menu Item Text	Go To URL
select a page	
Popular Herbs	popular_herbs.htm
Recipes	recipes.htm

d) View each web page document in a browser window.

e) Print a copy of each web page document from the browser.

Exercise 4   CACTUS

The CACTUS website was last modified in Chapter 6, Exercise 2. Modify the CACTUS website by completing the following steps:

    a) In Dreamweaver, open the CACTUS website for editing.

    b) Modify the types.htm web page document as follows:

        1. Place the insertion point at the end of the document after the period in the text roots of larger cacti. and press Enter.

        2. Create a form with labels, text fields, and buttons as follows:

        For each text field, include an appropriate TextField name. For the Multi line text field, set the Char width to 70 and Num Lines to 5. For the other text fields, set the Char width to approximate the examples above. For each button, include an appropriate Button name and set the appropriate action.

    d) View each web page document in a browser window.

    e) Print a copy of each web page document from the browser.

Exercise 5   Name Portfolio

Develop an electronic portfolio website for yourself, naming it Name Portfolio, replacing Name with your name. The website should include:

- a home page with your name, contact information, a brief greeting, and a photo if possible
- a web page document that contains your detailed academic history
- a web page document that contains your detailed work history
- at least one other web page document that presents information about accomplishments or experiences
- a web page document that contains a writing sample
- at least one other web page document that presents work samples or contains links to samples of your work on other websites

Preview the website in a browser. When satisfied with the website, print a copy of each web page document from the browser.

Exercise 6 ————————————————————————— Flash Logos

The Flash Logos website was created in Chapter 7, Exercise 6. Modify the Flash Logos website by completing the following steps:

a) Add another web page document to the website naming it orderform.htm. Modify the new web page document to include a table similar to the other web page documents in the website and the same buttons, footer, and other elements. Include links to the home page and other pages.

b) On each web page document except orderform.htm, add Flash text that reads Order Your Logo and that links to orderform.htm.

c) Add a form to orderform.htm that can be used to order a logo. Include form objects that allow the user to select the color, font, and finished size of the logo. Apply the Validate Form Action to appropriate fields.

Preview the website in a browser. When satisfied with the website, print a copy of each web page document from the browser.

Exercise 7 ————————————————————————— Rubrics

The Rubrics website was last modified in Chapter 7, Exercise 7. Use Dreamweaver to further modify the Rubrics website by completing the following steps:

a) In Dreamweaver, open the Rubrics website for editing.

b) Create a new web page document naming it: form_rubric.htm

c) Modify the index.htm web page document as follows:

   1. In the third row, place the insertion point at the end of the text Flash Rubric, press Enter, and then type the text: Form Rubric

   2. Link the text Form Rubric to form_rubric.htm.

d) Modify the form_rubric.htm web page document as follows:

   1. Link the rubric_style.css style sheet to the web page document.

   2. Change the page title to: Form Rubric

   3. Open the wpd_rubric.htm document, copy the entire table and paste it into the form_rubric.htm web page document.

   4. In the top cell, replace the text with: Form Rubric

   5. In the second row, replace the text single web page document with the text:

      Forms in a website

   6. Replace the first three criteria with these criteria:

      1. The form creates quality interaction between the user and the website.

      2. Labels and form objects include appropriate prompts.

      3. The form enhances the user's experience.

7. Brainstorm in small groups to generate two additional form rubric criteria. Replace the last two criteria in the rubric with these two.

    e) Check the spelling in the form_rubric.htm web page document.

    f) View the index.htm and form_rubric.htm web page documents in a browser window.

    g) Print a copy of index.htm and form_rubric.htm from the browser.

    h) In a browser window, view the web pages of a website that has a form and was created by a peer. Use the form rubric to evaluate the form.

    i) Reflect on the design of the rubric. Does it appropriately assess the form? Are there criteria that should be added or changed? Make any appropriate revisions and print a copy.

Exercise 8 —————————————————————————Local Club

The Local Club website was created in Chapter 4, Exercise 8. Modify the Local Club website by completing the following steps:

    a) Add another web page document to the website naming it joinform.htm. Modify the new web page document to include a table similar to the other web page documents in the website and the same buttons, footer, and other elements. Include links to the home page and other pages.

    b) On each web page document except joinform.htm, add Flash text that reads Join Our Club! and that links to joinform.htm.

    c) Add a form to joinform.htm that can be used to join the club. Include form objects that allow the user to submit their name, e-mail, and appropriate information that pertains to the topic of the club. Apply the Validate Form Action to appropriate fields.

Preview the website in a browser. When satisfied with the website, print a copy of each web page document from the browser.

Exercise 9 ————————————————————— Photographer

The Photographer website was created in Chapter 5, Exercise 9. Modify the Photographer website to include a feedback form at the bottom of one of the web pages. Include at least three of the following form objects:

- two text fields
- one radio button group
- two check boxes
- one List/Menu form object
- one button

Apply the Validate Form Action to appropriate fields. Preview the website in a browser. When satisfied with the website, print a copy of the modified web page document from the browser.

Chapter 8 Website Content and ColdFusion Technology

Publishing and Promoting a Website

T his chapter discusses publishing and promoting a website, and measuring its success. Maintaining a website and security issues are also discussed.

Publishing a Website

publishing a website

local sites
remote server

Publishing a website is the process of uploading a local site to a web server so that the site can be accessed on the World Wide Web. The websites developed in this text are referred to as *local sites* because the sites have been saved and edited on a local disk. A *remote server* can be a web server provided by an ISP, an intranet server, or a network server.

Before a website is published, it should be checked and tested:

- each web page document should be checked for misspellings and grammatical errors

- the download time of each web page document should be checked to ensure that they are not too long

- target browsers should be determined and then each web page document should be previewed in each target browser

- the HTML should be tested for target browser compatibility

- the site should be checked for broken and missing links

- the HTML should be checked for problems such as missing Alt text, empty tags, and untitled documents

After a website is published, it still needs attention:

- the website should be constantly maintained in order to keep the content updated

- the website will need to be promoted so that users are aware that the website is available

- some measure of success should be used to ensure that the website is serving its intended purpose

---

Web Server

A web server responds to requests from clients, usually a web browser, for HTML documents and any associated files or scripts. A web server is also called an HTTP server.

Checking Spelling and Grammar

A website with spelling or grammatical errors seems less credible. Just before a site is published, all web page documents in the site should be rechecked for spelling and grammatical errors because errors are often created from last minute changes.

Each web page document in a site has to be checked for spelling errors. To check spelling, open the web page document and select Text → Check Spelling.

Grammatical errors are found by proofreading each web page document. The web page documents should be printed from a browser because it is easier to proofread a hard copy than text on a screen. It is also a good idea to get another person to proofread the hard copy because it is often difficult to thoroughly proofread your own work.

Checking the Download Time

download time

weight of the page

Before a site is published, each web page document should be opened and the download time checked. The *download time* is the time it takes the web page document to load into a user's browser. The status bar at the bottom of a Document window displays the *weight of the page*, which is the web page document's file size and the estimated download time:

file size
estimated download time

File Size

File size is typically expressed in kilobytes (K) or megabytes (M). A kilobyte is approximately 1,000 bytes and a megabyte is approximately 1,000,000 bytes.

In the example above, the file size is 6K (kilobytes) and is estimated to take 1 second to download the page.

Changing the Connection Speed

Select Edit → Preferences and then select Status Bar in the Category list to change the connection speed used to calculate the download time.

Download time is calculated based on a connection speed. The default connection speed is 56 Kbps per second. The download time for a page is important because users will only wait about 12 seconds for a page to load before clicking a link or the Back button in their browser. A web page document that is estimated to take a long time to load may need to be separated into two web pages. Large image file sizes or many images in one document can also affect the download time.

① OPEN THE PUBLISHING WEB SITE FOR EDITING

a. Start Dreamweaver and open the PUBLISHING website for editing, which is a website provided with the data files for this text.

b. Familiarize yourself with the files and folders for this website.

c. Open the footer library item and replace the text Name with your name.

d. Save and close the library item, allowing Dreamweaver to update all the files.

e. Open the index.htm web page document and then view it in a browser.

f. Click the links to explore the two other web pages of the website.

g. Close the browser window. Dreamweaver is displayed.

② CHECK THE SPELLING

a. Open the index.htm web page document if it is not already displayed.

b. Select Text → Check Spelling. A dialog box is displayed that indicates website is not found in the dictionary.

    1. Select Ignore All. Another dialog box is displayed.

    2. In the Suggestions list, select Publishing.

    3. Select Change. Another dialog box is displayed.

    4. Select OK.

c. Save the modified index.htm.

d. Check the spelling in the other two web page documents, make any changes necessary, and then save any changes.

③ CHECK THE DOWNLOAD TIMES

a. Display index.htm and note the file size and download time.

b. Check the file sizes and download times for the other two web page documents.

Target Browsers

Browsers

Commonly used web browser applications include Internet Explorer, Netscape, Opera, Firefox, Amaya, and Safari.

A Dreamweaver website may include elements that are not supported by all browsers, such as JavaScript. A *target browser* is a browser and version, such as Internet Explorer 6.0, in which the website is designed to display correctly. The websites developed in this text have been designed using Internet Explorer 6.0 as the target browser.

A website is going to be viewed with different browsers, monitor sizes, screen resolutions, and connection speeds. Therefore, the site should be viewed and tested in more than one target browser and resolution.

One way to determine which browsers to target is to extend the definition of the target audience for the website by asking the following questions:

TIP There are websites that track browser use and provide statistics on the most common browsers.

1. What platforms will be used? Windows, Linux, or others?

2. What type of connections and speeds will be used? Dial-up, DSL, cable, or wireless and 56, 64, 128, or 1500 Kbps per second?

3. What browsers will be used? Internet Explorer, Firefox, or others?

4. What screen resolutions will be used? Perhaps 800x600 or 1024x768?

A website that is going to be published to a controlled environment, such as a company intranet, need only be tested using the browser and resolution that the company employees use.

Previewing in a Target Browser

Once the target browsers have been determined, the Preview in Browser command can be used to preview the site in the target browsers. When previewing the site in a target browser, check for:

Screen Resolution

When previewing in a target, browser, the screen resolution should be changed to view the site at different resolutions. To change the screen resolution, select **Appearance and Themes** in the Control Panel.

- fonts and colors displaying correctly
- tables and alignments displaying correctly and acting appropriately when the browser window is resized
- images displaying correctly

Select File → Preview in Browser to display a submenu with a list of browsers installed on the computer. To add a browser to the Preview in Browser submenu, select File → Preview in Browser → Edit Browser List, which displays the Preferences dialog box. Select Preview in Browser in the **Category** list to display those options:

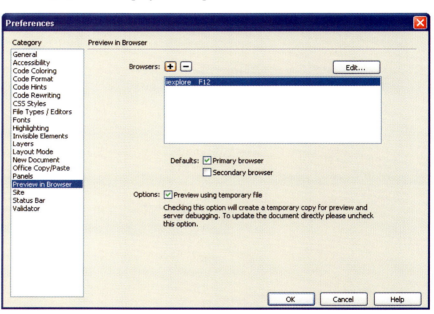

Downloading Browsers

In order to preview a website in a browser, the browser must be installed on the computer. Browsers are typically free of charge and can be downloaded from the browser company's website.

Click  to display the Add Browser dialog box:

Type a name for the browser in the **Name** box and click **Browse** to navigate to the browser application file. Up to 20 browsers can be listed.

Practice: PUBLISHING – part 2 of 4

Dreamweaver should be started and the PUBLISHING website should be the working site.

① **PREVIEW THE WEBSITE IN THE DEFAULT BROWSER**

    a. Open the index.htm web page document if it is not already displayed.

    b. Select File → Preview in Browser and select the primary browser, which is the first browser listed in the submenu. The web page document is displayed in the browser window. Note the way the fonts, colors, alignments, and images are displayed.

    c. Size the browser window larger and smaller by dragging the bottom-right window corner. Note how the layout adjusts as the browser is sized.

    d. Close the browser window.

② **PREVIEW THE WEBSITE IN A DIFFERENT BROWSER**

    a. If an additional browser is installed on the computer, select File → Preview in Browser and select the second browser in the submenu. The web page document is displayed in the browser window. Compare the way the fonts, colors, alignments, and images are displayed.

    b. Size the browser window larger and smaller by dragging the bottom-right window corner. Note how the layout adjusts as the browser is sized.

    c. Close the browser window.

Testing the HTML for Target Browser Compatibility

The HTML associated with a web page can be checked to see if any tags or attributes are not supported by selected target browsers. Unlike the Preview in Browser command, the target browser check commands do not require the browser and version to be installed on the local computer.

To select target browsers to check, click the No Browser/Check Errors button (⌨) on the Document toolbar and select Settings from the displayed menu. The Target Browsers dialog box is displayed:

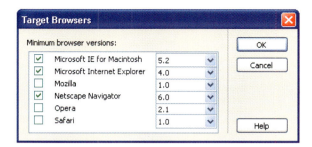

In the Minimum browser versions list, select the browsers and versions to test and then select OK. The current page can then be checked against the selected target browsers. Click the No Browser/Check Errors button (⌨) and select Show All Errors from the displayed menu. A report is displayed in the Target Browser Check panel in the Results panel group:

TIP Reports are temporary files, but can be saved in TXT format by selecting the Save Report button (🖫).

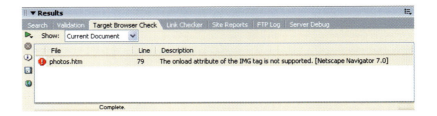

Checking an Entire Site

To check an entire site for target browser errors, select the website folder in the Files panel and then select File ➞ Check Page ➞ Check Target Browsers.

Check Browser and Check Plugin Actions

The Check Browser and Check Plugin actions support the fail gracefully technique by displaying a different web page depending on the user's browser. Both actions can be set in the Behaviors panel.

The report generates a list of tags and attributes that are not supported by the selected target browsers. Double-click an entry in the File column to display the current web page in Split view with the unsupported element and tag selected so that it can be edited.

A web page should be designed to *fail gracefully*, which is a design technique used to ensure that a site displays appropriately even when some elements are not supported. One "fail gracefully" technique is to design similar web pages with varying elements and then detect the user's browser using Dreamweaver's Check Browser action. Once the user's browser has been determined, an appropriate web page is displayed based on the level of browser support.

Testing for Broken Links and Missing Links

Document-relative links in an entire website can be checked for broken and missing links. Select the site's root folder in the Files panel and then select Site ➞ Check Links Sitewide. A report is displayed in the Link Checker panel in the Results group panel:

Broken Links report

A Broken Links report is displayed by default. Any broken links need to be fixed before the site is published. Double-click a broken link entry in the Files column of the Link Checker panel to open the appropriate web page document, select the broken link, and select the path and file name in the Property inspector. Correcting the link results in the entry being automatically removed from the list.

external links list
orphan files

A list of external or absolute links is displayed by selecting External Links in the Show list. External links are just listed, not checked. An *orphan file* has no links to it in the entire site. Select Orphaned Files in the Show list to display a list of orphan files, which may indicate missing links.

Checking for HTML Problems

Language References

If the code needs to be checked or edited before a site is published, the Reference panel in the Code panel group can be used to access information about markup languages, JavaScript, server technology, and cascading style sheets.

Accessibility

Section 508 of the Federal Rehabilitation Act stipulates that U.S. Federal agencies have to make their electronic and information technology accessible to individuals with disabilities. One requirement of this Act is that Alt (alternative) text in the form of labels or descriptors be provided for all graphics.

In Dreamweaver, a report can be generated that checks external links, accessibility, missing Alt text, and untitled documents. Select Site → Reports to display the Reports dialog box. To check the entire site, select Entire Current Local Site in the Report on list:

Select the appropriate HTML Reports and then select Run to create a report and display it in the Sites Reports panel in the Results panel group:

Double-click a file name in the File column to open the web page document so that it can be edited. Note that HTML errors listed in the report may be able to be corrected in the open web page document by selecting Commands → Clean up HTML.

Practice: PUBLISHING – part 3 of 4

Dreamweaver should be started and the PUBLISHING website should be the working site.

① **TEST THE HTML FOR BROWSER COMPATIBILITY**

a. Open the index.htm web page document if it is not already displayed.

b. On the Document toolbar, click the No Browser/Check Errors button (🔲) and select Settings from the displayed menu. Set the options to:

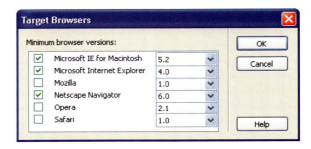

Note: your dialog box may have additional browsers listed.

c. Select OK.

d. Click the No Browser/Check Errors button () and select Show All Errors from the displayed menu. A report is displayed in the Target Browser Check panel. The report is empty, indicating all elements are supported by the selected target browsers.

② **CHECK FOR BROKEN OR MISSING LINKS**

a. Select Site ➡ Check Links Sitewide. A report is displayed in the Link Checker panel. The Broken Links report is empty, indicating that there are no link problems.

b. In the Link Checker panel, in the Show list, select External Links. The site's external links are listed.

c. In the Link Checker panel, in the Show list, select Orphaned Files. The Orphaned Files report is empty, indicating that there are no orphaned files.

③ **GENERATE A SITE REPORT**

a. Select Site ➡ Reports. A dialog box is displayed. Set the options to:

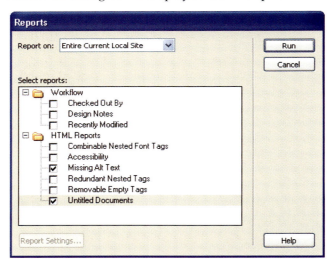

b. Select Run. A report is displayed in the Site Reports panel in the Results panel group. Note that the Site report lists two entries.

c. Double-click the index.htm entry, which indicates an untitled document. The HTML associated with index.htm is displayed.

d. On the Document toolbar, in the title box, replace the text Untitled Document with Publishing Home Page.

e. Check the spelling and then save the modified index.htm.

f. Double-click the preparing_for_publishing.htm entry, which indicates an image on the page is missing the Alt attribute. The HTML associated with preparing_for_publishing.htm is displayed.

g. Switch to Design view. Select the image in the top cell of the table if it is not already selected.

h. In the Property inspector, set **Alt** to: Publishing a website.

i. Check the spelling and then save the modified preparing_for_publishing.htm.

What is a Web Host?

TCP/IP software
HTTP software

A website on the Web has been published to a web server. A *web server* runs *TCP/IP software* (Transmission Control Protocol/Internet Protocol) in order to be connected to the Internet, and *HTTP software* (Hypertext Transfer Protocol) in order to handle the hyperlinks between web pages.

TIP Virtual hosts are used by companies and individuals that do not want to purchase and maintain a web server.

Web servers are often managed by *web hosting companies*, also called *virtual hosts*, which provide space on their server for a fee. Web hosts also provide services such as domain name registration and e-mail services. *Domain names*, such as www.lpdatafiles.com, are used to identify a particular web page and are made up of a sequence of parts, or subnames, separated by periods that may stand for the server, organization, or organization type.

IP Address

An IP address (Internet Protocol address) is a 32-bit binary number that identifies a computer or device connected to the Internet. An IP address is four numbers in the range of 0 to 255 separated by periods, such as 1.120.05.123.

The Domain Name System (DNS) is used because it is difficult to remember IP addresses. When a domain name is entered, it is automatically translated into an IP address.

A consideration when choosing a domain name is that users should associate it with the website, such as the business name or major topic that the site is about. It is also good if the domain name is easy to remember, and is one that users can probably guess. For example, GAP is a widely known clothing store. GAP's domain name is www.gap.com. Registering a domain name provides the exclusive right to use that name. A periodic renewal fee is required to keep the domain name.

Websites such as GeoCities and Angelfire provide free web hosting services. However, websites posted to these sites are identified by a subdirectory name on the host's domain and the domain name is not as easy to remember. For example, www.webhostname.com/sitename.

Publishing to a Web Server

uploading

Publishing a website requires obtaining a web host, defining the remote site, and then uploading the site. *Uploading* is the process of posting the files to a web server. To publish a website, select Site → Manage Sites, which displays the Manage Sites dialog box:

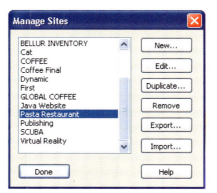

define a remote site Select a site and then Edit to display the Site Definition dialog box. Select the Advanced tab and then select the Remote Info category. In the Access list, select a method for connecting to the remote server:

FTP

FTP (File Transfer Protocol) is used to rapidly transfer (upload and download) files from one computer to another over the Internet.

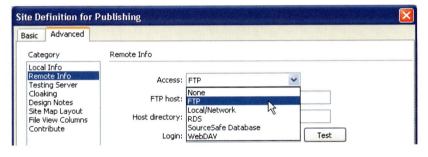

FTP is a common method of publishing to a web server. Select FTP to display additional options:

TIP Security features such as a password, firewall, and SFTP protocol can be selected to protect data as it is published.

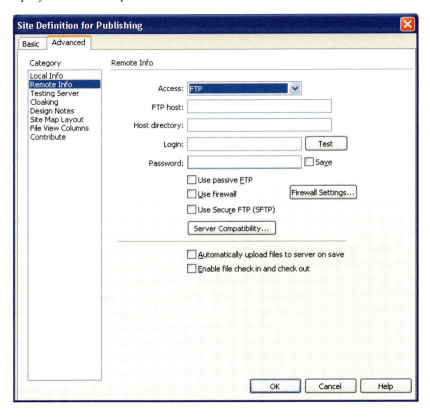

FTP Log

Dreamweaver keeps a record of all FTP activity. Select ▤ → View → Site FTP Log in the Files panel to view this activity.

- The FTP host box is used to indicate the hostname of the server, which usually starts with ftp.

- Information for the Host directory, Login, and Password boxes is provided by the web host.

Select OK to finish setting up the remote site, and then select Done to remove the Manage Sites dialog box.

upload the files The website is uploaded to the remote site by selecting the site's root folder in the Files panel and then clicking the Put File(s) button (⬆). All of the site's files are uploaded to the remote server. The site should then viewed at the appropriate URL and tested.

Publishing to a Local/Network Server

A website can be published to a local or network server instead of a remote web server. Intranets are on local servers. Publishing a website to a local or network server requires obtaining server space where the site can be set up, setting up the local/network site, and then uploading the site. To define the local/network site, select Site → Manage Sites, which displays the Manage Sites dialog box. Select a site and then Edit to display the Site Definition dialog box. Select the Advanced tab and then select the Remote Info category. In the Access list, select Local/Network, which displays additional options:

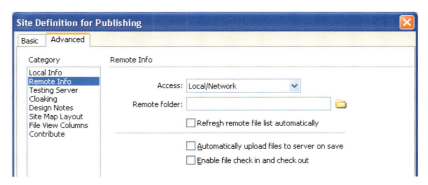

Click the folder icon (📂) to display the Choose remote root folder dialog box:

Navigate to the remote server folder location and click Select. The folder location is placed in the Remote folder box. Select OK to finish setting up the local/network site, and then select Done to remove the Manage Sites dialog box.

upload files   To upload the website to the remote site, select the site's root folder in the Files panel and then click the Put File(s) button (⬆). A dialog box is displayed:

Click OK to upload all of the site's files to the remote site. The site should then be viewed and tested.

Maintaining a Website

A website requires frequent updating in order to keep users coming back to the site. The parallel structure of the local site and the remote site makes maintaining a website simple. Both the local site and the remote site can be viewed and accessed from the Files panel.

viewing a remote site

To view the file structure of the remote site, select the Connects to remote host button () and then select Remote view in the Files panel:

TIP To select multiple files for downloading, hold down the Ctrl key while selecting files.

In Remote view, a file is downloaded from the remote site to the local site by selecting the file in the Files panel and then clicking the Get File(s) button ( ).

viewing a local site

In Local view, the local site folder is displayed in the Files panel. A web page document can be edited in the local site and uploaded to the remote site. Click the Put File(s) button ( ) to upload a selected file to the remote site. Edited pages should be viewed and tested in a browser. Note that the Put File(s) button automatically connects to the remote site if a connection is not already established.

Collaboration

Many websites are created in a *collaborative environment* where more than one person designs, develops, and maintains the same website. This approach allows for a site to be developed efficiently and take advantage of individual expertise, such as artistic abilities and technical expertise. Dreamweaver includes several collaboration features, including the Check In/Check Out feature and Design Notes.

Regardless of how website design and development responsibilities are divided, there is typically a need for team members to work on the same web pages. The Check In/Check Out feature ensures web pages are not improperly overwritten by letting team member know who is working on what file. To enable this feature, select the Enable file check in and check out check box when setting up the remote site:

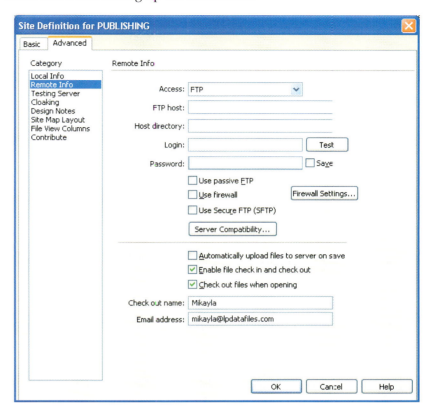

Checked out files are linked to a specified user name and e-mail address so that other team members know who has the file and how to contact them.

Once the Check In and Check Out feature is enabled, a team member can check out files from the remote site, modify the files, and check in the files when work is completed. Another person cannot work on the same file at the same time. Instead of using the Get File(s) and Put File(s) buttons, the Check Out File(s) button ( ) and the Check In button ( ) are used. In the Files panel, a green check mark indicates a checked out file that you are working on. Any associated dependent files are displayed with a padlock symbol ( ). Dependent files are also made read-only so that they cannot be modified until the file is checked in:

TIP Click the Expand/Collapse button ( ) to view additional information about checked out files.

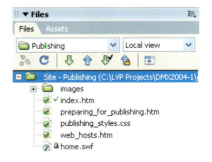

A red check mark indicates someone else is working on a checked out file.

Design Notes   A collaborative approach to website development requires a lot of organization and communication. Dreamweaver Design Notes is a feature that helps with organization and communication. A *Design Note* is a small file that can be attached to a web page.

To enable Design Notes, select Site → Manage Sites, which displays the Manage Sites dialog box. Select a site and then Edit to display the Site Definition dialog box. Select the Advanced tab and then select the Design Notes category, which displays additional options:

> ### Design Note Files
>
> Design Note files are saved in an automatically created notes folder in the website root folder. Design Notes are saved with the same file name as the file they are attached to, including the file's extension, but are also designated with an .mno extension. For example, index.htm.mno. The notes folder is not displayed in the Files panel.

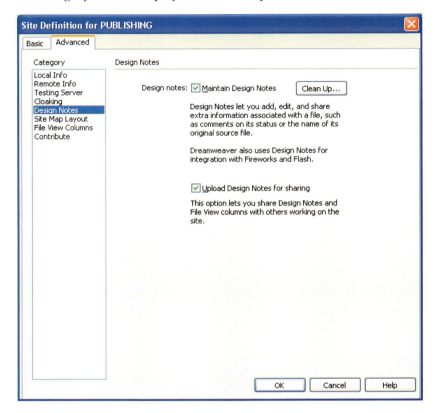

- Select the Maintain Design Notes check box to enable the Design Notes feature.

- Select the Upload Design Notes for sharing check box to transfer the design notes to the remote site for sharing with the team members.

Select OK to enable Design Notes.

Viewing Design Notes

Design notes can also be viewed by clicking the Expand/Collapse button (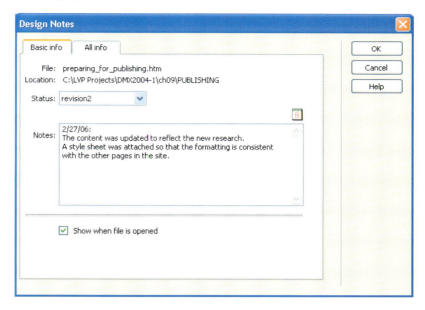) to expand the Files panel. In the expanded Files panel, the Notes column indicates that a Design Note exists for a particular file. If the Notes column is not displayed, select View → File View Columns and select Notes.

To add a Design Note to the active file, select File → Design Notes. A dialog box is displayed:

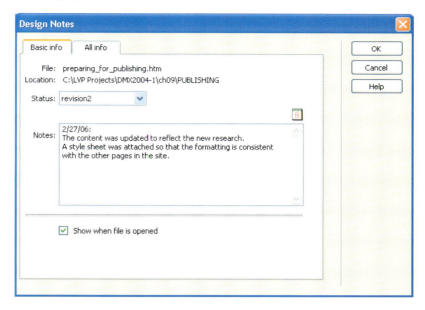

- Select a status for the web page from the Status list.
- Click ▣ to insert the current date in the Notes area.
- Type relevant information into the Notes area.
- Select the Show when file is opened check box to display the design note when the file is opened.

Promoting a Website

Once a website is published, there are various promotion techniques that can be used to help users find the site. One technique is to add additional meta tags to the home page of a website to increase the probability that a website is found by a search engine.

Meta tags appear in the HTML head section of a document. There are several different meta tags that are used to add meta data to a document. *Meta data* is information about the website contents and can be added to a document using several different meta tags.

keywords

One type of meta data is *keywords*, which are words or phrases that describe the site's content. Many search engines use keywords to index websites, so the keywords should be ones that may be used as search criteria. Another type of meta data is a *description*, which search engines use to display in the search results:

description

TIP Meta tags are not required, nor do they affect the layout of a web page.

TIP In Split view, click in the meta tag code to display meta properties in the Property inspector.

```
1  <!DOCTYPE HTML PUBLIC "-//W3C//DTD HTML 4.01 Transitional//EN"
2  "http://www.w3.org/TR/html4/loose.dtd">
3  <html>
4  <head>
5  <title>Publishing a Website</title>
6  <meta http-equiv="Content-Type" content="text/html; charset=iso-8859-1">
7  <meta name="keywords" content="publishing, web hosts, preparing for publishing, website publ
8  <meta name="description" content="How to publish a website, including preparing for publishi
9  </head>
```

Meta tags in Code view

The Content-Type meta tag is automatically added by Dreamweaver. The keywords and description meta tags can be added to the displayed web page document by clicking the Head button arrow in the HTML category in the Insert bar:

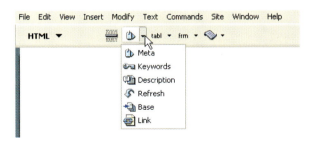

add keyword meta data   Click Keywords to display the Keywords dialog box:

Type keywords in the Keywords box, separating each keyword or phrase with a comma. Select OK to add the meta tag. Note that the most important keywords should be listed first because some search engines limit the number of keywords that can be specified.

add description meta data   Click Description to display the Description dialog box:

Type a description of the website in the Description box and then select OK to add the meta tag.

Other techniques for promoting a website include:

- listing it with search engines and directories. Some search engines and directories charge a fee for this service.

reciprocal links   - using *reciprocal links*, where websites with complementary information post links to each other's sites.

- advertising by e-mail or in printed media.

- adding the website address to company documents such as letterhead or business cards.

Practice: PUBLISHING – part 4 of 4

Dreamweaver should be started and the PUBLISHING website should be the working site.

① ENABLE DESIGN NOTES

Select Site ➡ Manage Sites. A dialog box is displayed.

1. Select PUBLISHING and then select Edit. Another dialog box is displayed.
2. Select the Advanced tab.
3. In the Category list, select the Design Notes.
4. Select the Maintain Design Notes check box if it is not already selected.
5. Select the Upload Design Notes for sharing check box if it is not already selected.
6. Select OK. Design Notes are enabled and the Manage Sites dialog box is displayed.
7. Select Done.

② ADD A META TAG WITH KEYWORDS

a. Open the index.htm web page document if it is not already displayed.
b. Switch to Design view.
c. In the HTML category in the Insert bar, click the Head button arrow and select Keywords. A dialog box is displayed.
   1. In the Keywords box, type: publishing, web hosts, preparing for publishing
   2. Select OK. A meta tag with keywords has been added to index.htm.

③ ADD A META TAG WITH A DESCRIPTION

a. In the HTML category in the Insert bar, click the Head button arrow and select Description. A dialog box is displayed.
   1. In the Description box, type: How to publish a website, including preparing for publishing and finding a web host.
   2. Select OK. A meta tag with a description has been added to index.htm.
b. Save the modified index.htm.

④ VIEW THE CODE

Switch to Code view. Note the newly added meta tags:

```
<meta name="keywords" content="publishing, web hosts, preparing for
publishing">
<meta name="description" content="How to publish a website, including
preparing for publishing and finding a web host.">
```

⑤ ADD A DESIGN NOTE

a. Switch to Design view.
b. Select File ➡ Design Notes. A dialog box is displayed.
   1. Select revision1 from the Status list.
   2. Click 🗓 to add the current date.
   3. In the Notes area, type: Keyword and description meta data was added.
   4. Select the Show when file is opened check box.
   5. Select OK.

a. Save the modified index.htm.

b. Close index.htm.

c. Open index.htm. The Design Notes dialog box is displayed.

d. Click OK. The Design Notes dialog box is removed.

e. Quit Dreamweaver.

Measuring Success

There are a several ways to measure the success of a website. One way is to have an online form and analyze the feedback from users to see if there are ways to improve the site.

web tracking software

Information can also be obtained from the web host if *web tracking software* is installed on the server. This software produces a report that contains information about users, such as the IP address, the URL requested, the browser, and the time spent at the site.

Negative feedback or a low amount of user traffic may require additional promoting of the site, changing site content, or changing the design of the site.

Website Security Issues

Website security is a concern for web developers, designers, hosts, and web users. For example, website content is protected by copyright, but it is difficult to monitor if users are downloading or copying the contents and using it as their own. Another concern, typically for large corporate sites, is a *denial of service attack*, which is an assault designed to disrupt website access. Antivirus and firewall software provide varying degrees of protection from this type of attack.

denial of service attack

encryption

A concern for website users is secure transactions over the Internet. Fortunately, most browsers use a level of protection for Internet transactions called *40-bit encryption*. *Encryption* translates data into a code before the data is sent over the Internet. A key or password is required to 'decrypt' the data. Banks, credit card companies, and online retailers use a higher level of encryption called *128-bit encryption*.

secure sites

Websites that use encryption techniques to secure data are called *secure sites*. Secure sites use a security protocol, such as Secure Sockets Layer (SSL). SSL encrypts all data that passes between a client and Internet server. SSL also requires the client to have a digital certificate. A *digital certificate* is a notice indicating that the website is legitimate. Digital certificates can be obtained from a *certificate authority*, such as VeriSign. Websites that contain SSL typically have an address that starts with https and display a padlock icon (🔒) on the status bar:

Ethical Issues

There are many ethical issues associated with maintaining a website, such as protecting client privacy, respecting copyrights, providing secure transactions, and posting accurate and unbiased content.

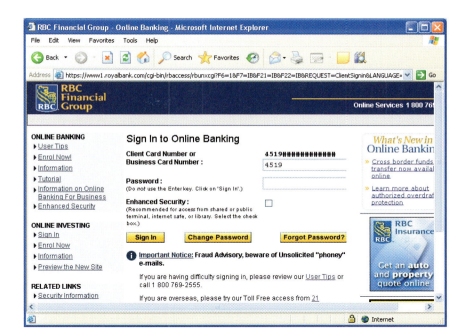

Website with SSL protection

TIP Pausing the pointer on the padlock icon displays the type of encryption.

There are also security and privacy issues associated with e-mail links. E-mail is not private and should be thought of as sending a postcard. However, e-mail can be encrypted by purchasing an e-mail encryption program. E-mail can also be protected by adding a digital signature. A *digital signature* is encrypted code that is attached to an e-mail message to verify that the message is authentic.

digital signature

Chapter Summary

Publishing a website is the process of uploading a local site to a web server so that the site can be accessed on the World Wide Web. A remote server can be a web server provided by an ISP, an intranet server, or a local/network server.

Before a site is published, there are a number of checks that need to occur:

- spelling and grammatical errors
- file size and estimated download time
- view the site in more than one target browser
- compatibility problems with target browsers
- external links, accessibility, missing Alt text, and untitled documents

A web server computer runs TCP/IP software in order to be connected to the Internet, and HTTP software in order to handle the hyperlinks between web pages. Web servers are often managed by web hosting companies, also called virtual hosts, which provide space on their server for a fee.

A website can be published to a web server or to a local/network server. A website requires frequent updating in order to keep users coming back to the site. Once a website is published, promotion techniques should be used to help users find the site. To increase the probability that a website is found by a search engine, the website should contain meta tags that specify keywords and a description. The success of a website can be measured with web tracking software and user feedback.

There are many security issues associates with websites, such as copyright protection and secure transactions. There are also security and privacy issues associated with e-mail links.

Vocabulary

Certificate authority A provider of digital certificates.

Collaborative environment Where more than one person designs, develops, and maintains the same website.

Denial of service attack An assault designed to disrupt website access.

Description A type of meta data that search engines use to display in the search results.

Design Note A small file that can be attached to a web page.

Digital certificate A notice indicating a website is legitimate.

Digital signature An encrypted code that is attached to an e-mail message to verify that the message is authentic.

Domain name Used to identify a particular web page and is made up of a sequence of parts separated by periods that may stand for the server, organization, or organization type.

Download time The time it takes the web page document to load into a user's browser.

Encryption A process of translating data into a code. Types of encryption include 40-bit and 128-bit encryption.

Fail gracefully A design technique used to ensure a site displays appropriately when some elements are not supported.

HTTP software Software that a web server runs in order to handle the hyperlinks between web pages.

Keyword A word or phrase that describes the site's content and may be used as search criteria to locate the site.

Local sites Sites that have been saved and edited on a local disk.

Meta data Information about the website contents.

Meta tags Tags that appear in the HTML head section of document used to add meta data to a document.

Orphan file A file that has no links to it in the entire website.

Publishing a website The process of uploading a local site to a web server so that the site can be accessed on the World Wide Web.

Reciprocal links A technique used to promote a website where websites with complementary information post links to each other's sites.

Remote server A web server provided by an ISP, an intranet server, or a local/network server.

Secure site A site that uses encryption techniques to secure data.

Target browser A browser and version, such as Internet Explorer 6.0, in which the website is designed to display correctly.

TCP/IP software Software that a web server runs in order to be connected to the Internet.

Uploading Posting files to a web server.

Virtual host *See* Web hosting company.

Web hosting company A company that manages a web server and provides space on their server for a fee.

Web tracking software Software installed on a server that allows a report to be produced containing information about users to the site such as the IP address, the URL requested, the browser, and the time spent at the site.

Weight of the page A web page document's file size and the estimated download time.

Dreamweaver Commands and Buttons

Check In button Uploads checked-out files to a remote server and removes the checked out mark(s). Found on the Files panel toolbar.

Check Links Sitewide **command** Checks the site for broken links and displays a report in the Link Checker panel in the Results group panel. Found in the Site menu.

Check Out File(s) button Downloads file(s) from a remote server and marks them as checked out. Found on the Files panel toolbar.

Check Spelling **command** Finds misspelled words in a web page document. Found in the Text menu.

Clean up HTML **command** Displays a dialog box used to correct HTML errors. Found in the Commands menu.

Connects to remote host button Connects to the remote server. Found on the Files panel toolbar.

Design Notes **command** Displays a dialog box used to add a Design Note to the active file. Found in the File menu.

Edit Browser List **command** Displays a dialog box used to add a browser to the Preview in Browser submenu. Found in File → Preview in Browser.

Folder icon Displays a dialog box used to select the remote root folder. Found in the Site Definition for Publishing dialog box.

Get File(s) button Downloads file(s) from a remote server to the local site. Found on the Files panel toolbar.

Head button Displays a menu used to add meta data to a web page. Found in the HTML category on the Insert bar.

Manage Sites **command** Displays a dialog box used to edit sites. Found in the Site menu.

No Browser/Check Errors button Displays a menu with target browser related commands. Found on the Document toolbar.

Preview in Browser **command** Displays a submenu used to select a browser to preview the web page document in. Found in the File menu.

Put File(s) button Uploads file(s) from the local site to a remote site. Found on the Files panel toolbar.

Reports **command** Displays a dialog box used to generate a report that checks external links, accessibility, missing Alt text, and untitled documents. Found in the Site menu.

1. a) Describe the process of publishing a website.
   b) Where are local sites saved and edited?

2. What should be checked and tested before a website is published?

3. Why should web page documents be checked for spelling and grammatical errors?

4. What does the "weight of the page" refer to?

5. What web page element may increase download time?

6. a) What is a target browser?
   b) Why should a website be viewed and tested in more than one target browser?

7. List four questions that could be asked about the target audience to help define which browsers to target when testing a website.

8. a) List the steps required to add a browser to the Preview in Browser submenu.
   b) How many browsers can be listed in the Preview in Browser submenu?

9. List the steps required to select two browsers and versions in the Target Browsers dialog box and then check the HTML associated with the open web page document.

10. What does "fail gracefully" mean?

11. List the steps required to check the document-relative links in a website for broken links.

12. What does the Orphaned Files report display?

13. a) What can be checked in the report that is generated by selecting Site → Reports?
    b) List the steps required to correct HTML errors if any are listed in a report that has been generated in the Site Reports panel.

14. Why does a web server run TCP/IP and HTTP software?

15. What do web hosting companies provide?

16. a) What are domain names used for?
    b) List one consideration when choosing a domain name.

17. a) What does publishing a website to a web server require?
    b) What does publishing a website to a local/network server require?

18. List the steps required to download files from the remote site to the local site.

19. What is a collaborative environment?

20. List two Dreamweaver features that help with collaboration.

21. a) Why should a meta tag be used?
    b) Give an example of three appropriate keywords for a pizza restaurant site.
    c) Give an example of appropriate description meta data for a pizza restaurant site.

22. List two ways to promote a website.

23. List two ways to measure the success of a website.

24. Describe two security issues associated with websites.

True/False

25. Determine if each of the following are true or false. If false, explain why.
    a) A website with spelling errors seems less credible.
    b) Typical users will wait about 50 seconds for a page to load.
    c) A website only needs to be previewed in one browser.
    d) Broken links affect the navigation structure of the website.
    e) Every website image should have Alt text.
    f) Companies can maintain their own web server.
    g) Uploading means to post files to a web server.
    h) Websites are always designed, developed, and maintained by one individual.
    i) Once published, a website does not need to be maintained.
    j) Meta tags must be added to a website.

Exercises

Exercise 1

Publish a previously created website to a Local/Network site by completing the following steps:

a. Check the spelling of each of the web page documents in the website.

b. Check the file size and download time of each of the web page documents in the website.

c. Determine which target browsers the website should be tested in.

d. Preview the website in more than one browser, if possible.

e. Test the HTML in each web page document for compatibility with at least three browsers.

f. Test the website for broken and missing links.

g. Check the website for Missing Alt Text and Untitled Documents.

h. Add keyword meta data with at least two appropriate keywords.

i. Add description meta data with an appropriate description of the website.

j. Publish the website to a Local folder.

Exercise 2

Use the Internet to research the steps required to publish a website that offers free web server space. Present the research in the form of technical documentation on an informational website. Publish the website to the free web server so that the information can be shared with your classmates.

Exercise 3

Use the Internet, newspapers, and local contacts and businesses to research the costs involved and steps required to publish a website to a virtual host. Compare at least two virtual hosts. Present the research in the form of an informational website.

Exercise 4

Use the Internet, newspapers, and local contacts and businesses to further research an ethical issue associated with websites. Present the research in the form of an informational website.

Exercise 5

Extend your knowledge on web servers and investigate the steps involved in setting up a web server by answering the following in a written report:

a) Compare two web server software applications. Include a description of the software's features, hardware requirements, and approximate price.

b) Investigate the technical needs of a web server including RAM, hard disk capacity, CPU speed, methods of connectivity.

c) Describe two electronic security methods for a web server that can be used to protect the server from unauthorized acccess.

d) Explain how password protection controls can be placed on individual websites to limit access to certain sites on a web server.

e) Compare two web tracking software applications that could be used to measure the success of a website. Include a description of the software's features, hardware requirements, and approximate price.

Exercise 6

Visit a local company that hosts websites. Interview an employee and present your findings in an informational website. Possible interview questions include:

- What services do they offer?

- What security features do they use?

- What technical knowledge is needed for positions in the company?

- What hours do the employees work?

- What is the biggest challenge to this type of business?

- What modes of advertising are used to promote the company?

Exercise 7

Collaborate with two peers to develop an informational website about browser software. Plan the website design so that a separate web page is used to describe each browser. Divide the responsibilities as follows:

- One person designs the website, defines the site, creates a style sheet, and creates web pages that have navigation bars.

- A second person researches different browsers available for purchase and for free. This person adds the information to the appropriate pages.

- A third person researches browser usage by surveying peers, family, and the community. It is their responsibility to present an analysis of the survey results on the website.

Chapter 9 Publishing and Promoting a Website

Appendix A
Banner Ads and ActionScript

Thishis appendix discusses banner ads and introduces ActionScript.

Banner Ads

It is common to find advertisements, called banner ads, on websites. A *banner ad* is an image that promotes a product or service and is usually a link to the advertiser's site. Most websites host banner ads for a fee. Banner ads are usually placed at the top, side, or bottom of a page. There are several standard banner ad sizes including 468x60 (Full Banner), 234x60 (Half Banner), and 120x240 (Vertical Banner) pixels.

rich media

Rich media banner ads are a type of banner ad that are designed to capture the user's attention by containing animated or dynamic content. They are also interactive in that they are designed to entice a user to click it, which in turn displays the advertiser's page. For example, clicking the banner ad below takes the user to the company's website:

TIP Sites that offer free hosting space typically require that banner ads be placed on the site or pop up in a new window when the site is viewed.

Many rich media banner ads on the Internet are created using the Flash application. Rich media ads can also be created using JavaScript or an animated GIF.

Creating a Banner Ad Using an Ad Template in Flash

Flash contains predefined templates that can be used to set the dimensions for a standard sized ad. To use a predefined template, select File ➜ New and then select the Templates tab in the New Document dialog box. Select Advertising in the Category list to display a list of ad templates in the Templates list:

IAB

The IAB (Interactive Advertising Bureau) is an organization that helps online companies increase their revenue. One aspect of the organization is to set standards and guidelines for rich media ad formats. Further information can be found at their website www.iab.net.

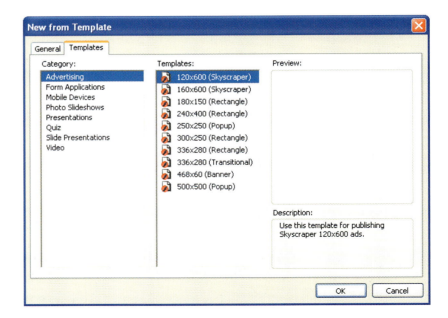

Click a template, such as 468x60 (Banner) to display a preview of the template in the Preview area and a description of the template in the Description area. Click OK to display the banner ad template on the Stage:

A 468x60 Banner Ad

Content can now be added to create the banner ad.

nested symbols

There are different methods of creating banner ad content. One method uses *nested symbols*, which places one symbol on top of another symbol. One symbol contains the banner ad content and is a frame-by-frame animation that has Movie Clip behavior, which allows the animation to play continuously like a banner ad. The other symbol is a button that covers the entire banner ad area and has Button behavior, which allows the banner ad to display another web page when it is clicked.

Adding Banner Ad Content

Banner Advertising Agencies

Banner advertising agencies create banner ads for a fee and find hosts for banner ads through its members, who are website publishers. Publishers hosting banner ads receive payment based on several factors:

Cost per action (CPA) The fee paid when a user clicks the ad and then completes a transaction with the advertiser.

Cost per click (CPC) The fee paid when a user clicks an ad.

Cost per thousand (CPM) The fee paid for every 1000 times an ad is viewed.

One measure of ad effectiveness is its click through rate (CTR), which is the percentage of users that click the ad. However, banner ads are often used to create product or logo awareness which cannot be measured by the CTR.

To create banner ad content, select Insert → New Symbol, which displays a dialog box. Type a descriptive name for the symbol and select Movie clip to create a movie clip symbol:

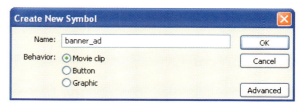

Click OK, which displays an empty Stage. Click the Rectangle tool ( ) and drag on the Stage to create a rectangle. In the Property inspector, set the width and height of the rectangle to the same dimensions as the banner ad. For example, to create a 468x60 banner ad, set W to 468 and set H to 60.

The image for the first frame of the banner ad can then be created by either drawing an image with the Tools panel or by importing an image. For example:

Frame-by-frame animation is then used to create an animated banner ad. Right-click a frame on the Timeline and select Insert Keyframe to add the image from the previous keyframe. The image in the new keyframe can then be modified to progress the animation. For example, the image in frame 30 could be modified to:

The process of inserting keyframes and modifying the image is repeated until the final frame of the application. Note that since the banner ad has Movie Clip behavior, it will therefore play continuously so static frames should be inserted after the final frame to create a pause before the banner loops back to the first frame.

Next, the button that will cover the entire area of the banner ad is created. Select Insert → New Symbol, which displays a dialog box where a descriptive name is typed and Button is selected to create a button symbol. Click OK to display an empty Stage with the button states displayed on the Timeline:

The banner ad should not change when the mouse is over or away from the banner ad so with the Playhead in the Up state, drag the banner ad from the Library panel onto the Stage. This creates an instance of the button over the entire area of the banner ad content. A button instance has to be named by typing a descriptive name, such as banner_button, in the Instance Name box in the Property inspector:

TIP An instance name cannot contain spaces.

Adding ActionScript

ActionScript can be added to the instance of the button to create a link to another web page when the banner ad is clicked. Press the F9 key to display the Actions panel and then select Window ➝ Behaviors to display the Behaviors panel. Click the Add Behavior button ( ) and select Web ➝ Go to Web Page:

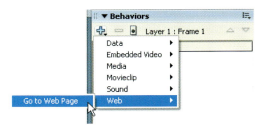

ActionScript

Scripts can be added to a Flash movie to make the movie interactive using a scripting language called ActionScript. A script is a list of commands that are automatically executed by a web browser.

A dialog box is displayed:

Replace the existing URL with the button's target URL and select an appropriate option in the Open in list. Select OK to display the automatically generated ActionScript for the button's behavior in the Actions panel:

Completing and Testing the Banner Ad

To complete the banner ad, click Scene 1 at the top of the page to return to the original banner ad template. From the Library, drag the button symbol onto the Stage. Select Control → Test Movie to test and view the banner ad. The banner ad can then be exported to be used in a web page document.

Other Types of Web Ads

Other types of web ads include interstitial, SUPERSTITIAL™, and Skyscraper ads. Interstitial ads appear in a separate browser window while a web page loads. One type of interstitial ad plays in a smaller browser window:

SUPERSTITIAL™ ads appear in a separate window and can be any size on the computer screen. These ads typically contain animation, sound, and graphics, but are considered "polite" since they only play when a user stops surfing:

Skyscraper ads are long vertical ads that appear on either the left or the right side of a web page:

More on ActionScript

TIP ActionScript 2 is an object-oriented language that follows the ECMA script language specifications.

ActionScript allows interactivity to be added to a Flash movie. Flash supports the latest version of ActionScript called ActionScript 2. The Actions panel provides an interface to add ActionScript. Press the F9 key to display the Actions panel:

ActionScript
toolbox

Script
navigator

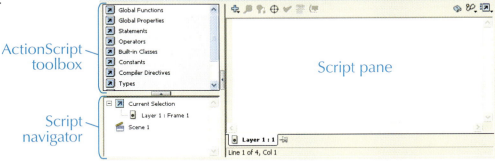

Script pane

- ActionScript actions are dragged or selected from the **ActionScript Toolbox** and placed in the Script pane.

- **Script navigator** displays all scripts associated with the movie.

- **Script pane** is the area where an ActionScript is composed.

To learn more about ActionScript, the Flash Help menu contains commands which can be used to access an ActionScript Dictionary, Flash ActionScript samples, tutorials, and other ActionScript support..

Digital cameras are widely available and affordable. Even the least expensive digital cameras can produce images of acceptable quality for use in web pages. Digital cameras have settings that affect the image files produced by the camera. This appendix explains some aspects of digital camera image files and how to use Fireworks to change image size and resolution.

Digital Camera File Formats

When a digital camera takes a photograph, a chip in the camera collects light and converts it to data. Settings in the digital camera determine what type of file the camera creates from the data that is collected. Common file settings in digital cameras are JPEG, TIFF, and RAW. The JPEG setting produces a JPG file and the TIFF setting produces a TIF file, which can then be transferred to a computer or printer. The TIF format has better quality than a JPG, but the file size is usually larger and a TIF must be converted to a JPG for use in a web page.

RAW   The RAW setting indicates that the photograph data is not processed in the camera. The data must be transferred to a computer that has software from the camera's manufacturer installed. The RAW file can then be manipulated using the software and saved in many image file formats. Manipulating a RAW file and saving the image in a different file format can be thought of as "developing the film," because it allows adjustments to be made such as exposure and color balance. RAW files have different extensions depending on the camera, for example .mrw is a Minolta RAW file, .crw is a Canon RAW file, and .nef is a Nikon RAW file.

Maintaining Image Quality in JPG Files

Setting a digital camera to process the photograph data as JPEG is a fast, convenient way to produce image files for use in a web page. However, every time a JPG image is saved it is compressed again and loses more data, because the JPG format has lossy compression.

TIP Images, image file formats, and Fireworks are discussed in Chapter 6.

To retain excellent image quality, the camera should set to process the photograph data as TIFF, and the TIF file can later be modified in a computer as needed and saved in JPG format. This way, the image will have

Megapixels and Resolution

One megapixel is one million pixels. The megapixel specification for a digital camera is dependent on the number of pixels on the chip in the camera that collect light and convert it to data. For example, a camera with a chip that is 1,600 pixels wide and 1,200 pixels tall has a total of 1,920,000 pixels and is considered to be a two megapixel camera with a resolution of 1,600 x 1,200.

much better quality than if it was a JPG that was modified and saved a few times. The TIF can also be saved in Fireworks as a PNG and then exported many times using different JPG settings without loss of quality.

When using a high-resolution digital camera such as a 3 or more megapixel camera, processing the photograph data as JPG is acceptable for use in a web page. In this case, the image is originally at a high resolution. After tranferring the image to a computer, it can be saved at a lower, proper resolution for use on a web page, and it will still retain sufficient quality.

Digital Camera Image Resolution

Digital cameras have settings that affect the resolution of the saved images. These settings may be called "File Size" or "Quality" or something similar and have settings such as Large, Medium, and Small, which affect the resolution of the image file processed by the camera. For example, selecting Large may result in images that are 1600 x 1200 pixels, and Small may result in images that are 640 x 480 pixels.

The file size (in kilobytes) of a Large quality image will be larger than the file size of the Small quality image because it contains more data. It is better to start off with the highest-quality image possible, and then reduce the size later if needed. However, sometimes compromises may need to be made because the larger file sizes of high-quality images require more space in memory, and therefore fewer images can be stored.

Changing Image Size and Resolution in Fireworks

Resolution

The word "resolution" is used to describe the dimensions of an image in pixels and the pixels per inch of an image. Both uses are correct, but when referring to images from a digital camera, resolution is the dimensions of the image in pixels. In Fireworks, resolution refers to the pixels per inch of the image.

Fireworks can be used to change the image size and resolution of an image file. Once an image file from a digital camera is opened in Fireworks, there are two main considerations in preparing the image for use in a web page: the image size (dimensions) in pixels, and the screen resolution in pixels per inch. Although the file size (in kilobytes) is important, the file size will be small if the image size and resolution are appropriate for a web page.

Most computer monitors display at a resolution of 72 pixels per inch. An image file used in a web page should therefore have a resolution of 72 pixels per inch. Any larger number includes image data that will not be able to be displayed on a screen, and therefore just increases the file size.

To modify an image in Fireworks, click the [Image Size...] button in the Property inspector or select Modify → Canvas → Image Size, which displays a dialog box:

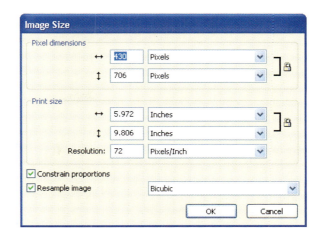

change dimensions

To change the physical dimensions of an image, make sure the Constrain proportions check box is selected and then change the Pixel dimensions of the image. Note that the Resolution does not change as this modification is made. Select OK to change the image dimensions.

change resolution

To change the resolution of an image, make sure the Resample image check box is cleared, which disables the Pixel dimensions boxes so that they cannot be changed. Change the Resolution and select OK to modify the resolution of the image.

Smaller, not Larger

The dimensions of an image should never be increased because the software extrapolates data information to fill in the additional needed pixels, which results in poor image quality. The resolution (dpi) of an image also should not be increased, because it would reduce the quality of the image.

If both the dimensions and resolution of an image need to be changed, first change the dimensions, select OK to apply the changes, and then click the [Image Size...] button again and change the resolution.

When modifications to an image are complete in Fireworks, use the Export Wizard to export the image to the images folder in a Dreamweaver website.

Appendix B Digital Camera Files

Website development in a collaborative environment requires different techniques to help manage and organize tasks. The use of templates is one technique that is helpful in a collaborative environment.

Templates

Many websites are created in a collaborative environment where more than one person designs, develops, and maintains the same website. For example, one person creates the website structure and page layout, and other people contribute content to the web pages. The use of templates is one technique that allows many contributors to add content to a website, yet maintain a consistent look in the site.

A *template* defines the structure, or layout, of a web page document. A designer will use a template to create the basic layout for the web pages of a website. The template "locks down" the design because web page documents created from a template are linked to the template. Other people then contribute by adding content to designated regions of the template. Layout elements, such as tables, cannot be changed without breaking the link to the template. Several templates may be needed for a site depending on the number and variety of web pages in the site.

editable region

The areas of a template that can be modified by adding content to a web page are marked by named editable regions. An *editable region* is a placeholder for content. The page below is a template with editable regions, which are marked with blue tabs:

> ### DWT
>
> A Dreamweaver template is a DWT file. The extension .dwt is automatically added to the file name.

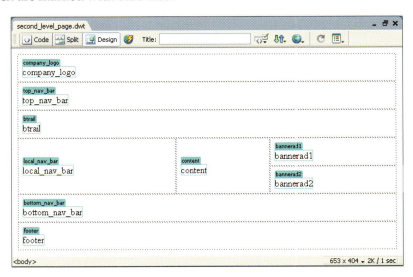

Creating a Template

TIP Dreamweaver includes several predesigned templates. Select File → New and then select one of the Page Designs categories.

The Assets panel can be used to create and apply templates. Click the Templates icon ( ) in the Assets panel to display the Templates category. Select → New Template to create a new template file. A new, untitled template is added to the list of templates in the Assets panel:

create a template

Click the Edit button ( ) at the bottom of the Assets panel to open a window. Tables and other "fixed" elements can then be added to the template. A template must also contain editable regions, discussed in the next section. After the completing the template, select File → Save to save the changes. Dreamweaver automatically adds a Templates folder to the website root folder when a template is created. A template may also be created from an existing web page by selecting File → Save As Template.

delete a template

To delete a template, select it in the Assets panel and then press the Delete key.

Adding Editable Regions

Although the structure presented in a template should not change, areas within the structure must be editable so that content can be added. To add an editable region, select Editable Region from the Templates button in the Common category in the Insert bar:

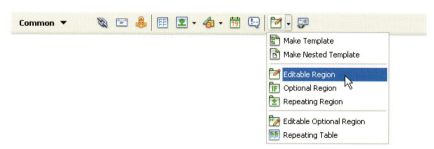

A dialog box is displayed:

TIP Editable region names should not contain special characters and must be unique within the document.

Type a descriptive name and then select OK to insert the region into the template.

Applying a Template to a Web Page Document

To apply a template to an open web page document, drag it from the Assets panel into the Document window or click Apply at the bottom of the Assets panel. The template appears with a yellow background in the web page document. The yellow background does not appear in a browser:

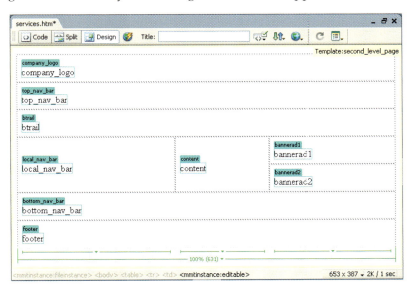

TIP To use a saved template from another site, select File → New and then select the Templates tab in the dialog box. A list of sites and their templates are displayed.

The editable regions can be modified to include content and the appropriate style sheet can be attached to format the web page document. The web page document is saved like any web page.

Appendix C Templates

HTML Tags and Attributes

Document Tags

<html> </html>
Indicates the start and end of an html document.

<head> </head>
Indicates the start and end of the head section.

<title> </title>
Used to display a title in the title bar of the browser's window.

<body> </body>
Indicates the start and end of the body section.
Attributes include:

> bgcolor="*value*"
> Sets the background color for the web page where value is a name or hexadecimal value.

Format Tags

<!--*comment*-->
Defines a comment.

<p> </p>
Defines the start and end of a paragraph. Attributes include:

> style="*value*"
> Indicates inline styles.

Inserts a line break.

<blockquote> </blockquote>
Indents text on both sides of a paragraph.

<ul> </ul>
Defines the start and end of a bulleted (unordered) list.

<ol> </ol>
Defines the start and end of a numbered list.

<li> </li>
Defines an item in a bulleted or numbered list.

<dl> </dl>
Defines the start and end of a definition list.

<dt>
Defines a definition term in a definition list.

<dd>
Defines a definition in a definition list.

<style> </style>
Defines an internal style.

Form Tags

<form> </form>
Inserts a form.

<input type="*button*">
Specifies an input field where *button* can be Reset, Submit, Checkbox, or Radio.

<select> </select>
Specifies the definition of a drop-down menu field.

<option> </option>
Specifies a menu option.

Graphic Tags

<img src="*file name*">
Inserts an image where *file name* is the file name of the graphic.

<img src="file name" alt="*value*">
Specifies alternate text for the graphic where value is the alternative text.

<hr>
Inserts a horizontal rule (line).

<object>
Embeds a generic object.

Image Maps

<map name="*value*"> </map>
Inserts an image map where *value* is the name of the image map.

<area href="*link*" shape="*shape*" coords="*w, x, y, z*">
Specifies an image map hotspot where *link* is a URL, *shape* is the hotspot shape default, rect, circle, or poly, and *w, x, y,* and *z* are the coordinates of the hotspot. Coordinates vary depending on the shape.

Links

`<a href="URL"> </a>`
Creates an external hyperlink where *URL* is the target URL.

`<a href="mailto:email_address"> </a>`
Creates an e-mail hyperlink where *email_address* is the target e-mail address.

`<a name="named_anchor"> </a>`
Creates a named anchor where *named_anchor* is the name of the location.

`<a href="#named_anchor"> </a>`
Creates a hyperlink to a named anchor where *named_anchor* is the target location.

`<a href="file name"> </a>`
Creates an internal hyperlink where *file name* is the file name of the target page.

Meta Tag

`<meta>`
Defines keywords used by search engines, expiration date, author, and page generation software.

Script Tags

`<script> </script>`
Inserts a script into the HTML.

`<noscript> </noscript>`
Defines the start and end of instructions for browsers that do not support scripts.

Table Tags

`<table> </table>`
Creates a table. Attributes include:

> `border="value"`
> Specifies the thickness of the cell border.
>
> `cellpadding="value"`
> Sets the amount of space between a cell's border and contents where value is a number.
>
> `cellspacing="value"`
> Specifies the amount of space between table cells where value is a number.
>
> `width="value"`
> Specifies the width of a table where value is a number in pixels or as a percentage of the document's width.

`<caption> </caption>`
Defines a table caption.

`<th> </th>`
Defines a table header, which is a normal cell with bold, centered text.

`<tr> </tr>`
Defines the start and end of a table row.

`<td> </td>`
Define the start and end of a table data cell.

`<tr valign="value">` or `<td valign="value">`
Specifies cell(s) vertical alignment where value is top, middle, or bottom.

`<td colspan="value">`
Specifies the number of columns a cell should span where value is a number.

`<td rowspan="value">`
Specifies the number of rows a cell should span where value is a number.

Text Tags

`<h1> </h1> ...<h6> </h6>`
Tag used to emphasize text. Heading 1 has the largest font size and is used to represent the most important information. Heading 6 has the smallest font size.

`<strong> </strong>`
Displays the text in bold.

`<em> </em>`
Emphasizes the text.

`<cite> </cite>`
Defines the start and end of a citation.

`<pre> </pre>`
Creates preformatted text in which all spaces and line endings are preserved.

`<abbr title="value"> </abbr>`
Displays the full version of an abbreviated word when the pointer rests on the word where value is the full version of the word.

`<acronym title="value"> </acronym>`
Displays the full version of an acronym when the pointer rests on the word where value is the full version of the word.

Color Constants and Corresponding Hexadecimal Values

Black	(#000000)	Olive	(#808000)
Silver	(#C0C0C0)	Yellow	(#FFFF00)
Gray	(#808080)	Navy	(#000080)
White	(#FFFFFF)	Blue	(#0000FF)
Maroon	(#800000)	Teal	(#008080)
Red	(#FF0000)	Aqua	(#00FFFF)
Purple	(#800080)	Fuchsia	(#FF00FF)
Green	(#008000)	Lime	(#00FF00)

Index

Symbols

\# 235, 240
\+ 16
.cfm 327
.com 9
.css 6
.doc 6
.dwt 383
.edu 9
.gov 9
.htm 6, 75
.lbi 134
.mno 360
.org 9
.swf 264
/ 42
// 9
<> 42
<a> 53
<applet> 61
<blockquote> 229
<body> 42, 43, 189

 47
<div> 240
<em> 221
<form> 326
<h1> 47, 226
<h2> 47
<h3> 47
<h4> 47
<h5> 47
<h6> 47, 226
<head> 42, 43
<hr> 48
<html> 43
<img> 55
<li> 229
<object> 61
<ol> 229
<p> 42, 47, 221
<param> 61
<script> 59
<strong> 221
<table> 80

<title> 42, 43
<ul> 229
> 120
_blank 93
_self 93
| 120
© 45, 136
– 16
128-bit encryption 364
40-bit encryption 364

A

About.com 16
above the fold 124
absolute hyperlink 93
absolute positioning 240
academic degrees 27
Acceptable Use Policy 23
Access, Microsoft 328
accessibility 55, 353
Accessibility options 80
Access Table 328
ActionScript 378
    adding 376
        Dictionary 378
        Toolbox 378
ActionScript 2 378
Actions panel 378
Active Server Page 326
Acts, disabilities 55, 161
Acts, protect privacy 22, 24
ad
        interstitial 377
        standards and guidelines 374
        SUPERSTITIAL 377
ADA Act 55, 161
Address bar 11
address bus 2
ads
        Skyscraper 377
advertising templates 373
AI 270
aligning objects 174
alignment
        change, in HTML document 57
        text 216

alignment buttons 173
Align Center button 168
Align command 174
Align Left button 168
Align Right button 168
Alpha transparency 177
AltaVista 16
alternative text 161, 182
Alt box 161
Alt text 347
ALU 2
Amaya 41, 349
Amazon.com Inc. 308
AMD 2
Americans with Disabilities Act 55, 161
anchor icon 235
anchor names 235
anchor points 267
anchor tag 53
AND 16
Angelfire 355
angle brackets (<>) 42
animated button 257, 258
animated GIF 373
animated text 257, 284
    steps for creating 285
animation
        defined 265
        export 269
        frame-by-frame 269, 375
        motion tweened 279
        preview 269
        shape tweened 276
        speeding up 270
        tweened 276
antialiasing 225
antivirus software 25, 364
AOL 16
applets
    parameters 61
applications software 2
Application panel 329
appropriateness 122, 123
Arial 213